Through
the Eyes of
LUKE

Through the Eyes of LUKE

A Devotional Commentary

KEITH CLOUTEN

Pacific Press®
Publishing Association

Nampa, Idaho | www.pacificpress.com

Cover design by Trent Truman
Cover design resources from GettyImages.com
Inside design by Aaron Troia

The author assumes full responsibility for the accuracy of all facts and quotations as cited in this book.

To order additional copies of this book call toll-free 1-800-765-6955, or visit AdventistBookCenter.com.

Library of Congress Cataloging-in-Publication Data

Names: Clouten, Keith, author.
Title: Through the eyes of Luke : a devotional commentary / Keith Clouten.
Description: Nampa, Idaho : Pacific Press, [2022] | Includes bibliographical references.
Identifiers: LCCN 2023000802 | ISBN 9780816369027 (paperback) | ISBN 9780816369034 (ebook)
Subjects: LCSH: Bible. Luke—Commentaries. | Bible. Luke—Devotional literature. | Luke, Saint.
Classification: LCC BS2595.53 .C56 2022 | DDC 226.4/077—dc23/eng/20230125
LC record available at https://lccn.loc.gov/2023000802

February 2023

Dedication

I dedicate this book to the memory of a dear daughter, Lin,
the loving mother of Jenny, Jeff, and Josh.

Contents

Part IV: Jesus at Jerusalem

Preface

My interest in Luke was piqued when our church pastor said something that shocked me. I had just agreed to write a simple Christmas play for the upcoming December service, and he responded, "Keith, did you know that Luke is the only Gospel writer who tells the beginning and end of Jesus' life on earth? Only Luke wrote about His birth, death, resurrection, and return to heaven. What's more, he is the only Gospel writer who never met Jesus and who wasn't a Jew."

No, I didn't know any of those things. However, as I explored Luke on my own, I discovered a lot more about this Gentile Gospel writer. In fact, his Gospel is part one of a two-part composition. Part two is The Acts of the Apostles. With the two combined, this prolific author wrote more of the New Testament than anyone else, including the apostle Paul. Luke's Gospel includes twenty-four parables—eighteen of which you will not find anywhere else.

The fact that Luke became a Christian quite a while after Jesus' time on earth raises an intriguing question. What led this brand-new Gentile Christian to undertake a project of writing the story of someone he had never met? And how and where did he gather all the information about Jesus? These are "mystery" questions that demand answers and draw us into his Gospel account. It takes an extraordinary person who has an extraordinary quest for adventure and is energized by the Holy Spirit to undertake such a project.

Luke was extraordinary in many ways. His writing portrays an educated and organized mind, a sequential thought process, a passion for history, and a talent for research. Luke's sense of adventure shows not only in his tackling the complex task of writing the story of Jesus but also in his numerous travels (check out his shipwreck story in Acts 27).

My reading and study of Luke have led me to some excellent and comprehensive commentaries on his Gospel. Biblical scholars have analyzed his writing, interpreted his many parables, and plumbed his theology both in the Gospel story and in Acts. Is there anything more to be said?

Yes! My background is not academic, but I like to approach the text of Luke with imagination and surprise. Like me, Luke is a Gentile, but he's one who discovered Jesus in some wonderful new ways. I love Luke's fascination with some of the funny stories that Jesus told. Some of them demand a sense of humor and an openness to discovering the unexpected.

I want to tell Luke's story like it is, in a conversational style, bordering on colloquial at times. I'd like you to hear it that way. I think you will stop sometimes and want to ask questions like these: How and where did Luke discover some of these stories? Who were the eyewitnesses that he found and interviewed? But most of all, what can I learn from this Spirit-guided account?

Now I invite you to find a comfy chair and sit alongside Luke's friend, Theophilus, in his comfortable Greek home. As you read by yourself or with a friend, I encourage you to carefully focus on the story and then spend a while reflecting on what you've read. Don't be surprised when you discover that you've just finished reading Luke's Gospel once more—or for the first time!

Who Was Luke?

Of the four Gospel writers, Luke is the odd man out. Matthew was a tax collector at Capernaum in Galilee until he left his lucrative employment to become a disciple of Jesus. John, with his brother James, was a fisherman in Galilee when Jesus called them to discipleship. Mark was a Jerusalem boy who became a follower of Jesus and later participated in evangelism with Paul and Peter. These three men—Matthew, Mark, and John—had personal associations with Jesus, so they were well equipped to write the story of His life, death, and resurrection.

But Luke? Nonbiblical sources tell us that Luke was a non-Jew, most likely living in Antioch, a Gentile city in Syria, to the north of Palestine.[1] In Antioch, Luke would have learned about Jesus and the gospel from early church evangelists like Paul and Barnabas, who both spent considerable time there, organizing and establishing the first Christian church outside Palestine. Luke tells us that believers in Antioch were the first believers to be given the name Christian (Acts 11:26). Luke later joined Paul in his missionary journeys to Western Asia, Greece, and Rome.

Biblical scholar and seminary professor Robert Stein introduces his commentary on Luke's Gospel with a concise summary of what is generally believed about Luke:[2]

- Luke "was not an apostle or follower of Jesus during His ministry."[3]
- He was well-educated, a gifted writer, and knew how to do research.
- Luke was a Gentile, as seen by his avoidance of certain Semitic words and the way he referred to Jews as if he was not one of them.
- He was a physician. Paul identifies him that way (Colossians 4:14). Luke recorded all of Mark's healing accounts, shared Matthew's healing of the centurion's slave, and added five more miraculous healings that are unique to his Gospel.[4]

It appears that Luke may have been a "God-fearer" before he became a Christian. If so, although a Gentile, he had likely read the Jewish scriptures, believed the teachings of Judaism, and kept the moral law but was never circumcised. In greetings at the end of his letter to the Colossians, Paul does not include Luke among "those of the circumcision" (Colossians 4:10, 11).[5]

Luke's is a wonderful story of conversion to the gospel, but some may inquire what qualified him to write the longest of the four accounts of Jesus' life here on earth. In fact, we have three strikes against Luke as a Gospel writer:

Strike one: He was a Gentile. In the society of that time, good Jewish men thanked God each day for three things: that they were not born a Gentile, a woman, or a slave. Gentiles were outsiders to God's people; they were "not us." They were considered ritually impure, which restricted their access to sacred spaces at the Jerusalem temple. Many Gentiles ate impure foods, came into regular contact with impure substances, were idolatrous, and committed defiling sexual acts. Consequently, Jews were forbidden to enter Gentile homes.[6]

Strike two: He was a physician. Although there were physicians in the time of Jesus, Jews had an unfortunate attitude toward them. It was commonly assumed that a person's disease or disability was caused by his or her sin and, therefore, was deserved. "Who sinned, this man or his parents, that he was born blind?" was a question Jesus' disciples asked their Master one day (John 9:2, NIV). Furthermore, Jewish purity laws forbid touching a dead or diseased body, including a leper, something that physicians did as part of their work. Also, there were men who claimed to be physicians but were in it only for the money. For all these reasons, Jewish society was critical of physicians and those who sought help from them.

Strike three: He never met Jesus. Luke was neither a Jew nor born in Judea. As an educated man, he evidently developed an interest in Judaism and its Scriptures but only learned about Jesus and the good news through the work of early Christian missionaries. The underlying question, however, is this: How could a non-Jew who never met Jesus write a detailed account of His life and ministry?

A quick preview of Luke's writings

We know some remarkable facts about Luke. He authored not only his Gospel, which is the longest of the four, but also its sequel, The Acts of the Apostles, which continues the story of Christ's disciples and Paul after Jesus' resurrection and ascension.

As a Gentile, Luke would have personally experienced what it was like to be an outsider in Jewish society. We won't be surprised, then, that Luke places more emphasis on Jesus' ministry to the down-and-out than any of the other Gospel writers. Luke's special focus is on Christ's ministry to outsiders—the poor, the sick, widows, women in general, Samaritans, lepers, the demon-possessed, hated tax collectors, and, yes, Gentiles. Our much-loved stories of the good Samaritan and the prodigal son are found only in Luke's Gospel. And as a physician, Luke was especially in tune with how Jesus ministered to the unclean—the raising of a widow's dead son and the healing of ten lepers—again, stories found only in Luke. Each of these characteristics makes Luke's Gospel unique.

Reflection

How do you respond to the fact that so much about Jesus' life and death was written by a non-Jew?

---

1. Mikeal C. Parsons, *Luke: Storyteller, Interpreter, Evangelist* (Peabody, MA: Hendrickson, 2007), 1, 2.
2. Parsons, 6.
3. Robert H. Stein, *Luke*, The New American Commentary, vol. 24 (Nashville, TN: Broadman, 1992), 20.
4. Stein, 20.
5. Darrell L. Bock, *Luke* (Grand Rapids, MI: Baker Academic, 1994), 6.
6. Eli Lizorkin-Eyzenberg, "Thank You, God, for Not Making Me a Woman," *Israel Bible Weekly*, April 30, 2021, https://weekly.israelbiblecenter.com/thank-not-making-woman/.

Part I

Beginnings

Luke 1:1–4:30

Chapter 1

Luke's Research and Travel

Luke 1:1–4

Luke may have guessed that someone picking up his account of the life of Jesus would ask how a person who had not even seen Jesus during His earthly ministry could write His story. So, Luke begins his Gospel with a short preface to explain how and why he wrote it. In Greek, the first four verses of Luke's Gospel are one long sentence. Read it carefully:

Inasmuch as many have undertaken to compile an account of the things accomplished among us, just as they were handed down to us by those who from the beginning were eyewitnesses and servants of the word, it seemed fitting for me as well, having investigated everything carefully from the beginning, to write it out for you in consecutive order, most excellent Theophilus, so that you may know the exact truth about the things you have been taught (Luke 1:1–4).

As a new Christian, Luke likely discovered that there were many accounts of Jesus' life. The early Christians were actively engaged in storytelling. As best we can tell, Luke wrote his Gospel before AD 68, when Mark's was the only other written account in existence. Sometime later, Matthew composed his work, drawing from Mark and possibly from a lost collection of sayings of Jesus that scholars refer to as "Q" or *Quelle*, meaning "source," to which Luke also had access. It was later, probably after AD 90, that John wrote his Gospel.

Luke, like any good historian of those times, searched for eyewitnesses of events in Jesus' life. In the days before printing and publishing, people commonly circulated their stories orally from one generation and one place to the next. While we may wonder about the accuracy of their verbal accounts, it is widely agreed that "oral transmission could be very accurate, especially among disciples of teachers in the east. Ancient memories were carefully trained, both among the educated and among uneducated reciters, and disciples of teachers ordinarily saw one of their chief roles as accurately communicating their teachers' message."[1]

Not everyone has an aptitude for chronology as we see it in Luke's writings. He was determined to write an "orderly"—logical and sequential—narrative about Jesus for his respected friend, Theophilus (verse 3). So, Luke set about to track down still-living eyewitnesses to events in Jesus' life and ministry as well as research what people had already written about Him. That meant traveling to sites where events had occurred and interviewing the witnesses he found. Either Luke was familiar with Mark and his written account of Jesus' life through their mutual friend and mentor, the apostle Paul, or Luke's research led him to Mark and his Gospel. Clearly, Luke believed Mark's writings were a reliable source, so he used much of Mark's work as he compiled his own version.

Scholars have long recognized Luke's literary ability, specifically as "an author of literary skill and rich imagination."[2] His knowledge of the Greek language was superb. Luke's propensity for history comes through clearly in The Acts of the Apostles. There he recounts the beginnings of the Christian church and the early work of Peter in Judea and surrounding areas and then focuses on Paul's missionary journeys to Greece and Rome. Luke writes almost nothing about the evangelistic endeavors of the other apostles who are reputed to have worked in Armenia, India, Egypt, Spain, and other places.*

A traveling man

Without access to libraries and archives, research requires travel, so we discover Luke in many different places around the Mediterranean. A friend of Paul, who was also perhaps his mentor, Luke accompanied Paul on some of his missionary journeys between about AD 49 and AD 61.

In the book of Acts, Luke describes how he sailed with Paul from Troas in Asia Minor (today's Turkey) to Philippi in Greece (Acts 16:6–12), a trip they took together in AD 49. Luke's "we" account ends at Philippi, so it's possible that he traveled independently from there.

Luke is back at Philippi about four years later, in AD 54, when he again accompanies Paul by ship to Caesarea by way of several Aegean ports and then overland to Jerusalem. Luke was in Jerusalem with Paul when the apostle was arrested and taken to Caesarea, where he was held in custody for two years (Acts 20:4–21:36).

Luke's "we" passages stop during the two years Paul was imprisoned at Caesarea. Undoubtedly, Luke spent those two years finding and interviewing Christian believers in Jerusalem and other Judean cities, collecting stories about Jesus as he compiled his Gospel.

The "we" passages recommence when he and Paul leave Caesarea on a voyage bound for Italy. Paul is on board as a prisoner to Rome, where he is placed under house arrest for the next two years (Acts 27; 28). At Rome, Luke finishes writing his Gospel and continues the story as he writes The Acts of the Apostles. He may have completed his writing by AD 64 because he does not tell of tumultuous events that were taking place during the mid-60s. Those included the executions of Paul and Peter and the Jewish revolt that culminated in the Roman destruction of Jerusalem in 70.

It's of more than the usual interest that Luke's "we" passages all relate to his sea travel with Paul. On each voyage that they took together, Luke describes exactly where they sailed, the weather conditions en route, and what he observes throughout the voyage. He writes much that seems inconsequential to us—like naming islands they sail by, identifying ports where they transfer from one ship to another, and describing intimate details of their brief shore excursions. It seems evident that Luke enjoyed sailing. Perhaps he spent a lot of his time on deck, fascinated by everything he observed. For example, read Luke's account of the almost catastrophic voyage from Crete to Malta to absorb his incredibly detailed narrative of the storm at sea (Acts 27).

Luke omitted all the extraneous detail when he was on shore with Paul or traveling independently. He liked to explore new places, perhaps seeking interviews with people who had been with Jesus.

During his travels, Luke finds eyewitnesses of Christ's life, death, and resurrection. He travels independently of Paul through parts of Asia Minor. Although we have Paul's letters to the people of Galatia and Colossae, we have nothing from Luke describing Paul's itineraries to these and other places. Later, writing from Rome, Paul sends greetings to the people of Colossae from "our dear friend Luke, the doctor"

---

* I sometimes wish Luke had tagged along with Thomas on his phenomenal missionary trip to southern India. That journey of at least 4,500 land miles would have made some of Paul's journeys around Asia Minor and Greece look like afternoon jaunts.

(Colossians 4:14, NIV), and in a separate letter to Philemon at Colossae, Paul again sends greetings from Luke (Philemon 24). Luke's independent travels likely included stops at cities like Ephesus and Colossae. When he reconnects with Paul at Philippi, he joins the apostle on the voyage to Caesarea.

At Ephesus, Luke would have met an important eyewitness of Jesus, the apostle John, who conducted missionary work in Ephesus and the surrounding cities and would have gladly shared some of his memories of Jesus' life, death, and resurrection. Several details of Passion Week and the Resurrection are unique to Luke's and John's Gospels.[3]

During his later visit to Jerusalem with Paul, Luke met James, the brother of Jesus and a leader of the early church (Acts 21:17, 18). James would have been another valuable eyewitness source.

Later, during two or more years in Rome, Luke likely became acquainted with Peter and his coworker Mark. Early Christian tradition states that it was Mark who transcribed Peter's stories of Jesus that became his Gospel.

Was Luke inspired?

An important question remains. Luke carried out research and interviewed eyewitnesses as he wrote the story of Jesus. Does that make Luke's writing inspired? Isn't it possible that any educated, spiritually minded person of Luke's time could have done the same thing?

We believe the Holy Spirit was heaven's agency in inspiring all the writers of Scripture. So, our question is this: Did the Holy Spirit use Luke as His servant to write the Gospel and the book of Acts? Was he guided by the Holy Spirit in his research and writing? "Luke has more to say about the Spirit in his Gospel than does any of the other Evangelists [Gospel writers]."[4] There are six references to the Holy Spirit in Mark, twelve in Matthew, seventeen in Luke, and more than forty in Acts of the Apostles, which might be more appropriately designated "the Acts of the Holy Spirit."[5] Furthermore, "the Spirit is a driving force for Luke's portrait of salvation, energizing and guiding events both in Luke and especially in Acts."[6] "True inspiration comes when the seeking mind of man joins with the revealing Spirit of God."[7] Let's dig into Luke's account!

Reflection

Based on the evidence, how would you describe Luke's personality? How might your perception of Luke affect the way you read his Gospel?

---

1. *NIV Cultural Backgrounds Study Bible* (Grand Rapids, MI: Zondervan, 2016), 1738.
2. Mikeal C. Parsons, *Luke: Storyteller, Interpreter, Evangelist* (Peabody, MA: Hendrickson, 2007), 15–17.
3. Leon Morris, *Luke: An Introduction and Commentary*, Tyndale New Testament Commentaries, vol. 3 (Downers Grove, IL: IVP Academic, 1988), 71, 72.
4. Morris, 56.
5. Robert H. Stein, *Luke*, The New American Commentary, vol. 24 (Nashville, TN: Broadman, 1992), 47.
6. Darrell L. Bock, *A Theology of Luke and Acts* (Grand Rapids, MI: Zondervan, 2012), 211, 212.
7. William Barclay, *The Gospel of Luke* (Philadelphia, PA: Westminster Press, 1975), 8.

Chapter 2

Birth of John Foretold

Luke 1:5–25

Having written his brief preface, Luke now writes what is unique to his Gospel—the birth narratives for both John the Baptist and Jesus, clearly showing us how ancient prophecies were being fulfilled. After the fall of Adam and Eve, God promised to send a Savior (Genesis 3:15). This promise was passed along to each new generation from Adam to Noah, Abraham, Isaac, and Jacob. Then, after their exodus from Egyptian bondage, the people of Israel watched for the arrival of Messiah, God's anointed One, who would free the world from the shackles of oppression and establish an eternal kingdom. The prophet Isaiah had written, "A voice cries out: 'In the wilderness prepare the way of the LORD, make straight in the desert a highway for our God' " (Isaiah 40:3, NRSV). "John paves the way; Jesus *is* the Way."[1]

The special moment has arrived. There will be no public announcements, but two very different people will be taken by surprise—first, an aging priest in the Jerusalem temple, then a peasant teenager in the small Galilean village of Nazareth.

The Christmas story is about to unfold! Since we associate Christmas with the opening of gifts, we are expectant. Yes, here are several packages wrapped and tied with cords of love. God hands the first to His lead angel, Gabriel. Open this one first, Gabriel.

The birth of John foretold

Luke records,

In the days of Herod, king of Judea, there was a priest named Zechariah, of the division of Abijah; and he had a wife from the daughters of Aaron, and her name was Elizabeth. They were both righteous in the sight of God, walking blamelessly in all the commandments and requirements of the Lord. And yet they had no child, because Elizabeth was infertile, and they were both advanced in years (Luke 1:5–7).

Nearly every good history starts at a "beginning." However, Luke's beginning is the continuation of a story that infiltrates the entire Old Testament. It is the fulfillment of a promise made first to Abraham that all the world would be blessed through his descendants. It's the outworking of the special covenant God made with Abraham.

We are immediately introduced to an aging priestly couple, Zechariah and Elizabeth. They are good people, but they've missed the special blessing of a family. Particularly in their day, childless parents lacked support in their old age, and they had no one to carry on the family name.

Luke states that the problem was with Elizabeth, who now was postmenopausal. Her childless state brought her shame and must surely have been some sort of punishment from God—well, that's what her neighbors thought. But the lack of children wasn't for the lack of earnest prayer and supplication through many years. Luke is careful to assure us that the aging couple "walk blamelessly" before God.

Now it happened that while he was performing his priestly service before God in the appointed order of his division, according to the custom of the priestly office, he was chosen by lot to enter the temple of the Lord and burn incense. And the whole multitude of the people were in prayer outside at the hour of the incense offering. Now an angel of the Lord appeared to him, standing to the right of the altar of incense. Zechariah was troubled when he saw the angel, and fear gripped him (verses 8–12).

As a priest, Zechariah serves in the Jerusalem temple for two one-week periods each year; but an overabundance of priests means that lots are cast for the special duty of burning incense at the morning and evening sacrifices. That day, in being allocated the duty of offering incense at the altar in the holy place, Zechariah is performing the once-in-a-lifetime act of his priestly career. Was it the morning or the evening sacrifice? Luke doesn't say, but it was usually the evening time that attracted a crowd of worshippers.* As Zechariah performed the solemn duty in front of the veiled entrance to the Holy of Holies, he was astonished and frightened when an angel suddenly appeared beside him.

But the angel said to him, "Do not be afraid, Zechariah, for your prayer has been heard, and your wife Elizabeth will bear you a son, and you shall name him John. You will have joy and gladness, and many will rejoice over his birth. For he will be great in the sight of the Lord; and he will drink no wine or liquor, and he will be filled with the Holy Spirit while in his mother's womb. And he will turn many of the sons of Israel back to the Lord their God. And it is he who will go as a forerunner before Him in the spirit and power of Elijah, TO TURN THE HEARTS OF FATHERS BACK TO THEIR CHILDREN, and the disobedient to the attitude of the righteous, to make ready a people prepared for the Lord" (verses 13–17).

Zechariah is stunned, shocked, and unbelieving when he hears, "Do not be afraid, Zechariah." The angel's message is good news—*very* good news—it's the fulfillment of the Messianic promise, something that will bring much joy to many people. But the old priest is barely comprehending the words. His wife, Elizabeth, is to have a son? Yes! Miracles like this have happened before. Remember how God opened the womb of Abraham's wife, Sarah? And Rachel, Jacob's wife? And Hannah, Elkanah's wife?

Zechariah said to the angel, "How will I know this? For I am an old man, and my wife is advanced in her years." The angel answered and said to him, "I am Gabriel, who stands in the presence of God, and I was sent to speak to you and to bring you this good news. And behold, you will be silent and unable to speak until the day when these things take place, because you did not believe my words, which will be fulfilled in their proper time" (verses 18–20).

This was not just any angel! This was Gabriel, who stands in the very presence of God! While God

---

* If Gabriel came to Zechariah at the time of the evening sacrifice with a Messianic announcement, it replicates a time long before when the same Gabriel came to Daniel at the time of the evening sacrifice with a prophetic message about the coming Messiah (Daniel 9:21–27).

calmed Zechariah's fears, there was a penalty for questioning the power of Almighty God. When God speaks, we must *listen*! As a result of Zechariah's disbelief, he would not be able to speak until the promise was fulfilled.

And meanwhile the people were waiting for Zechariah, and were wondering at his delay in the temple. But when he came out, he was unable to speak to them; and they realized that he had seen a vision in the temple, and he repeatedly made signs to them, and remained speechless. When the days of his priestly service were concluded, he went back home (verses 21–23).

The waiting crowd undoubtedly wondered why the old priest's duty took so long. When Zechariah reappears, speechless, they conclude he has had a vision. They remain in wonder as Zechariah returns to his country home in the Judean hills. I'm sure his disillusionment turned to joy, though, when Elizabeth announced that she was expecting a child.

Now after these days his wife Elizabeth became pregnant, and she kept herself in seclusion for five months, saying, "This is the way the Lord has dealt with me in the days when He looked with favor upon me, to take away my disgrace among people" (verses 24, 25).

God had promised that their son would be a unique prophet—the first after a silence of four hundred years, and the prophet who would announce the Messiah. Gabriel's words to Zechariah were directly from the prophet Malachi: "Behold, I am going to send you Elijah the prophet before the coming of the great and terrible day of the LORD. He will turn the hearts of the fathers back to their children and the hearts of the children to their fathers, so that I will not come and strike the land with complete destruction" (Malachi 4:5, 6). The special role of Zechariah and Elizabeth's son would be to prepare the way for the long-awaited Messiah, the One who will be called Jesus.

Meanwhile, though, Gabriel has a second package to open.

Reflection

It's easy to be critical of Zechariah, the aging priest, as an unbeliever of the angel's message, requiring a sign. Consider the situation faced by Abraham and Sarai in the Genesis record: Genesis 15:1–6 and 17:15–19. How did Abraham react to the news that Sarah would give birth?

---

1. Darrell L. Bock, *A Theology of Luke and Acts* (Grand Rapids, MI: Zondervan, 2012), 100, 101; emphasis added.

Chapter 3

Birth of Jesus Foretold

Luke 1:26–45

The birth message for John came to Zechariah while he stood in front of the curtain that separated him from the Holy of Holies. But John is only the *forerunner* of the Messiah, the world's Redeemer. And so the aged Elizabeth is in the sixth month of her pregnancy when Gabriel is given the directive to open his second Christmas package. We imagine an exclamation of surprise. He is now to go to a mere teenager at Nazareth in Galilee!

Recalling Nathanael's words, "Can anything good come out of Nazareth?" (John 1:46, NRSV), I wonder whether Gabriel asked God about the location. "Is there a mistake, Lord? Are you sending me to a teenage peasant girl in a village we haven't even heard of?" Yes, Gabriel. And Mary enters Luke's story almost as though she were an orphan—no family background is given. Clearly, we serve a God who plans the unexpected, a God who delights to surprise! The announcement will be simple, but the miracle will be great.

Now in the sixth month the angel Gabriel was sent from God to a city in Galilee called Nazareth, to a virgin betrothed to a man whose name was Joseph, of the descendants of David; and the virgin's name was Mary. And coming in, he said to her, "Greetings, favored one! The Lord is with you." But she was very perplexed at this statement, and was pondering what kind of greeting this was. And the angel said to her, "Do not be afraid, Mary, for you have found favor with God. And behold, you will conceive in your womb and give birth to a son, and you shall name Him Jesus. He will be great and will be called the Son of the Most High; and the Lord God will give Him the throne of His father David; and He will reign over the house of Jacob forever, and His kingdom will have no end" (Luke 1:26–33).

Don't be afraid, Mary. God will fulfill an ancient prophecy through you, as recorded by the prophet Isaiah: "Behold, the virgin will conceive and give birth to a son, and she will name Him Immanuel" (Isaiah 7:14).

More than likely, Mary was surprised and puzzled by Gabriel's appearance, especially as she heard the content of his message. She will give birth to a son who will be called "the Son of the Most High"? His kingdom will have no end? Why, that can only mean the Messiah! Yet, she had a problem.

But Mary said to the angel, "How will this be, since I am a virgin?" The angel answered and said to her, "The Holy Spirit will come upon you, and the power of the Most High will overshadow you; for that reason also the holy Child will be called the Son of God. And behold, even your relative Elizabeth herself has conceived a son in her old age, and she who was called infertile is

now in her sixth month. For nothing will be impossible with God." And Mary said, "Behold the Lord's bond-servant; may it be done to me according to your word." And the angel departed from her (Luke 1:34–38).

Mary was engaged to a Nazareth carpenter named Joseph. In first-century Jewish culture, a prospective bridegroom, after the engagement, or betrothal, announcement, returns to his parents' home and prepares a home for his bride. When the house is ready, which may take a year's time, the bridegroom will come for his bride and escort her to his new home. In first-century Jewish culture, betrothal was taken seriously. To break an engagement was akin to divorce. Until the marriage, then, Mary spent time alone, not with her future husband, Joseph, and in accordance with Jewish law, not having sex with any other man.[1]

So, the birth of God's Son to a young unmarried teenager will be unique in every way. If the conception of Jesus' forerunner, John, was a miracle against all odds and natural law for two aged parents, the conception of God's own Son, Jesus, will be a much greater miracle, something astounding and wonderful.

Unlike Zechariah, Mary didn't ask for a sign, but Gabriel offered one anyway. Her relative, Elizabeth, long childless, is also having a miracle son. Mary will immediately set out for the hill country of Judea to see the angel's sign fulfilled.

Now at this time Mary set out and went in a hurry to the hill country, to a city of Judah, and she entered the house of Zechariah and greeted Elizabeth. When Elizabeth heard Mary's greeting, the baby leaped in her womb, and Elizabeth was filled with the Holy Spirit. And she cried out with a loud voice and said, "Blessed are you among women, and blessed is the fruit of your womb! And how has it happened to me that the mother of my Lord would come to me? For behold, when the sound of your greeting reached my ears, the baby leaped in my womb for joy. And blessed is she who believed that there would be a fulfillment of what had been spoken to her by the Lord" (verses 39–45).

The two birth narratives are centered on God, not on the individuals who make up the stories. God is undoubtedly present throughout the narrative. When Elizabeth greeted Mary as "the mother of my Lord," she recognized that Mary's child would be the long-awaited Messiah. "Mary and Elizabeth's meeting brings together John and Jesus as represented through their mothers."[2] The fetal John testified to Jesus' divine presence by leaping in Elizabeth's womb—an acknowledgment that Jesus would be the greater of the two sons.

We are only forty-five verses into Luke's Gospel, and already the Holy Spirit has been mentioned three times. Even before his birth, John will be filled with the Holy Spirit (verse 15); the Holy Spirit will come upon Mary in the conception of Jesus (verse 35); and Elizabeth is filled with the Holy Spirit when Mary greets her (verse 41). Luke's writing, both in his Gospel and in Acts, emphasizes the activity of the Holy Spirit and the human response of prayer.

What Luke meant when he said he wanted to write an "orderly account" (verse 3, NIV) is beautifully illustrated in the way He put John's and Jesus' birth stories in parallel.[3] The same angel, Gabriel, appears to both Zechariah and Mary; both are troubled by the angel's visit, both are told not to be afraid, both are told of the future birth of a son, both births are associated with the work of the Holy Spirit. In both accounts, Gabriel gives the name for the son, and in both the angel states that the son will be great and his future role will be God-planned. Even more significant, though, are the differences: Jesus' birth will be far more miraculous than John's; Jesus will be the Messiah, John His forerunner; Jesus the greater, John the lesser.

Reflection

"A God who delights to surprise." We don't always enjoy or understand messages or events that surprise us. Has God ever surprised you during your life? Was it a good or bad surprise when it happened? What about later on?

---

1. *NIV Cultural Backgrounds Study Bible* (Grand Rapids, MI: Zondervan, 2016), 1740.
2. Darrell L. Bock, *Luke* (Grand Rapids, MI: Baker Academic, 1994), 132.
3. Robert H. Stein, *Luke*, The New American Commentary, vol. 24 (Nashville, TN: Broadman, 1992), 69.

Chapter 4

Mary's Song

Luke 1:46–55

Mary's Spirit-inspired song of praise filled the home of Zechariah and Elizabeth. The song is full of joy, thankfulness, and praise that magnifies God—hence it is called the Magnificat—with a deep sense of God's blessing and leading. It eliminates any doubts we might have had about God's choice of a peasant maid.

Luke included three poems in the birth stories of John and Jesus. Besides Mary's song, there's the song of Zechariah after the birth of his son and the words of an aging prophet, Simeon, when Baby Jesus is presented at the temple. There are some key words and thoughts to look for in each of these songs:

- *servant* or *service*
- *salvation* and *savior*
- *justice* coupled with *mercy*
- *peace*

I want to especially highlight the last word, *peace*. The Hebrew word *shalom* is usually translated as "peace" in our English Bibles, but it has a greater depth of meaning, including the concepts of salvation and reconciliation. In addition, *eirënë*—"peace" in Greek—"is used four times by Matthew . . . , once by Mark . . . , six times by John . . . , and twenty-one times by Luke," of which fourteen are in his Gospel and seven in Acts.[1]

And Mary said:

> **"My soul exalts the Lord,**
> **And my spirit has rejoiced in God my Savior.**
> **For He has had regard for the humble state of His bond-servant" (Luke 1:46–48).**

"I am the Lord's servant" were Mary's words when Gabriel approached her. In her song, she described herself as God's "bond-servant" (verse 48). Her song is an outburst of praise from a humble maiden. Mary began by identifying God as "my Savior," which echoes these words from the prophet Habakkuk, "I will exult in the God of my salvation" (Habakkuk 3:18, NRSV). She praises God that her Son will bring salvation to the world.

Mary recognized that she was a sinner like everyone else, and God's graciousness and mercy to a humble teenager brought her tremendous joy and a rich sense of blessing. In the thinking of the Jewish leadership at the time, "lowly" people didn't deserve honor or special favors. Life would not be easy, as neighbors and other people from her village would observe her pregnancy and assume there has been an adulterous relationship.

> **"For behold, from now on all generations will call me blessed.**
> **For the Mighty One has done great things for me;**
> **And holy is His name.**
> **And His mercy is to generation after generation**
> **Toward those who fear Him" (Luke 1:48–50).**

Continuing with her song, Mary sang of three things: God's power, His holiness, and His mercy. He is the "Mighty One" (verse 49), the divine Warrior who fights for His people, as He did for Israel when they were slaves in Egypt. Because God is holy, His name should be said reverently. God's justice is balanced with His mercy. When sin invaded the planet, God, in His great mercy, introduced a covenant relationship with humanity that is about to see its fulfillment in the birth of Mary's Child.

> **"He has done mighty deeds with His arm;**
> **He has scattered those who were proud in the thoughts of their hearts.**
> **He has brought down rulers from their thrones,**
> **And has exalted those who were humble" (verses 51, 52).**

Mary's song tells of a complete reversal of human values. "It is not *the proud* or *the mighty* or *the rich* who will have the last word. Indeed, through His Messiah, God is about to overthrow all these."[2] The powerful will be "brought down from their thrones" (verse 52), and the lowly will be lifted up. Caesar Augustus states his claim to be "the divine savior who has brought peace to the world." Jesus, who will become the ultimate Savior and peace-giver to all humanity, will be born in a lowly stable. Certainly, "what God has done for Mary—her election and miraculous conception—signifies a fundamental shift in history."[3]

> **"He has filled the hungry with good things,**
> **And sent the rich away empty-handed.**
> **He has given help to His servant Israel,**
> **In remembrance of His mercy,**
> **Just as He spoke to our fathers,**
> **To Abraham and his descendants forever" (verses 53–55).**

Notice the contrast in verse 53 between the poor ("the hungry") and the rich (sent away "empty"). The "hungry" are not just the unfortunate but the ones who are oppressed by those in power. This is a preview of Jesus' ministry, which will bring good news to the poor, release the oppressed, and provide mercy for those who are downtrodden by the wealthy in society.

These last verses of Mary's song verbalize the fulfillment of the Abrahamic covenant for the Israelite community. Mary knows that not only has God shown mercy to her, but also this mighty, merciful God will act out of His own self-giving nature to embrace men and women in a saving relationship.[4]

Mary's song also reveals something important about the significance of women. We will observe an emphasis in Luke on the place of women. Women were not highly esteemed in first-century Jewish society. They were consistently clumped with the poor, the disrespected, and the disreputable. As we press ahead into Luke's Gospel, get ready to meet widows, prostitutes, diseased and unclean women, a bent-over woman, a prophetess, and yes, several women who become disciples of Jesus.

Reflection

How have you experienced God's justice and mercy in your life?

---

1. Paul Borgman, *The Way According to Luke: Hearing the Whole Story of Luke-Acts* (Grand Rapids, MI: Eerdmans, 2006), 29n10.

2. Leon Morris, *Luke: An Introduction and Commentary*, Tyndale New Testament Commentaries, vol. 3 (Downers Grove, IL: IVP Academic, 1988), 93.

3. Joel B. Green, *The Gospel of Luke*, New International Commentary on the New Testament (Grand Rapids, MI: Eerdmans, 1997), 104.

4. Green, 105.

Chapter 5

The Birth of John

Luke 1:56–80

Now we must return to Zechariah, who waited silently for nine months. Perhaps some of his friends assumed he was also deaf and formed a habit of writing their questions down. Maybe Zechariah heard some things that were not intended for his ears.

Mary stayed with her about three months, and then returned to her home.

Now the time had come for Elizabeth to give birth, and she gave birth to a son. Her neighbors and her relatives heard that the Lord had displayed His great mercy toward her; and they were rejoicing with her (Luke 1:56–58).

Soon after Mary returned to her home in Nazareth, Elizabeth gave birth to her miracle child. The promised son came with the promised joy. Word of the baby's arrival drew a joyous crowd from the surrounding community. In a communal culture, privacy is not highly valued, and the townspeople invaded Elizabeth's home. Her neighbors were ecstatic, and everyone wanted to be present for the circumcision ceremony and the naming of the boy. Soon the event became interesting.

And it happened that on the eighth day they came to circumcise the child, and they were going to call him Zechariah, after his father. And yet his mother responded and said, "No indeed; but he shall be called John." And they said to her, "There is no one among your relatives who is called by this name." And they made signs to his father, as to what he wanted him called. And he asked for a tablet and wrote as follows, "His name is John." And they were all amazed (verses 59–63).

The hill country people confidently expected the child to be named after Zechariah. The name was already on the lips of the crowd when Elizabeth said, "No!" and Zechariah wrote on a tablet,* "His name is John." There is a double surprise. First, no one in the family has that name. Second, immediately the old priest's voice returned, and as he raised his voice in a song of praise to God, the community fell silent.

And at once his mouth was opened and his tongue freed, and he began speaking in praise of God. And fear came on all those who lived around them; and all these matters were being talked about in the entire hill country of Judea. All who heard them kept them in mind, saying, "What then will this child turn out to be?" For indeed the hand of the Lord was with him (verses 64–66).

The old priest's joy overflows in a song inspired by the Holy Spirit. "It weaves the stories of John and

---

* A wooden board with a wax surface was used as a writing tablet.

Jesus into the one tapestry of God's purpose."[1] In his song, look for these key words: *salvation, mercy, peace,* and *servant*; plus, we'll see a recognition of God's universal justice.

And his father Zechariah was filled with the Holy Spirit and prophesied, saying:

> **"Blessed be the Lord God of Israel,**
> **For He has visited us and accomplished redemption for His people,**
> **And has raised up a horn of salvation for us**
> **In the house of His servant David—**
> **Just as He spoke by the mouth of His holy prophets from ancient times—" (verses 67–70).**

Zechariah thanked God for visiting His people and bringing a mighty Savior whose coming was predicted by the "holy prophets from of old" (verse 70, ESV). Jesus would be the Messianic "Son of David," for whom Israel has waited for a long time. Animals use their horns in battle, so the "horn of salvation" represents the redemptive power of God.

> **"Salvation from our enemies,**
> **And from the hand of all who hate us;**
> **To show mercy to our fathers,**
> **And to remember His holy covenant,**
> **The oath which He swore to our father Abraham,**
> **To grant us that we, being rescued from the hand of our enemies,**
> **Would serve Him without fear,**
> **In holiness and righteousness before Him all our days" (verses 71–75).**

A divine rescue was anticipated in the words of Zechariah. He, along with most Jews of his time, wanted deliverance from "those who hate us," meaning the oppression of Rome. He connected that hope with the covenant promise God made with his ancestor, Abraham, requiring only that Abraham "walk before Me and be blameless" (Genesis 17:1, 2). God is remembering His covenant. He is raising up a powerful Messiah who will bring deliverance, but not of the political kind. Instead, spiritual deliverance from the oppression of sin is what the Holy Spirit has in mind.

> **"And you, child, also will be called the prophet of the Most High;**
> **For you will go on before the Lord to prepare His ways;**
> **To give His people the knowledge of salvation**
> **By the forgiveness of their sins" (Luke 1:76, 77).**

As Zechariah looked down at his baby boy, he recognized that John was God's gift for a special purpose. He would grow up to be a prophet who prepared the way for Jesus by preaching repentance and forgiveness. He would be "the prophet of the Most High" (verse 76).

> **"Because of the tender mercy of our God,**
> **With which the Sunrise from on high will visit us,**

To shine on those who sit in darkness and the shadow of death,
To guide our feet into the way of peace" (verses 78, 79).

As Zechariah finished his praise song, the gathered community of friends and neighbors recognized that the newborn had some special purpose. As they returned to their homes, they had much to think about as they wondered, "What then will this child turn out to be?" (verse 66).

Now the child grew and was becoming strong in spirit, and he lived in the deserts until the day of his public appearance to Israel (verse 80).

The youthful John finds his way into the wilderness. The area is probably the barren region on the western edge of the Jordan and the Dead Sea.[2] Since his parents were aged at his birth, we might wonder whether he soon found himself alone and sought a solitary lifestyle in the wilderness as he contemplated his mission.

Reflection

From the initial lack of faith in God's promise, Zechariah developed a mature faith during Elizabeth's pregnancy. Have your life experiences brought you to a more mature faith?

---

1. Joel B. Green, *The Gospel of Luke*, New International Commentary on the New Testament (Grand Rapids, MI: Eerdmans, 1997), 111.
2. Darrell L. Bock, *Luke* (Grand Rapids, MI: Baker Academic, 1994), 194.

Chapter 6

The Birth of Jesus

Luke 2:1–21

Joseph, here is your package. Life has not been easy for you. Mary's pregnancy by the Holy Spirit has brought you shame in the Nazareth community. The birth of Mary's child will not happen in the way you anticipated.

Like Joseph and Mary, we, too, are expectant, waiting for the birth of a boy whom they would call Jesus. His name—meaning "Yahweh Saves"—is a promise waiting for its glorious fulfillment. Luke has prepared his readers for this, and now we'll look at the story.

Now in those days a decree went out from Caesar Augustus, that a census be taken of all the inhabited earth. This was the first census taken while Quirinius was governor of Syria. And all the people were on their way to register for the census, each to his own city. Now Joseph also went up from Galilee, from the city of Nazareth, to Judea, to the city of David which is called Bethlehem, because he was of the house and family of David, in order to register along with Mary, who was betrothed to him, and was pregnant (Luke 2:1–5).

"Divine Augustus Caesar, son of a god, imperator of land and sea, the benefactor and savior of the whole world."[1] Augustus was the most powerful ruler ever known in the Mediterranean world,[2] but his proud claims were about to be challenged by the humble birth of a child. Caesar's demand for a census in Israel that required Joseph to register at his ancestral home, Bethlehem, was about to be overshadowed by God's purpose to have the ultimate Son of David born in the city of David, which is Bethlehem. Truly, "the Most High is sovereign over the kingdom of mortals" (Daniel 4:17, NRSV).

The purpose of a Roman census was for taxation and military service records. Although Jews were exempt from the military, they were required to register at their ancestral home. Since Joseph was a descendant of King David, he must travel nearly one hundred miles south to Bethlehem, David's birthplace. Did Mary have to go with him? No, but it was necessary for two reasons: her delivery time was approaching, and she would be the recipient of nasty gossip if she gave birth in Nazareth. Mary's pregnancy was shameful in the eyes of her home community because Joseph's betrothal with her had not been consummated.[3] Additionally, God had prophesied through the prophet Micah that the Messiah would be born in Bethlehem (Micah 5:2). With his decree, Caesar became the unknowing agent of God.

Luke describes Mary as "betrothed" to Joseph. In other words they were formally committed to marriage, but the couple did not yet live together as husband-and-wife. The Bible doesn't tell us when Joseph and Mary got married, but Matthew emphasized Jesus' virgin birth when he wrote that Joseph "kept her a virgin until she gave birth to a Son" (1:25). When they arrived in Bethlehem, they discovered there were no available rooms, so they may have bedded down in the public square which would have served as a caravansary for visitors during the census.

While they were there, the time came for her to give birth. And she gave birth to her firstborn son; and she wrapped Him in cloths, and laid Him in a manger, because there was no room for them in the inn (Luke 2:6, 7).

This was not the way they wanted it, but the stable was the only option in the crowded village. We assume it was a stable because of the presence of a manger, but Luke doesn't provide extra details. Most likely, Joseph's calloused hands assisted with the delivery, cutting and tying the umbilical cord. Then he watched as Mary swaddled her Son in strips of cloth to keep His limbs straight.[4] Telling us that this was Mary's "firstborn," Luke confirms her virginity.

In the same region there were some shepherds staying out in the fields and keeping watch over their flock at night. And an angel of the Lord suddenly stood near them, and the glory of the Lord shone around them; and they were terribly frightened. And so the angel said to them, "Do not be afraid; for behold, I bring you good news of great joy which will be for all the people; for today in the city of David there has been born for you a Savior, who is Christ the Lord" (verses 8–11).

We may well ask, *Lord, what were You thinking? Didn't You know that shepherds were considered disreputable and unclean in Jewish society?* Their humble occupation made them unable to keep all the requirements of the ceremonial law, like the ritual washing of hands.[5] Plus, they had a reputation for dishonesty, so most people wouldn't believe what a shepherd told them.[6] Surely, an angelic appearance at the temple in Jerusalem, witnessed by a crowd of worshippers, would be more appropriate! And yet, we must remember something the Lord said in Mary's song: "He has brought down the powerful from their thrones, and lifted up the lowly; he has filled the hungry with good things, and sent the rich away empty" (Luke 1:52, 53, NRSV). These shepherds represented the outcasts and sinners for whom Jesus would die. And it is very fitting that such outcasts were the first recipients of the good news. The future of the gospel message would be centered not in a temple but in the hearts of ordinary people. Good news had come to peasants, not rulers.[7]

"And this will be a sign for you: you will find a baby wrapped in cloths and lying in a manger." And suddenly there appeared with the angel a multitude of the heavenly army of angels praising God and saying,

> **"Glory to God in the highest,**
> **And on earth peace among people with whom He is pleased" (Luke 2:12–14).**

In the angelic announcement, we observe the same four things that came to old Zechariah and then to young Mary: (1) the appearance of an angel, (2) fear, (3) the announcement of a birth, and (4) a sign. But what sort of sign was this—a state of poverty, a baby in a hay trough who is wrapped in bands of cloth? In truth, "God's glory, normally associated with the temple, is now manifest on a farm! Luke puts us on notice that the new world coming is of a radically different shape than the former one."[8]

The glory song of "a multitude of the heavenly army of angels" swept across the night sky over those lonely sheep fields with brilliant light while majestic sound thundered across the hills. It was a light-and-sound spectacle like no other. Nothing like it had been seen before on this planet and will not be seen again until the end of time. On the little island of Patmos, the aged apostle John was treated to a preview of that end-time event as he heard

the voice of a great multitude, like the sound of many waters, and like the sound of mighty thunderpeals, crying out,

> "Hallelujah!
> For the Lord our God
>   the Almighty reigns.
> Let us rejoice and exult
>   and give Him the glory" (Revelation 19:6, 7, NRSV).

The angel brought the shepherds "good news of great joy" (Luke 2:10). God's "good news" is a theme of Luke's Gospel, and it is always an occasion for joy. Some describe Luke's account as a singing Gospel, and "the verb 'rejoice' occurs more often in Luke than in any other New Testament book."[9]

When the angels had departed from them into heaven, the shepherds began saying to one another, "Let's go straight to Bethlehem, then, and see this thing that has happened, which the Lord has made known to us." And they came in a hurry and found their way to Mary and Joseph, and the baby as He lay in the manger. When they had seen Him, they made known the statement which had been told them about this Child. And all who heard it were amazed about the things which were told them by the shepherds. But Mary treasured all these things, pondering them in her heart. And the shepherds went back, glorifying and praising God for all that they had heard and seen, just as had been told them (verses 15–20).

A late-night visit to Bethlehem by a bunch of excited, wild-eyed shepherds likely awakened the community. And their excitement only grew when the shepherds found heaven's newborn in a manger—just as the angel described. Perhaps a crowd soon gathered in the village square, where the shepherds tried to share what they had seen and heard. But how do you describe a heavenly happening in earthly language? The people were amazed.[10] Mary was amazed too. After the shepherds left and the silence returned, she contemplated everything they said.

And when eight days were completed so that it was time for His circumcision, He was also named Jesus, the name given by the angel before He was conceived in the womb (verse 21).

The child's name was not revealed to the shepherds. They were told of a "Savior" who is also "Christ the Lord." According to Jewish custom, a boy's name was not public information until the eighth day, when the circumcision was performed. That's when Joseph and Mary gave the child the name Jesus, as mandated by Gabriel to both Mary (Luke 1:31) and Joseph (Matthew 1:21).

Reflection

How have you celebrated the birth of Jesus? Will you celebrate the event differently in light of Luke's Spirit-guided account?

---

1. Myrian inscription.
2. *NIV Cultural Backgrounds Study Bible* (Grand Rapids, MI: Zondervan, 2016), 1743.
3. Paul Borgman, *The Way According to Luke: Hearing the Whole Story of Luke-Acts* (Grand Rapids, MI: Eerdmans, 2006), 23.
4. Robert H. Stein, *Luke*, The New American Commentary, vol. 24 (Nashville, TN: Broadman, 1992), 107.
5. William Barclay, *The Gospel of Luke* (Philadelphia, PA: Westminster Press, 1975), 22.
6. Ray Pritchard, "Shepherds: The Right Choice?" Christianity.com, May 21, 2010, https://www.christianity.com /jesus/birth-of-jesus/shepherds-and-angels/shepherds-the-right-choice.html. See also *NIV Cultural Backgrounds Study Bible*, 1744.
7. Darrell L. Bock, *Luke* (Grand Rapids, MI: Baker Academic, 1994), 213–219.
8. Joel B. Green, *The Gospel of Luke*, New International Commentary on the New Testament (Grand Rapids, MI: Eerdmans, 1997), 131.
9. Leon Morris, *Luke: An Introduction and Commentary*, Tyndale New Testament Commentaries, vol. 3 (Downers Grove, IL: IVP Academic, 1988), 56.
10. Borgman, *Way According to Luke*, 33.

Chapter 7

Simeon and Anna

Luke 2:22–38

Mary didn't yet understand the joy and the future pain she would experience in the days and years to come. We left Mary and Joseph with Baby Jesus in Bethlehem, where He was circumcised on the eighth day and named. Forty days after the birth, Mary, Joseph, and Baby Jesus arrive at the temple in Jerusalem.

And when the days for their purification according to the Law of Moses were completed, they brought Him up to Jerusalem to present Him to the Lord (as it is written in the Law of the Lord: "Every firstborn male that opens the womb shall be called holy to the Lord"), and to offer a sacrifice according to what has been stated in the Law of the Lord: "A pair of turtledoves or two young doves" (Luke 2:22–24).

Mary's purification took place before a priest in the temple, and it was required because Jesus was her first son (Exodus 13:2). She was ceremonially unclean for forty days after the birth and had to stay away from holy things for that time.[1] For her purification, she would normally offer the sacrifice of a lamb; but if she couldn't afford a lamb, a pair of doves or pigeons would suffice. Here we learn that while Joseph and Mary were humble and financially poor, they were also faithful and obedient—together they traveled to Jerusalem with their baby Son for the ceremony.

And there was a man in Jerusalem whose name was Simeon; and this man was righteous and devout, looking forward to the consolation of Israel; and the Holy Spirit was upon him. And it had been revealed to him by the Holy Spirit that he would not see death before he had seen the Lord's Christ (Luke 2:25, 26).

We don't know exactly who Simeon was, and there is no evidence that he was a priest. Luke simply described him as a righteous, upright man who looked forward to "the consolation of Israel" (verse 25). Like many Jews of his time, Simeon was looking forward to the coming Messiah, though many thought the Messiah would deliver Israel from the sovereignty of Rome. We picture an elderly saint who was shown by the Holy Spirit that he would live to see the Messiah.

And he came by the Spirit into the temple; and when the parents brought in the child Jesus, to carry out for Him the custom of the Law, then he took Him in his arms, and blessed God, and said,

> **"Now, Lord, You are letting Your bond-servant depart in peace,**
> **According to Your word;**
> **For my eyes have seen Your salvation,**

Which You have prepared in the presence of all the peoples:
A light for revelation for the Gentiles,
And the glory of Your people Israel" (verses 27–32).

On this particular day, Simeon was divinely led to the temple at the very time that Mary's Baby was presented there. Taking the Child in his arms, Simeon looked heavenward and spoke these Spirit-filled words, "My eyes have seen your salvation" (verse 30). A mighty deliverance would encompass all peoples. For Gentiles living in deep spiritual darkness (Isaiah 9:1, 2), Jesus would bring light. For the chosen nation of Israel, His advent represented a glorious moment, a realization of the ancient covenant with Abraham, kept alive through long centuries.[2]

Joseph and Mary were amazed to hear these wonderful words from a stranger who just happened to arrive, it seemed to them, at a deeply spiritual moment. Before he left, Simeon blessed them but added some prophetic words that dimmed a little of the light and joy.

And His father and mother were amazed at the things which were being said about Him. And Simeon blessed them and said to His mother Mary, "Behold, this Child is appointed for the fall and rise of many in Israel, and as a sign to be opposed—and a sword will pierce your own soul—to the end that thoughts from many hearts may be revealed" (Luke 2:33–35).

Simeon's last words were sobering and shocking. Would their sweet Baby be the cause of division and disruption? Would His ministry arouse grave opposition from some quarters? Yes, indeed. The birth of their Baby was "a sign" (verse 34)—that word again—that the nation of Israel would reject Jesus as their Messiah and Savior. Simeon's final words were addressed only to Mary: "A sword will pierce your own soul," he said (verse 35). Joseph would not be alive when Jesus was nailed to a cross; Mary, alone, would experience the pain of her son's crucifixion.

This is not the good news Mary and Joseph heard from the shepherds. Does it connect with the angels' message of joy and the choral anthem of glory? How do Simeon's chilling predictions relate to the Christmas story? Pondering the contrast, we turn again to the Isle of Patmos, where the apostle John is writing on a long scroll, describing what he has seen in vision. In Revelation 12, John's words portray Christ's birth as a cosmic event, part of an age-long controversy between God and Satan. Here is a birth narrative that is very different from the pen of Luke. The Holy Spirit has given Simeon a tiny glimpse of a "cosmic Christmas" that is set in the panorama of eternal realities.

Suddenly the troubling thoughts of the couple from Bethlehem were interrupted by the voice of an elderly woman.

And there was a prophetess, Anna, the daughter of Phanuel, of the tribe of Asher. She was advanced in years and had lived with her husband for seven years after her marriage, and then as a widow to the age of eighty-four. She did not leave the temple grounds, serving night and day with fasts and prayers. And at that very moment she came up and began giving thanks to God, and continued to speak about Him to all those who were looking forward to the redemption of Jerusalem (Luke 2:36–38).

In the Greek, it is unclear whether she lived eighty-four years after the death of her husband or whether she was eighty-four years old. Either way, she was "of a great age." That day the Holy Spirit led her to

Mary and Joseph, where she turned to face the temple crowds and broke into joyful praise for the Child who would bring salvation to her people—and the world.

The double testimony of an old man and an old woman came as Mary and Joseph dedicated their firstborn to the Lord. "When the testimony of the man and the woman is placed alongside the testimony of the shepherds, one can see a triad of witnesses. They come from the country and from the city; they represent both male and female; they picture the common person of the field along with the pious saints of great devotion. Many appreciate Jesus."[3]

Reflection

Jesus is portrayed as the object of Israel's fondest hopes and dreams (verses 25, 26, 29–32, 34, 38): consolation, salvation, glory, redemption. How and why will many of these hopes be dashed?

---

1. Darrell L. Bock, *Luke* (Grand Rapids, MI: Baker Academic, 1994), 234.
2. Darrell L. Bock, *A Theology of Luke and Acts* (Grand Rapids, MI: Zondervan, 2012), 122.
3. Bock, *Luke*, 254.

Chapter 8

The Boy Jesus

Luke 2:39–52

What a special glimpse of the birth of Jesus Luke provided for us in his account! But Luke didn't tell us everything that happened while Joseph and Mary made their temporary abode in Bethlehem. Instead, he wrote a brief summary.

And when His parents had completed everything in accordance with the Law of the Lord, they returned to Galilee, to their own city of Nazareth. Now the Child continued to grow and to become strong, increasing in wisdom; and the favor of God was upon Him (Luke 2:39, 40).

Perhaps the tasks of caring for their special Baby overwhelmed them, so they delayed the arduous hundred-mile journey north to their Nazareth home. Another Gospel writer, Matthew, tells the story of the wise men who travel from the East with gifts for Israel's new King. Their visit is quickly followed by a flight to Egypt to escape the wrath of Herod (Matthew 2). Finally, however, Mary and Joseph were ready for the journey north "to their own town of Nazareth" (Luke 2:39, NRSV).

His parents went to Jerusalem every year at the Feast of the Passover. And when He was twelve years old, they went up there according to the custom of the feast; and as they were returning, after spending the full number of days required, the boy Jesus stayed behind in Jerusalem, but His parents were unaware of it. Instead, they thought that He was somewhere in the caravan, and they went a day's journey; and then they began looking for Him among their relatives and acquaintances. And when they did not find Him, they returned to Jerusalem, looking for Him (verses 41–45).

Although it is a requirement for Jewish men to attend three festivals in Jerusalem every year, the distances from Jerusalem mean that many from Galilee attend only the important Passover festival, sometimes with their wives and children. This seems to be the case with Joseph and Mary. At the age of thirteen, a Jewish boy was expected to understand and begin observing the law. At twelve, Jesus is approaching that time. "Luke referred to the law four times in this passage" (verses 22, 23, 24, 27) and "clearly believed that the OT is still operative as a guide for Christian behavior."[1]

The journey to Jerusalem was minimally an eighty-mile trip from Nazareth. The journey often included roads that were watched by highway robbers, so the pilgrims often traveled in large caravans for protection.[2] Groups might cover twenty to twenty-five miles on foot in a typical day, so the journey from Nazareth could take four days each way. Typically, the men walked as a group with the older boys, while the women traveled together with the small children. Knowing this, we find it easy to understand why Joseph assumed that Jesus was with the women, and Mary, that He was with the men. At the first night's encampment on the return journey to Nazareth, they were shocked to discover that their boy was missing, and they spent the following day anxiously returning to Jerusalem to look for Him. The city was swarming with great crowds who, like themselves, had come for the Passover festival. I'm sure they wondered where in this crowded city they would find their precious Son.

Then, after three days they found Him in the temple, sitting in the midst of the teachers, both listening to them and asking them questions. And all who heard Him were amazed at His understanding and His answers (verses 46, 47).

Should Joseph and Mary be surprised that their twelve-year-old was sitting in the temple with the teachers of the law? Not really, Luke has already told us that this boy is "filled with wisdom" (verse 40, NRSV), and His parents surely recognized His wisdom. Jesus took the opportunity to learn from teachers of a higher caliber than Nazareth afforded. Sitting with them, Jesus listened and asked questions. The teachers were "amazed" at His level of understanding. Already we can see that amazement is one of Luke's favorite expressions. He has used it three times in the first two chapters of his Gospel, and it is almost always associated with God's presence. Does this imply that the temple teachers could discern that this twelve-year-old's wisdom came from a supernatural source?

When Joseph and Mary saw Him, they were bewildered; and His mother said to Him, "Son, why have You treated us this way? Behold, Your father and I have been anxiously looking for You!" And He said to them, "Why is it that you were looking for Me? Did you not know that I had to be in My Father's house?" And yet they on their part did not understand the statement which He had made to them (verses 48–50).

His parents had been beside themselves with worry. And, astonished to find Jesus in the temple, Mary is unhappy. She asks, "What are you doing here? Your father and I have been looking for you!"

Jesus responds, " 'Your father'? Don't you understand that I belong in the house of My Father?" Here we see that Jesus knew who His real Father was. "Already at the age of twelve he knew that He was God's Son. . . . He demonstrated a higher allegiance to his divine sonship than to Mary."[3] But they didn't comprehend what their Son was saying, in spite of Mary's prior knowledge. Twelve years of apparently normal family life has caused her to momentarily forget the reality of who Jesus is. Indeed, Mary was the only person in all of Israel who had intimate knowledge of Jesus' divine Sonship given by the Holy Spirit. It would take years of ministry before anyone else uttered the ultimate truth about Jesus being "the Son of God."

And He went down with them and came to Nazareth, and He continued to be subject to them; and His mother treasured all these things in her heart.

And Jesus kept increasing in wisdom and stature, and in favor with God and people (verses 51, 52).

In Luke's account, the first recorded words of Jesus show us that at the age of twelve, He knew He was the Son of God, and He tried to reveal that truth to His parents. Afterward, Jesus lived obediently with His parents in Nazareth. For the next eighteen years, we learn nothing about the day-to-day events in Jesus' life—these are the hidden years—but Luke gives us an important one-sentence summary: "Jesus grew in wisdom and stature, and in favor with God and man" (verse 52, NIV). This summary tells that Jesus had balanced growth—intellectual, physical, spiritual, and social—throughout His formative years.

Luke's special eyewitness

In his preface (Luke 1:1–4), Luke wrote that he depended on eyewitnesses as he compiled his Gospel. The only other Gospel writer who tells of Jesus' birth is Matthew, who almost certainly composed his Gospel after Luke and after the destruction of Jerusalem in AD 70. Matthew omits the events of Jesus' birth aside from emphasizing the role of Joseph and including the visit of the wise men from the East and the subsequent trip to and from Egypt (Matthew 2).

Where, then, did Luke learn all the wonderful and intimate details of the stories of John's birth and of Jesus' birth in Bethlehem and His boyhood visit to the temple? We find a clue in something The New American Commentary, volume 24, says about what the apostle John recorded about Jesus' words to him from the cross: "Now beside the cross of Jesus stood His mother. . . . So when Jesus saw His mother, and the disciple whom He loved standing nearby, He said to His mother, 'Woman, behold, your son!' Then He said to the disciple, 'Behold, your mother!' And from that hour the disciple took her into his own household" (John 19:25–27).

Thereafter, the apostle John took care of Mary, and when he moved to Ephesus to take up evangelistic work there and in the surrounding cities, he took Mary with him. We have evidence that Luke included Ephesus in his travels,[4] and a visit with Mary, perhaps in her seventies at the time, would have given him a genuine first-person account of the two birth narratives. What an incredible eyewitness Luke found in Jesus' mother!

Reflection

What thoughts might have been going through Mary's mind during Jesus' birth and His boyhood experiences (see Luke 1:31, 32, 2:17–19, 33, 51)? At the age of twelve, how much did Jesus know about His mission? Why would attendance at Passover be of special significance to Him?

---

1. Robert H. Stein, *Luke*, The New American Commentary, vol. 24 (Nashville, TN: Broadman, 1992), 119.
2. Darrell L. Bock, *Luke* (Grand Rapids, MI: Baker Academic, 1994), 264.
3. Stein, *Luke*, 124.
4. Refer back to chapter 1, "Luke's Research and Travel."

Chapter 9

John's Mission

Luke 3:1–6 (Matthew 3:1–3, Mark 1:2–4)

Thirty years have marched by since the two miracle births in the region of Judea. We know nothing aside from the glimpse of a twelve-year-old Boy who was wise beyond His years and His encounter with teachers at the temple. Everything we have read thus far comes uniquely from Luke's Gospel. He has carried us through the silent years with two brief statements:

- Of John: "The child grew and was becoming strong in spirit, and he lived in the deserts until the day of his public appearance to Israel" (Luke 1:80).
- Of Jesus: "Jesus kept increasing in wisdom and stature, and in favor with God and people" (Luke 2:52).

As they approached the age of thirty, the two cousins were strong, healthy young men, yet most of their lives was already over. Within two years, King Herod Antipas would behead John; and in three and a half years, Jesus would be crucified on a Roman cross. At age thirty, though, both men were qualified for public service. Historically, this was the age of maturity when Levites began their service as priests (Numbers 4:47).

Now in the fifteenth year of the reign of Tiberius Caesar, when Pontius Pilate was governor of Judea, and Herod was tetrarch of Galilee and his brother Philip was tetrarch of the region of Ituraea and Trachonitis, and Lysanias was tetrarch of Abilene, in the high priesthood of Annas and Caiaphas, the word of God came to John, the son of Zechariah, in the wilderness (Luke 3:1, 2).

Luke supplied all this political and religious background for the next part of his story. His purpose for sharing this information was to anchor the ministries of John and of Jesus on the time line of events in Rome and within Israel. Notice that Luke included a minor character—Lysanias, who ruled Abilene; this was a seemingly insignificant territory that bordered Syria. But perhaps Lysanias seemed important to Luke if he was indeed Syrian born.

Luke reminds his readers of Gabriel's message to John's aged father, Zechariah, whose Spirit-filled words were spoken at his birth: "And you, child, will be called the prophet of the Most High, for you will go on before the Lord to prepare His ways" (Luke 1:76). John's ministry was part of the divine plan, and his mission is God-directed.

There had been a time gap of four hundred years since there had been a prophet in Israel, so John's message increased the expectancy of the Jewish people in looking and longing for their promised Messiah. Luke showed how John, in a wonderful way, fulfilled some words of promise from Isaiah.

And he came into all the region around the Jordan, preaching a baptism of repentance for the forgiveness of sins; as it is written in the book of the words of Isaiah the prophet:

> "THE VOICE OF ONE CALLING OUT IN THE WILDERNESS,
> 'PREPARE THE WAY OF THE LORD,
> MAKE HIS PATHS STRAIGHT!
> EVERY RAVINE WILL BE FILLED,
> AND EVERY MOUNTAIN AND HILL WILL BE LOWERED;
> THE CROOKED WILL BECOME STRAIGHT,
> AND THE ROUGH ROADS SMOOTH;
> AND ALL FLESH WILL SEE THE SALVATION OF GOD!' " **(Luke 3:3–6).**

Luke alone presents the content of John the Baptist's teaching (verses 10–14) and cites the complete text of Isaiah 40:3–5, as quoted above.[1] In a contrasting poem, Isaiah employs the same metaphors to depict an evil influence:

> They do not know the way of peace,
> And there is no justice in their tracks;
> They have made their paths crooked,
> Whoever walks on them does not know peace (Isaiah 59:8).[2]

John's preaching would fulfill the prophet's Spirit-inspired words:

- "Every ravine will be filled, and every mountain and hill will be lowered" (Luke 3:5)—the proud would be humbled, as we saw in the words of Mary's song (Luke 1:52).
- "The crooked will become straight, and the rough roads smooth" (Luke 3:5)—John's preaching would correct the "crooked paths" (verse 5, CEV) of evildoers and flatten "rough places" (verse 5, ESV) of injustice.
- "All people will see God's salvation" (verse 6, NIV)—salvation is offered to everyone, Jew and Gentile.

Luke has already told us that John retreated to the desert as he contemplated his prophetic mission (Luke 1:80). Perhaps John spent some time at the Essene community of Qumran, a desert location near the western shore of the Dead Sea. The Essenes were a monastic Jewish cult that practiced ritual bathing to remove uncleanness. The Essenes invested much of their time copying the Scriptures, and when their existence was threatened by the Roman invasion, they hid their precious scrolls in nearby caves. In 1946, these were discovered and dubbed the Dead Sea Scrolls. They have proved valuable in verifying the accuracy of several Old Testament scriptures.

If John visited Qumran, he didn't adopt their monastic lifestyle, including their ritual bathing. The baptism that he introduced represented a life change that included repentance and acceptance of divine forgiveness. For thousands of years, Israelites had used washings and even immersion in water to represent spiritual cleansing. Speaking through Ezekiel, God said, "I will sprinkle clean water upon you, and you will be clean; I will cleanse you from all your filthiness and from all your idols. Moreover, I will give you a new heart and put a new spirit within you; and I will remove the heart of stone from your flesh and give you a heart of flesh" (Ezekiel 36:25, 26).

By the time of John's ministry, the Jews practiced a special baptism for proselytes—that is, Gentiles who wished to convert to Judaism, as did the Ethiopian eunuch in Acts 8. This involved total immersion, a practice almost identical to John's baptism. "The sting in John's practice was that he applied to Jews the ceremony they regarded as suitable for unclean Gentiles."[3] John's baptism was new in two ways: it was "a baptism of repentance for forgiveness of sins" (Luke 3:3), and it was administered by the prophet, in contrast to practices of self-dipping and bathing. The emphasis on repentance and forgiveness was continued by Jesus throughout His ministry and, later, by the apostles. In fact, *repentance* is used as a noun eleven times, and *repent* is used as a verb fourteen times in Luke and Acts.[4]

John baptized people in the waters of the Jordan, but the exact location is uncertain. Archaeological evidence points to a possible site on the eastern bank of the Jordan River, some five miles north of the Dead Sea.[5]

Reflection

How does baptism by total immersion symbolize repentance and a change in one's life direction?

1. Darrell L. Bock, *Luke* (Grand Rapids, MI: Baker Academic, 1994), 280.

2. Paul Borgman, *The Way According to Luke: Hearing the Whole Story of Luke-Acts* (Grand Rapids, MI: Eerdmans, 2006), 30.

3. Leon Morris, *Luke: An Introduction and Commentary*, Tyndale New Testament Commentaries, vol. 3 (Downers Grove, IL: IVP Academic, 1988), 112.

4. Robert H. Stein, *Luke*, The New American Commentary, vol. 24 (Nashville, TN: Broadman, 1992), 130.

5. "Baptism Site 'Bethany Beyond the Jordan' (Al-Maghtas)," UNESCO World Heritage Convention, accessed September 12, 2022, https://whc.unesco.org/en/list/1446/.

Chapter 10

John's Preaching

Luke 3:7–20 (Matthew 3:7–15; Mark 1:7, 8)

When the desert prophet began preaching in the Jordan wilderness, people came to listen. John's dynamic message about coming judgment and the need for repentance was compelling. We don't know how news of his preaching spread so quickly, but it did. Crowds left their comfortable homes in Jerusalem and the surrounding countryside to follow dusty trails that wound down through the mountains. Reports about John reached even the remote villages around Lake Galilee.

So he was saying to the crowds who were going out to be baptized by him, "You offspring of vipers, who warned you to flee from the wrath to come? Therefore produce fruits that are consistent with repentance, and do not start saying to yourselves, 'We have Abraham as our father,' for I say to you that from these stones God is able to raise up children for Abraham. But indeed the axe is already being laid at the root of the trees; so every tree that does not bear good fruit is cut down and thrown into the fire" (Luke 3:7–9).

John wasn't a passive preacher. His words were harsh, often shocking his listeners, " 'Do you really understand what my baptism is about,' you sons of snakes?"[1] When brush fires occur in the desert, snakes come out of the ground to escape the flames. It is a fitting illustration of coming judgment. The crowds recognized this preacher as an echo of former prophets like Joel, Isaiah, and Jeremiah—they, too, warned of judgment and likewise called for repentance and obedience. It had been at least four hundred years since the Jewish people had heard this kind of preaching. God had broken the silence. The Holy Spirit was active again.

The Jews had always placed their faith in their genealogy, looking back to their father Abraham, but this had to change. While they thought that because they were Jews and descendants of Abraham, they were safe, John told them, "Don't let that thought cross your mind. Becoming God's child is not a matter of inheritance. Your ancestry will not save you. It's the way you live that is important. Nor will baptism by itself save you. Your life must demonstrate your new way of thinking. Trees that don't bear fruit will be cut down."

And the crowds were questioning him, saying, "Then what are we to do?" And he would answer and say to them, "The one who has two tunics is to share with the one who has none; and the one who has food is to do likewise." Now even tax collectors came to be baptized, and they said to him, "Teacher, what are we to do?" And he said to them, "Collect no more than what you have been ordered to." And soldiers also were questioning him, saying, "What are we to do, we as well?" And he said to them, "Do not extort money from anyone, nor harass anyone, and be content with your wages" (verses 10–14).

The prophet's dire warnings of coming judgment, along with fire-and-brimstone preaching, produced results, and many asked, "What then are we to do?" The listeners came from all walks of life—the affluent, the poor, soldiers in the service of Herod, despised tax collectors, and even a few Pharisees (Matthew 3:7). Many were convicted by the prophet's appeals and asked what they should do. John's responses were quite practical:

- Share an item of clothing with a person in need. If you have an undershirt that you don't need, give it to someone who doesn't have one. And share your food with someone who is hungry.
- Tax collectors were unpopular in Jewish society. The prevailing system of "tax farming" (think pyramid scheme), which permitted a collector to add an unspecified surcharge as his wage, was open to abuse. "For assessment purposes, tax collectors were allowed to search anything except the person of a Roman lady; any property not properly declared was subject to seizure. In Egypt, tax collectors were sometimes so brutal that they were known to beat up an aged woman to try to learn where her tax-owing relatives were hiding."[2] John admonished them to be fair and honest.
- Soldiers who came to hear John were not Romans but Jewish military in the service of rulers like Herod Antipas or, perhaps, temple police. John told them they must avoid extortion, bribery, and violence.

True repentance responds to God and treats fellow humans justly. Many repented of their sinful ways and requested baptism. Changed lives were happening daily at the river.

Now while the people were in a state of expectation and they all were thinking carefully in their hearts about John, whether he himself perhaps was the Christ, John responded to them all, saying, "As for me, I baptize you with water; but He is coming who is mightier than I, and I am not fit to untie the straps of His sandals; He will baptize you with the Holy Spirit and fire. His winnowing fork is in His hand to thoroughly clear His threshing floor, and to gather the wheat into His barn; but He will burn up the chaff with unquenchable fire."

So with many other exhortations he preached the gospel to the people (Luke 3:15–18).

Some within the crowd wondered about this desert prophet who dressed funny and ate locusts and wild honey (Matthew 3:4). Who is he? Maybe he's the anticipated Messiah! But John firmly told them that he was not the Messiah. In Roman society, a child or a slave was often tasked with untying and removing a visitor's sandals. Using this as an illustration, John said he was not worthy to remove the Messiah's sandals. The stronger One to come will baptize with the Spirit, in contrast to John's water baptism.[3]

Emphasizing the judgment aspect, John spoke about winnowing forks and chaff burning with "unquenchable fire."* Was he accurately describing the kind of Messiah that Jesus would be? Perhaps his emphasis on judgment fit the broad expectation that Messiah's kingdom would end Roman authority within the Jewish realm. The people wanted a strong, dynamic Messiah, a king like David. Did John himself fully understand the nature of Christ's kingdom? Not completely, as we will later discover.

---

* The image of "unquenchable fire" fits the description of Gehenna, Jerusalem's garbage dump, where the fires never went out.

Luke closes this account by referencing "many other exhortations" of John, including "good news." This latter can only mean the message of forgiveness and the gospel—salvation is coming!

But when Herod the tetrarch was reprimanded by him regarding Herodias, his brother's wife, and regarding all the evil things which Herod had done, Herod also added this to them all: he locked John up in prison (Luke 3:19, 20).

While John preached righteousness, Satan continued his attempts to undermine God's mission. Luke informs us that King Herod would soon cut short John's ministry by imprisoning him. But until that happened, John continued to teach and baptize at the Jordan River. One day, Jesus arrived. It was the first time the two cousins met.

Reflection

"What then should we do?" was the question asked by people of different classes. In the following examples from Luke and Acts,[4] who were the questioners in each case, and what were the answers given? Luke 3:12; Luke 3:14; Luke 10:25; Luke 18:18; Acts 2:37; Acts 16:30; Acts 22:10.

1. Darrell L. Bock, *Luke* (Grand Rapids, MI: Baker Academic, 1994), 304, 305.
2. *NIV Cultural Backgrounds Study Bible* (Grand Rapids, MI: Zondervan, 2016), 1747.
3. Darrell L. Bock, *A Theology of Luke and Acts* (Grand Rapids, MI: Zondervan, 2012), 213–219.
4. Joel B. Green, *The Gospel of Luke*, New International Commentary on the New Testament (Grand Rapids, MI: Eerdmans, 1997), 177.

Chapter 11

Jesus Meets His Adversary

Luke 3:21–4:3 (Matthew 3:13–4:3; Mark 1:9–12)

Luke has completed his account of John and his mission in preparing the way for Jesus. He now carefully removes John from the public eye so that we can give our full attention to the arrival of Jesus and the start of His ministry.[1] Thanks to Luke, we already know the Christmas story of the angel's visit to Mary, the birth of Jesus in a manger, the angelic appearance to shepherds, the blessings of Simeon and Anna, and Jesus' visit to the temple when He was twelve.

Now when all the people were baptized, Jesus also was baptized, and while He was praying, heaven was opened, and the Holy Spirit descended upon Him in bodily form like a dove, and a voice came from heaven: "You are My beloved Son, in You I am well pleased" (Luke 3:21, 22).

Why did Jesus seek baptism from John? Did He need to repent? No, but Jesus "knew that he too must identify himself with his movement towards God. For Jesus the emergence of John was God's call to action."[2]

All four Gospel writers recorded the event of Jesus' baptism at the Jordan. Although Luke did not describe the event itself, he emphasized the anointing by the Holy Spirit and the public affirmation of His divinity. Luke is the only writer who tells us that Jesus prayed at His baptism, conscious that He was about to embark on His important mission.

When Jesus prayed, He relied on His Father for divine help and power in His ministry. We will find that many key events in Jesus' life are accompanied by prayer, which is a theme throughout Luke's Gospel and in Acts.[3] Something dramatic happened as Jesus came out of the water: the Holy Spirit descended on Him, and a voice from heaven confirmed for us what Mary knew: "You are My beloved Son." Heaven had spoken.

The words from heaven confirmed that Jesus is indeed God Incarnate, the Messiah. Now Luke is going to show us that Jesus is also human, with an ancestry.

Human ancestry of Jesus

Luke records the following:

When He began His ministry, Jesus Himself was about thirty years old, being, as was commonly held, the son of Joseph, the son of Eli, the son of Matthat, the son of Levi, the son of Melchi, the son of Jannai, the son of Joseph, the son of Mattathias, the son of Amos, the son of Nahum, the son of Hesli, the son of Naggai, the son of Maath, the son of Mattathias, the son of Semein, the son of Josech, the son of Joda, the son of Joanan, the son of Rhesa, the son of Zerubbabel,

the son of Shealtiel, the son of Neri, the son of Melchi, the son of Addi, the son of Cosam, the son of Elmadam, the son of Er, the son of Joshua, the son of Eliezer, the son of Jorim, the son of Matthat, the son of Levi, the son of Simeon, the son of Judah, the son of Joseph, the son of Jonam, the son of Eliakim, the son of Melea, the son of Menna, the son of Mattatha, the son of Nathan, the son of David, the son of Jesse, the son of Obed, the son of Boaz, the son of Salmon, the son of Nahshon, the son of Amminadab, the son of Admin, the son of Ram, the son of Hezron, the son of Perez, the son of Judah, the son of Jacob, the son of Isaac, the son of Abraham, the son of Terah, the son of Nahor, the son of Serug, the son of Reu, the son of Peleg, the son of Heber, the son of Shelah, the son of Cainan, the son of Arphaxad, the son of Shem, the son of Noah, the son of Lamech, the son of Methuselah, the son of Enoch, the son of Jared, the son of Mahalaleel, the son of Cainan, the son of Enosh, the son of Seth, the son of Adam, the son of God (verses 23–38).

Matthew also gives a genealogy for Jesus at the outset of his Gospel (Matthew 1:1–17), but there are several differences between his and Luke's accounts. Matthew begins at Abraham and moves forward from there to show Christ's Jewish lineage. In contrast, Greek genealogies, like this one by Luke, more often start with the present and trace back to earlier ancestors, in this case, all the way back to Creation and Adam, showing that everyone—Gentiles included—belonged in Jesus' ancestry.[4] It is significant that during His ministry, Jesus will most often identify Himself as "the Son of Man."

Luke's list of names between David and Jesus is sometimes different from Matthew's. Why? Some Bible scholars suggest that "Matthew gives us the genealogy of Joseph, the legal father of Jesus, while Luke gives that of Mary, the actual line of Jesus."[5] For that reason, perhaps, Luke omits Mary's name because he is speaking of a virgin birth. He begins his genealogy by saying that Jesus "was the son (*as was commonly held*) of Joseph." Traditionally, genealogies were never traced through the female line, but as we've already seen, Luke emphasizes the role of women in this departure from tradition.

Luke's genealogy of Jesus "runs through David for kingship, Abraham for promise, and uniquely back to Adam for the tie as 'son of God' directly created by God to be human."[6]

Now Jesus, full of the Holy Spirit, returned from the Jordan and was led around by the Spirit in the wilderness for forty days, being tempted by the devil. And He ate nothing during those days, and when they had ended, He was hungry. And the devil said to Him, "If You are the Son of God, tell this stone to become bread" (Luke 4:1–3).

Jesus received the Holy Spirit at His baptism. Now, "full of the Spirit," He goes to the wilderness to spend time in quiet reflection. Luke wanted us to understand that Satan would be tempting Jesus throughout His time in the wilderness. Jesus had just heard a voice from heaven calling Him "Son," and Satan would try to persuade Him to verify his Sonship by performing some miracles. Jesus' contemplation of His mission will be continually interrupted by an evil being with an agenda.

This is our first introduction to Satan. His existence as the adversary of God is alluded to but not expressly outlined in the Old Testament. Why? One theory is that because humans taught that the world was populated by many gods, so Jehovah emphasized His oneness: "Hear, Israel! The LORD is our God, the LORD is one!" (Deuteronomy 6:4). An exception is the account of Satan's appearance in a heavenly council where he challenges God to remove the hedge of protection around Job (Job

1; 2). Through the rest of that story, we find Job believing that all of his suffering comes from God. The author of the book was inspired to give us the inside story, but it is not clear whether or not Job or his friends knew of Satan's existence.[7]

Now, however, the salvation of humanity is at stake. Behind God's efforts at salvation for humankind stands the devil, who now steps out from behind the curtain for a direct confrontation. Behind Jesus, on the other hand, stands the Holy Spirit, so this will be a clash of cosmic proportions.[8] The surfacing of evil forces will characterize Jesus' entire ministry.

Reflection

Think of other Bible characters who spent time in the wilderness: Moses (Exodus 2:11–15; 3:1–9), David (1 Samuel 23:14–29), Elijah (1 Kings 19), and Paul (Galatians 1:13–18). What were the reasons for their wilderness sojourns, and what were the results?

---

1. Joel B. Green, *The Gospel of Luke*, New International Commentary on the New Testament (Grand Rapids, MI: Eerdmans, 1997), 184.
2. William Barclay, *The Gospel of Luke* (Philadelphia, PA: Westminster Press, 1975), 37.
3. Robert H. Stein, *Luke*, The New American Commentary, vol. 24 (Nashville, TN: Broadman, 1992), 51. The words *prayer* and *pray* are found thirteen times in Mark, seventeen times in Matthew, twenty-one times in Luke, and twenty-five times in Acts. What is significant is that prayer occurs at key times and places in Luke and Acts. Stein, 51.
4. *NIV Cultural Backgrounds Study Bible* (Grand Rapids, MI: Zondervan, 2016), 1747.
5. Leon Morris, *Luke: An Introduction and Commentary*, Tyndale New Testament Commentaries, vol. 3 (Downers Grove, IL: IVP Academic, 1988), 119.
6. Darrell L. Bock, *A Theology of Luke and Acts* (Grand Rapids, MI: Zondervan, 2012), 161.
7. Keith Clouten, *Breaking Through the Wall: How God Communicates With His Lost Creation* (Teach Services, 2018), 171, 172.
8. Green, *Gospel of Luke*, 192.

Chapter 12

Wilderness Temptations

Luke 4:3–13 (Matthew 4:3–11; Mark 1:13)

Jesus was alone in the wilderness when Satan came to challenge Him. In a community-based culture where being alone had negative overtones, this was a decisive moment in Jesus' life. Satan tempted Him to please and join the crowd as He interacted with people and tried to persuade Jesus that suffering and death on a Roman cross were not critical to human salvation, that there were less painful options.

And the devil said to Him, "If You are the Son of God, tell this stone to become bread." And Jesus answered him, "It is written: 'MAN SHALL NOT LIVE ON BREAD ALONE'" (Luke 4:3, 4).

Jesus' condition at the time of this encounter with Satan was one of physical weakness. He had had nothing significant to eat for forty days, so Satan began with a temptation to perform a miracle for Himself: "Use Your divine power to relieve Your hunger. You can do it! God has abandoned You out here in the desert, so You had better look out for Yourself." Satan wanted Jesus to use His power and authority for His own benefit, but Jesus chose to rely fully on His Father and the Holy Spirit. Thus, Satan's temptation failed. Furthermore, "Jesus' situation at his test contrasts with Adam's. Adam had not fasted at all, while Jesus had suffered lack for forty days. Adam could eat from any tree in the garden but one, while Jesus was denying himself food. Adam was in paradise, while Jesus was in the wilderness."[1]

And he led Him up and showed Him all the kingdoms of the world in a moment of time. And the devil said to Him, "I will give You all this domain and its glory, for it has been handed over to me, and I give it to whomever I want. Therefore if You worship before me, it shall all be Yours." Jesus replied to him, "It is written: 'YOU SHALL WORSHIP THE LORD YOUR GOD AND SERVE HIM ONLY'" (verses 5–8).

Instead of becoming the kind of political Messiah that most Jews and their leaders wanted to see, Jesus chose a cross, not a crown.

And he brought Him into Jerusalem and had Him stand on the pinnacle of the temple, and said to Him, "If You are the Son of God, throw Yourself down from here; for it is written:

'HE WILL GIVE HIS ANGELS ORDERS CONCERNING YOU, TO PROTECT YOU,'

and,

**'ON THEIR HANDS THEY WILL LIFT YOU UP,
SO THAT YOU DO NOT STRIKE YOUR FOOT AGAINST A STONE.'"**

And Jesus answered and said to him, "It has been stated, 'You shall not put the Lord your God to the test'" (verses 9–12).

In this temptation, Satan quoted Psalm 91:11, 12, but he ignored verse 1, which specifies protection for "he who dwells in the shelter of the Most High" (ESV). Satan was persuasive. "Come on, now. Instead of Jerusalem being the place of Your suffering and death, it can be the place of Your glory." But Jesus rejected his temptation.

Jesus responded to the temptations from the book of Deuteronomy, all of which reference the wilderness experience of Israel. The Israelites had traveled through the wilderness for forty years, and they failed each of the tests that Satan was now bringing to Jesus:

- The test of hungering in the wilderness (Deuteronomy 8:2, 3). Jesus quoted verse 3: "Man shall not live on bread alone, but man shall live on everything that comes out of the mouth of the Lord."
- The test of worshiping only God (Deuteronomy 6:4–15). Jesus quoted verse 13: "You shall fear only the Lord your God; and you shall worship Him."
- Blaming God for their thirst at Massah—"Is the Lord among us, or not?" (Exodus 17:7). Again, Jesus quoted words from Deuteronomy: "You shall not put the Lord your God to the test, as you tested Him at Massah" (Deuteronomy 6:16).

The three temptations of Christ are also described by Matthew, but the order of the last two is reversed (Matthew 4:1–11). For ancient writers, though, chronological sequence is secondary to purpose when telling a story.[2] Luke emphasized the role of the temple, so he brought us to Jesus standing on the pinnacle of the temple in Jerusalem. Matthew links events in Jesus' life with mountains, so the last test happens on a mountaintop. Knowing the sequence of the temptations is less important than discerning the purposes of the writers.

And so when the devil had finished every temptation, he left Him until an opportune time (Luke 4:13).

Throughout His wilderness ordeal, Jesus was not acting on His own. He allowed God to lead Him through the Holy Spirit. The experience in the wilderness established Jesus' competence and authority. His success in the wilderness contrasts with Israel's failure there. Jesus won this victory over His enemy, but the battle would continue throughout His ministry. "By facing these tests and proving his fidelity, Jesus has demonstrated unequivocally his faithful obedience to God and thus his competence to engage in ministry publicly as God's Son."[3]

Reflection

In Christ's second temptation, Satan quoted from Psalm 91:11, 12. When we are tempted, what other promises found in Psalm 91 may we claim?

1. Darrell L. Bock, *Luke* (Grand Rapids, MI: Baker Academic, 1994), 371.
2. E. Randolph Richards and Brandon J. O'Brien, *Misreading Scripture With Western Eyes* (Downers Grove, IL: Inter-Varsity, 2012), 149, 150.
3. Joel B. Green, *The Gospel of Luke*, New International Commentary on the New Testament (Grand Rapids, MI: Eerdmans, 1997), 196.

Chapter 13

Jesus Defines His Mission

Luke 4:14–22 (Matthew 4:12–17; Mark 1:14, 15)

Luke begins,

And Jesus returned to Galilee in the power of the Spirit, and news about Him spread through all the surrounding region. And He began teaching in their synagogues and was praised by all (Luke 4:14, 15).

Jesus returned from the wilderness empowered by the Holy Spirit. He bested all the tests thrown at Him by Satan. And then He returned to Galilee, His home territory. I imagine that He was well known to the townspeople of Capernaum and other towns strung along the shores of the lake. Perhaps they have long admired the fine young Man who frequently jogged down the steep trail from the high country around Nazareth to spend time with the locals. It seemed that He had an uncanny ability to turn up wherever help was needed—to assist in hauling a boat onto the beach, to carry a load of grain for a widow who had gleaned behind reapers, to repair a leaking roof with new thatch—always with a ready smile and a kind word. And no one could top this young Man in His knowledge of the Scriptures.

Now, though, a different Jesus returned to Galilee. In "the power of the Spirit," He began a teaching tour in the synagogues that culminated with a Sabbath sermon in the small synagogue of His home village, Nazareth. Luke says that it was His custom to worship in a synagogue each Sabbath (verse 16).

And He came to Nazareth, where He had been brought up; and as was His custom, He entered the synagogue on the Sabbath, and stood up to read. And the scroll of Isaiah the prophet was handed to Him (verses 16, 17).

Coming at the beginning of His ministry, the service at Nazareth is of enormous significance. Luke has already given us reliable witnesses to who Jesus is—"a devout priest and his wife, the angel Gabriel, an angel of the Lord [to some shepherds], the righteous Simeon, and prophets such as Anna and John the Baptist. . . . Now, however, *Jesus himself* answered the question, 'Who is this One?' "[1] Luke tells the story of this Nazareth visit in great detail, showing us what kind of Messiah He is and what His mission will be. His words to His home congregation became His mission statement.

A synagogue service comprised several elements. It included reciting the *Shema* (Deuteronomy 6:4–9) together, which begins with "Hear, Israel! The LORD is our God, the LORD is one!" This was typically followed by set prayers, a reading from the five books of Moses (Torah), then a reading from the prophets, which led into a period of instruction or a sermon and ended with a benediction. On this day, Jesus gave the reading from the prophets, followed by the sermon.

We saw that the ministry of John the Baptist was defined by prophetic words from Isaiah 40:3–5.

Other words from Isaiah will now define the ministry of Jesus. On this Sabbath morning at Nazareth, He was handed the scroll of Isaiah, and standing before the congregation, He selected and read aloud from a Messianic passage in Isaiah 61:1, 2:

> "THE SPIRIT OF THE LORD IS UPON ME,
> BECAUSE HE ANOINTED ME TO BRING GOOD NEWS TO THE POOR.
> HE HAS SENT ME TO PROCLAIM RELEASE TO CAPTIVES,
> AND RECOVERY OF SIGHT TO THE BLIND,
> TO SET FREE THOSE WHO ARE OPPRESSED,
> TO PROCLAIM THE FAVORABLE YEAR OF THE LORD" (Luke 4:17–19).

Jesus added words from other parts of Isaiah, "to let the oppressed go free, and break every yoke" (Isaiah 58:6), and "the eyes of those who are blind will be opened" (Isaiah 35:5). But He also omitted some words from Isaiah 61:2: "and the day of vengeance of our God." The omission is intentional. "The present time is one of grace and opportunity. . . . Yet by its very nature the 'today' of grace implies a 'tomorrow' when that grace will be withdrawn and judgment will come."[2]

And He rolled up the scroll, gave it back to the attendant, and sat down; and the eyes of all the people in the synagogue were intently directed at Him. Now He began to say to them, "Today this Scripture has been fulfilled in your hearing" (Luke 4:20, 21).

Jesus returned the scroll to the attendant and sat down to teach, as was customary. All eyes were on Him as He said, "Today this Scripture has been fulfilled in your hearing." Those words announced "jubilee" and "Messiah" to the Nazareth congregation. They remembered God's words through Moses (Leviticus 25:10–13, 23–55) introducing laws of social justice for the poor. Every fiftieth year—designated a year of jubilee—"each of you shall return to his own property, and each of you shall return to his family" (Leviticus 25:10). If anyone, because of poverty, sold himself as a slave, he was given his freedom at the jubilee.

Let's imagine that you are an Israelite among your people in the Promised Land. Famine and sickness have taken their toll on you and your family. You've had to sell your precious piece of land to one of your affluent neighbors. No longer able to afford food, your wife sells herself as a servant—slave, really—to a respectable family. So, what future do you have? Well, coming up soon is a jubilee year—every fiftieth—and that spells relief. You will then be able to move back onto your land, and your wife will be a free person again.

How does this relate to Christ's mission? The words Jesus quoted from Isaiah create a picture of freedom:

- good news for the poor—those of low status in society—widows, children, disabled, the destitute, outsiders
- release from Satan's captivity, including demon-possession
- recovery of sight for the spiritually blind
- restitution and wholeness for humanity

Jesus, filled with the Holy Spirit and so recently victorious over Satan, defined His mission with these words from Isaiah—who He was, why He was there, and what He would accomplish. He had come as the world's Redeemer. He would ultimately sacrifice Himself to buy back our lost freedom.

The Nazareth congregation understood this to mean the dawn of God's new age of salvation through a Messiah. However, the freedom they wanted was liberty from the controlling power of Rome. They had it all wrong—God had a very different purpose in Jesus' mission. "The citation in Luke, then, is not a call to fulfill literally the legal requirement of Jubilee. Rather, the passage takes that picture of freedom to show what God is doing spiritually and physically through his commissioned agent, Jesus."[3]

And all the people were speaking well of Him, and admiring the gracious words which were coming from His lips; and yet they were saying, "Is this not Joseph's son?" (Luke 4:22).

The immediate response of the Nazareth villagers is positive amazement. They approve of what He has said, but then they ask, "Isn't He Joseph's son?" Unfortunately, "this question shows that they wish to respond to Jesus in terms of his human origin rather than his divine mission. When Jesus detects their motive, he knows that his own people will never take him seriously enough."[4] Jesus is *not* Joseph's son. He is God's Son. The Nazareth villagers were not going to like what He was about to tell them.

Reflection

Do you have a personal mission statement? It should come when you ask yourself these questions: Why am I here? What is my purpose in life? What are my goals? Your mission statement will have something to do with your interests, talents, and abilities. Here are some examples of personal mission statements:

- I will use my writing skills to inspire and educate others to make a change.
- I will use my gifts as a speaker to improve the self-worth of people around the world.
- I will create music that helps people struggling with mental illness feel calm, loved, and in control.

---

1. Robert H. Stein, *Luke*, The New American Commentary, vol. 24 (Nashville, TN: Broadman, 1992), 160; emphasis in original.
2. Stein, 160.
3. Darrell L. Bock, *Luke* (Grand Rapids, MI: Baker Academic, 1994), 410.
4. O. C. Edwards Jr., *Luke's Story of Jesus* (Philadelphia, PA: Fortress, 1981), 35.

Chapter 14

Gentiles Too?

Luke 4:23–30

The Nazareth congregation liked what they heard from Jesus. Doubtless, they felt a sense of pride in having Him there to participate in their synagogue service. After all, this fine young Man was a local boy from a respected family in their village community. They anticipated He would make Nazareth His home once again. He could even become the leader of their synagogue.

The Nazareth villagers were also proud of their Jewish heritage. They were children of Abraham through a long line of prophets and kings—members of God's chosen people, proud of ancestors like Isaac, Jacob, and Samuel, and reaching a climax with King David.

And He said to them, "No doubt you will quote this proverb to Me: 'Physician, heal yourself! All the miracles that we heard were done in Capernaum, do here in your hometown as well.' " But He said, "Truly I say to you, no prophet is welcome in his hometown" (Luke 4:23, 24).

Jesus read the thoughts of His hometown people. If He was the one fulfilling the words of Isaiah, they expected Him to show them signs and wonders as evidence. Likely, stories of miraculous events in Capernaum had reached Nazareth, and they wanted Him to "do at home what You have done elsewhere." They wanted Jesus to demonstrate that He was their Nazareth prophet.

"But I say to you in truth, there were many widows in Israel in the days of Elijah, when the sky was shut up for three years and six months, when a severe famine came over all the land; and yet Elijah was sent to none of them, but only to Zarephath, in the land of Sidon, to a woman who was a widow" (verses 25, 26).

The listeners at Nazareth knew the story well. In the time of Elijah, when the people of Israel were worshiping the god Baal, believing that *he* provided the seasonal rains for their crops, God permitted a lengthy drought to deplete their harvest, causing widespread famine. This was a particularly tough time for widows, who depended on handouts from friends and neighbors. In the midst of the famine, God instructed Elijah to go to the foreign country of Sidon where He would provide for him through a widow and her son (1 Kings 17).[1]

"And there were many with leprosy in Israel in the time of Elisha the prophet; and none of them was cleansed, but only Naaman the Syrian" (Luke 4:27).

The second story dates from the time of Elisha. Leprosy was a common disease in the ancient world. With no known cure for the disease, victims were social outcasts, forced to survive on the fringes of civilized life. In the enemy kingdom of Syria, an army captain, Naaman, became leprous and faced a future without hope until a captive Jewish maid persuaded him to go to Israel, where the prophet Elisha prescribed seven washings in the Jordan River. Naaman returned to Syria healed and happy (2 Kings 5).

And all the people in the synagogue were filled with rage as they heard these things; and they got up and drove Him out of the city, and brought Him to the crest of the hill on which their city had been built, so that they could throw Him down from the cliff. But He passed through their midst and went on His way (Luke 4:28–30).

Why did the congregation become so angry? Their vision didn't extend beyond the boundaries of Judaism. The Elijah story tells of God's concern for a destitute individual—a woman, a widow, a Gentile, in a foreign country—during a time of famine. The second story is about the miraculous healing of Naaman—a Syrian, a leper, a Gentile, and an army general of an enemy nation. The Nazareth congregation is furious. They want a Messiah who will respond to *their* needs, cure *their* sicknesses—not waste His energy with foreign widows, lepers, Gentiles, and other enemies!

Jesus recounted those stories to illustrate what His mission statement meant in practical terms. His ministry will be good news for the poor of *all* nations, recovery of sight for *all* the spiritually blind, release for *all* captives of Satan, and freedom from *all* social and religious oppression. No one will ever be excluded from God's grace.

Luke is unique in his retelling of the two Old Testament stories. I wonder if his eyewitness source was James, a half-brother of Jesus, who was almost certainly in the synagogue congregation with his family that Sabbath. After a period of uncertainty about Jesus, James became a firm believer, and in the time of Luke's writing, he was the leader of the fledgling Christian church in Jerusalem. Luke had the wonderful opportunity of meeting James when he accompanied Paul to Jerusalem (read about it in Acts 21:17–19).

The rejection and attempt by the Nazarenes to kill Jesus was a portent of what would take place in His rejection and death at Jerusalem. "From the beginning Jesus was aware that he, like the prophets, would be rejected by his own (4:24), and the rejection in Nazareth is programmatic of the future rejection in Jerusalem. . . . The incident also foreshadows the future mission to the Gentiles, for even as Gentiles were the recipients of God's grace in the ministry of Elijah and Elisha . . . , so it would be Gentiles who would be the primary recipients of the gospel's words of grace."[2]

Reflection

A key element in Jesus' mission statement is His loving concern for every person, no matter their sex, race, creed, color, age, or nationality. How should I relate to those who belong to a different category than I do? Do I have a responsibility?

---

1. Darrell L. Bock, *Luke* (Grand Rapids, MI: Baker Academic, 1994), 418.
2. Robert H. Stein, *Luke*, The New American Commentary, vol. 24 (Nashville, TN: Broadman, 1992), 160, 161.

Part II

Galilean Ministry

Luke 4:31–9:50

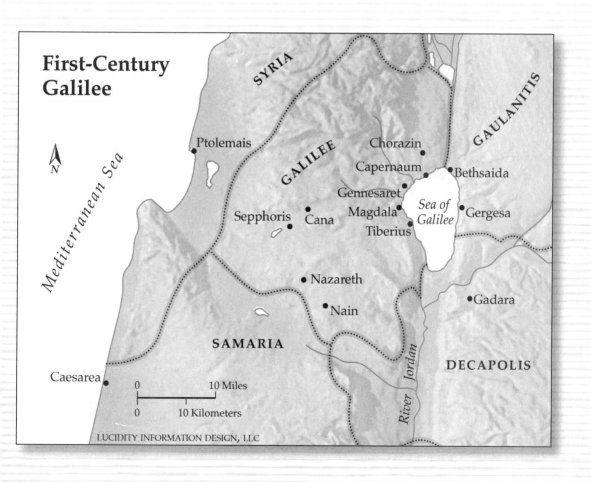

First-Century Galilee

SYRIA

Ptolemais

GALILEE

Chorazin

Capernaum

Bethsaida

GAULANITIS

Gennesaret

Magdala

Sea of Galilee

Gergesa

Sepphoris

Cana

Tiberius

Mediterranean Sea

N

Nazareth

Nain

Gadara

SAMARIA

DECAPOLIS

River Jordan

Caesarea

0   10 Miles

0   10 Kilometers

LUCIDITY INFORMATION DESIGN, LLC

Chapter 15

The Galilean Ministry of Jesus

Jesus spent His early ministry in the province of Galilee. Six chapters of Luke's Gospel follow Jesus' itinerary through Galilee (Luke 4:14–9:50). There are a few noteworthy characteristics about the province of Galilee in the time of Jesus. Study the map of Galilee Province on page 55, and notice several things. First, the Lake of Galilee was not entirely within the borders of the province. Its eastern shore was outside the provincial boundary. Most of Galilee was a chunk of land extending westward from the Jordan River almost to the Mediterranean Sea.

The lake lies in a deep trench, seven hundred feet below sea level. High mountains rise quite abruptly from the lake on its eastern and western shores. Since Nazareth is approximately 1,100 feet above sea level, a walk from Capernaum on the lakeshore to Nazareth will involve an overall ascent of nearly 2,000 feet.

In addition, Galilee was separated from the more heavily populated southern province of Judea, including Jerusalem, by the unfriendly territory of Samaria, which was also bounded on its east by the Jordan River.

For much of Israel's history, the kingdom was divided. Judah, in the south, was the home of Israel's worship at Jerusalem and the temple. It was where Jews went several times a year for the festivals. Galilee, in the north, was historically part of a separate kingdom, Israel, which also encompassed Samaria.

As we think about the ministry of Jesus in both Galilee and Judea, we should be aware of several important differences between the two provinces:

- Galilee was an agricultural region, producing grapes, figs, olives, and wheat, as well as providing pasturage for sheep and goats. In addition, the lake was a busy hub for fishermen. So, we would expect to find Jesus using these settings in His teachings and travels while He is in Galilee. By contrast, most of Judea is unproductive land. The climate there is dryer, and many farms are ranch-like, where wealthy landowners employ servants or own slaves.
- Galilee was basically a peasant culture with small village markets. Many people lived near the poverty line, relying on subsistence farming, exchanging any surplus for other necessities. Galilee was a province of the poor, in contrast with the urban rich in much of Judea.
- Galilee was a racial melting pot. Historically, the region was invaded and ruled by foreign powers, including the empire of Assyria in the eighth century BC. At that time, many Jews from the north were forcibly removed to the Assyrian capital, their places taken by refugees brought in from other conquered nations. Galilee thus became known as the "region of the Gentiles." Jews became only one of many nations represented, and as a result, Galileans weren't respected among the Jews in the south.
- Religiously, the Galileans tended to be lax in following some Jewish rituals and often failed to attend

the annual Passover festival in Jerusalem. Their shortest route to Jerusalem was through Samaria, which was unfriendly territory. The alternative was a longer journey through Jericho, ending with a long, hard ascent to Jerusalem.

• Linguistically, Galileans had an accent and were considered slovenly in their speech. At the trial of Jesus, Peter was identified as a Galilean by his speech. Galileans were considered uneducated by the urban dwellers in Judea, so they were looked upon as "country cousins."

Isn't it strange, then, that Jesus came from Galilee? Pharisees would correctly argue that "no prophet arises out of Galilee" (John 7:52). "The prevailing thought was that if a prophet were to come out of Israel, he would most definitely come out of Judea, the heart of Israel's worship."[1]

Bible scholar Dick France, commenting on how Jesus might expect to be viewed in Jerusalem, wrote: "Even an impeccably Jewish Galilean in first-century Jerusalem was not among His own people; he was as much a foreigner as an Irishman in London or a Texan in New York. His accent would immediately mark Him out as 'not one of us,' and all the communal prejudice of the supposedly superior culture of the capital city would stand against his claim to be heard even as a prophet, let alone as the 'Messiah,' a title which, as everyone knew, belonged to Judea (cf. John 7:40–42)."[2]

So then, why was Jesus born a Galilean, and why was so much of His ministry accomplished in the northern province? We may find an answer in a prophetic vision of the prophet Isaiah as he looked ahead to the promised Messiah. Isaiah speaks about two rather isolated Israelite tribes in the north of Israel:

In the past he humbled the land of Zebulun and the land of Naphtali, but in the future he will honor Galilee of the nations, by the Way of the Sea, beyond the Jordan—

> The people walking in darkness
>   have seen a great light;
> on those living in the land of deep darkness
>   a light has dawned. . . .
> For to us a child is born,
>   to us a son is given,
>   and the government will be on his shoulders.
> And he will be called
>   Wonderful Counselor, Mighty God,
>   Everlasting Father, Prince of Peace.
> Of the greatness of his government and peace
>   there will be no end.
> He will reign on David's throne
>   and over his kingdom (Isaiah 9:1–7, NIV).

That first sentence refers to "the Way of the Sea." The Way of the Sea, named Via Maris by the Romans, was one of the ancient trade routes, dating from the early Bronze Age. It linked Egypt with the northern empires of Syria, Anatolia, and Mesopotamia, passing through the historical Fertile Crescent. In Palestine, it came northward near ancient Dothan to Megiddo, cut a path northeastward through the province of

Galilee, passing close to Nazareth, and then crossed the upper Jordan to Syria (recall the story of Joseph, in Genesis 37:17–28, when his brothers, sheepherding near Dothan, sold him to a caravan of Midianite traders traveling the Way of the Sea en route to Egypt).

Through Isaiah, God promised that the Messiah, the future Davidic king, would "make glorious the Way of the Sea, the land beyond the Jordan, Galilee of the nations" (Isaiah 9:1, NRSV). It was a promise that Galilee, a territory seemingly forgotten, war-torn, and severely ravaged by Assyria in the time of Isaiah, would one day give birth to a Prince of Peace.

We worship a God who loves to surprise us. His best surprise was having one member of the holy Trinity come to earth to become a human, like one of us. We recall Luke's birth narrative of Jesus—how a humble Galilean teenager became His mother, how the first news of His birth came to simple shepherds. The major events of Jesus' ministry—the launching of His mission at Nazareth, most of His healing miracles, the calling of His disciples, His Sermon on the Mount, the feeding of five thousand, His transfiguration—none of these occurred at Jerusalem in the heartland of Judaism but in "Galilee of the Gentiles." I think God wants to tell us that the Savior came for humanity of every color, language, and culture in every part of our planet.

Reflection

Galilee was a province of mixed races and cultures. According to Matthew, Jesus' pedigree includes several unsavory characters, most of them Gentile women. Find them in the first chapter of Matthew's Gospel.

---

1. Brian Dye, "The Unlikely Disciples," Legacy Disciple, May 2, 2018, https://legacydisciple.org/index.php/2018/05/02/the-unlikely-disciples/.

2. R. T. France, *The Gospel of Matthew*, The New International Commentary of the New Testament, ed. Ned B. Stonehouse, F. F. Bruce, and Gordon D. Fee (Grand Rapids, MI: Eerdmans, 2007), 6.

Chapter 16

One Sabbath Day at Capernaum

Luke 4:31–44 (Matthew 8:14–17, 4:23–25; Mark 1:21–39)

At the northern end of Lake Galilee, just west of the point where the upper Jordan River flows into the lake, are the archaeological remains of Capernaum. In Roman times, this was a substantial lakeside town. The most prominent structure at the site today is what remains of a fifth-century synagogue built over the basalt foundation stones of an older synagogue, which was almost certainly the one in which Jesus taught and performed a miracle.[1] Luke shares the story of that miracle as he recounts the events of one Sabbath day at Capernaum.

We remember that it was on a Sabbath in Nazareth that Jesus officially introduced His mission. There is no biblical record that He ever returned to His hometown. During His Galilean ministry, Jesus seems to have regarded the town of Capernaum as His "home" at the lake (Matthew 4:13; 9:1; Mark 2:1). Prior to His baptism and the formal beginning of His work, Jesus doubtless made numerous visits to the lake and met some of the lake fishermen, including the brothers Simon and Andrew. It is possible that He made Simon's home at Capernaum His Galilean home base.[2]

And He came down to Capernaum, a city of Galilee; and He was teaching them on the Sabbath; and they were amazed at His teaching, because His message was delivered with authority (Luke 4:31, 32).

After escaping from an angry mob of villagers at Nazareth (verses 28–30), Jesus journeyed down through the mountains to Lake Galilee and Capernaum. On Sabbath, Jesus taught in the Capernaum synagogue. He was no stranger to the people, but as they listened to Him, they were awestruck by His divinely inspired words.

In the synagogue there was a man possessed by the spirit of an unclean demon, and he cried out with a loud voice, "Leave us alone! What business do You have with us, Jesus of Nazareth? Have You come to destroy us? I know who You are—the Holy One of God!" But Jesus rebuked him, saying, "Be quiet and come out of him!" And when the demon had thrown him down in the midst of the people, it came out of him without doing him any harm. And amazement came upon them all, and they began talking with one another, saying, "What is this message? For with authority and power He commands the unclean spirits, and they come out!" And the news about Him was spreading into every locality of the surrounding region (verses 31–37).

Suddenly, the service is interrupted by a scream from somewhere in the congregation: "Let us alone! Have you come to destroy us? I know who you are, the Holy One of God!" The interruption came from a man who shuddered in demonic terror.

"Be silent! Come out of him!" Jesus delivered these words with authority. The angry demon threw the man to the floor as it fled the scene. Everyone watched breathlessly as the man got up, unharmed; then, they found their voices. "This Jesus has power over evil spirits!" "They obey Him!" "What authority He has!" "We have never seen anything like this before."

"The very thing the devil promised to give Jesus, 'authority,' has come to Jesus as a consequence of His resisting the devil and operating in the sphere of the Holy Spirit, with the result that He now exercises authority and power against the forces of evil."[3]

Then He got up and left the synagogue, and entered Simon's home. Now Simon's mother-in-law was suffering from a high fever, and they asked Him to help her. And standing over her, He rebuked the fever, and it left her; and she immediately got up and served them (verses 38, 39).

The synagogue service over, Jesus accompanied Simon to his house in town. Mark adds that Simon's brother, Andrew, lived there too (Mark 1:29). Two other fishermen, brothers James and John, were also visiting this afternoon, and we can imagine that the topic of conversation centered around the demonic outburst at the synagogue and the authority of Jesus over evil forces. However, the family is about to witness the same authority in healing sickness. Simon's mother-in-law was sick with a "high fever," and in His second miracle of the day, Jesus "rebuked" the fever and restored the woman to wellness. In fact, she got up and prepared food for everyone. What rejoicing there was in the home that Sabbath afternoon! From Luke's and Mark's Gospel accounts, we conclude that this lady is a widow with no living sons to support her, so Simon had graciously taken her into his home. We will soon learn more about Simon Peter and his fishing mates, James and John.

Luke does not name Simon's brother, Andrew, in these early accounts, but Mark tells us that Andrew lived with Simon, and they fished together. Throughout his writing, Luke chose to focus on Simon Peter as Christ's leading disciple. In Acts, Luke gives prominence to Peter as an apostle and evangelist,[4] and in naming the twelve disciples, Luke starts with "Simon, whom He also named Peter" (Luke 6:14).

Now while the sun was setting, all those who had any who were sick with various diseases brought them to Him; and He was laying His hands on each one of them and healing them (Luke 4:40).

As the sun set that Sabbath evening, a crowd of townspeople gathered at Simon's house. They brought their sick to Jesus, and His healing touch restored many to wholeness.

Demons also were coming out of many, shouting, "You are the Son of God!" And yet He was rebuking them and would not allow them to speak, because they knew that He was the Christ (verse 41).

The people of Capernaum had already witnessed the power of Jesus in their synagogue that morning, so some came to be released from the power of demons. The people recognized Jesus' miracle-working power, and the demons knew with certainty that He was the Son of God and that they had to obey when Jesus told them to be quiet. He did not want positive testimony from such inglorious figures. Isn't it strange that only unearthly beings recognized Jesus for who He is?[5]

Now when day came, Jesus left and went to a secluded place; and the crowds were searching for Him, and they came to Him and tried to keep Him from leaving them. But He said to them, "I must also preach the kingdom of God to the other cities, because I was sent for this purpose."
So He kept on preaching in the synagogues of Judea (verses 42–44).

At Capernaum, we have seen Jesus put His mission statement into practice. He has brought release to captives of Satan (verse 18). Now, after a busy day of miracles, Jesus sought rest and prayer empowerment. He withdrew to a quiet place to converse with His Father. The Capernaum crowds found Him the next morning and tried to persuade Him to remain in their city. Jesus, however, had other plans. He explained to the townspeople how His mission would be put into practice: "I must proclaim the good news of the kingdom of God to the other cities also; for I was sent for this purpose" (verse 43, NRSV). This is the first of thirty-one references to the "kingdom of God" mentioned in Luke's Gospel. Unlike political jurisdictions, God's kingdom has no territorial boundaries. You get your membership card when you accept the "good news" of personal salvation in Jesus Christ.

Reflection

The word *authority* carries negative overtones in our society. In what ways should we recognize the authority of Jesus in our lives? What are some positive aspects of His authority?

---

1. *NIV Cultural Backgrounds Study Bible* (Grand Rapids, MI: Zondervan, 2016), 1750.
2. Biblical Archaeology Society Staff, "The House of Peter: The Home of Jesus in Capernaum?" Biblical Archaeology Society, October 13, 2022, https://www.biblicalarchaeology.org/daily/biblical-sites-places/biblical-archaeology-sites/the-house-of-peter-the-home-of-jesus-in-capernaum/.
3. Joel B. Green, *The Gospel of Luke*, New International Commentary on the New Testament, vol. 3 (Grand Rapids, MI: Eerdmans, 1997), 221.
4. Robert H. Stein, *Luke*, The New American Commentary, vol. 24 (Nashville, TN: B & H, 1992), 168.
5. James M. Dawsey, *The Lukan Voice: Confusion and Irony in the Gospel of Luke* (Macon, GA: Mercer University Press, 1986), 7.

Chapter 17

The Calling

Luke 5:1–11 (Matthew 4:18–22; Mark 1:16–20)

We don't know if Luke ever visited Galilee, but we see evidence that he referenced an early manuscript of Mark's Gospel in his account of Jesus' early ministry at Capernaum and other lakeside localities.* We may be certain that the Holy Spirit guided Luke in his writing and the retelling of Christ's ministry for his friend Theophilus and, ultimately, for us.

Now it happened that while the crowd was pressing around Him and listening to the word of God, He was standing by the lake of Gennesaret; and He saw two boats lying at the edge of the lake; but the fishermen had gotten out of them and were washing their nets. And He got into one of the boats, which was Simon's, and asked him to put out a little distance from the land. And He sat down and continued teaching the crowds from the boat (Luke 5:1–3).

Gennesaret was another name for Lake Galilee, but it was also a town west of Capernaum on the lakeshore. Lake Galilee measures eight miles from east to west and fourteen miles north to south. Fishermen used all parts of the lake in their work, so it won't surprise us that Simon and his workmates have their boats at the village of Gennesaret on this particular day.

Wherever He went in Galilee, Jesus drew a crowd of people coming to see and hear Him. There was a freshness and relevance about His teaching that put Him at variance with the instruction of the scribes. One day, as He taught at the lakeshore, the crowd pressed in on Him, eager to hear the words from God. Jesus observed two boats that were pulled up at the shore, and nearby, Simon and Andrew were washing their nets. Jesus stepped into Simon's boat and asked him to move the boat out a little from the shore so that He could sit and teach from the boat.

Now when He had finished speaking, He said to Simon, "Put out into the deep water and let down your nets for a catch." Simon responded and said, "Master, we worked hard all night and caught nothing, but I will do as You say and let down the nets" (verses 4, 5).

When Jesus finished teaching, He gave Peter some strange instructions: "Let down your nets for a catch." David Bivin identifies the nets that these fishermen use as trammel nets,[1] which were made of linen, visible to fish during the day, so used only at night. The nets were heavy, so two or more men were needed to use them, and they required washing after use.

We might well wonder what went through Peter's mind when Jesus asked him to use the linen nets in broad

---

* Note, for example, Luke's reference in Luke 4:44 to Jesus' preaching "in the synagogues of Judea" when it is apparent that he was itinerating in Galilee.

daylight! He had seen ample evidence that Jesus was an agent from God, but he must have wondered what a carpenter brought up in Nazareth knew about nets and fishing! In fact, what Jesus requests is absurd—a waste of time and effort. But Peter is polite: "Master, we fished all last night and didn't catch a thing. But we will do as you say." So, he and Andrew loaded the wet nets and rowed out into deeper water with Jesus.

And when they had done this, they caught a great quantity of fish, and their nets began to tear; so they signaled to their partners in the other boat to come and help them. And they came and filled both of the boats, to the point that they were sinking. But when Simon Peter saw this, he fell down at Jesus' knees, saying, "Go away from me, Lord, for I am a sinful man!" For amazement had seized him and all his companions because of the catch of fish which they had taken; and likewise also were James and John, sons of Zebedee, who were partners with Simon (verses 6–10).

The catch was huge, and the heavy nets began to break, so a second boat, belonging to James and John, approached to help contain the astonishing haul of fish. All the men were amazed, but Peter's immediate response was to fall at Jesus' feet, saying "I am a sinful man, Lord." Like every individual in the presence of Jesus, Peter recognized that he was a sinner.

And Jesus said to Simon, "Do not fear; from now on you will be catching people" (verse 10).

Jesus' response to Simon is warming and wonderful: "Peter, don't be afraid. From now on, you are going to help me catch people." What a remarkable call to discipleship! "Jesus does not turn His back on the sinner, but includes the sinner in his task. What a reversal and what a token of God's grace this is."[2]

When they had brought their boats to land, they left everything and followed Him (verse 11).

The four men at the lakeshore were incredulous, but they sensed a calling they could not ignore. As soon as they brought their boats to the beach, Peter, Andrew, James, and John knew exactly what they would do. Leaving behind a lucrative fishing business in Galilee was an economic sacrifice,[3] but "they left everything and followed Him" (verse 11).

Discipleship involves a life choice and a commitment—it's all about relationships. It is a change of life direction that will require prayerful preparation. My family experienced such a life change when we accepted a call to migrate from Australia to Canada, where God unfolded a plan that led me in pathways of service I never anticipated. Peter discovered that discipleship meant being a willing student of Jesus Christ, making mistakes along the way but learning from the Master Teacher and relying on the Holy Spirit as an indispensable Guide. In his later ministry, he caught thousands of men and women with the gospel net. There was no turning back.

Reflection

It has often been said that "God doesn't call the equipped—He equips the called." How was this demonstrated with the fishermen whom Jesus called to follow Him? (Read Hebrews 13:20, 21).

1. Joel B. Green, *The Gospel of Luke*, New International Commentary on the New Testament, vol. 3 (Grand Rapids, MI: Eerdmans, 1997), 232.
2. Darrell L. Bock, *Luke* (Grand Rapids, MI: Baker Academic, 1994), 459.
3. *NIV Cultural Backgrounds Study Bible* (Grand Rapids, MI: Zondervan, 2016), 1751.

Chapter 18

The Healing

Luke 5:12–26 (Matthew 8:1–4; 9:1–8; Mark 1:40–45; 2:1–12)

Jesus continued His itinerary through Galilean towns and villages, always drawing a crowd. In this and the following accounts, Luke appears to draw from Mark's Gospel but made the stories his own by his choice of words and emphasis.

While He was in one of the cities, behold, there was a man covered with leprosy; and when he saw Jesus, he fell on his face and begged Him, saying, "Lord, if You are willing, You can make me clean" (Luke 5:12).

Leprosy was the name given in Bible times to a number of skin diseases—many of them uncurable. Quarantine for the sufferer was the primary way to treat the disease. Leprosy was considered a "social disease" because victims were forbidden to approach anyone and had to cry out, "Unclean!" when someone came near. Sufferers were forbidden to enter villages and towns, and their livelihood depended on charity, usually from family members. It was commonly believed that leprosy was God's punishment for sin, so lepers were burdened with shame as well as illness. Lepers were hated by others until they came to hate themselves. Shunned and despised, lepers sometimes took their own lives.[1]

The sufferer in Luke's story was "covered with leprosy," so his disease was highly visible. Hearing reports of Jesus' healing miracles, he made a risky decision to disobey the rules and enter the town where Jesus was known to be. Feeling wretched and dirty, he approached Jesus, knowing that if the Master ignored him, he would lose whatever self-respect he had left. Coming as close as he dared, he bowed low and said bravely, "Lord, if you choose, you can make me clean." Knowing leprosy is a dirty disease, he wanted to be clean, so he approached the One with healing ability.

And He reached out with His hand and touched him, saying, "I am willing; be cleansed." And immediately the leprosy left him. And He ordered him to tell no one, saying, "But go and show yourself to the priest, and make an offering for your cleansing, just as Moses commanded, as a testimony to them." But the news about Him was spreading even farther, and large crowds were gathering to hear Him and to be healed of their sicknesses. But Jesus Himself would often slip away to the wilderness and pray (verses 13–16).

Here Jesus ignored the rules. He reached out to the leper, touched him, and with compassion, said, "I am willing. Be made clean." Jesus could have kept His distance and simply spoken the words. After all, to stretch out His hand and touch the leper violated the law, but it communicated acceptance and reentry into the community.[2] Jesus did not, however, wholly ignore the law. He instructed the man to follow the law's requirement by going to a priest, who acted as a health inspector and was qualified to declare the man cured. "The believer's need to keep the law is an especially important emphasis for Luke."[3]

Jesus touched the untouchable. "When we despise ourselves, when our hearts are filled with bitter shame, let us remember, that, in spite of all, Christ's hand is still stretched out. . . . It is of the very essence of Christianity to touch the untouchable, to love the unlovable, to forgive the unforgiveable. Jesus did—and so must we."[4]

Jesus ordered the healed leper to "tell no one" about his healing, but an ex-leper with a clean body and a wide-open smile was all the evidence people needed. Jesus did not want people to believe in Him because of miracles, so as crowds began to gather, He again withdrew to the wilderness for a time of prayer. He saw conflict just ahead.

Healing a paralytic

Soon Jesus was back in Capernaum, and as word spread that He was "at home" (Mark 2:1), the crowds gathered. He was probably staying at Simon Peter's house, which was apparently large in comparison to most dwellings in the town,[5] but so many came to see the miracle worker that the house quickly filled with people. When some scribes and Pharisees turned up, everyone made room for them, and the crowd overflowed into the street. Inside, Jesus was teaching—in fact, He was teaching teachers.

One day He was teaching, and there were some Pharisees and teachers of the Law sitting there who had come from every village of Galilee and Judea, and from Jerusalem; and the power of the Lord was present for Him to perform healing. And some men were carrying a man on a stretcher who was paralyzed; and they were trying to bring him in and to set him down in front of Him. But when they did not find any way to bring him in because of the crowd, they went up on the roof and let him down through the tiles with his stretcher, into the middle of the crowd, in front of Jesus (Luke 5:17–19).

Suddenly four men (Mark 2:3) arrived, carrying a paralyzed man on some kind of stretcher—determined to get their friend to Jesus. This was not possible because of the crowd, but that did not deter them. Galilean town houses had flat roofs, often with an exterior stairway to the rooftop. The roof was likely constructed of poles, clay, and thatch. Mark described it that way, but Luke portrayed a house like one in which Theophilus lives, with a tile roof.[6] The unconventional method of bringing the paralytic to Jesus produced surprise and undoubtedly some dust, but they lowered him on his bed right in front of Jesus.

And seeing their faith, He said, "Friend, your sins are forgiven you." The scribes and the Pharisees began thinking of the implications, saying, "Who is this man who speaks blasphemies? Who can forgive sins, except God alone?" But Jesus, aware of their thoughts, responded and said to them, "Why are you thinking this way in your hearts? Which is easier, to say: 'Your sins are forgiven you,' or to say, 'Get up and walk'? But so that you may know that the Son of Man has authority on earth to forgive sins," He said to the man who was paralyzed, "I say to you, get up, and pick up your stretcher, and go home" (Luke 5:20–24).

It took significant effort to bring the man to Jesus, but now there was an obstacle of a different character. Jesus looked at the paralytic and then at the hopeful faces of his four friends. What faith they had! Jesus knew about the deep-felt needs of the man in front of Him. He needed physical healing, yes, but sin had affected his spiritual and emotional health too. Addressing him, Jesus said, "Your sins are forgiven."

Jesus said what? Pharisees and scribes were present! Some of them had come all the way from Jerusalem to check out this Teacher and Miracle-Worker. As guardians of biblical law, they took their religion seriously, knowing very well that only God can forgive sins. Jesus read their thoughts and addressed them, "Is what I said troubling you? Which is easier to say: 'Your sins are forgiven'? or 'Stand up and walk'?" His question is ultimately about *power* and *authority*. Some ancient prophets, like Elijah and Elisha, were given miraculous powers of healing, but no prophet had ever been given the authority to forgive sins! What Jesus said is regarded in Judaism as blasphemy, which was punishable by death. However, to demonstrate His authority to forgive sins, Jesus commanded the paralytic, "Stand up, pick up your bed, and go home."

And immediately he got up before them, and picked up what he had been lying on, and went home glorifying God. And they were all struck with astonishment and began glorifying God. They were also filled with fear, saying, "We have seen remarkable things today!" (verses 25, 26).

The healing was immediate. The paralytic got up, picked up his bed, and walked out of the room, glorifying God. Everyone else glorified God too, and there was great joy on the faces of the four friends who had carried the crippled man to Jesus. It was another amazing day in Capernaum!

In this incident, we witness the first reaction to Jesus from organized Judaism. The healing was the first of five controversial events in this and the next chapter of Luke. The evil one was at work. As Jesus continued His ministry in the province of Galilee, crowds continued to wrestle with the question of who He was.

"Who exactly is this One who claims to minister for God?"[7] A carpenter from Nazareth? A Teacher? A Prophet? The long-awaited Messiah? Jesus referred to Himself as the "Son of Man," taking His listeners back to the prophet Daniel, who in vision saw "One like a son of man" coming to the "Ancient of Days" to receive glory and an everlasting kingdom (Daniel 7:13).[8]

Isn't it ironic that Jesus used "Son of Man" as His self-designation (twenty-six times in Luke), while unearthly beings such as evil spirits recognized Him as the "Son of God"?[9] When will Jesus be identified that way by people in His society?

Reflection

Sin may be compared to leprosy. How has Jesus healed you: Spiritually? Physically? Emotionally?

---

1. William Barclay, *The Gospel of Luke* (Philadelphia, PA: Westminster Press, 1975), 58.

2. Joel B. Green, *The Gospel of Luke*, New International Commentary on the New Testament, vol. 3 (Grand Rapids, MI: Eerdmans, 1997), 238.

3. Robert H. Stein, *Luke*, The New American Commentary, vol. 24, (Nashville, TN: B & H, 1992), 173.

4. Barclay, *Gospel of Luke*, 58.

5. Biblical Archaeology Society Staff, "The House of Peter: The Home of Jesus in Capernaum?" Biblical Archaeology Society, October 12, 2021, https://www.biblicalarchaeology.org/daily/biblical-sites-places/biblical-archaeology-sites/the-house-of-peter-the-home-of-jesus-in-capernaum/.

6. Stein, *Luke*, 176.

7. Darrell L. Bock, *Luke* (Grand Rapids, MI: Baker Academic, 1994), 464.

8. Darrell L. Bock, *A Theology of Luke and Acts* (Grand Rapids, MI: Zondervan, 2012), 163.

9. James M. Dawsey, *The Lukan Voice: Confusion and Irony in the Gospel of Luke* (Macon, GA: Mercer University Press, 1986), 73.

Chapter 19

Eating With Tax Collectors

Luke 5:27–32 (Matthew 9:9–13; Mark 2:13–17)

Near the entry gates into a town or city stood a tollbooth where a government-appointed officer collected entry fees. The tax collector was authorized to search anyone's possessions and to impose customs duties on goods passing through the town.[1] Luke picked up the story with Jesus leaving Capernaum.

After that He went out and looked at a tax collector named Levi sitting in the tax office, and He said to him, "Follow Me." And he left everything behind, and got up and began following Him (Luke 5:27, 28).

The Romans farmed out the collection of taxes. A district was assessed at a certain cash value, and the highest bidder was given the right to collect that amount. As long as the tax collector handed over the assessed figure at year's end, he was allowed to keep whatever extra money he could extract from the people. In truth, "a tax-collector could bid a man stop on the road and unpack his bundles and charge him well nigh what he liked."[2]

Tax collectors were considered social outcasts, sinners. Everybody knew that they were dishonest and practiced extortion. Remember that John the Baptist acknowledged the sins of tax collectors and admonished them to practice honesty and integrity (Luke 3:12, 13). But now, we find Jesus calling one of these rogues to be His disciple.

Who was Levi anyway? His identification in Greek indicates that he was a lower-level tax collector in the tax farming system. He reported to a chief tax collector like Zacchaeus, whom we'll meet in a later story. Mark identifies the man as "Levi son of Alphaeus" (Mark 2:14, NRSV), and Matthew identified the tax collector as himself, "Matthew the tax collector" (Matthew 10:3). In his listing of the twelve disciples, Luke also called him Matthew.

Luke's account is brief and simple. Jesus stopped at Levi's tax booth and called him to become His follower. Levi got up, left his job, and followed Jesus. The Greek words may also mean "he began to follow him,"[3] which makes sense when we read that Levi soon threw a party and invited Jesus. He could well afford to do that.

And Levi gave a big reception for Him in his house; and there was a large crowd of tax collectors and other people who were reclining at the table with them. The Pharisees and their scribes began grumbling to His disciples, saying, "Why do you eat and drink with the tax collectors and sinners?" And Jesus answered and said to them, "It is not those who are healthy who need a physician, but those who are sick. I have not come to call the righteous to repentance, but sinners" (Luke 5:29–32).

Levi wanted his teammates to meet his new Master, so he prepared a feast for them and a few other friends. We already know that Jesus forgave sinners, but would He also eat with them? Sinners such as tax collectors were considered ceremonially unclean. Pharisees would never share a meal with such rabble. They wouldn't be at Levi's dinner, but they grumbled that Jesus and His disciples were having table fellowship with sinners. They were yet reticent to challenge Jesus directly, so they addressed His newly minted disciples: "Why do you eat and drink with tax collectors and sinners?"

But Jesus responded to their question, "Healthy people don't need to see a physician. Those who are sick do." Then He added the clincher, "I have come to call not those who think they are righteous, but those who know they are sinners and need to repent" (verse 32, NLT). When Luke wrote that Levi "left everything" (verse 28), he is letting us know that the tax collector had experienced a life change.[4]

Clearly, "what Jesus' actions show is the extent of his compassion and the depth of God's grace. The Physician seeks out the sick and calls them into the hospital room of God's care."[5] Did the Pharisees get the point? Probably not. Like most of the Jewish leadership of the day, they drew a thick boundary line between themselves and the rejects of society—outsiders that included Gentiles, Samaritans, the wretched poor, lepers, widows, the sick and blind, the physically imperfect, the ceremonially unclean, women in general, children, and of course, tax collectors.

What kind of Messiah would spend time with these outcasts, let alone eat with them? Pharisees needed to get accustomed to the reality that Jesus spent much of His time with the outcasts of society. He would eat with Pharisees, too, when they invited Him, and He'd tell them parables about the meaning of spiritual leadership. Pharisees prided themselves as strict law-keepers—law-protectors, actually—but they had not learned the meaning of grace.[6]

Jesus was a unique individual—nothing like what the Jewish people expected the Messiah to be. He would be loved by sinners and hated by those who were self-righteous. Truly, "God's invitation to experience his grace can be offered only to those who realize that they are sinners in need of God's help. Everyone experiences God's healing grace the same way—because they realize they need it, not because they earn it through their own merit."[7] "The church is the only fellowship in the world where the one requirement for membership is the unworthiness of the candidate."[8]

Reflection

How does Jesus' participation in Levi's banquet fit with His mission statement (Luke 4:18, 19) and His reply to some Pharisees (Luke 5:32)?

---

1. *NIV Cultural Backgrounds Study Bible* (Grand Rapids, MI: Zondervan, 2016), 1688.
2. William Barclay, *The Gospel of Luke* (Philadelphia, PA: Westminster Press, 1975), 64.
3. Robert H. Stein, *Luke*, The New American Commentary, vol. 24 (Nashville, TN: Broadman, 1992), 181.
4. Joel B. Green, *The Gospel of Luke*, New International Commentary on the New Testament, vol. 3 (Grand Rapids, MI: Eerdmans, 1997), 246.
5. Darrell L. Bock, *Luke* (Grand Rapids, MI: Baker Academic, 1994), 500.
6. Darrell L. Bock, *A Theology of Luke and Acts* (Grand Rapids, MI: Zondervan, 2012), 248.
7. Bock, *Luke*, 492.
8. Leon Morris, *Luke: An Introduction and Commentary*, Tyndale New Testament Commentaries, vol. 3 (Downers Grove, IL: IVP Academic, 1988), 140.

Chapter 20

Questions and Conflict

Luke 5:33–6:5 (Matthew 9:14–17; 12:1–8; Mark 2:18–28)

Some people were not happy with Jesus and His disciples because they seemed to be enjoying themselves too much.

Fasting

The scribes saw a sharp contrast between the apparent lifestyle of Jesus' disciples and the followers of John the Baptist. Jesus' disciples had just attended Levi's feast, where there was much eating and drinking. In contrast, John's disciples followed a habit of formal prayers and fasting as they modeled the religious behavior of their mentor.

And they said to Him, "The disciples of John often fast and offer prayers, the disciples of the Pharisees also do the same, but Yours eat and drink." And Jesus said to them, "You cannot make the attendants of the groom fast while the groom is with them, can you? But the days will come; and when the groom is taken away from them, then they will fast in those days" (Luke 5:33–35).

The only fasting prescribed in the Law happened on the annual Day of Atonement. Self-righteous Pharisees, though, typically fasted twice a week, on Mondays and Thursdays, but never on Sabbaths or festival days. Back in the days of the prophet Isaiah, fasting was highly regarded as an act of worship, but God said it was a worthless act if the pious did not practice compassion for the needy (Isaiah 58:1–7). Scribes and Pharisees emphasized external piety in their worship of God, but they failed to practice love for their neighbors.

But a new era had come to Judaism. Jesus introduced a kingdom that differed from the old. It involved a new view of Judaism, a unique and different worldview that would overturn many traditional practices. Note that fasting is part of the emphasis on external piety and is sometimes linked with mourning. However, you don't fast at a wedding because it's a time of rejoicing.[1] Jesus told the scribes and Pharisees, "You can't make the wedding guests fast while the bridegroom is with them, can you?" In fact, Jesus Himself rarely fasted during His earthly ministry. His new kingdom would bring joy, not gloom.

And He was also telling them a parable: "No one tears a piece of cloth from a new garment and puts it on an old garment; otherwise he will both tear the new, and the patch from the new garment will not match the old" (Luke 5:36).

Jesus is an agent of change. Using the examples of cloth and wineskins, He illustrated how His kingdom differed from both old and contemporary Judaism. Just as it is not a good practice to attach a piece of new cloth to an old garment, so Jesus' new movement could not mix with the old without the new movement being lost.

"And no one pours new wine into old wineskins; otherwise the new wine will burst the skins and it will be spilled out, and the skins will be ruined. But new wine must be put into fresh wineskins. And no one, after drinking old wine wants new; for he says, 'The old is fine' " (verses 37–39).

Jesus used a second illustration of pouring new wine into old wineskins. At this time, people employed animal skins, especially goatskins, as containers for fluids. "New wine must have new wineskins to last. . . . Those attached to old wine will not like the taste of the new wine and will prefer the old."[2] Luke emphasizes the newness of the kingdom brought by Jesus. The "new" wine of the gospel could not be placed within the "old" wineskin of Pharisaic Judaism. "The reader is asked to pick which wineskin to draw from: the one containing Judaism's old wine or the one containing Jesus' new wine."[3] Jesus is advocating change, but making a lifestyle change is not easy. "A man drinking old wine does not want even to try the new. *The old is good*, he says."[4]

Sabbath

One Sabbath day in Galilee, Jesus and His disciples walked near the edge of a grain field, closely watched by a few Pharisees.

Now it happened that Jesus was passing through some grainfields on a Sabbath, and His disciples were picking the heads of grain, rubbing them in their hands, and eating them. But some of the Pharisees said, "Why are you doing what is not lawful on the Sabbath?" (Luke 6:1, 2).

The Old Testament law permitted what the disciples were doing: "When you enter your neighbor's standing grain, you may pluck the heads of grain with your hand, but you are not to use a sickle on your neighbor's standing grain" (Deuteronomy 23:25). But that day was Sabbath, and this changed everything. Among the thirty-nine specific tasks that the Jewish Mishnah prohibits on Sabbath are reaping, threshing, winnowing, and preparing food. The disciples were "plucking" grain (that's reaping), "rubbing them in their hands" (that's threshing), throwing away the husks (that's winnowing), and eating (that's preparing food). They are committing a quadruple offense. Incidentally, though, the Mishnah comments that "the rules about the Sabbath . . . are as mountains hanging by a hair, for Scripture is scanty and rules many,"[5] but the watching Sabbath police do not see it as unimportant. They asked, "Why are you breaking the Sabbath by harvesting grain for yourselves?"

The Pharisees addressed the disciples, but a teacher is responsible for the behavior of his students, so Jesus replied by referencing a story about David in 1 Samuel 21, when he took consecrated bread from Ahimelech, the priest.

And Jesus, answering them, said, "Have you not even read what David did when he was hungry, he and those who were with him, how he entered the house of God, and took and ate the consecrated bread, which is not lawful for anyone to eat except the priests alone, and gave it to his companions?" (Luke 6:3, 4).

Let's imagine the scene:

David: Listen, I'm on a special mission for King Saul—a secret mission. So, my men are here, and I need some bread for them.

Ahimelech: I don't have any common bread; all I have is this shewbread that I baked for the table of the Lord. It is holy to the Lord. Only the priest is permitted to eat it.

David: I understand, but give me five loaves for me and my men.

Ahimelech: Are the men clean? Have they touched women?

David: We've not been around women for at least the last three days.

Ahimelech: All right, I'll give you these loaves.

Pharisees knew their Scriptures very well. What David did when he took the sacred bread from the tabernacle was an embarrassment in their thinking. In Pharisaical eyes, David violated the law. They failed to understand that ceremonial restrictions must give way to compassion and genuine need. The Sabbath was never meant to be a master over people; it was meant to serve them (Mark 2:27). By using the Old Testament illustration, Jesus essentially said, "If you condemn My disciples, you are condemning David."

And He was saying to them, "The Son of Man is Lord of the Sabbath" (Luke 6:5).

Jesus finished the conversation with a staggering claim: "The Son of Man is Lord of the Sabbath." It's not so "staggering" when we recall the Old Testament words of Daniel 7:

> "One like a son of man was coming, . . .
> And to Him was given dominion,
> Honor, and a kingdom,
> So that all the peoples, nations, and populations of all languages
> Might serve Him.
> His dominion is an everlasting dominion
> Which will not pass away" (Daniel 7:13, 14).

- The origin of the Sabbath takes us back to Creation when God rested on the seventh day and pronounced it holy (Genesis 2:1–3).
- If the pre-incarnate Christ was the Creator, as testified by Paul and other New Testament writers (Colossians 1:15–17; John 1:1–4; Hebrews 1:1, 2), He could legitimately claim lordship of the Sabbath on that basis alone.

The Pharisees were influential law-keepers and law-guardians, and people were in awe of them. They emphasized the externals of law-keeping rather than coming to love God with their hearts. Sabbath was intended to be a day of joy instead of a burden with dozens of petty rules. "Jesus' ministry restores to the Sabbath command its profound significance: *restoration* of human beings in their integrity as part of God's creation."[6] The Sabbath incident in the grain fields heightened the conflict the Pharisees had with Jesus. They began looking for an excuse to remove Him from the community.

Reflection

Which of these illustrates what Jesus meant by His remarks about the Sabbath?

- Most Old Testament laws were only for the Jews.
- The moral law (the Ten Commandments) is for all time.
- You can break the law if you are hungry.
- Rules are OK when they help you to enjoy the Sabbath.
- Love and compassion have priority over law observance.
- Sabbath is holy time.

1. *NIV Cultural Backgrounds Study Bible* (Grand Rapids, MI: Zondervan, 2016), 1754.

2. Darrell L. Bock, *Luke* (Grand Rapids, MI: Baker Academic, 1994), 509.

3. Bock, 532.

4. Leon Morris, *Luke: An Introduction and Commentary*, Tyndale New Testament Commentaries, vol. 3 (Downers Grove, IL: IVP Academic, 1988), 142.

5. Bock, *Luke*, 523.

6. Joel B. Green, *The Gospel of Luke*, New International Commentary on the New Testament, vol. 3 (Grand Rapids, MI: Eerdmans, 1997), 256.

Chapter 21

Doing Good on Sabbath

Luke 6:6–11 (Matthew 12:9–14; Mark 3:1–6)

It's another Sabbath day, and Jesus, as was His custom, attended one of the Galilean synagogues.

On another Sabbath He entered the synagogue and taught; and a man was there whose right hand was withered. Now the scribes and the Pharisees were watching Him closely to see if He healed on the Sabbath, so that they might find a reason to accuse Him. But He knew what they were thinking, and He said to the man with the withered hand, "Get up and come forward!" And he got up and came forward (Luke 6:6–8).

It also became customary for scribes and Pharisees to be present in the congregation, silently watching Jesus. The Greek word translated here as "watch" carries the idea of "spying." They would really like to catch Him breaking some Sabbath rules, such as healing on the holy day. Under rabbinical law, there was to be no healing or medical work on Sabbath unless someone's life was in danger, a child was being born, or a circumcision needed to be performed because it was the eighth day after birth. This brings the question: "Since one can circumcise and thus sanctify one member of the body on the Sabbath, how much more can one save a life (and the whole body!) on the Sabbath"?[1]

In the congregation that day was a man whose hand and arm had become useless, incapacitated, "withered." Luke, the physician, informs us that it was the man's *right* hand. One of the apocryphal Gospels—*The Gospel According to the Hebrews*, which never gained admission into the New Testament—tells that the man begged help from Jesus: "I was a stone mason earning my living with my hand; I beseech you, Jesus, give me back my health that I may not have to beg my bread with shame."[2] Without income, the man faced the shameful life of a beggar. What would Jesus, the Lord of the Sabbath, do? The man's condition didn't require urgent treatment. The healing could wait until the next day. This was another test of Jesus' authority. He knew exactly what His opponents were thinking. When Jesus asked the man with the defective hand to come forward and stand where he could be seen by everyone, the man obeyed.

And Jesus said to them, "I ask you whether it is lawful to do good on the Sabbath or to do harm, to save a life or to destroy it?" And after looking around at them all, He said to him, "Stretch out your hand!" And he did so; and his hand was restored. But they themselves were filled with senseless rage, and began discussing together what they might do to Jesus (verses 9–11).

Jesus put a question to the entire congregation, but it's especially for the ears of the scribes and Pharisees. It was a carefully worded question: "Is it lawful to do good on the Sabbath or to do harm, to save a life or to destroy it?" (verse 9). This is not a yes or no question. Put yourself in the shoes of a Pharisee. If you say it is lawful to do good on the Sabbath, you have weakened your case if Jesus heals the man. On the other hand, how can anyone say that it's lawful to do harm on the Sabbath? It is a no-win situation. Jesus' opponents gritted their teeth and said nothing. The point Jesus makes is that not doing good is actually doing evil.[3] We may think of this statement from the apostle James: "So for one who knows the right thing to do and does not do it, for him it is sin" (James 4:17).

Jesus looked around at the congregation before He instructed the man to stretch out his hand. He wasn't physically able to do this, so he might have responded, "Sir, I can't." But his heart grasped onto faith, he slowly stretched out his right arm, and everyone saw that it was restored. Healing had occurred. The man has been made whole again. Were the people amazed? Luke doesn't tell us, perhaps because his and their joy was momentarily overshadowed by the reaction of some scribes and Pharisees, who were at their wits' end. They were "filled with fury" and discussed among themselves what they might do to destroy Jesus.

In these recent stories, we have witnessed five consecutive instances of conflict in which Pharisees and scribes have opposed the ministry of Jesus. They came to Galilee from distant places, including Jerusalem (Luke 5:17), in order to evaluate Jesus, asking questions like, "What authority does this Teacher believe He has? Surely it cannot be God-given, but where does it come from?" Their reaction to Jesus had risen from perplexity to hatred and anger:

- They cried "blasphemy" when Jesus offered forgiveness to a paralytic in Capernaum (verses 17–25).
- They were appalled when Jesus and His disciples attended a feast with tax collectors and other sinners (verses 27–32).
- They accused Jesus and His disciples of lax behavior in not fasting as they did (verses 33–39).
- They accused Jesus and His disciples of breaking multiple Sabbath rules as they walked through a grain field on Sabbath (Luke 6:1–5).
- They were "filled with senseless rage" when Jesus healed a man on Sabbath (verses 6–11).

More conflict lay ahead of Jesus and His followers, but let's not overlook the joy we have witnessed in these five stories:

- the joy of a leper who is now cleansed (Luke 5:12–15)
- the joy of forgiveness experienced by the paralytic (verses 17–26)
- the joy of table fellowship at Levi's feast (verses 27–29)
- the joy of God's love for sinners, which includes tax collectors (verses 30–32)
- the joy of being with Jesus, the "bridegroom" (verses 33–39)

Reflection
Jesus asked the question, Is it lawful to do good on the Sabbath? How would you define "doing good"?

---

1. Darrell L. Bock, *Luke* (Grand Rapids, MI: Baker Academic, 1994), 528.
2. William Barclay, *The Gospel of Luke* (Philadelphia, PA: Westminster Press, 1975), 72.
3. Robert H. Stein, *Luke*, The New American Commentary, vol. 24 (Nashville, TN: Broadman, 1992), 190.

Chapter 22

Choosing Twelve

Luke 6:12–16 (Matthew 10:1–4; Mark 3:13–19)

In spite of much conflict and opposition, Jesus had many followers. Some He called to follow; others were captivated by the fresh, Spirit-inspired teaching; many were attracted by the miracles they witnessed. From among all these, Jesus chose twelve for future church leadership.

Now it was at this time that He went off to the mountain to pray, and He spent the whole night in prayer with God. And when day came, He called His disciples to Him and chose twelve of them, whom He also named as apostles: Simon, whom He also named Peter, and his brother Andrew; and James and John; and Philip and Bartholomew; and Matthew and Thomas; James the son of Alphaeus, and Simon who was called the Zealot; Judas the son of James, and Judas Iscariot, who became a traitor (Luke 6:12–16).

Contemplating the task, Jesus left the busy towns and villages and climbed one of the mountains that overlooked the lake. Luke alone tells how He spent this night in prayer with His Father. The next morning, from among His followers, Jesus selected a small group that would emerge as "the early church's leadership, and this [Luke's] account makes it clear that they are divinely chosen, the product of an evening of prayer."[1]

The list of the twelve disciples is the same in the three synoptic Gospels as well as in Acts 1:13. However, some disciples might be identified by a nickname or the father's name or their place of origin.[2] Let's review the list and glean something about each one:[3]

- Simon Peter was called from his fishing occupation. Peter is outspoken, fearless, and deeply committed to his Master. He would make many mistakes, even denying his Lord at a critical moment, but would emerge as Christ's first preaching evangelist. The biblical record in Acts locates him at various times in Antioch, Syria; in Corinth, Greece; and finally, in Rome. Sometime between AD 64 and 68, Peter was crucified, by Emperor Nero, for his faith.
- Andrew was Peter's brother but lacked his brother's outspoken personality. Luke mentioned Andrew this one time in his Gospel, so we rely on John's Gospel for more information about him. It seems likely that Andrew is the younger of the two brothers, and the Gospel accounts indicate he was a quiet, serious thinker and seeker of truth. He went out to the wilderness to hear John the Baptist, became one of John's disciples, and was thus introduced to Jesus. Andrew immediately became a follower of Christ and introduced Peter to Him (John 1:35–42). In later accounts, Andrew brought a little boy with a picnic lunch of fish and bread to Jesus (John 6:8), and later still, he brought several inquiring Greeks to Jesus (John 12:20–22).
- James and John, the fishing brothers, sons of Zebedee, were possibly cousins of Jesus because it

appears that their mother was a sister of Mary, Jesus' mother.[4] Luke says that James was the first of the apostles to be martyred by King Herod Agrippa (Acts 12:1, 2). His brother John became an evangelist in the provinces of Asia Minor and was imprisoned on the Island of Patmos in the Aegean Sea (Revelation 1:9).

- Philip was from Bethsaida and a friend of Andrew's, who likely introduced him to Jesus. "The next day He [Jesus] decided to go to Galilee, and He found Philip. And Jesus said to him, 'Follow Me' " (John 1:43). Philip is believed to have evangelized in Egypt later on.
- Bartholomew, better known as Nathanael, was from the city of Cana in Galilee (John 21:2). He is a friend of Philip, who told him that he had found the Messiah, "Jesus of Nazareth." Nathanael responded, "Can anything good come from Nazareth?" (John 1:46, NLT). "Come and see," Philip replied. When Jesus told Nathanael that He knew him as a student of the Scriptures, Nathanael responded with the best answer yet of who Jesus is: "Rabbi, You are the Son of God; You are the King of Israel!" (John 1:48, 49). Tradition records that Nathanael eventually became a missionary to Armenia.
- Matthew, whom Luke introduced as Levi, was a tax collector at Capernaum when Jesus called him to follow. Later in life, Matthew wrote the Gospel that bears his name and possibly took the gospel message to Ethiopia.
- Thomas, sometimes called "doubting Thomas," was a sincere searcher for truth. Not certain that Jesus had been resurrected, Thomas was invited to touch the scars on Jesus' hands and side, and he then responded, "My Lord and my God!" (John 20:27, 28). There is evidence that Thomas traveled all the way to southern India, where he preached the gospel.
- James the son of Alphaeus may have been Matthew's brother if his father was the same Alphaeus that is named as Levi's father (Mark 2:14). James is believed to have taken the gospel to Egypt.
- Simon, "who was called the Zealot," is referred to as "Simon the Canaanite" in Matthew and Mark. The Zealots were a Jewish faction who strongly opposed Rome and tried to take Judea by force in the lead-up to the destruction of Jerusalem by Rome in AD 70. Simon likely had nationalistic, political leanings when Jesus called him. "It is one of the miracles of the power of Christ that Matthew the tax-collector and Simon the Zealot could live at peace in the close company of the apostolic band."[5]
- Judas, or Jude, son of James, may have preached the Cross in Judea, Samaria, and Syria. It is believed he was martyred in Lebanon.
- Judas Iscariot, identified as "the traitor," is likely the only non-Galilean among Jesus' disciples. "Iscariot" appears to mean "of Cariot," an ancient site in southern Judea. Unlike the other eleven disciples, Judas would become infamous for betraying Jesus.

Jesus chose twelve rather ordinary men to form the nucleus of His followers. Among them were several fishermen, a tax collector, a political revolutionary, a skeptical man, and even a traitor. "No Rabbi ever paid them attention before. Most assuredly, no Rabbi would ever entrust them with a mission. But Jesus knew it would not be their education or stature that would change the world. They were uneducated, common men, but they had been with Jesus (Acts 4:13). And that was all that would matter."[6]

Reflection
Read 1 Corinthians 1:26–31. Ask yourself, Can God use me to share the good news about Jesus?

1. Darrell L. Bock, *Luke* (Grand Rapids, MI: Baker Academic, 1994), 538.
2. *NIV Cultural Backgrounds Study Bible* (Grand Rapids, MI: Zondervan, 2016), 1755.
3. Ken Curtis, "Whatever Happened to the Twelve Apostles?" Christianity.com, April 28, 2010, https://www.christianity.com/church/church-history/timeline/1-300/whatever-happened-to-the-twelve-apostles-11629558.html.
4. James Callen, "Could the Disciples James and John Have Been First Cousins of Jesus?" James Callen, March 16, 2019, http://toliveischrist.com/were-james-and-john-cousins-of-jesus/.
5. William Barclay, *The Gospel of Luke* (Philadelphia, PA: Westminster Press, 1975), 75.
6. Brian Dye, "The Unlikely Disciples," Legacy Disciple, https://legacydisciple.org/index.php/2018/05/02/the-unlikely-disciples/.

Chapter 23

The Great Reversal

Luke 6:17–26 (Matthew 5:1–12)

After a night of prayer on the mountain, Jesus met with an unspecified number of His followers and selected twelve of them for His inner circle. Descending with them to a relatively level space—perhaps a plateau area with a view to the lake—Jesus found a large crowd waiting for Him. He went up to pray to His Father; He came down to meet with people.

And then Jesus came down with them and stood on a level place; and there was a large crowd of His disciples, and a great multitude of the people from all Judea and Jerusalem, and the coastal region of Tyre and Sidon, who had come to hear Him and to be healed of their diseases; and those who were troubled by unclean spirits were being cured. And all the people were trying to touch Him, because power was coming from Him and healing them all (Luke 6:17–19).

Three distinct groups were with Jesus that day:

- His newly chosen twelve, the inner circle.
- A larger group of disciples, many of whom will continue to follow Him. Some may later be among seventy messengers that Jesus will send out in an upcoming story.
- A much larger crowd has gathered from places as far away as Judea, Jerusalem, and even the coastlands of Tyre and Sidon. The province of Galilee housed people of mixed races—an aftermath of the Assyrian invasion and resettlement seven centuries earlier. So, the crowd with Jesus likely included some Gentiles.

Jesus' fame as a teacher and healer had spread quickly and widely. Crowds came from a large area to meet this bearer of good news. His desire was to teach them, but attention to their physical needs must precede their attentiveness to things of the Spirit. Some in the crowd were troubled by "unclean spirits"; others were "sick" in a variety of ways. Jesus healed all of them, and then everyone was ready to listen to the Teacher. This segment of Christ's teaching is often referred to as the "Sermon on the Mount" (Matthew 5–7). Here Luke presents a shorter version while keeping parts to present later on in his narrative. Many scholars think that both Matthew and Luke drew from an early manuscript of Jesus' sayings identified as "Q," a compilation of much of what Jesus publicly taught.

And He raised His eyes toward His disciples and began saying, "Blessed are you who are poor, for yours is the kingdom of God. Blessed are you who are hungry now, for you will be satisfied. Blessed are you who weep now, for you will laugh. Blessed are you when the people hate you, and when they

exclude you, and insult you, and scorn your name as evil, on account of the Son of Man. Rejoice on that day and jump for joy, for behold, your reward is great in heaven. For their fathers used to treat the prophets the same way" (Luke 2:20–23).

"He raised His eyes toward His disciples" (verse 20). In these next few verses, Jesus spoke primarily to His newly minted disciples, those who "left all" to become His followers, but the entire crowd was listening. Keep this in mind as we look at the four beatitudes, or blessings, that Luke recorded.

- "Blessed are you who are poor" (verse 20). Many of the listeners in the Galilean region were economically poor, but "poor" also means spiritually needy or simply being held in contempt by many in Jewish society who associate poverty with social trash. Some of Jesus' disciples were literally poor because they abandoned their livelihoods and had no resources. Whatever their situation, the poor may experience inner happiness. "Taste and see that the LORD is good; how blessed is the man who takes refuge in Him!" (Psalm 34:8).
- "Blessed are you who are hungry now" (Luke 6:21). Some hunger for food, but all are promised a meal at God's future banquet table. "You prepare a table before me in the presence of my enemies" (Psalm 23:5).
- "Blessed are you who weep now" (Luke 6:21). The day is coming when these people will laugh with joy. "Weeping may last for the night, but a shout of joy comes in the morning" (Psalm 30:5). Recall that rejoicing is a theme in Luke's Gospel.
- "Blessed are you when people hate you, . . . exclude you, and insult you, and scorn your name as evil" (Luke 6:22). Some of Jesus' close followers had already experienced opposition and suffering. It would come for all His followers. Take comfort, said Jesus, because the prophets of old endured persecution for their faith. "If you are insulted for the name of Christ, you are blessed, because the Spirit of glory, and of God, rests upon you" (1 Peter 4:14).

Is Jesus saying that poor, hungry, grieving, mistreated people are blessed? What does He mean? When we look at the Greek word here translated as "blessed," it is *makarios*, which quite literally means "happy," "contented," or, as we might say, having no cares in the world. God has a future like that for those who are faithful now. Looking back to Mary's song when she was visiting Elizabeth, we noticed how she expressed thoughts that parallel these four beatitudes from Jesus:

- Poverty: Mary herself was poor, but God "has brought down rulers from their thrones, and has exalted those who were humble" (Luke 1:52).
- Hunger: "He has filled the hungry with good things" (verse 53).
- Weeping: There will be joy, "My spirit has rejoiced in God my Savior" (verse 47).
- Hatred and scorn: "He has scattered those who were proud in the thoughts of their hearts" (verse 51).

Matching the four blessings are four woes. This represents a great reversal of values, a huge paradigm shift from the way the world works to the values of God's kingdom. The beatitudes speak of future reward, the woes of future judgment. The word *woe* might be better translated as "Alas!" or "How sad!" because it carries the thought of compassion, not anger.

But woe to you who are rich, for you are receiving your comfort in full. Woe to you who are well-fed now, for you will be hungry. Woe to you who laugh now, for you will mourn and weep. Woe to you when all the people speak well of you; for their fathers used to treat the false prophets the same way (Luke 6:24–26).

Let's look briefly at each one, seeing how they reverse the Beatitudes.

- How sad for "you who are rich" (verse 24). Is Jesus teaching that wealth is sin? No, but Jewish society commonly believed that there was a limited cache of money around, so taking too much of it meant that others would be poor.[1] The wealthy may enjoy life now, feeling self-sufficient, but in the time of judgment, they may find a scribbled note saying, "Reward received on earth."
- How sad for you who are full now (verse 25). The rich are seen as arrogant, haughty, and dishonest. Later, they will experience spiritual hunger, an emptiness of the soul. We see an example of this in Luke's story of the rich man and the beggar, Lazarus (Luke 16:19–31).
- How sad for you who are laughing now (Luke 6:25). This refers to derisive laughter, not the deep joy of life with Jesus. "You will cry out from a painful heart, and you will wail from a broken spirit" (Isaiah 65:14).
- How sad when all "speak well of you" (Luke 6:26). Jesus likens these people to the false prophets of old who were held in high regard until their words proved false. "The prophets prophesy falsely. . . My people love it this way! But what will you do when the end comes?" (Jeremiah 5:31).

The Beatitudes and woes of Jesus were revolutionary statements. "The people whom Jesus called happy the world would call wretched," and vice versa.[2] I titled this chapter "The Great Reversal," and it is exactly that. Paul the apostle makes the same future commitment: "We do not lose heart. . . . For our momentary, light affliction is producing for us an eternal weight of glory far beyond all comparison" (2 Corinthians 4:16, 17).

People were listening to the words of Jesus. But did they perceive the great reversal between the existing worldview and the new values of the kingdom of God? They listened. How would they respond as Jesus launched into the major thrust of His sermon?

Reflection

If you have a friend who has never experienced Jesus and would like to study the Bible with that person, what can you learn from how Jesus approached people?

---

1. E. Randolph Richards and Brandon J. O'Brien, *Misreading Scripture With Western Eyes* (Downers Grove, IL: Inter-Varsity, 2012), 41.
2. William Barclay, *The Gospel of Luke* (Philadelphia, PA: Westminster Press, 1975), 76.

Chapter 24

Love My Enemies?

Luke 6:27–38 (Matthew 5:38–48)

Jesus continued to instruct His disciples with a large crowd of people listening in. This scenario will be repeated many times in Luke because crowds were drawn to Jesus wherever He was. They wanted to hear everything He said, even when Jesus was focused on His disciples or even a single individual.

Now Jesus has a message for everyone. He addressed it to "you who hear," but His opening words would shock the listeners.

"But I say to you who hear, love your enemies, do good to those who hate you" (Luke 6:27).

Love my enemies? This was a radical statement then, and it's still radical for us today. For the crowd listening to Jesus, Rome was their number-one enemy. They chafed under a foreign power that took their money, punished lawbreakers with cruelty, and threatened their very existence as a nation.

Love for neighbor was always understood as a clear mandate (Leviticus 19:18), but often we think *neighbor* refers to someone who thinks as we do. And what does it mean to love the people who hate me? Which of the four kinds of love did Jesus refer to? "Jesus was not asking for *storgē*, natural affection, nor for *erōs*, romantic love, nor for *philia*, the love of friendship. He was speaking of *agapē*, which means love even of the unlovely, . . . which proceeds from the fact that the lover chooses to be a loving person."[1] This degree of love is possible only if we have experienced God's forgiveness and love. We see this *agapē* love in Jesus on the cross—"Father, forgive them"—and in Stephen at his stoning—"Lord, do not hold this sin against them!" (Luke 23:34; Acts 7:60). The ultimate in enemy-love is described by Paul: "While we were God's enemies, we were reconciled to him through the death of his Son" (Romans 5:10, NIV). Truly,

we cannot love our enemies as we love our nearest and dearest. To do so would be unnatural, impossible and even wrong. But we can see to it that, no matter what man does to us, even if he insults, ill-treats and injures us, we will seek nothing but his highest good.

. . . This love towards our enemies is not only something of the heart; it is something of the will.[2]

"Bless those who curse you, pray for those who are abusive to you. Whoever hits you on the cheek, offer him the other also; and whoever takes away your cloak, do not withhold your tunic from him either. Give to everyone who asks of you, and whoever takes away what is yours, do not demand it back. Treat people the same way you want them to treat you" (Luke 6:28–31).

"Pray for those who abuse you" (verse 28). This is "tough love" in the sense that it's a reversal of our natural instincts. When someone treats me badly—perhaps even a friend or a coworker—I'm inclined to pray something like "Lord, please bless me, and *change him*." But we should practice the more difficult prayer: "Please bless him, Lord, and change *me*."[3] When I can truly pray that prayer, I can say with Paul, "It is no longer I who live, but Christ lives in me" (Galatians 2:20).

If someone punches me in the jaw? Jesus says, "Don't fight back," which I am inclined to do. If someone takes my coat, I'm to offer him my undershirt. Is this what meekness means? It is the *spirit* of Jesus' saying that is important. A very poor woman might have just one coat; to surrender it might leave her naked. Beggars and robbers are always ready to take possessions from those who won't fight back. Paul warned some lazy believers in Thessalonica, "If anyone is not willing to work, then he is not to eat, either" (2 Thessalonians 3:10). Jesus sometimes used hyperbole in His discourses. The bottom line is that love means being vulnerable and forgiving, open to abuse but able to decide in an individual case whether to give or withhold.[4]

The entire instruction is summed up in the golden rule of Luke 6:31: Do unto others what you would like them to do to you. The concept exists in many writings in the negative form, but the Christian ethic is positive. "It does not consist in *not doing* things but in *doing* them."[5] Jesus put a positive spin on what dozens of His contemporaries said in the negative. Rabbi Hillel, for example, said, "What is hateful to you, do not do to your neighbor."[6]

"If you love those who love you, what credit is that to you? For even sinners love those who love them. And if you do good to those who do good to you, what credit is that to you? For even sinners do the same. And if you lend to those from whom you expect to receive, what credit is that to you? Even sinners lend to sinners in order to receive back the same amount. But love your enemies and do good, and lend, expecting nothing in return; and your reward will be great, and you will be sons of the Most High; for He Himself is kind to ungrateful and evil people. Be merciful, just as your Father is merciful" (verses 32–36).

Disciples' love is different in quality from sinners' love. Here are some illustrations of how sinners act toward each other: "I loan so that I might get a loan in the future." "I loan to protect myself, not to meet a need." "I give so I will receive a gift in return." "I'll scratch your back if you scratch mine."[7] For the Christian, there are to be no strings attached to our giving.

Summing it up, Jesus says, "Love your enemies, do good, and lend, expecting nothing in return" (verse 35, NRSV). Such behavior demonstrates that one is a child of God, whose character is love and mercy. There will be a reward, but that is not the primary motivation.

"Do not judge, and you will not be judged; and do not condemn, and you will not be condemned; pardon, and you will be pardoned. Give, and it will be given to you. They will pour into your lap a good measure—pressed down, shaken together, and running over. For by your standard of measure it will be measured to you in return" (verses 37, 38).

Luke gives us a summary of Jesus' sermon with a bunch of pithy statements. By telling us not to judge, Jesus does not forbid the legitimate exercise of judgment in law courts. He is warning us against criticizing and condemning one's neighbor. The one who judges others invites God's judgment on himself. Instead of condemning or diminishing my neighbor, I must pray, "Lord, please bless him and change me."

As a disciple of Jesus, I am to give and give and give. It may deplete my resources now, but there is an eternal reward. For Galilean peasants, Jesus used an illustration they understood very well. It involved purchasing grain in the village market square. There, the customer must beware of false balances or having chaff put in with the grain, as the prophet Amos vividly described the merchants of his time doing (see Amos 8:5, 6). By contrast, God's measure is "pressed down, shaken together, running over."

The crowd listened to Jesus in awed silence. Jesus introduced a paradigm shift of staggering dimensions. God's new kingdom is certainly different from the way this world works. What thoughts were troubling the minds of some of Jesus' disciples? Were James and John, the "sons of thunder," wanting to deliver a double punch to anyone who threw one at them? Was Simon the Zealot confused by Jesus' command to love our enemies? How should he react to Rome's absolute power? Was Judas silently wishing Jesus would preach a prosperity gospel instead of giving away the farm?

Reflection

Loving enemies is a challenge. Very often, my enemy is not someone who hates me or threatens violence but a friend, coworker, or neighbor who criticizes, gossips, puts me down, or boasts about himself/herself. That is when I must learn to pray, "Bless them, Lord, and change me."

---

1. Leon Morris, *Luke: An Introduction and Commentary*, Tyndale New Testament Commentaries, vol. 3 (Downers Grove, IL: IVP Academic, 1988), 149.

2. William Barclay, *The Gospel of Luke* (Philadelphia, PA: Westminster Press, 1975), 78, 79.

3. Janice Jean Springer, *I Know We're All Welcome at the Table, But Do I Have to Sit Next to You?* (Gonzalez, FL: Energion Publications, 2018), 18.

4. *NIV Cultural Backgrounds Study Bible* (Grand Rapids, MI: Zondervan, 2016), 1755.

5. Barclay, *Gospel of Luke*, 79; emphasis in original.

6. Darrell L. Bock, *Luke* (Grand Rapids, MI: Baker Academic, 1994), 596.

7. Bock, 601.

Chapter 25

Living Is Also Doing

Luke 6:39–49 (Matthew 7)

In His sermon, Jesus talked in practical terms about living what we would call the Christian life with love as the guiding principle. He challenged His audience to choose the loving response in every circumstance of life, to respond to every need—even if the recipient hates you—with love and mercy. Jesus climaxed His sermon by emphasizing that *doing* is an essential part of *living*: "Why do you call me 'Lord, Lord,'" He asked, "and do not *do* what I say?" (Luke 6:46; emphasis added).

Now He also spoke a parable to them: "A person who is blind cannot guide another who is blind, can he? Will they not both fall into a pit? A student is not above the teacher; but everyone, when he has been fully trained, will be like his teacher. Why do you look at the speck that is in your brother's eye, but do not notice the log that is in your own eye? How can you say to your brother, 'Brother, let me take out the speck that is in your eye,' when you yourself do not see the log that is in your own eye? You hypocrite, first take the log out of your own eye, and then you will see clearly to take out the speck that is in your brother's eye" (verses 39–42).

Jesus finished His sermon with some parables, though we might think of them more as proverbs, all with an emphasis on doing. Each focuses on a pair of something: two blind people (verse 39), a teacher and his pupil (verse 40), two siblings (verses 41, 42), good and bad trees (verses 43, 44), good and evil people (verse 45), and two house-builders (verses 46–49).

What happens when a blind person leads another blind individual? They will both fall and get hurt. Once, when Jesus healed a blind man, some Pharisees exclaimed, "We are not blind too, are we?" (John 9:40). Yes, Jesus replied. A disciple should respect his teacher, so he must choose his teacher wisely. In the days before libraries and books, a disciple had only his rabbi as his source of information. "One should choose one's teachers carefully, making sure one is going in the right direction, and not be too quick to set others straight."[1]

Be careful about correcting others when you yourself have a serious eye problem. You think you see clearly enough to take a speck out of your neighbor's eye, but you have a large plank jutting out of your own eye. This example shows Jesus' sense of humor. I imagine that when He exaggerated to make His point, the crowd was in a fit of laughter.[2] But they got His point.

"For there is no good tree that bears bad fruit, nor, on the other hand, a bad tree that bears good fruit. For each tree is known by its own fruit. For people do not gather figs from thorns, nor do they pick grapes from a briar bush. The good person out of the good treasure of his heart brings forth what is good; and the evil person out of the evil treasure brings forth what is evil; for his mouth

speaks from that which fills his heart" (Luke 6:43–45).

I'm guessing the crowd started laughing again when Jesus told them not to look for figs on a thorn tree, or grapes on a bramble bush. Our actions and words should match, and I must evaluate what my heart is producing. Jesus' words about good and bad fruit are reminiscent of John's message to the people who came to him in the wilderness—trees that fail to produce good fruit will eventually be cut down (Luke 3:8, 9). I sometimes need to take an honest look at myself and ask, *Am I practicing the lessons that I hear from my Teacher?* Jesus taught His followers that a person's "mouth speaks from that which fills his heart" (Luke 6:45).

"Now why do you call Me, 'Lord, Lord,' and do not do what I say? Everyone who comes to Me and hears My words and acts on them, I will show you whom he is like: he is like a man building a house, who dug deep and laid a foundation on the rock; and when there was a flood, the river burst against that house and yet it could not shake it, because it had been well built. But the one who has heard and has not acted accordingly is like a man who built a house on the ground without a foundation; and the river burst against it and it immediately collapsed, and the ruin of that house was great" (verses 46–49).

Jesus finished His sermon with a parable about two builders. Matthew recounted the same parable in his Sermon on the Mount (Matthew 7:24–27), but the two Gospel writers told it differently. Matthew's house was a simple, Palestinian-style construction, built on a rock in the first case and on the sand in the second. Luke contextualized his house for Gentile readers and particularly for his friend, Theophilus. Greek houses typically had basements, so Luke's first builder "dug deep" for a house with a basement on solid rock. The account in Matthew envisions a storm in Palestine that produces rising streams or wadis swollen with rainwater descending down the hills. In contrast, Luke described rain that causes a river to rise and a flood to "burst against" the house (Luke 6:49).[3]

The parable warned the reader not only to hear Jesus but also to put into practice the lessons presented. A time of judgment is coming—those who listen and obey have nothing to fear from the coming storm, but failure to obey will bring personal disaster. The sermon ends with echoes of the roar of floodwaters as a house collapses in a great heap.

Reflection

Jesus warned about making judgments against others. Ask yourself, What are some of the ways in which I may be unintentionally judgmental?

---

1. Darrell L. Bock, *Luke* (Grand Rapids, MI: Baker Academic, 1994), 609.
2. Leon Morris, *Luke: An Introduction and Commentary*, Tyndale New Testament Commentary, vol. 3 (Downers Grove, IL: IVP Academic, 1988), 154.
3. Robert H. Stein, *Luke*, The New American Commentary, vol. 24 (Nashville, TN: Broadman, 1992), 215.

Chapter 26

A Centurion and His Slave

Luke 7:1–10 (Matthew 8:5–13)

We have seen how Jesus is unconventional in His teachings. Concepts like loving your enemy and being kind to your abuser were considered bizarre by His hearers—including the Twelve—as we will come to see. In fact, these ideas still cause quite a stir.

Jesus was also unconventional in His attitude toward the outsiders in Jewish society—the poor, sinners, the disabled, prostitutes—the social trash of contemporary Judaism. Jesus repeatedly broke out of the tightly drawn social and religious boundaries.

When He had completed all His teaching in the hearing of the people, He went to Capernaum. Now a centurion's slave, who was highly regarded by him, was sick and about to die. When he heard about Jesus, he sent some Jewish elders to Him, asking Him to come and save the life of his slave (Luke 7:1–3).

Back in Capernaum, there was a centurion who had a very sick slave. A centurion was a Roman officer who commanded a unit of one hundred soldiers (though sometimes his authority was different in rural communities like Galilee).

This is our first encounter with a slave in Luke's Gospel. Slaves were not a regular commodity in the province of Galilee. Peasants couldn't afford to keep them and didn't require their help anyway. Slaves appear increasingly in Luke's Gospel as we move south with Jesus into Judea—where affluent farmers and businessmen had many.

Why did this officer care about his slave? After all, a slave was nothing more than a living tool. If he was broken, a replacement came cheap.[1] But Luke's story describes a military officer who was humane, humble, and knew the meaning of faith. In the mind of the officer, the slave's humanity was worth much more than his muscles.

The centurion had heard reports of Jesus' healing power and may even have witnessed a miracle himself, so he approached some local Jewish elders and asked them to inform Jesus about his sick slave. Would the elders be willing to do that? Did they honestly expect that Jesus would respond to the wishes of a Gentile and his slave?

When they came to Jesus, they strongly urged Him, saying, "He is worthy for You to grant this to him; for he loves our nation, and it was he who built us our synagogue" (Luke 7:4, 5).

As it turned out, this centurion had an unusually warm relationship with the people of Capernaum. "This man loves our people," the elders informed Jesus, "and he has even built the synagogue for us." Some commentators wonder whether this military officer is what is known as a "God-fearer," meaning "a Gentile who believed in the teachings of Judaism and kept the moral law but who had not become a Jewish proselyte."[2] Or perhaps he built the synagogue merely to win favor with the townspeople so that they would be obligated to "owe him one."

Whichever the situation, Jesus immediately responded to the centurion's request for mercy. That likely surprised the Jewish elders, who "are captive to a world system whose basis and practices run counter to the mercy of God."[3] Had they already forgotten what Jesus said in His sermon about loving one's enemies?

Now Jesus started on His way with them; but already, when He was not yet far from the house, the centurion sent friends, saying to Him, "Lord, do not trouble Yourself further, for I am not worthy for You to enter under my roof; for that reason I did not even consider myself worthy to come to You; but just say the word, and my servant shall be healed. For I also am a man placed under authority, with soldiers under myself; and I say to this one, 'Go!' and he goes, and to another, 'Come!' and he comes, and to my slave, 'Do this!' and he does it" (verses 6–8).

Jesus set off with the elders toward the centurion's home, followed by a curious crowd of townspeople, but there was a problem. Gentile houses were ritually impure, so how could Jesus enter one? However, this centurion was aware of Jewish religious cultural rules, so he sent a couple of his friends to intercept the procession. "Lord, do not trouble yourself, for I am not worthy to have you come under my roof. But only speak the word, and let my servant be healed" (verse 6, NRSV).

"Only speak the word." This military officer understood authority, and he sincerely believed that Jesus possessed a level of authority that was way above his. Using his own position as an example, "I am also a man who has been given authority," he explains. "When I say 'Go!' or 'Come!' my slave obeys me."

Now when Jesus heard this, He was amazed at him, and turned and said to the crowd that was following Him, "I say to you, not even in Israel have I found such great faith." And when those who had been sent returned to the house, they found the slave in good health (verses 9, 10).

Jesus expressed amazement about this man's faith. He turned to face the crowd of onlookers who overheard the conversation and said, "I tell you, not even in Israel have I found such faith" (verse 9, NRSV). Were the townspeople astonished? Or did they feel ashamed for their own lack of faith? Back at the house, the slave was found in good health. The healing power was even in the words Jesus spoke!

For the Gospel writer—himself a Gentile—the story of Jesus and the centurion whose faith exceeded anything found in Israel must have been very encouraging. And it foreshadows what occurs in Acts as the gospel spread into the Gentile world. In the story of the centurion's slave, Luke wanted his readers—then and now—to learn true faith and receive spiritual healing from Jesus.

Reflection

On three different occasions, Jesus performed miraculous healing without seeing the sick person. Read the other two accounts, neither of which are reported by Luke, in Mathew 15:21–28 and John 4:46–54. What do these stories teach you?

1. William Barclay, *The Gospel of Luke* (Philadelphia, PA: Westminster Press, 1975), 84.
2. Robert H. Stein, *Luke*, The New American Commentary, vol. 24 (Nashville, TN: Broadman, 1992), 219.
3. Joel B. Green, *The Gospel of Luke*, New International Commentary on the New Testament (Grand Rapids, MI: Eerdmans, 1997), 287.

Chapter 27

A Widow's Son

Luke 7:11–17

Soon afterward Jesus went to a city called Nain; and His disciples were going along with Him, accompanied by a large crowd (Luke 7:11).

Today, Nain (present day, Nein) is a small Arab village near the southern border of the former province of Galilee. Find it on the map of Galilee province on page 55. It's six miles southeast of Nazareth and sits at an elevation of 750 feet above sea level. Jesus and His disciples were walking from Capernaum on the northern shore of Lake Galilee, at nearly 700 feet below sea level. The thirty-mile walk for Jesus and His followers included an uphill climb and may have required two or more days of travel.

Why was Jesus making this trip? We're about to discover a widow living on the fringe of Jewish society. She is mourning the death of her only son, and we arrive with Jesus just minutes ahead of his burial.

Now as He approached the gate of the city, a dead man was being carried out, the only son of his mother, and she was a widow; and a sizeable crowd from the city was with her (verse 12).

Jesus and His entourage arrived in Nain at the same moment that a funeral procession was on its way to the cemetery. The burial customs of that time dictated that "first, a person was not prepared for burial until death was certain. . . . Second, a family tore their garments as a sign of mourning and closed the eyes of the corpse to show that death has come. . . . The body was anointed and buried quickly. . . . The corpse was wrapped in cloth and placed on a burial plank, not in a coffin."[1] The bereaved walked in front of the platform, or bier, which was carried by up to four men and followed by mourners. The burial would then take place in a family cemetery outside the village.

When the Lord saw her, He felt compassion for her and said to her, "Do not go on weeping." And He came up and touched the [bier]; and the bearers came to a halt. And He said, "Young man, I say to you, arise!" And the dead man sat up and began to speak. And Jesus gave him back to his mother (verses 13–15).

On this day, as Jesus and His group met the widow as she was about to bury her only son, truly, "the Way of Life" is meeting "the way of death."[2] Childless widows were utterly defenseless, and "with his passing, she is relegated to the status of dire vulnerability—without a visible means of support and, certainly, deprived of her access to the larger community and any vestiges of social status within the village."[3] The compassionate Jesus addressed her, "Do not weep" (verse 13, NRSV). In a moment, His comfort will be more than simply words.

What happened next is one of the loveliest episodes in the Gospels. Jesus moved forward and touched the plank where the corpse lay. This is considered an impure act, but Jesus values mercy over ceremonial purity. Everyone came to a stop. Jesus didn't touch the corpse, but He now speaks to it: "Young man, I say to you, arise!" Everyone watched in amazement as the dead man sat up and spoke, clear evidence that he was now alive. Luke does not tell us what he said, but I imagine that if I woke up at my own funeral, I would certainly say something!

Throughout this episode, Jesus' focus is on the widow—count how many times the words "she" and "her" appear in the account. The resurrected young man stood up, and "Jesus gave him to his mother" (Luke 7:15, NRSV). This act represents her restoration to the community, an extension of Jesus' "good news" to the socially marginalized and vulnerable. Jesus' authority not only heals but also overrides death.[4]

Fear gripped them all, and they began glorifying God, saying, "A great prophet has appeared among us!" and, "God has visited His people!" And this report about Him spread throughout Judea and in all the surrounding region (verses 16, 17).

The fear that settled over the crowd refers to a "deep awe," and those who witnessed this event glorified God. They recognized in Jesus a "great prophet," perhaps seeing a fulfillment of these words of God to Moses, "I will raise up for them a prophet from among their countrymen like you" (Deuteronomy 18:18). The ex-funeral crowd at Nain proclaimed, "A great prophet has risen among us! God has looked favorably on his people!" (Luke 7:16, NRSV). Luke says that their report "spread throughout Judea and all the surrounding country" (verse 17).

In making this proclamation, the people were equating Jesus with the prophets Elijah and Elisha in the Old Testament. Both prophets were given the power to raise people from death. Elijah once raised the son of a widow in the Phoenician city of Zarephath (1 Kings 17), and Elisha raised the son of a woman at Shunem (2 Kings 4).

Reflection

The first two healings in Luke 7 parallel two Old Testament stories that Jesus reiterated for the congregation in Nazareth (Luke 4:25–27). Compare the Elijah story (1 Kings 17:8–24) with the raising of the widow's son at Nain.

---

1. Darrell L. Bock, *Luke* (Grand Rapids, MI: Baker Academic, 1994), 651.
2. Bock, 649.
3. Joel B. Green, *The Gospel of Luke*, New International Commentary on the New Testament, vol. 3 (Grand Rapids, MI: Eerdmans, 1997), 291.
4. Green, *Gospel of Luke*, 290.

Chapter 28

"Should We Look for Someone Else?"

Luke 7:18–35 (Matthew 11:2–19)

The ministry of John the Baptist was cut short when Herod Antipas, the ruler of the Galilean province, arrested and imprisoned him. This happened after John publicly berated Herod for unlawfully marrying the wife of his half-brother, Philip. Herod reacted by putting John in prison (Matthew 14:3–5), as Luke mentioned earlier in his account (Luke 3:19, 20). The Baptist's faith was strong, but his patience may have been wearing thin. His own disciples reported to him about the recent healing ministry of Jesus at Capernaum and Nain. While Jesus' actions are praiseworthy, they aren't the baptizing with fire that John talked about (Luke 3:16).[1]

The disciples of John also reported to him about all these things. And after summoning two of his disciples, John sent them to the Lord, saying, "Are You the Coming One, or are we to look for another?" When the men came to Him, they said, "John the Baptist has sent us to You, to ask, 'Are You the Coming One, or are we to look for another?' " (Luke 7:18–20).

Doubt seeps through in these questions. In John's thinking, Jesus was not doing some of the things he expected and prophesied that the Messiah would do. Jesus was followed by people who were being healed, cured of demon possession, and even raised from the dead. But this was not the picture of a Messiah that John preached about. "The axe is already being laid at the root of the trees," he had warned, and "He will burn up the chaff with unquenchable fire" (Luke 3:9, 17). Where is the mention of judgment in Jesus' ministry? When would He publicly condemn the Roman oppression? He would like to hear Jesus say something like, "My armies are massing. Caesarea, the headquarters of the Roman government, is about to fall. The sinners are being obliterated. And judgment has begun."[2]

John's inquiry was on the lips of many people. Who was this Jesus of Nazareth? Some saw Him as a great teacher and healer. Some Pharisees talked of blasphemy and wanted Him removed. Others spoke of "a great prophet among us." One or two disciples dared to address Him as "Lord." John and Jesus represent two different styles of ministry. "One ministered in the desert as an ascetic, while the other roamed freely among the people and approached the rejected and sinful of society."[3] Some observed how John's disciples fasted with formal prayers while Jesus ate with tax collectors and sinners. Years later, the apostle Paul encountered disciples of John's baptism who eagerly accepted Jesus when Paul shared with them (see Acts 19:1–7).

At that very time He cured many people of diseases and afflictions and evil spirits; and He gave sight to many who were blind. And He answered and said to them, "Go and report to John what you have seen and heard: people who were blind receive sight, people who limped walk, people

with leprosy are cleansed and people who were deaf hear, dead people are raised up, and people who are poor have the gospel preached to them. And blessed is anyone who does not take offense at Me" (Luke 7:21–23).

"Should we look for someone else?" Jesus does not answer John's question. Instead, He simply instructed the two messengers to go tell John what they saw Him doing. "Report what you have seen and heard" is an expression that occurs several times in Luke and Acts. Judaism did not expect the Messiah to do miraculous works. Like John, they anticipated a Messianic freedom-fighter: "You shall break them with a rod of iron, you shall shatter them like earthenware" (Psalm 2:9). John "had prophesied that the Coming One would do some striking works of judgment. . . . But Jesus was doing nothing of the sort. He was engrossed in works of mercy."[4] Jesus' own description of His ministry in Luke 7:22 is a symphony of echoes from Isaiah:[5]

- "On that day those who are deaf will hear . . . , and . . . the eyes of those who are blind will see" (Isaiah 29:18).
- "Then the eyes of those who are blind will be opened, and the ears of those who are deaf will be unstopped. Then those who limp will leap like a deer" (Isaiah 35:5, 6).
- "Hear, you who are deaf! And look, you who are blind, so that you may see" (Isaiah 42:18).
- "Because the LORD anointed me to bring good news to the humble . . . , to proclaim release to captives" (Isaiah 61:1).

Jesus' mission statement at Nazareth (Luke 4:18, 19) echoed those same words from Isaiah.

When the messengers of John had left, He began to speak to the crowds about John: "What did you go out into the wilderness to see? A reed shaken by the wind? But what did you go out to see? A man dressed in soft clothing? Those who are splendidly clothed and live in luxury are found in royal palaces! But what did you go out to see? A prophet? Yes, I tell you, and one who is more than a prophet. This is the one about whom it is written: 'BEHOLD, I AM SENDING MY MESSENGER AHEAD OF YOU, WHO WILL PREPARE YOUR WAY BEFORE YOU' " (Luke 7:24–27).

We've heard what John thinks about Jesus, but what does Jesus think about John? He asks His hearers a series of questions. What led you to go out into the desert? Was it to see a "reed shaken by the wind"? (verse 24). The reed was an emblem on the coin of Herod Antipas, who had imprisoned John.[6] Did you go out to see someone dressed like a prince? John was not a city dresser; he wore camels' hair clothing and ate locusts and wild honey (Mark 1:6). No, people followed the paths into the wilderness to hear the words of a prophet; in fact, he was "more than a prophet." He was the last of the long line of biblical prophets. "John belonged to the time of promise." Jesus belongs to the time of fulfillment.[7]

"I say to you, among those born of women there is no one greater than John; yet the one who is least in the kingdom of God is greater than he." When all the people and the tax collectors heard this, they acknowledged God's justice, having been baptized with the baptism of John. But the Pharisees and the lawyers rejected God's purpose for themselves, not having been baptized by John (Luke 7:28–30).

How can anyone be greater than someone who is the greatest? This sounds contradictory. There is more than one answer to that question. On the one hand, John would not live to see salvation come to the human race through Jesus' death and resurrection or to witness the apostolic preaching at Pentecost. But on the other hand, those reborn in the kingdom of grace that Jesus proclaimed are greater than the greatest person born only in the flesh.[8]

Next, Luke interjected his own comments parenthetically (verses 29, 30, NRSV). Sinners who accepted John's baptism of repentance and forgiveness acknowledged a just God; the scribes and Pharisees, who refused to repent, rejected God's purpose for their lives.

"To what then shall I compare the people of this generation, and what are they like? They are like children who sit in the marketplace and call to one another, and say, 'We played the flute for you, and you did not dance; we sang a song of mourning, and you did not weep.' For John the Baptist has come neither eating bread nor drinking wine, and you say, 'He has a demon!' The Son of Man has come eating and drinking, and you say, 'Behold, a gluttonous man and a heavy drinker, a friend of tax collectors and sinners!' And yet wisdom is vindicated by all her children" (verses 31–35).

Still talking to the crowd, Jesus threw in a little parable that told of a common scene in any village marketplace: children come out of their dingy, gloomy houses and congregate in the plaza to play their silly games, like pretend weddings or funerals. John's lifestyle was too ascetic for those uncomfortable with his message, and Jesus' teachings were too radical for others. Jesus likens the contemporary generation to a bunch of spoiled children who will play only if they can make the rules.

But in truth, "despite its different appearance, the message of Jesus and John was the same. It was not therefore the form of the message that caused its rejection but rather its content. The message was rejected because it demanded repentance."[9]

Reflection

In what ways are you "greater" than John the Baptist?

1. *NIV Cultural Backgrounds Study Bible* (Grand Rapids, MI: Zondervan, 2016), 1759.
2. William Barclay, *The Gospel of Luke* (Philadelphia, PA: Westminster Press, 1975), 89.
3. Darrell L. Bock, *Luke* (Grand Rapids, MI: Baker Academic, 1994), 658.
4. Leon Morris, *Luke: An Introduction and Commentary*, Tyndale New Testament Commentaries, vol. 3 (Downers Grove, IL: IVP Academic, 1988), 162.
5. Joel. B. Green, *The Gospel of Luke*, New International Commentary on the New Testament, vol. 3 (Grand Rapids, MI: Eerdmans, 1997), 297.
6. *NIV Cultural Backgrounds Study Bible*, 1759.
7. Morris, *Luke*, 163.
8. Bock, *Luke*, 675, 676.
9. Robert H. Stein, *Luke*, The New American Commentary, vol. 24 (Nashville, TN: Broadman, 1992), 233.

Chapter 29

Who Loves the Most?

Luke 7:36–8:3

The Gospels of Matthew, Mark, and John record a story that, at first glance, closely resembles one shared in Luke (see Matthew 26:6–13, Mark 14:3–9, and John 12:1–8). But New Testament scholars have examined both stories carefully and believe that Luke's story is unique and strikingly different from the account of the other writers. The following list summarizes how the accounts of the two stories differ:

- The second instance occurred in the final week of Jesus' life.
- It occurred near Jerusalem, not in Galilee.
- It took place in the house of a leper, where Pharisees would never dine.
- A leper could not be a Pharisee.
- The audience in the second story comprises Jesus' disciples.
- The name Simon is one of the most common names of that period.
- In Matthew's and Mark's accounts, the woman anoints Jesus' head, not His feet.
- The one anointing is Mary of Bethany, sister of Martha and Lazarus.
- The reaction to the anointing is different; in the second account, the complaint is of a waste of perfume; in Luke's account, it is the association with a "sinner."
- In the later story, the woman's act is seen as a preparation for Jesus' burial.
- The conclusions differ. In the second account, Jesus says the woman's act will be memorialized, in contrast to the controversy that Jesus' forgiveness causes in Luke's story.[1]

The comparison makes clear that Matthew, Mark, and John describe a particular event in the final week of Jesus' life, while Luke records a distinct event during Jesus' Galilean ministry.

Now one of the Pharisees was requesting Him to eat with him, and He entered the Pharisee's house and reclined at the table. And there was a woman in the city who was a sinner; and when she learned that He was reclining at the table in the Pharisee's house, she brought an alabaster vial of perfume, and standing behind Him at His feet, weeping, she began to wet His feet with her tears, and she wiped them with the hair of her head, and began kissing His feet and anointing them with the perfume (Luke 7:36–38).

Even before we get very far into this story, we have questions. How dare this woman—a "sinner" at that—gate-crash a formal meal at a Pharisee's house! We've already seen that Pharisees wanted nothing to do with "sinners." So, what is she doing at Jesus' feet? Let's explore for some answers.

Luke doesn't say where in Galilee the event took place. Some think Nain, where the widow's son was raised, but I wonder if this story happened at Magdala, a town on the western shore of Lake Galilee, where there was an important synagogue in Jesus' time. There, a Pharisee invited Jesus to his house for a meal with several other Pharisees (verse 36). It was not unusual for a local spiritual leader "to invite a visiting rabbi or teacher to the Sabbath meal after he had taught in the synagogue."[2] "It was the custom that when a Rabbi was at a meal in such a house, all kinds of people came in—they were quite free to do so—to listen to the pearls of wisdom that came from his lips."[3]

Houses of the upper classes were often built around an open courtyard. Those invited to the lunch weren't sitting at a table as we know it; rather, each person lay on his side, facing a low table, but with body and feet angling away from the table—which explains how the woman could come behind Jesus and anoint His feet.[4]

Luke says the woman who came to the Pharisee's house was a "sinner" but does not elaborate further. The word *sinner* had a multitude of meanings. Was her problem demon-possession? Was she a widow forced into prostitution to survive? It's evident that she lived locally and was known to the community. She was not a welcome visitor, especially when everyone observed what she was doing. Standing behind Jesus, she wept, and as her tears wet His feet, she unbound her hair (itself a shameful act in public) and used it to dry His feet. Finally, as people watched in silent disgust, she kissed Jesus' feet and anointed them with an expensive perfume.

Now when the Pharisee who had invited Him saw this, he said to himself, "If this Man were a prophet He would know who and what sort of person this woman is who is touching Him, that she is a sinner!"

And Jesus responded and said to him, "Simon, I have something to say to you." And he replied, "Say it, Teacher" (verses 39, 40).

Simon, the host Pharisee, had thoughts about what was happening: *Either Jesus doesn't know what the rest of us know about this woman, or else He knows and yet permits this sinful woman to touch and make Him impure. Whichever is true, He is surely not a prophet.* Simon's thoughts are interrupted by Jesus. Jesus shared a parable with him. Everyone listens.

"A moneylender had two debtors: the one owed five hundred denarii, and the other, fifty. When they were unable to repay, he canceled the debts of both. So which of them will love him more?" Simon answered and said, "I assume the one for whom he canceled the greater debt." And He said to him, "You have judged correctly" (verses 41–43).

Two individuals have debts. One owed his creditor ten times more than the other. It is better to figure the debt in terms of basic wages—about two months' wages versus one-and-three-quarter-years' wages, assuming a six-day work week. That comparison graphically illustrates the gap between the two debts.[5] When the moneylender freely forgave both debtors, the listeners were shocked because it never happens that way in real life. The lesson is coming, and it will illustrate how great God's forgiveness is.

And turning toward the woman, He said to Simon, "Do you see this woman? I entered your house; you gave Me no water for My feet, but she has wet My feet with her tears and wiped

them with her hair. You gave Me no kiss; but she has not stopped kissing My feet since the time I came in. You did not anoint My head with oil, but she anointed My feet with perfume. For this reason I say to you, her sins, which are many, have been forgiven, for she loved much; but the one who is forgiven little, loves little" (verses 44–47).

Jesus gently rebuked, "Simon, do you see this woman? Are you not aware that this woman has confessed her many sins and has been forgiven? That is why she is showing great love. But one to whom little is forgiven loves little."

Evidently, this woman had interacted with Jesus on a previous occasion. Perhaps she was among the crowds that followed Him from place to place. Drawn to Jesus, she felt His power in her life and experienced genuine repentance, forgiveness, and a life-change. Now, when Jesus came to her hometown, her heart overflowed with love for her Savior.

And He said to her, "Your sins have been forgiven." And then those who were reclining at the table with Him began saying to themselves, "Who is this man who even forgives sins?" And He said to the woman, "Your faith has saved you; go in peace" (verses 48–50).

Now there was a stirring among the table guests, "Who is this who even forgives sins? He is unquestionably an amazing teacher. He works great miracles. He is 'Jesus of Nazareth,' but is He a prophet? A great prophet even? The Messiah?" We, Luke's readers, are still waiting for someone to acknowledge that the "Son of Man" is also the Son of God.

Soon afterward, Jesus began going around from one city and village to another, proclaiming and preaching the kingdom of God. The twelve were with Him, and also some women who had been healed of evil spirits and sicknesses: Mary who was called Magdalene, from whom seven demons had gone out, and Joanna the wife of Chuza, Herod's steward, and Susanna, and many others who were contributing to their support out of their private means (Luke 8:1–3).

Jesus continued His itinerary through Galilee, in company with the Twelve. Although women, in general, were not wealthy since funds were usually controlled by their fathers, husbands, or sons, some women were blessed with accessible resources. Here we learn that several women were faithful disciples of Jesus. This was regarded as unusual in the time of Jesus, but Luke habitually emphasized the role of women, who were often marginalized in Jewish society.[6] We have already encountered Elizabeth, wife of the priest Zachariah; Mary, the mother of Jesus; Anna, a prophetess; Peter's mother-in-law; a widow at Nain; and the unnamed woman who washed Jesus' feet. Who was the unnamed woman? Did you notice that one of the women in Luke's list is "Mary, called Magdalene," which is another way of saying "Mary of Magdala"? We cannot be certain, but it is possible that the unnamed woman in the story is Mary Magdalene, later identified as the first person who saw the resurrected Jesus and carried the wonderful news to the Twelve (Luke 24:1–12; John 20:1, 2).

Reflection

What picture do you have of Simon in this story? Contrast his faith with that of the woman.

---

1. Darrell L. Bock, *Luke* (Grand Rapids, MI: Baker Academic, 1994), 689–691.
2. Robert H. Stein, *Luke*, The New American Commentary, vol. 24 (Nashville, TN: Broadman, 1992), 235, 236; *NIV*

Cultural Backgrounds Study Bible (Grand Rapids, MI: Zondervan, 2016), 1760.

3. William Barclay, *The Gospel of Luke* (Philadelphia, PA: Westminster Press, 1975), 94.

4. Leon Morris, *Luke: An Introduction and Commentary*, Tyndale New Testament Commentaries, vol. 3 (Downers Grove, IL: IVP Academic, 1988), 166. See also, Bock, *Luke*, 694.

5. Darrell L. Bock, *A Theology of Luke and Acts* (Grand Rapids, MI: Zondervan, 2012), 231.

6. *NIV Cultural Backgrounds Study Bible*, 1761.

Chapter 30

Lessons From the Farm

Luke 8:4–21 (Matthew 12:46–50; 13:1–23; Mark 4:1–25)

Jesus' words to the woman at the Pharisee's house were, "Your faith has saved you; go in peace" (Luke 7:50). The Greek word translated "saved" can also be translated as "healed," in which case, "Jesus not only *heals* in a physical sense but also *saves* in a spiritual sense."[1] Faith is the essential ingredient for both healing and salvation. In Luke 8, we will discover that faith is sometimes absent, sometimes minimal, and occasionally mature, but it always has room to grow.

Now when a large crowd was coming together, and those from the various cities were journeying to Him, He spoke by way of a parable: "The sower went out to sow his seed; and as he sowed, some fell beside the road, and it was trampled underfoot, and the birds of the sky ate it up. Other seed fell on rocky soil, and when it came up, it withered away because it had no moisture. Other seed fell among the thorns; and the thorns grew up with it and choked it out. And yet other seed fell into the good soil, and grew up, and produced a crop a hundred times as much." As He said these things, He would call out, "The one who has ears to hear, let him hear" (verses 4–8).

Everyone loves a story, and for the Galileans, this one brought a familiar picture. Every year, in late fall or early winter, the people saw farmers sowing a new crop of wheat and barley. The sower carried a bag of grain over his shoulder, and from this bag, he tossed the seed in rows across his field. Of course, not all the seed reached the field. Some fell on the path, where it got walked on by people or snatched up by birds looking for food. There were large patches of stony ground that had a light cover of soil. And some varieties of prickly weeds grow very quickly in Palestinian soils. In Galilee, even today, sowing seed often precedes plowing.[2] Jesus' listeners could picture what He's describing.

Finishing the story with the assurance of a good crop, Jesus says loudly, "Let anyone with ears to hear listen!" (Luke 8:8, NRSV). Indeed, "hearing" and "listening" are key words in this story. Count how many times these related words occur in Luke 8:4–21.

Now His disciples began asking Him what this parable meant. And He said, "To you it has been granted to know the mysteries of the kingdom of God, but to the rest they are told in parables, so that while seeing they may not see, and while hearing they may not understand" (verses 9, 10).

The disciples didn't get it, and we probably don't, either. Did Jesus not want people to understand His words? The parable has to be more than a simple story. What did Jesus mean when He referred to "mysteries" (verse 10)? In a moment, Jesus would interpret the parable, but He also wanted His disciples to understand why some of His illustrations weren't clear to the listeners. He referred to a strange message that God gave to the prophet Isaiah centuries earlier:

"Go, and tell this people:

> 'Keep on listening, but do not understand;
> And keep on looking, but do not gain knowledge.'
> Make the mind of this people insensitive,
> Their ears dull,
> And their eyes blind,
> So that they will not see with their eyes,
> Hear with their ears,
> Understand with their hearts,
> And return and be healed" (Isaiah 6:9, 10).

In that strange passage, God used irony to describe people who chose not to hear and understand what Isaiah was telling them. Jesus said His parables are like that. As in Isaiah's day, the people of Jesus' time were steeped in tradition. Their minds were closed to new truths about God's kingdom. Luke later recounted in Acts how Paul quoted those same words from Isaiah in his very last address to Jewish leaders in Rome (Acts 28:25–27). So Jesus used parables because they "both conceal and reveal truth: they reveal it to the genuine seeker who will take the trouble to dig beneath the surface and discover the meaning, but they conceal it from him who is content simply to listen to the story."[3]

"Now this is the parable: the seed is the word of God. And those beside the road are the ones who have heard, then the devil comes and takes away the word from their heart, so that they will not believe and be saved. Those on the rocky soil are the ones who, when they hear, receive the word with joy; and yet these do not have a firm root; they believe for a while, and in a time of temptation they fall away. And the seed which fell among the thorns, these are the ones who have heard, and as they go on their way they are choked by worries, riches, and pleasures of this life, and they bring no fruit to maturity. But the seed in the good soil, these are the ones who have heard the word with a good and virtuous heart, and hold it firmly, and produce fruit with perseverance" (Luke 8:11–15).

Jesus interprets the parable for His disciples and the larger audience. The seed, He said, is the Word of God, but it doesn't always take root.

This parable of the sower is really the "parable of the seed among the soils."[4] Each of us represents a particular soil into which the Word of God comes. "If we take it in, a rich harvest results, but if we react like the path, the rock, or the thorns, we finish with nothing."[5] There was a lesson here for the disciples who would soon be sent out on their first missionary journey. As they used divine power to heal and teach, they would be preparing the soil. Their teaching will uproot some of the rocks of stubbornness and clear away the weeds of selfish ambition. Hearts will be open to the good news.

"Now no one lights a lamp and covers it over with a container, or puts it under a bed; but he puts it on a lampstand so that those who come in may see the light. For nothing is concealed that will not become evident, nor anything hidden that will not be known and come to light. So take care how you listen; for whoever has, to him more will be given; and whoever does not have, even what he thinks he has will be taken away from him" (verses 16–18).

The crowd likely began laughing. Their peasant homes were small and dark, and it would be ludicrous to light the lamp and then put it under the bed. But there's also a serious lesson here—Jesus said they might be doing that very thing spiritually by concealing the light of the gospel message! "So," Jesus added, "pay attention to how you listen!" There is a difference between hearing and listening. *Hearing* needs only a pair of ears; *listening* requires a mind that is open to what is being said. When I was a boy, when my father said, "Listen up!" I knew I must pay full attention to him.

Listen up! That is how understanding takes place. "To those who have, more will be given" (verse 18, NRSV). Faith grows that way. The gospel light is not meant to be hidden. Letting it shine is the role of every disciple.

Now His mother and brothers came to Him, and they were unable to get to Him because of the crowd. And it was reported to Him, "Your mother and Your brothers are standing outside, wishing to see You." But He answered and said to them, "My mother and My brothers are these who hear the word of God and do it" (verses 19–21).

What was the motive for Mary and Jesus' brothers coming? Luke doesn't say. But Jesus does not immediately go to them. He was teaching about the importance of listening and responding to what is heard, so He told the crowd, "My family are those who hear and do the word." Like everybody else, Jesus' own family must be responsive to God's message through Him.

Reflection

Listening requires patience. Value the person speaking by

- listening without judging,
- listening without jumping in with my story,
- listening without problem-solving, and
- listening with an open heart.[6]

Consider ways you can implement intentional listening in your relationships.

---

1. John Brunt, *A Day for Healing* (Nampa, ID: Pacific Press®, 2016), 26; emphasis in the original.
2. Leon Morris, *Luke: An Introduction and Commentary,* Tyndale New Testament Commentaries, vol. 3 (Downers Grove, IL: IVP Academic, 1988), 170.
3. Morris, 171.
4. Darrell L. Bock, *Luke* (Grand Rapids, MI: Baker Academic, 1994), 739.
5. Morris, *Luke*, 172.
6. Janice Jean Springer, *I Know We're All Welcome at the Table, But Do I Have to Sit Next to You?* (Gonzalez, FL: Energion Publications, 2018), 109.

Chapter 31

The Storm

Luke 8:22–25 (Matthew 8:23–27; Mark 4:35–41)

During a visit to Galilee several years ago, I sailed across the lake to the village of Migdal on its western shore, close to the archaeological site of ancient Magdala. At Migdal, we visited the Yigal Alon Museum to inspect a fishing boat that dates from the time of Jesus.

In 1986, drought significantly reduced the water level of the lake. Two brothers from a nearby kibbutz (agricultural community) who occasionally fished the lake were examining the exposed beach when they stumbled across the remains of a boat partly buried in the shore mud. Archaeologists were contacted, and a team of specialists successfully unearthed and preserved the boat by submerging it in a wax-like bath for twelve years before placing it in a museum. Measuring 27 feet by 7.5 feet, the ancient fishing boat has a flat bottom with a shallow draft. It has been carbon-dated to 40 BC.[1] It was exciting to think that Jesus may have traveled in that boat—or certainly one like it.

The Yigal Alon boat is a reminder that Lake Galilee has been the basis of a successful fishing industry for thousands of years, as well as being an important communication link between lakeside communities. For Jesus and His disciples, the Gospels confirm that boats were sometimes their favored means of transportation between lakeside towns and villages. Most lake trips took place without incident, but Luke described one lake crossing that had almost fatal consequences.

Now on one of those days Jesus and His disciples got into a boat, and He said to them, "Let's cross over to the other side of the lake." So they launched out. But as they were sailing along He fell asleep (Luke 8:22, 23).

Jesus was weary. Mark's account puts this event at the close of a day when Jesus had taught a crowd of people near the shore of Galilee. "On that day, when evening had come, he said to them, 'Let's go over to the other side' " (Mark 4:35, WEB). We're not told where the lakeside preaching took place, but the instruction to "go across to the other side of the lake" indicates they may have departed from somewhere on the western or northwestern shore of the lake—perhaps Gennesaret or Magdala. The lake is about eight miles wide at that point.

We discover from the ongoing story that their destination on "the other side of the lake" was Gentile territory that comprised the entire eastern shore of Lake Galilee and was outside the legal boundaries of the Roman province of Galilee. As night fell, Jesus and the twelve disciples climbed aboard one of the boats and pushed off from the shore. The evening was pleasant, the lake was calm, and Jesus was soon asleep at the stern of the boat.

A fierce gale of wind descended on the lake, and they began to be swamped and to be in danger.

They came up to Jesus and woke Him, saying, "Master, Master, we are perishing!" (Luke 8:23, 24).

The lake of Galilee occupies a deep trench, almost 700 feet below sea level, with steep mountains rising on its eastern and western sides. Cool air sometimes rushes down the ravines and hills and collides with warm air above the lake, creating severe storms on the water.[2] Fishermen are accustomed to such phenomena, but there was something different about the storm that night. This storm was violent. I imagine the thunder crashed, the wind was wild, and waves erupted, flowing into the boat. There seemed to be something demonic about this storm. The disciples were afraid, and they made frantic attempts to keep the craft stable. Just imagine the rush of adrenaline! But the men have forgotten something—Someone. A mighty crash, a blinding flash, and they saw the face of Jesus, but He was sound asleep! Their desperate cry came out of the terror and turbulence: "Master! Master! We're drowning!"

And He got up and rebuked the wind and the surging waves, and they stopped, and it became calm. And He said to them, "Where is your faith?" But they were fearful and amazed, saying to one another, "Who then is this, that He commands even the winds and the water, and they obey Him?" (verses 24, 25).

Awakening, Jesus rose and stood steady in the violently pitching boat; His words sounded above the roar of the gale: "Quiet! Be still!" There was a moan in the rigging as the wind died and quietness again stole over the dark water. Luke said that Jesus "rebuked" the storm (verse 24). This is the third time he has used that word to describe something that Jesus did. In the synagogue at Capernaum, He "rebuked" an unclean spirit (Luke 4:35); in Peter's house, he "rebuked" the sickness in a woman (verse 39); now, He "rebuked" a storm. Clearly, "any force hostile to humans can be rebuked by Jesus, whether spirit, disease, or natural forces."[3]

"Where is your faith?" (Luke 8:25). The words were not spoken in anger but likely with sadness. The men, their hearts still pumping with fear, looked at one another in amazement, asking, "Who then is this, that He commands even the winds and the water, and they obey Him?" (verse 25). Will these men reflect later on David's dramatic words in Psalm 107?

> He spoke, and the winds rose,
> > stirring up the waves.
> Their ships were tossed to the heavens
> > and plunged again to the depths;
> > the sailors cringed in terror.
> They reeled and staggered like drunkards,
> > and were at their wits' end.
> "LORD, help!" they cried in their trouble,
> > and he saved them from their distress.
> He calmed the storm to a whisper
> > and stilled the waves (Psalm 107:25–29, NLT).

Jesus' authority extends to the whole creation. Prophets like Jonah and Paul never had that kind of authority in their sea sagas. As we leave this story, some words are still playing on the lips of twelve weather-beaten men. "Who then is this?" (Luke 8:25).

Reflection

"Where is your faith?" is the question Jesus asked of His disciples. Have you ever claimed the promise of Psalm 107:29 during a "storm" event in your life? Share about it.

1. Dan Fisher, "Israeli Archeologists Rush to Excavate 'Jesus Boat' From Sea of Galilee," *Los Angeles Times*, February 26, 1986, https://www.latimes.com/archives/la-xpm-1986-02-26-mn-54-story.html.

2. *NIV Cultural Backgrounds Study Bible* (Grand Rapids, MI: Zondervan, 2016), 1762.

3. Darrell L. Bock, *Luke* (Grand Rapids, MI: Baker Academic, 1994), 762.

Chapter 32

The Release

Luke 8:26–39 (Matthew 8:28–34; Mark 5:1–20)

It's "the morning after the night before" as Jesus and His disciples pull their boat onshore at an unspecified location in "the country of the Gerasenes, which is opposite Galilee" (Luke 8:26).[1] This was Gentile territory. We are about to discover why Jesus wanted to cross the lake and why Satan did *not* want Jesus to cross the lake.

Then they sailed to the country of the Gerasenes, which is opposite Galilee. And when He stepped out onto the land, a man from the city met Him who was possessed with demons; and he had not put on clothing for a long time and was not living in a house, but among the tombs (verses 26, 27).

No sooner had Jesus stepped on shore when He was approached by a wretched semblance of humanity. Naked, dirty, crazed, and inhabited by numerous demons, the man was a frightening picture of degradation. Socially isolated, he was often manacled and chained, but with demonic strength, he broke the chains and was driven by demons to the cemetery. He had crossed the boundaries of human decency into an existence that was worse than death. This poor man was a pawn in a cosmic spiritual battle. But Jesus came with divine power and authority to release this man from his evil prison.

And seeing Jesus, he cried out and fell down before Him, and said with a loud voice, "What business do You have with me, Jesus, Son of the Most High God? I beg You, do not torment me!" For He had already commanded the unclean spirit to come out of the man. For it had seized him many times; and he was bound with chains and shackles and kept under guard, and yet he would break the restraints and be driven by the demon into the desert. And Jesus asked him, "What is your name?" And he said, "Legion"; because many demons had entered him. And they were begging Him not to command them to go away into the abyss (verses 28–31).

Stumbling his way toward Jesus, the man fell at His feet and shouted, "What have you to do with me, Jesus, Son of the Most High God?" (verse 28, NRSV). The falling down was not worship, nor was the voice his own, but the demons recognized an authority that demanded obeisance. Jesus asked his name, and a voice responded, "Legion." A Roman legion was a military unit of approximately 5,600 men.[2] In short, Jesus was totally outnumbered by this man's collection of evil spirits.

The disciples were terrified and cried, "Quick! Get back in the boat!" But Jesus was in command of the situation. With authority, He commanded all the unclean spirits to come out of the man. They were forced to do so, but they begged Jesus not to consign them to "the abyss"—the final destiny of Satan and his angels—described in Revelation as a "bottomless pit" (Revelation 20:1–3, NKJV) but may also signify a "watery grave."[3]

Now there was a herd of many pigs feeding there on the mountain; and the demons begged Him to permit them to enter the pigs. And He gave them permission. And the demons came out of the man and entered the pigs; and the herd rushed down the steep bank into the lake and was drowned (Luke 8:32, 33).

A large herd of swine was feeding on a nearby hillside. The demons asked for permission to enter the swine, so Jesus gave them permission. Coming out of the man, they entered the large herd of pigs, which suddenly rushed down a steep bank into the lake, where they drowned. The surprising reaction of the pigs was not something Jesus intended, but it speaks volumes about how an animal responds when it becomes a lodging for devils.

This is Jesus' first excursion into Gentile territory. Everything here is impure for Jews. Pigs are unclean, tombs are places of death, and Gentiles themselves are regarded as impure. Perhaps Luke included this story because it foreshadows what would happen when the gospel spread throughout the Roman empire, as recorded in Luke's second book, Acts.

Now when the herdsmen saw what had happened, they ran away and reported everything in the city, and in the country. And the people came out to see what had happened; and they came to Jesus and found the man from whom the demons had gone out, sitting down at the feet of Jesus, clothed and in his right mind; and they became frightened. Those who had seen everything reported to them how the man who had been demon-possessed had been made well. And all the people of the territory of the Gerasenes and the surrounding region asked Him to leave them, because they were overwhelmed by great fear; and He got into a boat and returned (verses 34–37).

The incident caused quite a stir among the swineherds. They ran into town to tell everyone what had happened. This was not something that happened to your average pig herd, and they needed to explain the absence of a large herd! Their story needed corroboration, so the townspeople came out to see for themselves. "The trip confirms the herders' report. In a complete reversal of the previously possessed man's demeanor, he is now clothed, whereas before he had been naked; he is now seated, whereas before he had been roaming; he is now associating with others as he sits at Jesus' feet."[4] The townspeople were afraid, but this was not the fear that leads to faith. What had occurred was beyond their understanding, so they asked Jesus to depart.

But the man from whom the demons had gone out was begging Him that he might accompany Him; but Jesus sent him away, saying, "Return to your home and describe what great things God has done for you." So he went away, proclaiming throughout the city what great things Jesus had done for him (verses 38, 39).

Meanwhile, the man was sitting at the feet of Jesus, learning from Him. As Jesus and the disciples prepared for departure, he begged to go with them, but Jesus had an assignment for him: "Return to your home, and declare how much God has done for you" (verse 39, NRSV). "Sometimes when the answer to a request is no, God has other things in mind. . . . Jesus' reply reveals something about the mission of believers; some are to travel with Jesus away from their home, while others are to remain where they are and testify to him there. . . . Not all believers are to serve Jesus in the same way."[5] The restored demoniac became Christ's first foreign missionary. Luke describes how he went back to his city and told everyone what Jesus did for him. His knowledge was limited, and his faith was small, but he rejoiced in his release from Satanic captivity and shared his story with others.

Satan was determined to stop Jesus from crossing the lake, so he sent the great storm to drown everyone. However, he could not compete with the authority of the Son of God. "Perhaps the devil, who is the *prince of the power of the air,* and who *raiseth winds* by the permission of God, had some suspicion, from some words which Christ might let fall, that he was coming over the lake now on purpose to cast that legion of devils out of the poor man on the other side, and therefore poured this storm upon the ship he was in, designing, if possible, to have sunk him and prevented that victory."[6]

The story reminds us of Jesus' own words when He defined His mission statement: "He has sent Me to proclaim *release to captives . . . , to set free those who are oppressed*" (Luke 4:18; emphasis added).

Reflection

People everywhere love stories. Think back over your spiritual history. What story could you tell that would affirm your own faith and stir the faith of those listening?

---

1. *NIV Cultural Backgrounds Study Bible* (Grand Rapids, MI: Zondervan, 2016), 1695. The site visited may have been Gergesa, rather than Gerasa.

2. Joel B. Green, *The Gospel of Luke*, New International Commentary on the New Testament, vol. 3 (Grand Rapids, MI: Eerdmans, 1997), 339.

3. *NIV Cultural Backgrounds Study Bible*, 1762.

4. Darrell. L. Bock, *Luke* (Grand Rapids, MI: Baker Academic, 1994), 777.

5. Bock, 780.

6. Matthew Henry, *Commentary on the Whole Bible*, Luke 8:22–39, BibleGateway, accessed September 14, 2022, https://www.biblegateway.com/resources/matthew-henry/Luke.8.22-Luke.8.39; emphasis in original.

Chapter 33

Two Faith Healings

Luke 8:40–56 (Matthew 9:18–26; Mark 5:21–43)

And as Jesus was returning, the people welcomed Him, for they had all been waiting for Him (Luke 8:40).

Jesus returned to Galilee of the Jews, probably again at Capernaum. "He had been in a situation that epitomized ritual impurity—interacting with a demoniac who made the tombs his abode, in close proximity to a herd of pigs, with no hint of any observance of the Mosaic law."[1]

And a man named Jairus came, and he was an official of the synagogue; and he fell at Jesus' feet, and began urging Him to come to his house; for he had an only daughter, about twelve years old, and she was dying. But as He went, the crowds were pressing against Him (verses 41, 42).

The last person who fell at Jesus' feet was a wretched, naked demoniac. Now, it's an orthodox Jewish leader, the local synagogue ruler. Jesus was back in familiar territory, and the crowds were there to welcome Him. They were "pressing in" on Him, which is understandable when we think of the narrow streets and lanes of Galilean villages and towns. And two individuals in this crowd were anxious to get near Jesus. One of them was Jairus, the local synagogue leader, a respected man in the community. He "was responsible for the arrangements at synagogue the services. He would select, for example, those who will lead in prayer, read the Scripture and preach."[2] But that day, his only daughter was very sick. Jairus knew about Jesus' healing power, so he maneuvered his way through the crush of people and fell humbly at Jesus' feet, begging Him to come to his house.

And a woman who had suffered a chronic flow of blood for twelve years, and could not be healed by anyone, came up behind Him and touched the fringe of His cloak, and immediately her bleeding stopped. And Jesus said, "Who is the one who touched Me?" And while they were all denying it, Peter said, "Master, the people are crowding and pressing in on You." But Jesus said, "Someone did touch Me, for I was aware that power had left Me" (verses 43–46).

The second person who wanted to get near to Jesus that day was a woman who had suffered from vaginal bleeding for the past twelve years—this made her ceremonially unclean and, therefore, a social outcast. Anyone who touched her would likewise become impure (Leviticus 15:27). Mark's Gospel tells that she "had endured much under many physicians," which had cost all her money, and she was no better but worse (Mark 5:26, NRSV). Luke was kinder to his profession but agreed that no one could cure her.

The woman was desperate. Coming up behind Jesus, she touched the fringe of His garment, "the tassel on the end of the square garment that was thrown over the left shoulder and hung down the back."[3] Just her touching the garment would transfer her impurity to Jesus, but what happened next was exactly the opposite—healing power from Jesus was transferred to the woman, cleansing her disease. Jesus stopped and asked, "Who touched me?" (Luke 8:45, NRSV). Peter figured that was a silly question in the crush and said so. But Jesus knew this was not a common touch.

Now when the woman saw that she had not escaped notice, she came trembling and fell down before Him, and admitted in the presence of all the people the reason why she had touched Him, and how she had been immediately healed. And He said to her, "Daughter, your faith has made you well; go in peace" (verses 47, 48).

We might say, "Jesus, You have embarrassed this poor woman. She is trembling with fear, realizing that now everyone knows of her malady." But she told it all, desperately hoping that touching Jesus was acceptable and He would not reverse the cure. But His response says everything, "Daughter, your faith has made you well" (verse 48). By calling her "daughter," Jesus gave her enviable status and restored her to community acceptance.[4] Her faith had brought physical restoration as well as spiritual healing.[5]

While He was still speaking, someone came from the house of the synagogue official, saying, "Your daughter has died; do not trouble the Teacher anymore." But when Jesus heard this, He responded to him, "Do not be afraid any longer; only believe, and she will be made well" (verses 49, 50).

Jairus likely found it hard to be patient, and bad news was coming. "Your daughter is dead" (verse 49, NRSV). Perhaps he thought there was no point in bringing Jesus to his house now. Death was the end, wasn't it? Caught with sudden fear, Jairus heard comforting words. "Don't be afraid, Jairus. Make an act of faith. Believe."

When He came to the house, He did not allow anyone to enter with Him except Peter, John, and James, and the girl's father and mother. Now they were all weeping and mourning for her; but He said, "Stop weeping, for she has not died, but is asleep." And they began laughing at Him, knowing that she had died. He, however, took her by the hand and spoke forcefully, saying, "Child, arise!" And her spirit returned, and she got up immediately; and He ordered that something be given her to eat. Her parents were amazed; but He instructed them to tell no one what had happened (verses 51–56).

Some in the crowd laughed at Jesus' response. His words, like some seeds in the parable, were being choked by thorns and thistles. Already, professional mourners were at Jairus's house; some perhaps played a dirge on their flutes; others wept and wailed.[6] "Don't weep," Jesus said, "she is only sleeping," meaning the sleep of death that is described by Paul and Luke (1 Thessalonians 4:13–18; Acts 7:60).

Only the parents and three disciples, Peter, James, and John, were permitted in the room as Jesus took the girl by the hand and said, "Child, get up!" (Luke 8:56, NRSV). She got up at once. Like a physician who takes the pulse of a recovering child and prescribes food, Jesus directed the mother to give her daughter something to eat. The parents, of course, were astounded and overjoyed. But Jesus told the parents not to broadcast the child's recovery. He would rather be known and followed for the truths that He taught than for the miracles He performed. Here we see that "several issues stand out in the Jairus account: Jesus' power, faith's importance, and the patience of the one who is called to trust in God. God will do his work in his time."[7]

Chapter 8 of Luke has given us story pictures of fear and faith. We have seen Jesus busy

- teaching about faith to a large crowd from many villages (verses 4–21),
- demonstrating His authority over demonic forces at sea and on land (verses 22–39), and
- performing physical and spiritual healing (verses 40–56).

But Satan was busy too:

- trying to drown Jesus and the disciples in a storm
- demonstrating his power over a poor man of the Gerasenes
- bringing twelve years of bleeding to a woman and death to an only child

Reflection

God does everything "in His time." In many cultures, then and now, time is about relationship, not meeting a deadline.[8] That is hard for us in Western cultures to understand and accept. Read a story in John's Gospel that illustrates how God's timing was the best in John 11:1–44.

---

1. Joel. B. Green, *The Gospel of Luke*, New International Commentary on the New Testament, vol. 3 (Grand Rapids, MI: Eerdmans, 1997), 344.

2. Leon Morris, *Luke: An Introduction and Commentary*, Tyndale New Testament Commentaries, vol. 3 (Downers Grove, IL: IVP Academic, 1988), 177.

3. Morris, 178.

4. Morris, 179.

5. Robert H. Stein, *Luke*, The New American Commentary, vol. 24 (Nashville, TN: Broadman, 1992), 262.

6. *NIV Cultural Backgrounds Study Bible* (Grand Rapids, MI: Zondervan, 2016), 1763.

7. Darrell L. Bock, *Luke* (Grand Rapids, MI: Baker Academic, 1994), 806.

8. E. Randolph Richards and Brandon J. O'Brien, *Misreading Scripture With Western Eyes* (Downers Grove, IL: Inter-Varsity, 2012), 137.

Chapter 34

Apprenticeship

Luke 9:1–11 (Matthew 9:35–10:4; 14:1–12; Mark 6:6–29)

It was time. Since their calling, Jesus' disciples had been watching, listening, and learning. They were men in training, and the watching, listening, and learning would continue as long as Jesus was with them. Now, though, it was time for them to put into practice what they had learned. They were ready for their first missionary adventure.

Now He called the twelve together and gave them power and authority over all the demons, and the power to heal diseases. And He sent them out to proclaim the kingdom of God and to perform healing (Luke 9:1, 2).

"Jesus *called the twelve together*. We should not think that the disciples were together all the time. Some of them had homes and families in Capernaum and we need not doubt that they spent some of the time at their homes."[1] But now, Jesus gave them a task, and in a special sense, they would no longer be mere disciples but apostles—meaning they had been *called*; now they were being *empowered* and *sent*. Jesus gave them two things—power and authority—and asked them to *do* two things—preach and heal. The healing included dealing with demon possession. Luke saw no clear distinction between exorcism and healing.[2]

The disciples were not given power that resided in themselves. How divine power sometimes operates through a human agent is nicely illustrated in a twentieth-century story. Pastor David received a midnight call from parents whose baby was near death in a hospital. "When he arrived at the hospital, he found a very sick seven-month-old baby with sores all over his body" and parents in shock. "He's been diagnosed with acute leukemia. The doctor said all his blood cells are immature. He will not live through the night." Pastor David "placed his hand on little Mike's head and prayed for a miracle." While the pastor prayed, he felt an electric shock run down his arm. After the prayer, much to his own surprise, he said, "Your baby is healed." When doctors came and took blood samples in the morning, they were shocked at the results. Baby Mike's blood cells were mature. Prayer opened the divine power circuit and brought healing to baby Mike.[3]

And He said to them, "Take nothing for your journey, neither a staff, nor a bag, nor bread, nor money; and do not even have two tunics. And whatever house you enter, stay there until you leave that city. And as for all who do not receive you, when you leave that city, shake the dust off your feet as a testimony against them." And as they were leaving, they began going throughout the villages, preaching the gospel and healing everywhere (verses 3–6).

The men were to travel light—no staff, no knapsack, no food, no money, no extra clothing. This would be a unique experience in trusting God to take care of all their needs. As they visited the homes of peasants, they were not to be mistaken for wandering cynic philosophers who made a living by door-to-door pitches and carried a bag or purse for the money they received.[4] When they entered a village, they were to accept the hospitality of one family and not move to any other home. They might normally carry a staff to use "as a walking stick or for protection against bandits," but now they were to trust God for protection.[5]

So, the twelve departed on their first missionary journey, bringing "good news" and "curing diseases everywhere" (verse 6, NRSV). Not everyone would welcome them, of course. Like the sower in the parable, they would encounter a variety of "soils" as they scattered the gospel seed. If they were not welcomed in a village, they were to shake the dust from their feet as they departed. In that culture, "proper hospitality included offering water for guests to wash their feet; here the travelers' feet remain conspicuously unwashed."[6]

Now Herod the tetrarch heard about all that was happening; and he was greatly perplexed, because it was said by some that John had risen from the dead, and by some that Elijah had appeared, and by others that one of the prophets of old had risen. Herod said, "I myself had John beheaded; but who is this man about whom I hear such things?" And he kept trying to see Him (verses 7–9).

As the disciples moved from village to village in Galilee, they aroused a lot of interest. Herod Antipas, a son of Herod the Great by a Samaritan wife, was the ruler of the Galilean province, the territory where Jesus had been doing most of His work. From his palace at Tiberias on the western shore of the lake, I imagine Herod heard about what the Twelve were doing as they proclaimed Jesus, and he was bothered by his thoughts. Some time ago, he had put John the Baptist in prison, and more recently, in a rash moment of drunken foolishness, he had ordered him decapitated. Some people now were saying that Jesus was John the Baptist, raised from the dead. Naturally, this disturbed Herod. He preferred to believe that Jesus might be the prophet Elijah, as some were claiming, based on a prophecy from Malachi 4:5, 6. "Who then is this?" Herod asked (Luke 9:9, NABRE). He wanted to see Jesus for himself.

When the apostles returned, they gave an account to Him of all that they had done. And taking them with Him, He withdrew privately to a city called Bethsaida. But the crowds were aware of this and followed Him; and He welcomed them and began speaking to them about the kingdom of God, and curing those who had need of healing (verses 10, 11).

The Twelve had stories to share, but they needed a quiet place away from the crowds that always surrounded Jesus. They desired to meet together for rest, fellowship, and focus. A city like Bethsaida would offer no privacy, but Jesus had a nearby site in mind. So, He and the Twelve took a boat around the lake to the secluded place He had selected (Mark 6:32). Alas! The crowds made their way there too. But would Jesus send them away? Never. He welcomed them, and soon a large number of people heard Jesus teach about the kingdom of God and received miracles of healing.

Reflection

Although not given "apostolic" power and authority, today, men and women of faith are commissioned by God to spread the gospel message, sometimes to distant lands but more often at home. What talents do you have for such a purpose?

1. Leon Morris, *Luke: An Introduction and Commentary*, Tyndale New Testament Commentaries, vol. 3 (Downers Grove, IL: IVP Academic, 1988), 182.

2. Joel B. Green, *The Gospel of Luke*, New International Commentary on the New Testament, vol. 3 (Grand Rapids, MI: Eerdmans, 1997), 358.

3. Dalores Broome Winget, "The Anointing," in *Color My World With Love* (Nampa, ID: Pacific Press®, 2020), 313.

4. Morris, *Luke*, 182.

5. Robert H. Stein, *Luke*, The New American Commentary, vol. 24 (Nashville, TN: Broadman, 1992), 268.

6. *NIV Cultural Backgrounds Study Bible* (Grand Rapids, MI: Zondervan, 2016), 1764.

Chapter 35

Who Is This Man?

Luke 9:12–20 (Matthew 14:13–21; 16:13–23; Mark 6:30–44; 8:27–33; John 6:1–14)

At a remote site near the town of Bethsaida, Jesus taught a large crowd about the kingdom of God and healed many diseases. He may have chosen this place to spend quiet time with the Twelve following their missionary experiences, but it did not turn out that way. The intrusive crowd followed them here. Jesus typically chose quiet places for prayer, but if a period of prayer with His disciples was His intention, it had to be postponed (Luke 9:18).[1]

Now the day was ending, and the twelve came up and said to Him, "Dismiss the crowd, so that they may go into the surrounding villages and countryside and find lodging and get something to eat; because here, we are in a secluded place." But He said to them, "You give them something to eat!" But they said, "We have no more than five loaves and two fish, unless perhaps we go and buy food for all these people." (For there were about five thousand men) (verses 12–14).

The miracle of the feeding of five thousand is the only miracle, other than the resurrection, that is reported in all four Gospels. Jesus taught the people, but they faced a problem when the day grew late. The disciples, bless them, were sensitive to the physical needs of this large number of people.

So, the Twelve came to Jesus and said, "Lord, it's getting late. Send the crowd away so they can buy food in nearby towns and villages. Some people have come from far away and may need lodging tonight." Visitors might normally hope for hospitality in surrounding villages, but the region could not support thousands of visitors. The disciples' advice appears sensible and caring, but Jesus had a surprising response: "*You* give them something to eat. *You* provide food for them."

Were the disciples surprised? Absolutely. The request seems unreasonable, but they took it seriously and began to consider their options (John 6):

- They could share whatever food they had—Andrew found a boy with some barley loaves and a couple of fish. Nice kid, but this was not going to work!
- They could buy enough food to feed the crowd. Philip, who comes from nearby Bethsaida, knew a place where he could probably buy a lot of food, but it would cost at least 200 denarii—that's six months' wages—and he didn't have that kind of money.

So, the disciples told Jesus it would take lots of food and money to feed all these people. Did they forget that on their recent missionary journey, Jesus instructed them to take nothing—no food or money? Yet everything was supplied. So, perhaps there's a third option: ask Jesus! This was a test of their faith. "They need to realize that for them to minister they need to rely on Jesus."[2]

But He said to His disciples, "Have them recline to eat in groups of about fifty each." They did so, and had them all recline. And He took the five loaves and the two fish, and, looking up to heaven, He blessed them and broke them, and gave them to the disciples again and again, to serve the crowd. And they all ate and were satisfied; and the broken pieces which they had left over were picked up, twelve baskets full (Luke 9:14–17).

Five barley loaves—that's what the poor ate—and two fish. A small boy's lunch is all that Jesus required to feed five thousand men. For the disciples, the event was also a lesson in organization. Having the people sit in small groups made the food distribution effective. All were fed, and there were twelve baskets full of leftovers. Jesus does "immeasurably more than all we ask or imagine, according to his power" (Ephesians 3:20, NIV). And "the abundance witnesses both to Jesus' power and to his grace."[3]

How did the crowd respond? Some wanted to make Jesus their earthly king to ensure a permanent supply of food (John 6:15). Others reflected on Isaiah's promise of a future Messianic banquet (Isaiah 25:6).

Trek to Caesarea Philippi

The long day was over, and Jesus again sought time alone with the Twelve. Although Luke does not tell us where they went, both Matthew and Mark identify the location as Caesarea Philippi, a community farther north, close to the foot of Mount Hermon and near a cave that is a source of the Jordan River. After the miraculous feeding of the five thousand, Jesus and the Twelve made their way northward to this remote and beautiful region.

And it happened that while He was praying alone, the disciples were with Him, and He questioned them, saying, "Who do the people say that I am?" They answered and said, "John the Baptist, and others say Elijah; but others, that one of the prophets of old has risen." And He said to them, "But who do you say that I am?" And Peter answered and said, "The Christ of God" (Luke 9:18–20).

Luke noted that while the Twelve were with Jesus, He was praying alone. "Luke has shown that it is in prayer that Jesus solidifies his relationship with God and receives guidance and empowerment from God."[4] His solitary times of prayer often occurred before a key moment in His ministry—like this one.

Now, for the first time, Jesus asked the disciples what people were saying about Him. It was an appropriate question, coming so soon after the disciples had been scattered throughout Galilee on their missionary journeys; they knew what people were saying. So, what did they hear people say about their Master? Their responses echoed what Herod had also heard from the populace: a resurrected John the Baptist or the prophet Elijah or another of the ancient prophets.

"But," and here comes the key question, "who do *you all* say that I am?" Peter was the group's spokesman, and he stated, "The Christ of God" (verse 20). That response is worlds away from the fear and astonishment of these same men after the demonic storm on the lake, when they wondered, "Who then is this?" (Luke 8:25). Nor does it "mean that Peter and the others understand fully the nature of Jesus and his mission, only that they have moved from their former incomprehension, and certainly beyond the helpful but inadequate perspectives of the crowds."[5]

The confession at Caesarea Philippi has been described as a turning point in the ministry of Jesus and His relationship with the Twelve. From this point onward, Jesus began to instruct the disciples directly and prepare them for His departure and suffering. "Though the apostles know who Jesus is, as their confession of him as Christ shows, they do not yet know the character of his messianic ministry."[6] Jesus would try to prepare them for the suffering that lay ahead for Him and for them, too.

Reflection

"Who do *you* say that I am?" is a question for you and me, too. Who is Jesus to you? Is He the center of your life? Explain.

---

1. Joel B. Green, *The Gospel of Luke*, New International Commentary on the New Testament, vol. 3 (Grand Rapids, MI: Eerdmans, 1997), 362, 363.

2. Darrell L. Bock, *Luke* (Grand Rapids, MI: Baker Academic, 1994), 835.

3. Robert H. Stein, *Luke*, The New American Commentary, vol. 24 (Nashville, TN: Broadman, 1992), 274.

4. Green, *Gospel of Luke*, 368.

5. Green, 368.

6. Bock, *Luke*, 837.

Chapter 36

"This Is My Son"

Luke 9:21–36 (Matthew 16:21–23; 17:1–13; Mark 8:31–33; 9:2–13)

Peter's confession that Jesus is "the Christ of God" represents a turning point in Luke's Gospel. Luke tells us that Jesus was praying immediately before He popped the question to the Twelve: "Who do *you* say that I am?" (Luke 9:18–20; emphasis added).

But He warned them and instructed them not to tell this to anyone, saying, "The Son of Man must suffer many things and be rejected by the elders and chief priests and scribes, and be killed and be raised on the third day" (verses 21, 22).

Peter's confession clearly states who Jesus is. He is Christ, the promised Messiah. Surely, the disciples should tell everyone who He is. But Jesus "warned and instructed" the disciples not to tell anyone what they have confessed. Why? Because "such a proclamation would have disastrous consequences; for to Jesus, 'Christ/Messiah' meant suffering and death as God's Anointed, whereas among the people it signified the Anointed King who would throw off the Roman yoke, smite the Gentiles, and bring political independence and greatness to Israel."[1] Public proclamation of Jesus as Messiah would bring about an immediate confrontation between Jesus and Rome.

Jesus would soon depart for Jerusalem and the cross. Was there anyone who really knew who He was?[2] The disciples didn't yet understand the kind of Messiah that Jesus would be or "what is in store for those who follow him in his journey of rejection, exaltation, and glory. God's plan for Messiah is contrary to the disciples' expectations about Messiah. God's people will not experience a glorious messianic rescue from physical enemies in the near future."[3] That was not how God planned to save humanity. It would be through a cross, followed by a resurrection and a future kingdom of glory.

It would take Jesus' resurrection for the disciples to accept the truth about Him. Then, their minds would be open to understand (Luke 24:44, 45); after His ascension, they would be empowered to proclaim the "good news" of salvation to everyone (Acts 1:8).

And He was saying to them all, "If anyone wants to come after Me, he must deny himself, take up his cross daily, and follow Me. For whoever wants to save his life will lose it, but whoever loses his life for My sake, this is the one who will save it. For what good does it do a person if he gains the whole world, but loses or forfeits himself? For whoever is ashamed of Me and My words, the Son of Man will be ashamed of him when He comes in His glory and the glory of the Father and the holy angels. But I say to you truthfully, there are some of those standing here who will not taste death until they see the kingdom of God" (Luke 9:23–27).

The road ahead for Jesus' followers will not be easy. When someone saw a man from his village take up a cross and then go off with a little band of Roman soldiers, he knew it was a one-way journey. He would not be coming back. So, what does taking up a cross mean for a follower of Jesus? A disciple was not expecting to die for his rabbi.[4] When Jesus talked about daily cross-bearing, He taught that discipleship means making a 180-degree turn from a system of enslavement to self-indulgence and, instead, choosing a very different road—the way of Jesus and self-denial.[5] This is also a one-way journey. There will be no turning back.

The disciples were not really hearing what Jesus was saying. He talked about future suffering, being killed, and being raised to life again. And who wants to contemplate life with an ugly cross? The idea was horrifying. Yes, there would be trouble and persecution for followers of Jesus. But what did He mean by saying that someone "wanting to save his life will lose it" while someone "willing to lose his life for Jesus will save it"? They didn't understand. "To seek to save one's life is to seek the world's acceptance. To lose one's life is to identify with Jesus and face rejection by the world for making the choice."[6]

But there is great hope at the end of the road. Jesus finished with a promise that some standing before Him would catch a glimpse of His glory. There is about to be a preview.[7]

Transfiguration

From their stop at Caesarea Philippi, the little group turned southward. Several days later, they reached the foot of one of the mountains of Galilee, traditionally Mount Tabor. Jesus planned to climb the mountain for a time of prayer, and He chose three—Peter, James, and John—to accompany Him. The remaining nine would await their return the next day.*

About eight days after these sayings, He took along Peter, John, and James, and went up on the mountain to pray. And while He was praying, the appearance of His face became different, and His clothing became white and gleaming (verses 28, 29).

Again, we see the role of prayer in Jesus' ministry. "In Luke, when prayer is present, something significant usually follows."[8] At the mountain summit, under the stars, the three disciples observed Jesus in prayer a short distance away before they fell asleep. They were suddenly awakened, though, as a brilliant light illuminated Jesus, His clothing a dazzling white—the three disciples were witnessing a preview of His coming glory.

And behold, two men were talking with Him; and they were Moses and Elijah, who, appearing in glory, were speaking of His departure, which He was about to accomplish at Jerusalem. Now Peter and his companions had been overcome with sleep; but when they were fully awake, they saw His glory and the two men who were standing with Him (verses 30–32).

As they watched, Moses and Elijah appeared with Jesus—Moses, the great lawgiver, and Elijah, one of God's greatest prophets. Luke shares that the subject of their conversation is Jesus' upcoming "departure," *exodos*, in Greek (verse 31)—His death will release humanity from the bondage of sin in the same way the historic Exodus ended Israel's bondage in Egypt; and His departure to heaven would follow His resurrection. Obviously, "the vision on the mountain set the seal of divine approval on the step he was about to take."[9]

---

* The transfiguration probably happened at night. See Leon Morris, *Luke: An Introduction and Commentary,* Tyndale New Testament Commentaries, vol. 3 (Downers Grove, IL: IVP Academic, 1988), 191.

And as these two men were leaving Him, Peter said to Jesus, "Master, it is good that we are here; and let's make three tabernacles: one for You, one for Moses, and one for Elijah"—not realizing what he was saying. But while he was saying this, a cloud formed and began to overshadow them; and they were afraid as they entered the cloud. And then a voice came from the cloud, saying, "This is My Son, My Chosen One; listen to Him!" And when the voice had spoken, Jesus was found alone. And they kept silent, and reported to no one in those days any of the things which they had seen (verses 33–36).

Overcome with what they were seeing, Peter did not want the moment to slip away and tried to preserve it by proposing the construction of tents, or booths, for Jesus, Moses, and Elijah. He was recalling the ancient Feast of Tabernacles, when Israelites constructed booths or tents to commemorate the Exodus and their journey through the wilderness.

Peter's outburst was interrupted as a cloud of glory enveloped Jesus and the heavenly visitants. Suddenly feeling excluded and abandoned, the disciples were seized with fear. Just as suddenly, though, a voice was heard from somewhere in the cloud: "This is my Son, my Chosen; listen to Him!" (verse 35, NRSV). Those words confirmed that Jesus is the divine Son of God.

The voice quieted, the cloud dissipated, and darkness and silence crept across the mountaintop. The three disciples were silent too. Words did not come easily to describe what they had experienced. Nothing was said as the four descended into the dawn of a new day. "But the eyes and ears of the three disciples have begun to be opened, so they will begin to comprehend what they have seen."[10] The last three words spoken that night were for them: "Listen to Him!"

Only after the Resurrection would the three disciples be able to grasp the real significance of the event. When John commenced his Gospel, he wrote, "We saw His glory, glory as of the only Son from the Father, full of grace and truth" (John 1:14). In his second epistle, Peter described the event: "When He received honor and glory from God the Father, such a declaration as this was made to Him by the Majestic Glory: 'This is My beloved Son with whom I am well pleased'—and we ourselves heard this declaration made from heaven when we were with Him on the holy mountain" (2 Peter 1:17, 18). The third disciple, James, was executed by Herod in the early struggles of the Christian church, so his memories of the holy experience weren't preserved for us, but he doubtless shared them with others before his death.

Reflection

Reflect upon a "mountaintop" experience in your life. Are words capable of describing experiences that move us deeply?

---

1. Robert H. Stein, *Luke*, The New American Commentary, vol. 24 (Nashville, TN: Broadman, 1992), 277.
2. William Barclay, *The Gospel of Luke* (Philadelphia, PA: Westminster Press, 1975), 119.
3. Darrell L. Bock, *Luke* (Grand Rapids, MI: Baker Academic, 1994), 846.
4. *NIV Cultural Backgrounds Study Bible* (Grand Rapids, MI: Zondervan, 2016), 1764.
5. Leon Morris, *Luke: An Introduction and Commentary*, Tyndale New Testament Commentaries, vol. 3 (Downers Grove, IL: IVP Academic, 1988), 189.
6. Darrell L. Bock, *A Theology of Luke and Acts* (Grand Rapids, MI: Zondervan, 2012), 232.
7. Bock, *Luke*, 859.
8. Bock, 866.
9. Morris, *Luke*, 190.
10. Joel B. Green, *The Gospel of Luke*, New International Commentary on the New Testament, vol. 3 (Grand Rapids, MI: Eerdmans, 1997), 384, 385.

Chapter 37

Stumbling

Luke 9:37–50 (Matthew 17:14–23; 18:1–6; Mark 9:14–41)

Back at the foot of the mountain, there was trouble, a scene of disorder. Have you noticed that a mountaintop "high" is often followed by a plunge into a valley "low"? Despite a series of high points for the disciples—a successful missionary event, feeding five thousand people, their confession of Jesus as "Messiah," and for three of them, a vision of future glory—Luke now records four short incidents that reveal that these men were still weak in faith and slow to learn. The stories reinforce God's command to "listen to Him" (Luke 9:35).

On the next day, when they came down from the mountain, a large crowd met Him. And a man from the crowd shouted, saying, "Teacher, I beg You to look at my son, because he is my only son, and a spirit seizes him and he suddenly screams, and it throws him into a convulsion with foaming at the mouth; and only with difficulty does it leave him, mauling him as it leaves. And I begged Your disciples to cast it out, and they could not." And Jesus answered and said, "You unbelieving and perverse generation, how long shall I be with you and put up with you? Bring your son here." Now while he was still approaching, the demon slammed him to the ground and threw him into a convulsion. But Jesus rebuked the unclean spirit, and healed the boy and gave him back to his father. And they were all amazed at the greatness of God (verses 37–43).

Mark tells the story in greater detail (Mark 9:14–29). A large crowd met Jesus at the foot of the mountain, and things were not going well. A man brought forward his son with a severe case of demon possession. This was Luke's third account of an "only" child (Luke 7:11–17; 8:40–42)—a critical factor in a society where family survival depended on male offspring.

The distraught father told Jesus loudly and clearly what he had already shared with the nine disciples. Whenever a spirit seized the boy, he shrieked, foamed at the mouth, was thrown about, and injured. "I begged your disciples to cast it out," he reported, "but they could not." (Luke 9:40, NRSV). The case was distressing, and the contrast striking. "On the one hand we have those who rejoiced in the light of God on the mountain top, on the other those defeated by the powers of darkness on the plain."[1]

In Mark's account, Jesus asked the father how long this had been happening to the boy. He replied, "From childhood," and then appealed, "If you are able to do anything, have pity on us and help us" (Mark 9:21, 22, NRSV). Jesus asked, *"If you are able?"* (verse 23, NRSV; emphasis added). The father replied, "Lord, I believe; help my unbelief!" (verse 24, NKJV). Jesus rebuked the demon, and the boy lay, corpselike, on the ground. Jesus took the boy's hand, helped him stand up, and returned him to his father. All were astounded at God's power and greatness!

But what went wrong? Did the disciples forget that prayer is needed to open heaven's power circuit?

They were embarrassed as the scribes ridiculed them. Jesus' words were for them and everyone present, "You faithless and perverse generation! How much longer must I be with you?" (Luke 9:41, NRSV). What happened to their faith? Shortly before, the disciples were given power over demons during their recent missionary tour, but the power is not residual in them. The power comes only with constant faith and prayer.

But while everyone was astonished at all that He was doing, He said to His disciples, "As for you, let these words sink into your ears: for the Son of Man is going to be handed over to men." But they did not understand this statement, and it was concealed from them so that they would not comprehend it; and they were afraid to ask Him about this statement (verses 43–45).

The crowds continued to be amazed at all that Jesus had been doing in miracles and teaching, but the disciples must not be misled by all this popular attention. A reversal was coming. "Let these words sink into your ears" (verse 44). Jesus wanted them to listen to His words, but it would take a long while for them to understand and accept things they didn't want to hear.

Now an argument started among them as to which of them might be the greatest. But Jesus, knowing what they were thinking in their hearts, took a child and had him stand by His side, and He said to them, "Whoever receives this child in My name receives Me, and whoever receives Me receives Him who sent Me; for the one who is least among all of you, this is the one who is great" (verses 46–48).

It seems that "while Jesus is telling the disciples of His approaching suffering and death, they are arguing about their relative importance."[2] Rivalry for greater honor was common among ancient Mediterranean men.[3] Because position and status were important symbols in Jewish society, "so long as the Twelve thought of Jesus' kingdom as an earthly kingdom it was inevitable that they should be in competition for the highest places in it."[4]

To answer the question, Jesus called a child to His side. In Jewish culture, a child had low status—he was considered helpless and unimportant. Not so, Jesus said. When you accept a child as a member of God's family, you accept Jesus. "Greatness comes from God, and it can even come on one as little as a child."[5] The disciples' greatness would come only through their connection to Jesus.

John answered and said, "Master, we saw someone casting out demons in Your name; and we tried to prevent him, because he does not follow along with us." But Jesus said to him, "Do not hinder him; for the one who is not against you is for you" (verses 49, 50).

After a very important lesson, John changed the subject. He had seen a man casting out demons in Jesus' name and told him to stop because "he doesn't belong to us." Jesus responded, "Why would you do that?" There is no neutrality in the war against evil. Divine power is not given to just one agency or Christ-centered community. Anyone who operates in Jesus' name in accordance with His Word is His servant. We ought to appreciate all who bring souls to the feet of Jesus. "This has been the error of Christians in every age and it is interesting to see it in the very first generation of Jesus' followers."[6]

In this concluding section of the Galilean ministry, Satan was doing whatever he could to discourage Jesus. He did this by showing that the disciples didn't seem to have learned much since He called them and taught them. They must keep listening and learning.

Reflection

After a time on the mountain, we must get back to the routine of life. Doubt and discouragement are two of Satan's tools to undermine faith. How are we to deal with these "down" times?

1. Leon Morris, *Luke: An Introduction and Commentary*, Tyndale New Testament Commentaries, vol. 3 (Downers Grove, IL: IVP Academic, 1988), 192.

2. Darrell L. Bock, *Luke* (Grand Rapids, MI: Baker Academic, 1994), 894.

3. *NIV Cultural Backgrounds Study Bible* (Grand Rapids, MI: Zondervan, 2016), 1765.

4. William Barclay, *The Gospel of Luke* (Philadelphia, PA: Westminster Press, 1975), 127.

5. Bock, *Luke*, 891.

6. Morris, *Luke*, 195.

Part III

Journey to Jerusalem

Luke 9:51–19:28

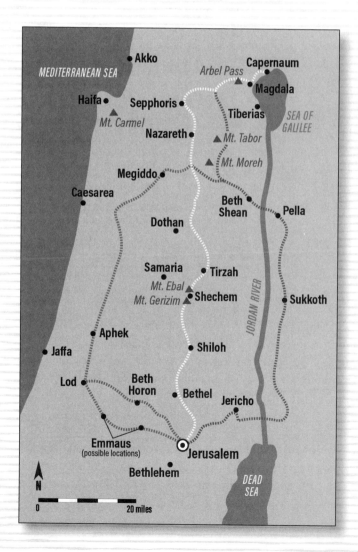

Chapter 38

Journey to Jerusalem

Luke 9:51 (Matthew 19:1, 2; Mark 10:1)

Luke begins this section,

When the days were approaching for His ascension, He was determined to go to Jerusalem (Luke 9:51).

With that simple statement, Luke begins part 2 of his Gospel. Up to now, almost all of Jesus' ministry has taken place in the province of Galilee, near where He grew up. We've become acquainted with several places along the shoreline of Lake Galilee—Capernaum, Gennesaret, Magdala, Bethsaida, Tiberius, Gergesa—and places in the high country to the west—Nazareth, Nain, Cana, and Mount Tabor. But the time had come for Jesus to leave His home territory and head south, so He began a meandering trek toward His ultimate destination, Jerusalem. The next ten chapters of Luke comprise the "travel section" of Jesus' ministry.

Luke has not told us about Jesus' short visits to Jerusalem from Galilee. Instead, Luke focused on His Galilean ministry and only mentioned Jesus' trip to Jerusalem as a twelve-year-old for the Passover festival (Luke 2:41–50). John tells us that He attended important feasts in Jerusalem during His Galilean ministry.

As Luke wrote about Jesus' ministry in Galilee, he closely followed Mark's account of most events. Now, his dependence on Mark ceased as he turned his attention to the next phase of Christ's ministry. At Luke 9:51, we find that Luke set aside Mark's account and did not pick it up again until Luke 18:14.[1] In between those points, where did Luke find the stories and teachings that fill nine chapters of his Gospel?

Some Bible scholars think that Luke relied, to some extent, on a now-nonexistent manuscript that they dub "Q" or "Quelle," which is German for "source." They also think that Matthew had access to "Q" when he later wrote his Gospel. What is most interesting, though, is that more than half of what we read between Luke 9:51 and 18:14 is unique to Luke, found nowhere else.[2] This includes, for example, the stories of the good Samaritan, the prodigal son, and the rich man and Lazarus. Where did Luke find these wonderful stories, including the many parables that Jesus told along the way? I believe the answer is Luke's successful, Spirit-guided search for eyewitnesses of Jesus' ministry and teaching during His journey through the Judean countryside. We must remember, too, that Luke had at least two years to interview people in Judea while his friend Paul was imprisoned in Caesarea.

A change of scene

As we spent time with Jesus in and around Galilee, we were exposed to now-familiar themes—the nature of Jesus' mission, His gathering of disciples, His teachings at the lakeshore and on hillsides, thirteen healing miracles, and the adoring crowds that were always with Him. We also saw the start of opposition to His authority and teachings. And widely different groups of people have considered the same question: "Who is this Man?"

Now, as we leave the peasant farms and fishing villages of Galilee, we will experience communities and styles of living that are significantly different. We will encounter wealthy landowners whose possessions prioritize their lives. We will meet businessmen who employ slaves to manage their financial affairs. We will certainly encounter greater numbers of scribes, Pharisees, and other leaders who challenge what Jesus is saying and doing.

The upcoming chapters of Luke will be largely concerned with Jesus' teachings and not so much with activity. He teaches in synagogues on some Sabbath days, sometimes with meal invitations from Pharisees, but more often, He teaches out in the open—perhaps in town and village public plazas and marketplaces. "Luke is concerned to show that teaching takes place in settings where a sense of intimacy with the teacher is established."[3]

In these talks and sermons, Jesus will use many parables—seventeen, in fact, of which fifteen are unique to Luke's Gospel. Several stories will contrast the new way of Jesus, characterized by compassion for the poor and downtrodden, with the self-righteous attitudes of the Jewish leadership. Scribes and Pharisees will make frequent appearances as conflict escalates. We will often be reminded of Simeon's prediction that Mary's child would bring division in Israel (Luke 2:34, 35). As Jesus works His way toward Jerusalem, He faces rejection by Jewish leadership that will culminate in His death on a cross. Throughout this journey, we will also observe the consistent resistance of Christ's disciples to the idea that their Master will endure suffering.

The journey to Jerusalem will not be made in a straight line, and these chapters from Luke are not a travel narrative. Study the map on page 121, which highlights three possible paths that Jesus probably used in His meanderings southward. We find few geographical markers as the journey unfolds. The route began through Samaria, which is the most direct road linking Galilee with the southern province of Judea. Much later, on the final leg of His journey, we will find Jesus at Jericho, which is on the longer route south through the Jordan valley.

So, what is Luke's purpose in these nine chapters? Instead of a travelogue, this section of Luke's Gospel will emphasize some forceful concepts:

- the sovereign rule of God over history
- the kingdom of God—"now," but also "not yet"
- the great reversal: "the last shall be first, and the first last"
- the priority of prayer in the Christian's life
- the role of wealth and possessions[4]

Let's now join Jesus and His disciples on their journey. Surrounded by the crowds that often follow Him, we will listen to His stories and prepare to follow the way of the Cross as we also await His kingdom of glory.

Reflection

How would you characterize the expectations of the disciples and the crowd as they followed Jesus to Jerusalem?

1. Robert H. Stein, *Luke*, The New American Commentary, vol. 24 (Nashville, TN: Broadman, 1992), 296.
2. Darrell L. Bock, *Luke* (Grand Rapids, MI: Baker Academic, 1994), 23, 24.
3. Darrell L. Bock, *A Theology of Luke and Acts* (Grand Rapids, MI: Zondervan, 2012), 244.
4. Stein, *Luke*, 45–54.

Chapter 39

Not Today

Luke 9:52–62 (Matthew 8:19–22)

Jesus was accompanied by His disciples and an unknown number of followers as they set out on a long winding journey toward Jerusalem. There He would fulfill His "departure," which Moses and Elijah talked about with Him on the mount of transfiguration (Luke 9:31).

Jesus' choice of route begins by going through Samaria. This was the fastest way to Judea, but Jews were often not welcomed by the Samaritans. Some of Jesus' disciples are liable to react if they encounter animosity.

Jews and Samaritans don't like each other. The mutual hatred goes back to the time when Israel's "united kingdom was divided after Solomon's death due to the foolishness of his son, Rehoboam (1 Kgs 12). The ten northern tribes formed a nation known variously as Israel, Ephraim, or . . . Samaria. [When this northern kingdom] fell to the Assyrians, . . . [its] leading citizens were exiled and dispersed throughout the Assyrian Empire. [Other displaced persons] were then brought into Samaria. Intermarriage resulted, the 'rebels' became 'half-breeds' in the eyes of the [Judeans]," and bitterness developed.[1]

The map shows how Samaria effectively blocked Judea from the northern province of Galilee, so although the road through Samaria is the shortest route between Galilee and Jerusalem, Jewish travelers often avoided Samaria by taking the longer route along the Jordan valley. But not Jesus.

And He sent messengers on ahead of Him, and they went and entered a village of the Samaritans to make arrangements for Him. And they did not receive Him, because He was traveling toward Jerusalem. When His disciples James and John saw this, they said, "Lord, do You want us to command fire to come down from heaven and consume them?" But He turned and rebuked them. And they went on to another village (Luke 9:52–56).

The Jerusalem journey began with a negative experience of rejection as the group trekked through Samaria. When Jesus sent unnamed messengers ahead to a Samaritan town, seeking lodging for the night, the request was denied. Some Samaritans may have heard about the prophet from Nazareth, but if His sights are set on Jerusalem and its temple, they want nothing to do with Him. Jesus simply accepted no for an answer, and they went on to another village.

This Samaritan story, which is unique to Luke, reveals that at least two disciples haven't yet gotten it. When the people of the village rejected the request for a night stay, James and John were ready to call down fire and have them all incinerated. But Jesus said, no! It wasn't a time for judgment. The two "sons of thunder" should have remembered their missionary apprenticeship when they simply shook the dust from their feet if a village did not welcome them. They would soon learn that the Samaritans were their neighbors. Jesus does not draw boundaries—all are precious in His sight.

Gathering followers

Leaving Samaria, Jesus and His entourage continued along a road somewhere in Judea. Since Luke was not brought up in Palestine, he wasn't familiar with the geography of the places where Jesus went. Luke may not have traveled in Galilee since he followed Mark's narrative quite closely in most of Christ's Galilean ministry.

As they were going on the road, someone said to Him, "I will follow You wherever You go." And Jesus said to him, "The foxes have holes and the birds of the sky have nests, but the Son of Man has nowhere to lay His head." And He said to another, "Follow Me." But he said, "Lord, permit me first to go and bury my father." But He said to him, "Allow the dead to bury their own dead; but as for you, go and proclaim everywhere the kingdom of God." Another also said, "I will follow You, Lord; but first permit me to say goodbye to those at my home." But Jesus said to him, "No one, after putting his hand to the plow and looking back, is fit for the kingdom of God" (verses 57–62).

As Jesus and His group walked along the road, people noticed their passing. Jesus invited people to join Him, but not all responded in a positive way. Some were working in the fields; some stood outside their wayside houses as this Rabbi and His band of disciples walked by. One man was drawn to follow Jesus, and he said, "I will follow You anywhere You want me to go." Jesus responded, "Foxes have holes and birds have nests for their homes. I have nowhere to lay my head."

As another man scrutinized the travelers, Jesus invited him to follow. He appeared interested but responded, "Not today; I will follow you after my father passes away." Jews consider that a son's greatest obligation is to honor his parents, and burying them is the greatest expression of that obligation.[2] This man's request to "first bury my father" may be a polite plea for delay in following Jesus. The response, "Let the dead bury their own dead," may mean, " 'Let the [spiritually] dead bury their own [physical] dead,' but you go and proclaim the kingdom of God."[3] The spiritually dead are those who choose not to follow Jesus.

A third man was quite positive, "Yes, I will follow you, Lord, but just give me time to say goodbye to my family." Elisha was given permission to do just that when he followed Elijah (1 Kings 19:20). "But following Jesus means more than following Elijah," and we are left wondering, Does the man's reply conceal "some reluctance to take the decisive step"?[4]

As they passed a farmer working in his field, Jesus summarized the nature of His call and its priority: "Once you put your hand to the plow, you don't look back." When I was a teenager, a local hobby-farmer offered me ten cents an hour to guide his horse-drawn plow by holding the reins. The problem was I kept turning around to see if we were going straight, and you can guess what happened. Looking backward is not the way to follow a straight line.

Luke doesn't talk about those who heeded the call and joined Jesus' band of followers on this trip to Jerusalem. It's costly to follow Jesus. The significance of these brief travel stories at the beginning of the Jerusalem journey is that they portray what looms ahead for Jesus: rejection.

Reflection

Discipleship begins when one becomes a follower of Jesus. Is it easy to make that decision? Why is it easy to find reasons (excuses) why today isn't the right time to follow Jesus—or to accept responsibility in the church?

1. Robert H. Stein, *Luke*, The New American Commentary, vol. 24 (Nashville, TN: Broadman, 1992), 318.

2. *NIV Cultural Backgrounds Study Bible* (Grand Rapids, MI: Zondervan, 2016), 1766.

3. Stein, *Luke*, 301.

4. Leon Morris, *Luke: An Introduction and Commentary*, Tyndale New Testament Commentaries, vol. 3 (Downers Grove, IL: IVP Academic, 1988), 199.

Chapter 40

The Seventy Messengers

Luke 10:1–16

Now after this the Lord appointed seventy-two others, and sent them in pairs ahead of Him to every city and place where He Himself was going to come (Luke 10:1).

Luke is the only Gospel writer who tells about the sending out of this large band of disciples, which number "seventy" in some manuscripts and "seventy-two" in others. Seventy "was held to be the number of nations in the world" (see Genesis 10), and Luke may be thinking of the day when people of every nation will be Christ's followers.[1]

Where did Jesus gather all these willing disciples? Luke told us about two or three who declined Jesus' invitation to "follow" (Luke 9:57–62), but there may well have been a larger number who embraced His call. Perhaps seventy includes a few from Galilee who are faithfully following Him on the journey to Jerusalem. Many have been drawn to Jesus by the freshness of His teaching; others, by the miracles. Were the twelve apostles included in the Seventy? Perhaps they accompanied the others as mentors.

And He was saying to them, "The harvest is plentiful, but the laborers are few; therefore plead with the Lord of the harvest to send out laborers into His harvest. Go" (Luke 10:2, 3).

As the seventy willing recruits gathered around Jesus for instructions, He used the analogy of reaping a harvest of grain, but their mission was really about spreading the kingdom of God.[2] There are two opposing kingdoms in this world—Jesus leads God's kingdom, which will ultimately overthrow the kingdom of Satan. In this sense, the Seventy will be God's infantrymen, going as foot soldiers to towns and villages, preparing the way for Jesus. There is an interesting parallel here between the mission of John the Baptist and the task Jesus gives to this group of faithful followers. Just as John was sent by God to prepare the way for Jesus, Seventy were sent ahead of Jesus to announce the arrival of His kingdom.

There was excitement about this bold missionary enterprise. "Now he will send out the disciples, not with a mood of gloom, but of excitement, authority, revelation, and opportunity."[3] The men would go in pairs and must expect to encounter opposition from Satanic forces, but the Holy Spirit would accompany them.

"Behold, I am sending you out like lambs in the midst of wolves. Carry no money belt, no bag, no sandals, and greet no one along the way. And whatever house you enter, first say, 'Peace be to this house.' And if a man of peace is there, your peace will rest upon him; but if not, it will return to you. Stay in that house, eating and drinking what they provide; for the laborer is deserving of his wages. Do not move from house to house. Whatever city you enter and they receive you, eat what is served to you; and heal those in it who are sick, and say to them, 'The kingdom of God has come near to you' " (verses 3–9).

Jesus gave careful instructions to His new recruits. Unlike the mission of the Twelve in Galilee, this group wasn't sent to preach but to spread the word about Jesus and to perform miracles of healing. As they went into the towns and villages, the kingdom of God would "come near" (verse 9), and their faithful work will foreshadow the future collapse of Satan's kingdom.

The missionary enterprise would be a novel experience for many of these men. They were to be on their best behavior, remaining at the home that first welcomed them, enjoying table fellowship there, not fussing about the food or contemplating better fare at other homes. Nor will they accept money. Jesus gave them the authority to heal sickness and exhibit the presence of God.

It is clear that "hospitality was one of the chief virtues in Mediterranean antiquity, and Jewish travelers could normally count on Jewish hospitality."[4] So let's picture what happened when two messengers entered a village. In the public street or plaza, everyone gathered to meet the strangers. Who were they? They don't carry knapsacks, so they may need a place to stay. Seeing everyone's curious faces, the men said who they were and why they'd come: "Have you heard about Jesus of Nazareth? You've got to meet Him and listen to Him when He comes to your village. We are His ambassadors. He is gracious to everyone and has given us some of His authority to heal anyone who is sick. Tomorrow morning, we will tell you how we met Jesus and how special He is. Please plan to come, and spread the word to others!"

Perhaps a dear widow invited the men to stay at her small house. The beds were lumpy, but she would do her best for them. Two other people offered to host the strangers at their houses, but the messengers had already accepted the kindness of the widow, and they brought a special benediction of peace to her humble cottage.

"But whatever city you enter and they do not receive you, go out into its streets and say, 'Even the dust of your city which clings to our feet we wipe off in protest against you; yet be sure of this, that the kingdom of God has come near.' I say to you, it will be more tolerable on that day for Sodom than for that city" (verses 10–12).

Let's now imagine a different scenario. Two messengers arrived at a village, and people gathered in the public square to find out who they were. They weren't carrying anything so may have needed a place to stay. They said they were messengers for Jesus of Nazareth, which began a noisy discussion. One or two appeared interested, but most were negative and unwelcoming. The messengers showed disappointment as someone spoke loudly for the villagers: "We don't want you here. Just go away!"

Above the ruckus, the two men spoke: "We're sad you don't want us to tell you about Jesus. We will be on our way, but know that God's kingdom comes with Jesus, and you will miss out." As the two messengers left, they wiped the dust of the street from their sandals, which the locals understood as a symbolic act. Paul and Barnabas later did the same thing at Antioch (Acts 13:51).[5] Perhaps someone threw a handful of gravel at the messengers as they left the village.

The prospect of inhospitality led Jesus to talk about other places that have rejected the gospel. Some Galilean towns had rejected the good news about God's kingdom.

"Woe to you, Chorazin! Woe to you, Bethsaida! For if the miracles that occurred in you had occurred in Tyre and Sidon, they would have repented long ago, sitting in sackcloth and ashes. But it will be more tolerable for Tyre and Sidon in the judgment than for you. And you, Capernaum, will not be exalted to heaven, will you? You will be brought down to Hades!" (Luke 10:13–15).

Jesus spoke rhetorically as He reflected on the inadequate responses of many to God's call. He expressed sadness for cities where He preached and healed but where people held on to their traditional ways of thinking; they were "holding to a form of godliness although they have denied its power" (2 Timothy 3:5). Chorazin was a city just north of Capernaum, and though not mentioned by Luke in Jesus' Galilean travels, it is evident that He performed miracles there. It was in the vicinity of Bethsaida that He fed the five thousand.

Capernaum received special emphasis because Jesus spent so much time there, preaching in its synagogue and performing many miracles. Matthew described Capernaum as Jesus' "own city," or hometown, as we might say (Matthew 9:1). These Galileans enjoyed multiple blessings of God's presence in Jesus, yet few made the commitment to discipleship. In the judgment, it would be worse for Capernaum than it would be for Tyre and Sidon, which never had the blessing of Jesus' presence.

"The one who listens to you listens to Me, and the one who rejects you rejects Me; but the one who rejects Me rejects the One who sent Me" (Luke 10:16).

Jesus' final words to the seventy messengers as they set out on their mission told of His relationship to His heavenly Father. "To reject Jesus' messengers is to reject Jesus and his message. To reject Jesus is to reject God. To reject God is to align oneself with Satan, and to align oneself with Satan is to place oneself in a position to be cast down in the judgment."[6]

Reflection

Jesus chose His disciples and His messengers from among the poor and uneducated in the communities. Ask yourself, Does anything disqualify me from being a messenger for Jesus?

---

1. William Barclay, *The Gospel of Luke* (Philadelphia, PA: Westminster Press, 1975), 133.
2. Darrell L. Bock, *A Theology of Luke and Acts* (Grand Rapids, MI: Zondervan, 2012), 205, 206.
3. Darrell L. Bock, *Luke* (Grand Rapids, MI: Baker Academic, 1994), 986.
4. *NIV Cultural Backgrounds Study Bible* (Grand Rapids, MI: Zondervan, 2016), 1767.
5. Bock, *Luke*, 1002.
6. Joel B. Green, *The Gospel of Luke*, New International Commentary on the New Testament (Grand Rapids, MI: Eerdmans, 1997), 411.

Chapter 41

Times of Joy

Luke 10:17–24 (Matthew 11:25–27)

Mission accomplished. The seventy messengers returned to Jesus, and the broad smiles on their faces told the story—it's been a successful mission.

Now the seventy-two returned with joy, saying, "Lord, even the demons are subject to us in Your name!" And He said to them, "I watched Satan fall from heaven like lightning. Behold, I have given you authority to walk on snakes and scorpions, and authority over all the power of the enemy, and nothing will injure you. Nevertheless, do not rejoice in this, that the spirits are subject to you, but rejoice that your names are recorded in heaven" (Luke 10:17–20).

Jesus had given these messengers power in His name to heal sickness. Perhaps they did not think it included the power to cast out demons, but indeed it had, for they exclaimed, "Lord, even the demons submit to us in your name!" Ancient exorcists coaxed and threatened spirits and sometimes used incantations or odorous roots to expel them, but the name of Jesus was instantly effective.[1] He heard their excitement and understood what this meant for the future defeat of Satan's kingdom. The prophet Isaiah had been given a picture of the original fall of Satan: "How you have fallen from heaven, you star of the morning, son of the dawn!" (Isaiah 14:12). Now, recalling Satan's fall, Jesus stated, "I watched Satan fall from heaven like a flash of lightning." The " 'lightning' indicates not brightness but the suddenness of the fall."[2]

As the returning missionaries shared their experiences, Jesus helped them understand what it meant for kingdom victory. "Look, I have given you authority to tread on snakes and scorpions" (Luke 10:19, NET). The snake as a symbol of Satan originates in Genesis 3, where we have the story of humanity's fall. A special promise given to Adam and Eve was that the serpent's head would be crushed (Genesis 3:15). The serpent symbol carries all the way through to the book of Revelation, where "the great dragon" is defined as "the serpent of old who is called the devil and Satan, who deceives the whole world" (Revelation 12:9).

While the men expressed their joy, Jesus told them that real joy would come, not from their missionary accomplishments but from their eternal salvation. "Rejoice that your names are written in heaven," He said. They had joined God's kingdom. On this note, Luke finished his account of these specially commissioned disciples—their sending, their return, and how Jesus interpreted their accomplishments.

At that very time He rejoiced greatly in the Holy Spirit, and said, "I praise You, Father, Lord of heaven and earth, that You have hidden these things from the wise and intelligent and have revealed them to infants. Yes, Father, for doing so was well pleasing in Your sight" (Luke 10:21).

Now it's Jesus' turn to be joyful. The successful mission of the Seventy brought Him encouragement.

Their Spirit-directed achievement enabled Him to look ahead to the ultimate victory over evil, and we have here a rare glimpse of Jesus experiencing joy. More often, we picture Him saddened as people, especially the religious leaders, rejected His teaching. Yet we have this magnificent statement of Paul, speaking of Christ, "who for the joy set before Him endured the cross, despising the shame" (Hebrews 12:2). Jesus "rejoiced in the Holy Spirit" as He began praying to His Father. He thanked His Father, "Lord of heaven and earth," for granting divine wisdom, not to those who *think* themselves wise, but to the "little ones," the "infants." The "infants" include the seventy messengers, the ones who listened to the words of Jesus and responded with their hearts.

Once again, we hear some words Jesus used in His mission statement: "He anointed Me to bring good news to the poor. He has sent Me to proclaim release to captives, and recovery of sight to the blind" (Luke 4:18).

"All things have been handed over to Me by My Father, and no one knows who the Son is except the Father, and who the Father is except the Son, and anyone to whom the Son determines to reveal Him" (Luke 10:22).

In His prayer, Jesus acknowledged the sovereignty of God and of Himself as co-regent with the Father in the divine purpose and authority (John 10:30). To Jesus belonged the unique role of revealing God to the human race. "No one can really understand the Father or what God is about without listening to the Son and his revelation."[3]

Turning to the disciples, He said privately, "Blessed are the eyes that see the things you see; for I tell you that many prophets and kings wanted to see the things that you see, and did not see them, and to hear the things that you hear, and did not hear them" (Luke 10:23, 24).

"You are blessed in a special way," Jesus told the Twelve. Prophets like Isaiah and Jeremiah were faithful spokesmen for God and were shown in vision the future coming of the Messiah, but they did not live to see how the kingdom of God was revealed in Jesus.[4] His specially selected men were eyewitnesses to great events. Faithful disciples and followers of Jesus are immeasurably blessed.

Reflection

Ask yourself, Am I a joyful disciple? How do you define joy? How does it differ from "pleasure" and "happiness"? One writer suggests that "true joy is a limitless, life-defining, transformative reservoir waiting to be tapped into. It requires the utmost surrender and, like love, is a choice to be made."[5]

1. *NIV Cultural Backgrounds Study Bible* (Grand Rapids, MI: Zondervan, 2016), 1767.
2. Robert H. Stein, *Luke*, The New American Commentary, vol. 24 (Nashville, TN: Broadman, 1992), 310.
3. Darrell L. Bock, *Luke* (Grand Rapids, MI: Baker Academic, 1994), 1012.
4. Joel B. Green, *The Gospel of Luke*, New International Commentary on the New Testament, vol. 3 (Grand Rapids, MI: Eerdmans, 1997), 424.
5. "What's the Difference Between Joy and Happiness?" Compassion International, accessed September 28, 2022, https://www.compassion.com/sponsor_a_child/difference-between-joy-and-happiness.htm.

Chapter 42

The Compassionate Samaritan

Luke 10:25–37

And behold, a lawyer stood up and put Him to the test, saying, "Teacher, what shall I do to inherit eternal life?" And He said to him, "What is written in the Law? How does it read to you?" And he answered, "You shall love the Lord your God with all your heart, and with all your soul, and with all your strength, and with all your mind; and your neighbor as yourself." And He said to him, "You have answered correctly; do this and you will live" (Luke 10:25–28).

Jesus may still have been conversing privately with the Twelve when He was interrupted by a lawyer who had a question for Him. This fellow wanted to test Jesus' attitude toward the law of Moses. He may have heard rumors that Jesus was soft on law-keeping, so his question focused on "doing" what the law requires: "What do I have to *do* to get eternal life?"

He didn't anticipate that Jesus would respond with a question of His own. "How does it read to you?" (verse 26) is another way of asking, "What is your understanding of what it says?"[1] Every pious Jew recited the *Shema* two times a day: "Hear, Israel! The Lord is our God, the Lord is one! You shall love the Lord your God with all your heart and with all your soul and with all your strength" (Deuteronomy 6:4, 5).

The lawyer was quick to answer Jesus' question by repeating those words of the *Shema*: "You shall love the Lord your God with all your heart, and with all your soul, and with all your strength," and he added, "and with all your *mind*" (Luke 10:27; emphasis added). Then, perhaps to display his superfluous knowledge, he added something found elsewhere in the law of Moses, "But you shall love your neighbor as yourself" (Leviticus 19:18).

Jesus applauded the lawyer's response, adding, "Do this, and you will live" (Luke 10:28). Confident that he was already doing everything required of him by the law but perhaps wanting to display his superiority, the lawyer asked a follow-up question: "Who is my neighbor?"

But wanting to justify himself, he said to Jesus, "And who is my neighbor?" (verse 29).

Well, the answer to that question is a no-brainer, isn't it? Every Jew knew who his neighbors were. Jewish law taught that your neighbors are the people of the covenant, your fellow Jews. Others are simply "non-neighbors." Had the questioner conveniently forgotten that the same chapter of Leviticus talks about "the stranger who resides with you . . . , you shall love him as yourself"? (Leviticus 19:34). But he was looking for the minimum obedience required.

Truly, "knowledge of what God requires is not enough. Such knowledge needs to be put into practice."[2] So, Jesus told a story. It's specifically for the lawyer, but everyone who listens will benefit.

Jesus replied and said, "A man was going down from Jerusalem to Jericho, and he encountered robbers, and they stripped him and beat him, and went away leaving him half dead. And by coincidence a priest was going down on that road, and when he saw him, he passed by on the other side. Likewise a Levite also, when he came to the place and saw him, passed by on the other side" (Luke 10:30–32).

The ancient road from Jerusalem to Jericho was about thirty miles long, winding downward through rugged desert terrain, descending three thousand feet from the high plateau of Jerusalem to the Jordan valley, where Jericho lies below sea level.[3] Bandits were a problem on many roads in the time of Jesus, and the ruggedness and steep passes along the road to Jericho provided many natural hideouts for robbers.[4]

So, it happened that a nameless Jew who traveled alone down to Jericho was suddenly attacked by robbers who beat him and left him by the roadside. The first traveler to happen onto the scene was a priest, representing the height of piety, but his fear of becoming unclean by possibly touching a corpse led him to pass by "on the other side." He was followed soon afterward by a Levite, a religious leader and temple assistant. This man feared the robbers might be watching *him* at that very moment, so he likewise continued his journey "on the other side."

Pious Judaism has had two tries to respond, and both failed. "Who will love this dying man?"[5]

"But a Samaritan who was on a journey came upon him" (verse 33).

A Samaritan? We might wonder, *James and John, are you listening? Remember how you wanted to incinerate a Samaritan village a while back?* (Luke 9:54). The Samaritan was considered ceremonially unclean and to be avoided. Surely, he's the last person who would help a wounded Jew. If the roles were reversed, the Jew might spit in his direction. It seems a given that this traveler will also pass by on the other side.

"And when he saw him, he felt compassion, and came to him and bandaged up his wounds, pouring oil and wine on them; and he put him on his own animal, and brought him to an inn and took care of him. On the next day he took out two denarii and gave them to the innkeeper and said, 'Take care of him; and whatever more you spend, when I return, I will repay you' " (Luke 10:33–35).

Wonder of wonders, this Samaritan, who is very likely a traveling merchant, has a heart of compassion. Jesus described seven actions of this kind traveler:[6]

1. He went directly to the wounded man.
2. He anointed the man's cuts with soothing olive oil and wine to disinfect them.
3. He bound his wounds, perhaps ripping up some of his own clothing for bandages.
4. He loaded the injured man on his donkey and walked alongside.
5. He took the man to a wayside inn.
6. He cared for the man throughout the night.
7. The next morning, before continuing on his way, he left money with the innkeeper—two denarii, enough for a poor man's bed and food for twenty-four days. "If you need to spend more, I will pay when I return. The man was robbed, so he cannot pay his bill." Innkeepers

had a reputation as being untrustworthy, so the Samaritan provided a financial incentive for the innkeeper to care for the man.[7]

"Which of these three do you think proved to be a neighbor to the man who fell into the robbers' hands?" And he said, "The one who showed compassion to him." Then Jesus said to him, "Go and do the same" (verses 36, 37).

The lawyer's original question, "What must I *do* to inherit eternal life?" has been answered. Salvation is not earned by reciting the law; it is by grace through faith (Ephesians 2:8, 9). It is expressed in the way we live, the way we show love to a stranger.

Neighbor-love knows no boundaries. And it's not just a matter of whom I must love, but what should my love *look like* when I love a neighbor? "The quality of love manifested in the behavior of the Samaritan is love for another that is equal to love for the self."[8]

I wonder why Jesus chose the road from Jerusalem to Jericho for His story. Did He foresee that His own journey to Jerusalem would end on that same road, except that it would start at Jericho and be an uphill climb ending on a hill called Calvary?

Reflection

How might you show neighborly love to a refugee family looking for a place to live in your community?

---

1. *NIV Cultural Backgrounds Study Bible* (Grand Rapids, MI: Zondervan, 2016), 1768.
2. Darrell L. Bock, *Luke* (Grand Rapids, MI: Baker Academic, 1994), 1027.
3. Sergio and Rhoda in Israel, "Jericho to Jerusalem, Walking the Ancient Trail of the Good Samaritan," YouTube, 24:16, June 23, 2019, https://www.youtube.com/watch?v=q6Uz9gIdm68.
4. Bock, *Luke*, 1029.
5. Bock, 1031.
6. Bock, 1032, 1033.
7. *NIV Cultural Backgrounds Study Bible*, 1768.
8. O. C. Edwards Jr., *Luke's Story of Jesus* (Philadelphia, PA: Fortress, 1981), 57.

Chapter 43

At the Feet of Jesus

Luke 10:38–42

Luke rarely pinpoints where Jesus is located during the journey to Jerusalem. Some Bible students wonder whether He and His team were somewhere near Jericho when He told the parable about four travelers on the downhill road from Jerusalem. The first traveler was robbed and beaten half to death. The last one, a generous Samaritan, showed mercy to the dying man.

Luke follows that story with Jesus' visit to "a certain village" that he does not identify, but we can make an educated guess by matching it to a story in John's Gospel that it is Bethany, a rural hamlet on the eastern slopes of the Mount of Olives, less than two miles from Jerusalem (John 11).

Now as they were traveling along, He entered a village; and a woman named Martha welcomed Him into her home. And she had a sister called Mary, who was also seated at the Lord's feet, and was listening to His word (Luke 10:38, 39).

Jesus was visiting the Bethany home of Martha, Mary, and Lazarus. From other stories in John's Gospel, we discover that the three siblings were close friends of Jesus. He may have stayed at their home on multiple occasions. When Lazarus fell ill at a later time, Martha sent an urgent message to Jesus to please come because "he whom You love is sick" (John 11:3). On the occasion of the visit Luke describes, Martha was a busy woman in the kitchen, preparing a special meal for her guest. Right away, we have a problem.

But Martha was distracted with all her preparations; and she came up to Him and said, "Lord, do You not care that my sister has left me to do the serving by myself? Then tell her to help me." But the Lord answered and said to her, "Martha, Martha, you are worried and distracted by many things; but only one thing is necessary; for Mary has chosen the good part, which shall not be taken away from her" (Luke 10:40–42).

While Martha was toiling in a hot kitchen, Mary was inside, sitting at Jesus' feet and listening to His every word. This irritated Martha to the point that she approached Jesus and spoke her mind: "Lord, don't You care that I'm slaving away while my sister is just sitting here? Tell her to come and help me."

Luke's audience was almost certainly on Martha's side. They understood the high value their society placed on hospitality. Of course, it's right for Martha to be preparing a meal for her guest, and it's OK to ask for help—but wait.

Jesus' response was soft and kind. He wanted Martha to understand something about priorities. "Martha, Martha, you are busy with many good things. But there is something even better, and that's what Mary has chosen." While there are many good things to be done, there is nothing more important than spending time with Jesus. It is easy to be so busy doing good things that we neglect to do "the one thing that is needful."

Martha is a "doing" person. In Luke's previous story, a lawyer asked Jesus what he must *do* to inherit eternal life. The compassionate Samaritan showed his love for the wounded stranger by *doing* a number of things. Perhaps Luke placed the story of Martha and Mary right after the parable "as a safeguard against any of his readers coming under the misapprehension that salvation is by works."[1]

Darrell Bock points out that Martha's behavior fits cultural expectations. What Mary did was countercultural. Women did not sit at the feet of a rabbi as a disciple.[2] It was not done. Luke, though, wanted his readers to understand that women must never be marginalized or treated as inferior. Men and women are of equal worth, and Luke has already provided three examples—Mary Magdalene, Joanna, and Susanna—of women who were faithful disciples of Jesus (Luke 8:1–3).

There is an interesting parallel between the lawyer's question in the previous story: "What must I do to inherit eternal life?" and the example of Mary, who was a candidate for eternal life as she sat at the feet of Jesus. In order to be inheriting eternal life, one must listen to the word of God and do it.[3]

Another important lesson from Jesus' visits to Bethany is that "no one in the history of the universe has ever carried an agenda as momentous as our Lord. His life here on earth was so brief, His ministry so crammed into three short years, His priorities so critical for our salvation. Yet He periodically took time out to travel to an obscure village for a visit with friends. It is a refreshing journey that we often need to take as well."[4] Praise God; there is room for us at the feet of Jesus!

Reflection

Put yourself in Martha's position. She wanted to provide the best possible meal for a very special guest. Is there anything wrong with that? How do you prioritize the tasks of your day?

---

1. Leon Morris, *Luke: An Introduction and Commentary*, Tyndale New Testament Commentaries, vol. 3 (Downers Grove, IL: IVP Academic, 1988), 210.
2. Paul Borgman, *The Way According to Luke: Hearing the Whole Story of Luke-Acts* (Grand Rapids, MI: Eerdmans, 2006), 97, 104.
3. Borgman, 104.
4. Keith Clouten, *Journeys: Devotions for Travelers* (Winepress, 2011), 142.

Chapter 44

Teach Us to Pray

Luke 11:1–13 (Matthew 6:9–13; 7:7–11)

"Inheriting eternal life, entering God's kingdom, requires hearing and doing the will of God, as we have just seen [in the previous two stories]. But this is impossible without help from God. And so it is that prayer is a constant refrain throughout Luke's two-volume story."[1] At Bethany, Mary listened to Jesus. Now Jesus listened to His Father, drawing on His source of power.[2]

Luke emphasized that prayer was a central part of Jesus' life. As the disciples observed Jesus' consistent reliance on prayer, they noticed that there was something magnetic about the Master's prayer life because it demonstrated a thriving relationship with His Father. One day, the disciples waited until Jesus finished praying, and then one of them made a request.

It happened that while Jesus was praying in a certain place, when He had finished, one of His disciples said to Him, "Lord, teach us to pray, just as John also taught his disciples." And He said to them, "When you pray, say:

> **'Father, hallowed be Your name.**
> **Your kingdom come.**
> **Give us each day our daily bread.**
> **And forgive us our sins,**
> **For we ourselves also forgive everyone who is indebted to us.**
> **And do not lead us into temptation' " (Luke 11:1–4).**

We recognize this as the Lord's Prayer. Matthew describes Jesus reciting the prayer during His sermon on the mount in Galilee (Matthew 6:9–15). The version in Luke is slightly shorter, and it's shared at a different time and place in response to the request from His disciples: "Lord, teach us to pray, as John taught his disciples" (Luke 11:1, NRSV). From this, we gather that John the Baptist taught his disciples a formal or fixed prayer (Luke 5:33), and Jesus' disciples wanted to be taught a prayer like that. Jesus responded by outlining a corporate prayer, which many Christian churches have used in their liturgy for centuries.

The prayer is addressed to "Father." "As a title for God, 'Father' is found only fifteen times in the entire OT" and rarely in connection with prayer.[3] In the Greco-Roman world, a father had virtually unlimited authority over his children as long as he lived. "Would a newborn child be reared in the family? Sold? Exposed? Killed? Would the children be scourged? Pawned? Allowed or refused marriage or divorce?"[4] All this was a father's prerogative. Jesus wants His disciples to have a very different understanding of God, not only as their Father but also as their Friend. It is to a loving, caring God that they are to pray and make requests.

The prayer, as Jesus taught His disciples, has five brief but distinct parts:

1. "Hallowed be Your name." God's name is holy. It signifies His character, which is love. He is the Creator God, enthroned and ruling the universe.
2. "Your kingdom come." Jesus announced that the "kingdom of heaven is at hand," making it both now and not yet.
3. "Give us each day our daily bread." This request is not just about bread. This is about dependence on God for all our needs, day by day. Ask, and know it will be supplied as it was when the disciples were sent on their first missionary trip without money.
4. "Forgive us our sins." We receive forgiveness, but only as we offer forgiveness to others. "An unforgiving heart is not in a condition that it can accept forgiveness."[5]
5. "Do not lead us into temptation." Testing will come, but we don't ask for it. We crave spiritual protection. "This request reflects a spirit of dependence on God, as does the whole prayer."[6]

God of abundance

Luke was a product of the social customs and cultural values found in his corner of the Roman world, and this shows in his writing. Luke depicts two cultural values in Christ's discussion of prayer with the Twelve:*

1. *Friendship* was an important cultural value in the Hellenistic world. Luke highlights friendship in several of his stories. Friendship is commonly seen in social relationships among equals, but it can also be practiced between those who are not equal, such as between humans and God.
2. *Relationship* between those not equal was also commonly observed between patrons and clients in the Roman world. "A patron has social, economic, and political resources that are needed by a client. In return, a client can give expressions of loyalty and honor that are useful for the patron."[7] In this type of relationship, God is seen as the supreme Patron. We, His clients, make requests of Him by means of prayer; He responds with blessings and mercies; we reciprocate with praise and gratitude.

Continuing on, Parsons observes how these cultural values are depicted in a funny little story that Jesus used to illustrate how we can be bold in our approach to God.

And He said to them, "Suppose one of you has a friend, and goes to him at midnight and says to him, 'Friend, lend me three loaves, because a friend of mine has come to me from a journey and I have nothing to serve him'; and from inside he answers and says, 'Do not bother me; the door has already been shut and my children and I are in bed; I cannot get up and give you anything.' I tell you, even if he will not get up and give him anything just because he is

---

* Parsons believes Luke's audience will understand this story culturally as a patron-client relationship. The sleeper is the patron, the petitioner the client. Mikael C. Parsons, *Luke: Storyteller, Interpreter, Evangelist* (Peabody, MA: Hendrickson, 2007), 53–60.

his friend, yet because of his shamelessness he will get up and give him as much as he needs" **(Luke 11:5–8).**

Put yourself in the story. Imagine that you live in a rural village, where the simple mud-brick houses are close together. Each is a one-room home in which the whole family makes their bed on a floor mat. Sometimes, the mat may be spread across a raised bench to sleep apart from the animals. Each night, you bring the hens, the goats, and the other livestock into your one-room house.

Like other peasant families, you bake bread daily, just enough for your immediate needs—generally three small loaves for each adult's evening meal. There are no evening shops in the village, and a disturbance at midnight would awaken the whole family, including the animals. A loud conversation would also awaken your neighbors.

Late one night, a friend arrives at your little house, so you make him a bed on the floor. The poor guy hasn't eaten all day, but you have nothing to offer him. It will take a lot of nerve to wake your next-door neighbor to ask for some bread, which he always has in abundance. It's absurd to consider banging on his door at midnight, but the village culture of hospitality demands it. The honor of your village is at stake, so you wake your neighbor in order to feed your friend.[8]

God is the reliable patron or friend who answers the requests of His petitioners. "The host plans to pay back his groggy neighbor." However, "the point of the parable is that if an irritated person responds to boldness, so you can be bold with the Gracious One."[9] *How much greater* is the Father's graciousness than the kindest act of a sinner?

"So I say to you, ask, and it will be given to you; seek, and you will find; knock, and it will be opened to you. For everyone who asks receives, and the one who seeks finds, and to the one who knocks, it will be opened. Now which one of you fathers will his son ask for a fish, and instead of a fish, he will give him a snake? Or he will even ask for an egg, and his father will give him a scorpion? So if you, despite being evil, know how to give good gifts to your children, how much more will your heavenly Father give the Holy Spirit to those who ask Him?" (verses 9–13).

Let's paraphrase these words of Jesus to the disciples, who must have been in awe of the gracious Father they have.

- Be bold with God in *asking*, even when you don't truly know what your needs are.
- Be bold in *searching* for answers to the questions that bother you. God is always listening and ready to help.
- Be bold in *knocking* at God's door—even if it's midnight!

So, Andrew, if your son asks for an egg for breakfast, would you put a scorpion on his plate? I would never do that, Lord! Nathanael, when your baby boy wants a cup of milk, will you give him sour wine? Of course not! Well, can you imagine *how much kinder* God is than any of you fathers? Your heavenly Father is longing for you to ask Him for the gift of the Holy Spirit. That is a gift of eternal value, and He is eager to bestow it on all who ask Him.

Reflection

A Christian blogger lists some problems with how we pray, including these: (1) I work on solving my problems without asking God to help; (2) "I make decisions and then ask God to bless them"; (3) "I tell God how to solve [my] problems"; (4) "I spend more time talking than listening."[10] Discuss.

1. Paul Borgman, *The Way According to Luke: Hearing the Whole Story of Luke-Acts* (Grand Rapids, MI: Eerdmans, 2006), 111.

2. Borgman, 111.

3. Robert H. Stein, *Luke*, The New American Commentary, vol. 24 (Nashville, TN: Broadman, 1992), 324.

4. Joel B. Green, *The Gospel of Luke*, New International Commentary on the New Testament, vol. 3 (Grand Rapids, MI: Eerdmans, 1997), 438.

5. Leon Morris, *Luke: An Introduction and Commentary*, Tyndale New Testament Commentaries, vol. 3 (Downers Grove, IL: IVP Academic, 1988), 213.

6. Darrell L. Bock, *Luke* (Grand Rapids, MI: Baker Academic, 1994), 1056.

7. Green, *Gospel of Luke*, 202.

8. *NIV Cultural Backgrounds Study Bible* (Grand Rapids, MI: Zondervan, 2016), 1769.

9. Bock, *Luke*, 1057, 1058.

10. Henry Neufeld, "Some Problems With Prayer," *Threads From Henry's Web*, January 20, 2018, https://henryneufeld.com/threads/2018/01/20/some-problems-with-prayer/.

Chapter 45

Two Kingdoms

Luke 11:14–26 (Matthew 12:22–30, 43–45)

As Jesus continued His journey through Judea, He encountered crowds and controversy. People in Judea were not like the eager villagers and townspeople of Galilee, ever chasing the footsteps of the Master, acclaiming Him as teacher and healer. These southerners questioned the source of His power to heal, and they wondered who gave Him authority. Controversy was blowing in the wind.

And He was casting out a mute demon; when the demon had gone out, the man who was previously unable to speak talked, and the crowds were amazed. But some of them said, "He casts out the demons by Beelzebul, the ruler of the demons." Others, to test Him, were demanding of Him a sign from heaven (Luke 11:14–16).

Whenever and wherever Jesus performed a healing miracle, people were amazed—that's one of Luke's favorite words—but the religious leaders questioned His authority (Matthew 12:22–24). In Judean society, magical formulas were often utilized to manipulate and cast out spirits.[1] Some thought that was what Jesus was doing. "Jesus [was] either wrong, crazy, lying, or sent from God—there are no other options."[2]

It's interesting that the Bible says little about demon possession before and after the time of Jesus, but it's certainly a hot topic during His ministry.[3] Should we be surprised? Have you ever baited for cockroaches and watched them come in hordes to their death? Satan's aim to constrain Jesus Christ and remove His authority drew out all the evil spirits. In the story of the seventy missionaries, we heard them rejoicing because they had cast out demons through divine power. Praise God that in the power of the Holy Spirit, evil gets defeated and Jesus is victorious.

One day, Jesus released a man from a demon that had kept him mute. The miracle created wonder because Jewish leaders claimed that you couldn't cast out a mute demon. They thought that you could only coax spirits out of a person who could name his demon. Since a mute person can't speak, people said it was impossible to cast out his demon.[4] But Jesus did it!

Some who watched Jesus perform this miracle argued that He got His special authority from someone they call Beelzebul, also known as Satan.* By making this blasphemous accusation, they tried to minimize Jesus' effectiveness and influence. Others were amazed by what Jesus had done, and they wanted to see Him perform more signs and wonders. They seemed to think that casting out demons wasn't enough evidence for them to believe that Jesus was from God.

---

* The name Beelzebul goes back to a description of the old Canaanite god, Baal, or in its English form may refer to Baal-Zebub, the Philistine god of Ekron (1 Kings 1:2, 3). Darrell L. Bock, *Luke*, (Grand Rapids, MI: Baker Academic, 1994), 1074.

But He knew their thoughts and said to them, "Every kingdom divided against itself is laid waste; and a house divided against itself falls. And if Satan also has been divided against himself, how will his kingdom stand? For you claim that I cast out the demons by Beelzebul. Yet if by Beelzebul I cast out the demons, by whom do your sons cast them out? Therefore, they will be your judges. But if I cast out the demons by the finger of God, then the kingdom of God has come upon you" (Luke 11:17–20).

Jesus presented His opponents with a counterargument based on simple logic. Think of two opposing kingdoms; in this case, one kingdom belongs to Satan. Let's imagine for a moment that Jesus belonged to Satan's kingdom and kept busy by casting Satan's own demons out of people. That would mean Satan was fighting against himself, which wouldn't make any sense. In that case, Satan's kingdom would self-destruct.

In turn, Jesus asked, "By whom do your sons cast them out?" His disciples—"your sons"—had been given divine authority to cast out demons. "Why don't you ask them regarding the source of their power? They will tell you that they are empowered by God."[5] "So," Jesus replied, "when you see Me casting out demons by the power of God, you know for certain that I represent the other kingdom, which is the kingdom of God." The exercise of divine power is evidence that God's kingdom is present and real.[6]

"When a strong man, fully armed, guards his own house, his possessions are secure. But when someone stronger than he attacks him and overpowers him, that man takes away his armor on which he had relied and distributes his plunder. The one who is not with Me is against Me; and the one who does not gather with Me scatters" (verses 21–23).

There is a war in progress. Satan, "a strong man," is guarding his castle against attack. But the time is coming when someone "stronger than he" will overpower the prince of evil and destroy both his castle and his kingdom. Every person is called upon to align himself for battle. You cannot be in God's kingdom if you are secretly supporting the enemy—there is no neutral ground. Jesus now told a simple story to illustrate.

"When the unclean spirit comes out of a person, it passes through waterless places seeking rest, and not finding any, it then says, 'I will return to my house from which I came.' And when it comes, it finds it swept and put in order. Then it goes and brings along seven other spirits more evil than itself, and they come in and live there; and the last condition of that person becomes worse than the first" (verses 24–26).

So, we are to imagine that a person was dispossessed of his demon by an exorcist, but the newly freed individual didn't follow Jesus. The demon was lonely and, after wandering in a thirsty desert for a while, decided to return to "my house" (verse 24), which he found empty and nicely swept. Wanting company, he invited all his friends to come join him. This is what happens when a person is relieved of his demon but not led into God's kingdom.

Clearly, you cannot live in a moral vacuum. "An empty soul is a soul in peril."[7] When a person gets rid of an evil spirit but puts nothing in its place, he is in a worse place than at the beginning. The little parable also illustrates the danger of experiencing God's work in your life but then falling back onto your own resources, which brings the threat of a renewed satanic attack.

Reflection

You are just a pawn in a cosmic war unless you join the army of God. What weapons does the Holy Spirit offer you?

1. "Healing Miracles in the New Testament," *NIV Cultural Backgrounds Study Bible* (Grand Rapids, MI: Zondervan, 2016), 1771.

2. Darrell L. Bock, *Luke* (Grand Rapids, MI: Baker Academic, 1994), 1067.

3. Leon Morris, *Luke: An Introduction and Commentary*, Tyndale New Testament Commentaries, vol. 3 (Downers Grove, IL: IVP Academic, 1988), 129.

4. David Guzik, *The Enduring Word Bible Commentary*, Luke 11, accessed September 28, 2022, https://enduringword .com/bible-commentary/luke-11/.

5. Joel B. Green, *The Gospel of Luke*, New International Commentary on the New Testament, vol. 3 (Grand Rapids, MI: Eerdmans, 1997), 456.

6. Darrell L. Bock, *A Theology of Luke and Acts* (Grand Rapids, MI: Zondervan, 2012), 205, 206.

7. William Barclay, *The Gospel of Luke* (Philadelphia, PA: Westminster Press, 1975), 149.

Chapter 46

A Wicked Generation

Luke 11:27–36 (Matthew 12:38–42; 6:22, 23)

The crowd surrounding Jesus grew larger and noisier. There was an increasing element of criticism and negative thinking about this teacher from Galilee. Jesus was still pinpointing the lesson from His dynamic little parable about an unclean spirit's return to an empty house when, suddenly, a woman's loud voice broke the tension of confrontation.

While Jesus was saying these things, one of the women in the crowd raised her voice and said to Him, "Blessed is the womb that carried You, and the breasts at which You nursed!" But He said, "On the contrary, blessed are those who hear the word of God and follow it" (Luke 11:27, 28).

This woman was brave to speak up in a society where women are not expected to be heard publicly, but as we have noted previously, Luke emphasized the role of women in his writings. She pronounced a blessing on the mother of Jesus and indirectly on Jesus Himself. Responding, Jesus did not try to correct her, but He had a response for everyone: "Blessed rather are those who hear the word of God and obey it!" (verse 28, NRSV). Do those words of Jesus sound familiar to you? Think back to a day in Galilee when Jesus was teaching a large crowd, and someone similarly interrupted to tell Him that His mother and brothers were waiting to see Him. Jesus gave this almost identical response: "My mother and My brothers are *these who hear the word of God and do it*" (Luke 8:21). The lesson is simple: listen and obey.

Now as the crowds were increasing, He began to say, "This generation is a wicked generation; it demands a sign, and yet no sign will be given to it except the sign of Jonah. For just as Jonah became a sign to the Ninevites, so will the Son of Man be to this generation. The Queen of the South will rise up with the men of this generation at the judgment and condemn them, because she came from the ends of the earth to listen to the wisdom of Solomon; and behold, something greater than Solomon is here. The men of Nineveh will stand up with this generation at the judgment and condemn it, because they repented at the preaching of Jonah; and behold, something greater than Jonah is here" (Luke 11:29–32).

As the crowd grew larger, there were increased demands for Jesus to show them a sign. They wanted to see another miracle. But Jesus told them, "This generation is a wicked generation; it demands a sign" (verse 29). What did He mean by "a wicked generation"? By "this generation," He is not referencing a chronological age or peer group; instead, He is portraying the nation of Israel as stubborn and rebellious.[1] As John recorded, "Unless you people see signs and wonders, you simply will not believe" (John 4:48).

Sadly, the crowd continued to clamor for a sign. People wanted spectacular evidence when they should have been listening to His teaching. In essence, Jesus told them, "You already have the sign of Jonah." The people of Nineveh did not witness the sign of Jonah in the fish's belly, but they listened to his preaching and repented (Jonah 3:5).[2] Years before that, the Queen of Sheba heard reports about the wisdom of King Solomon. She traveled all the way to Jerusalem to hear and see for herself and exclaimed, "The half of it was not reported to me" (1 Kings 10:7). She became a powerful witness to the greatness of Solomon's God.

The unhappy crowd was painfully aware that both the Ninevites and the inhabitants of Sheba were Gentiles, whom they despised, yet *those people* listened and believed. Repentant Gentiles would testify against unrepentant Israelites at the judgment.[3] "History does not speak kindly of rejecting God's messengers. Neither will the final judgment. Here is a warning to heed Jesus' message and respond to him."[4]

Jesus was not going to perform for this noisy bunch of people. The stories from Israel's past, well known to the Jews, should have been adequate evidence of God's goodness and greatness. Now, Someone greater than Jonah and Solomon was present, calling for repentance and faith.

"No one lights a lamp and puts it away in a cellar nor under a basket, but on the lampstand, so that those who enter may see the light. Your eye is the lamp of your body; when your eye is clear, your whole body also is full of light; but when it is bad, your body also is full of darkness. So watch out that the light in you is not darkness. Therefore if your whole body is full of light, without any dark part, it will be wholly illuminated, as when the lamp illuminates you with its light" (Luke 11:33–36).

Jesus switched to a metaphor of light. Jesus Himself is the Light of the world (John 8:12). In the days before electric light and large windows, houses were typically dark places. If you wanted to avoid bumping into objects or to look for something, you needed to light your oil lamp and place it where everything in the room was visible. Jesus is the Lamp, the source of spiritual light.

But there is also a responsibility for each individual: "Your eye is the lamp of your body." Healthy eyes are needed to see clearly. Eyes that are unhealthy place one in spiritual darkness. Jesus counseled His followers, "Examine your eyes, then, to be sure you are not living in darkness." Eyes of faith are needed to see who Jesus is. A good pair of spiritual eyes represents understanding that leads to faith and obedience. The product of faith is total reliance on God and what He has promised.[5] You should not need to depend on miracles.

Reflection

Think about the role of faith in our high-tech society, where biblical style miracles are a rare occurrence. Why are miracles more often witnessed in primitive cultures?

1. Joel B. Green, *The Gospel of Luke*, New International Commentary on the New Testament, vol. 3 (Grand Rapids, MI: Eerdmans, 1997), 463.
2. *NIV Cultural Backgrounds Study Bible* (Grand Rapids, MI: Zondervan, 2016), 1770.
3. *NIV Cultural Backgrounds Study Bible*, 1770.
4. Darrell L. Bock, *Luke* (Grand Rapids, MI: Baker Academic, 1994), 1099.
5. Darrell L. Bock, *A Theology of Luke and Acts* (Grand Rapids, MI: Zondervan, 2012), 268.

Chapter 47

Lunch With Pharisees and Lawyers

Luke 11:37–54

Whenever Jesus accepted a meal invitation from someone with wealth or power, it inevitably led to conflict. His attendance at Levi's banquet at Capernaum led to public criticism for eating with tax collectors and sinners (Luke 5:27–32). A Pharisee's invitation to a Sabbath lunch brought conflict when a sinful woman gate-crashed the fellowship (Luke 7:36–39). Next, Jesus accepted another Pharisee's meal invitation, and they were going to chew more than food.

Now when He had spoken, a Pharisee asked Him to have lunch with him; and He went in and reclined at the table. When the Pharisee saw this, he was surprised that Jesus had not first ceremonially washed before the meal. But the Lord said to him, "Now you Pharisees clean the outside of the cup and of the dish; but your inside is full of greed and wickedness. You foolish ones, did He who made the outside not make the inside also? But give that which is within as a charitable gift, and then all things are clean for you" (Luke 11:37–41).

Not all Pharisees were out to get Jesus into trouble, but plenty of them kept a close eye on Jesus. As self-appointed keepers of the law, they may have respected Jesus for His phenomenal knowledge of the Mosaic law, but they were upset when He disregarded some of its requirements. We saw this happen when He violated some of their own Sabbath regulations (Luke 6:1–5).[1]

On the present occasion, there was no apparent hostility at first, but Jesus was being watched carefully, and when the host Pharisee observed that Jesus did not ceremonially pour the equivalent of one-and-a-half eggshells of water over His hands before reclining at the table,[2] Jesus responded, "You Pharisees are so careful about externals. You are fastidious about washing the outside of your cups and plates, but do you ever think of giving what is on your plate to the poor and destitute?"

At a luncheon, it was easy for Jesus to draw an illustration from the dinnerware. His table companions emphasized ceremonial purity and the cleanliness of their plates and dishes, but had they thought about sharing some of their eatables with the destitute and hungry? One of their prophets, Micah, put it succinctly: "What does the LORD require of you but to do justice, to love kindness, and to walk humbly with your God?" (Micah 6:8). Justice, love, and humility are missing components from the self-righteous law keepers.

The relationship of Pharisees with the common people was another case of patron-client affiliation. It was fashionable for Pharisees to give alms to the poor in reciprocation for praiseful recognition in the marketplace, but their concern with social status governed whom they chose to help. At this luncheon, Jesus launched into a denunciation of the hypocrisy of His table companions. He pronounced three "woes," or warnings, for the Pharisees. "Woe" is an expression of regret or sadness, not vindictiveness. In these Luke 11 texts, I am substituting "what sorrow awaits you" for "woe."

"But [what sorrow awaits] you Pharisees! For you pay tithes of mint, rue, and every kind of garden herb, and yet you ignore justice and the love of God; but these are the things you should have done without neglecting the others" (verse 42).

There is nothing wrong with tithing precisely; in fact, it was commanded in Leviticus 27:30. And "it was meant to be a joyful offering of love, but this calculation of one tenth of all the stalks of garden herbs made a burdensome mockery of it."[3] But Jesus told the Pharisees they needed to get their priorities straight. They shouldn't be selective in choosing to follow minor rules while disregarding justice and love.

"[What sorrow awaits] you Pharisees! For you love the seat of honor in the synagogues and personal greetings in the marketplaces" (Luke 11:43).

"You love the chief seats" (verse 43, ASV). What mockery of love and humility! These self-centered spiritual leaders enjoyed seats of honor in the synagogues and the attention they got wherever the "inferior" poor congregated. This was clearly the sin of pride.

"[What sorrow awaits] you! For you are like unseen tombs, and the people who walk over them are unaware of it" (verse 44).

Essentially, "Hey! Be careful where you walk in the Judean countryside. Tens of thousands have died and been buried here since the time of Abraham and even before that! There are unmarked graves everywhere. You'll be ceremonially unclean until you find a place to perform some ritual washing." And what did Jesus add? "You Pharisees are like those unmarked graves." "The Pharisees, who saw themselves as the paragon of purity, are in fact leaders of spiritual uncleanness."[4]

While the Pharisees were chewing on that, a lawyer spoke up.

One of the lawyers said to Him in reply, "Teacher, when You say these things, You insult us too" (verse 45).

Who are these lawyers? The other Gospel writers call them "scribes"—professional rabbis who give their complete attention to the interpretation of the law. A scribe's schooling has three stages:

1. A beginner scribe was "simply a pupil who would watch even the gestures of his teacher."
2. Later, as "an 'unordained scholar,' . . . he had mastered [the collective body of Jewish religious law] and could make personal decisions on given questions."
3. At ordination, "he became a full scholar. . . . He could . . . make religious decisions, act as a judge in civil matters . . . , and become a recognized teacher of Torah," the entire law of Moses.[5]

Luke figured that this professional fellow was, in Gentile parlance, a "lawyer" and identified him that way for his friend, Theophilus. At the Pharisee's lunch, a lawyer spoke up publicly for his profession, and Jesus now had three woes for the scribes.

But He said, "[What sorrow awaits] you lawyers as well! For you load people with burdens that are hard to bear, while you yourselves will not even touch the burdens with one of your fingers" (verse 46).

Law-keeping was heavy stuff for the common people of the day. By emphasizing strict compliance with religious law, these scribes took all the joy out of obedience.

"[What sorrow awaits] you! For you build the tombs of the prophets, and it was your fathers who killed them. So you are witnesses and you approve of the deeds of your fathers; because it was they who killed them, and you build their tombs. For this reason also, the wisdom of God said, 'I will send them prophets and apostles, and some of them they will kill, and some they will persecute, so that the blood of all the prophets, shed since the foundation of the world, may be charged against this generation, from the blood of Abel to the blood of Zechariah, who was killed between the altar and the house of God; yes, I tell you, it shall be charged against this generation' " (verses 47–51).

We are talking about graves again, but these are clearly marked tombs. Jewish leaders were building tombs to honor some famous prophets.[6] They were designed and constructed as memorials for long-dead prophets. Looking His listeners right in the eye, Jesus told them, "It was your ancestors who killed those prophets, and now you try to make up for it by building beautiful tombs for them." It does no good to mouth pious words to cover the evil deeds of your ancestors. Instead, start listening to the prophet's messages.[7] A day of judgment is coming when the record will show how Israel killed its prophets from the time Cain killed Abel onward.

"[What sorrow awaits] you lawyers! For you have taken away the key of knowledge; you yourselves did not enter, and you hindered those who were entering" (verse 52).

The scribes professed to enlighten people about the meaning of Scripture, but it had the opposite effect. "The disconnect between exterior show and interior darkness is serious. The consistent call of Jesus to listen contrasts with the compulsion of Israel's leaders to silence the prophets by killing them—by shutting up the very possibility of God's word being made clear."[8]

When He left that place, the scribes and the Pharisees began to be very hostile and to interrogate Him about many subjects, plotting against Him to catch Him in something He might say (verses 53, 54).

The temperature in the room rose considerably during this luncheon. As everyone left the house, the leaders engaged Jesus in a rancorous discussion. Feeling humiliated, they decided to trap Jesus.

Here we see that the "long condemnation [of Pharisees and scribes] destroys the popular portrait of Jesus as a mild-mannered teacher who avoids confrontation. Though not blatantly immoral, the Jews have a form of piety that does not honor God. That is what Jesus condemns here."[9]

Reflection

Ask yourself, Is there a danger that I could sometimes be right but unloving?

1. Robert H. Stein, *Luke*, The New American Commentary, vol. 24 (Nashville, TN: Broadman, 1992), 188, 189.

2. Leon Morris, *Luke: An Introduction and Commentary*, Tyndale New Testament Commentaries, vol. 3 (Downers Grove, IL: IVP Academic, 1988), 221.

3. Morris, 222.

4. Darrell L. Bock, *Luke* (Grand Rapids, MI: Baker Academic, 1994), 1117.

5. Bock, 678.

6. *NIV Cultural Backgrounds Study Bible* (Grand Rapids, MI: Zondervan, 2016), 1772.

7. Bock, *Luke*, 1120.

8. Paul Borgman, *The Way According to Luke: Hearing the Whole Story of Luke-Acts* (Grand Rapids, MI: Eerdmans, 2006), 146.

9. Darrell L. Bock, *A Theology of Luke and Acts* (Grand Rapids, MI: Zondervan, 2012), 146.

Chapter 48

Disciple Talk

Luke 12:1–12 (Matthew 10:28–33)

Jesus has just denounced the hypocrisy of the Pharisees and scribes, and He knows He faces a growing conflict with the spiritual leaders of Judaism. With this in mind, Jesus sensed the need to talk to His disciples and prepare them to face times of persecution.

Under these circumstances, after so many thousands of people had gathered together that they were stepping on one another, He began saying to His disciples first of all (Luke 12:1).

This would not be a private conversation with the Twelve, though. A large crowd has again found Jesus, and "they were stepping on one another" (verse 1) to get close to Him. His teaching is so different from what they heard from their religious leaders and so relevant to the times that the people were always eager to listen to Jesus. However, Jesus knew that His popularity was temporary.

So, while Jesus focused His remarks on His disciples, a larger group also listened. The Twelve must see their Master's teaching as for them first, whatever application it may also have to the rest. Some of the teachings in this chapter are also found in Mark or Matthew, though framed in different circumstances. It is quite reasonable to think "that Jesus repeated His teaching on different occasions" for different audiences.[1] In these first verses of Luke 12, Jesus hits five related topics that bring warnings and assurances for His disciples. Let's look briefly at each one.

1. Preach the truth from rooftops.

"Beware of the leaven of the Pharisees, which is hypocrisy. But there is nothing covered up that will not be revealed, and hidden that will not be known. Accordingly, whatever you have said in the dark will be heard in the light, and what you have whispered in the inner rooms will be proclaimed upon the housetops" (verses 1–3).

Hypocrisy is playacting. Having just come from denouncing Pharisees for their hypocrisy, Jesus told His followers, "Don't be like them." Their influence was subtle and inconspicuous. Just like leaven becomes invisible when it infiltrates the dough, false ideas are concealed when people live double lives. The things that are whispered behind closed doors, in private, are not what should be preached on housetops. That's where the truth about Jesus ought to be proclaimed. The Twelve were to be bold in proclaiming Christ.

2. Fear God, not humans.

"Now I say to you, My friends, do not be afraid of those who kill the body, and after that have nothing more that they can do. But I will warn you whom to fear: fear the One who, after He has killed someone, has the power to throw that person into hell; yes, I tell you, fear Him!" (verses 4, 5).

Jesus was aware that hostile Pharisees and scribes were already stalking Him, and this posed a threat to His followers, so He instructed the disciples on behavior appropriate to times of persecution.[2] "Do not fear those who kill the body" (verse 4, NRSV), Jesus said. His disciples might ultimately face martyrdom for their faith, but Jesus told them not to fear because they would have an eternal hope of glory (Ephesians 1:18).

The Jews had various views of "hell." They typically associated it with the valley of Gehinnom near Jerusalem, a ravine where children were offered as sacrifices to the god Moloch in Israel's past. The site was declared unclean by King Josiah and converted into "Gehenna," a place where trash was burned. Over time, Gehenna came to be associated with the fiery judgment of final punishment.[3] Jesus confirmed that there would be a real end-time judgment, which is clearly described in Revelation 20:11–15.

3. God cares.

"Are five sparrows not sold for two [cents]? And yet not one of them has gone unnoticed in the sight of God. But even the hairs of your head are all counted. Do not fear; you are more valuable than a great number of sparrows" (Luke 12:6, 7).

Jesus wanted to reassure His disciples, not frighten them. In the market, two sparrows cost one penny, but if you spent two pennies, you got five sparrows: the extra one was thrown in for nothing. Jesus says not one of these cheapest of birds is forgotten by God—not even the free one! The faithful "who are *of more value than many sparrows* should face life without fear." They need not worry about how God will care for them.[4]

4. Be faithful to Jesus.

"Now I say to you, everyone who confesses Me before people, the Son of Man will also confess him before the angels of God; but the one who denies Me before people will be denied before the angels of God. And everyone who speaks a word against the Son of Man, it will be forgiven him; but he who blasphemes against the Holy Spirit, it will not be forgiven him" (verses 8–10).

The disciples ought to be able to witness for Jesus before other people, even in threatening situations. He assured them that He would be standing with them when they faced opposition and human judgment. The faithful Stephen was shown such a picture before his death, "Behold, I see the heavens opened and the Son of Man standing at the right hand of God" (Acts 7:55, 56). In contrast, the one who denies Jesus will be denied in heaven. Is Jesus referring to a single incident or a life pattern? Peter's denial of Jesus at His trial followed by his public repentance after Jesus' resurrection reveal the grace of forgiveness for a failure.[5]

Jesus' statement about the blasphemy of the Holy Spirit is a commonly misunderstood statement. It looks at the totality of a person's response to the Holy Spirit, not just a single moment. It is a persistent rejection of Jesus Christ. A sin becomes unforgivable only when repentance is impossible. Sadly, that occurs when a person has lost any consciousness of sin.[6]

5. Assurance of the Spirit.

"Now when they bring you before the synagogues and the officials and the authorities, do not worry about how or what you are to speak in your defense, or what you are to say; for the Holy Spirit will teach you in that very hour what you ought to say" (Luke 12:11, 12).

Jesus' followers are not to fear the Holy Spirit, for He is their helper. "He is present with God's people, especially with God's persecuted people, to give them the assistance they need when they stand before the authorities."[7] The believer need not fear because God cares.

Reflection
How do you reconcile "fear" with "joy" in living the Christian life?

---

1. Leon Morris, *Luke: An Introduction and Commentary*, Tyndale New Testament Commentaries, vol. 3 (Downers Grove, IL: IVP Academic, 1988), 225.
2. Joel B. Green, *The Gospel of Luke*, New International Commentary on the New Testament, vol. 3 (Grand Rapids, MI: Eerdmans, 1997), 477.
3. Green, 482; Morris, *Luke*, 227.
4. Morris, 228; emphasis in original.
5. Darrell L. Bock, *Luke* (Grand Rapids, MI: Baker Academic, 1994), 1139, 1140.
6. William Barclay, *The Gospel of Luke* (Philadelphia, PA: Westminster Press, 1975), 162.
7. Morris, *Luke*, 229.

Chapter 49

Possessions

Luke 12:13–34 (Matthew 6:19–21, 25–34)

While Jesus instructed the disciples, the crowd pressed in to listen to everything He said. Then, a man in the crowd interrupted what Jesus was saying. He called out for help with a problem.

Now someone in the crowd said to Him, "Teacher, tell my brother to divide the family inheritance with me." But He said to him, "You there—who appointed Me a judge or arbitrator over the two of you?" But He said to them, "Beware, and be on your guard against every form of greed; for not even when one is affluent does his life consist of his possessions" (Luke 12:13–15).

Apparently, this fellow had an older brother who, he believed, was not dividing the inherited property fairly, Moses had specified inheritance rights (Deuteronomy 21:15–17), and apparently this young man thought Jesus would take an interest in his situation as other rabbis of the time may have. By addressing Jesus as "Teacher," the young man acknowledges Him as a rabbi. However, he didn't ask Jesus to arbitrate the case, which would involve hearing both sides of the dispute. Instead, he just wanted Jesus to decide in his favor. Jesus, of course, refused to get involved in the dispute; "He came to bring people to God, not property to people."[1]

The large crowd heard the young man's request and wanted to hear what Jesus would say. So, turning to the crowd, Jesus used the interruption to talk about greed and selfishness. He shared a parable to illustrate the lesson.

And He told them a parable, saying, "The land of a rich man was very productive. And he began thinking to himself, saying, 'What shall I do, since I have no place to store my crops?' And he said, 'This is what I will do: I will tear down my barns and build larger ones, and I will store all my grain and my goods there. And I will say to myself, "You have many goods stored up for many years to come; relax, eat, drink, and enjoy yourself!" ' But God said to him, 'You fool! This very night your soul is demanded of you; and as for all that you have prepared, who will own it now?' Such is the one who stores up treasure for himself, and is not rich in relation to God" (Luke 12:16–21).

Wealthy landowners generally lived in cities or on large estates while impoverished tenant farmers worked their land. Excavations have shown that landowners often built large silos to store excess grain.[2] In the parable, the rich man had been blessed abundantly by God. The harvest was exceptional, the yield unexpected, and the returns were gained honestly. He was prudent and formulated a plan. He would tear down his barn, build larger ones, and store his crop. Then, when famine hit the community, he would get a high price for his grain.

Count how many times "I" and "my" occurred in the rich man's self-talk.[3] He never saw beyond himself or his world. When someone asked a schoolboy what parts of speech "my" and "mine" are, he said they are "aggressive pronouns."[4]

God does not condemn planning and wealth. The farmer's plan makes economic sense, but it is morally wrong. He overlooked his moral responsibility to care for the needs of the surrounding peasants who, in a subsistence economy, struggle to make ends meet. Grain withheld would mean higher prices in the local markets.[5] Truly, "the danger of the pursuit of possessions is that it can make one insensitive to people. . . . The definition of life is not found in objects, but relationships, especially to God and his will."[6] Embedded in an indulgent lifestyle, the wealthy hoarder has forgotten that his life is on loan from God. Such is the danger of attachment to wealth. It can leave us self-focused and detached from God.

"Luke has written more on the topic of wealth than any other NT writer," and it is always in relation to the treatment of the poor in society.[7] The rich fool of Jesus' parable was the recipient of good fortune, but he planned selfishly and foolishly. In his death, he is left with nothing. We saw the reverse scenario in Jesus' parable of the compassionate Samaritan, who used his income to save the life of a wounded Jew on the roadside (Luke 10:30–37).

And He said to His disciples, "For this reason I tell you, do not worry about your life, as to what you are to eat; nor for your body, as to what you are to wear. For life is more than food, and the body is more than clothing. Consider the ravens, that they neither sow nor reap; they have no storeroom nor barn, and yet God feeds them; how much more valuable you are than the birds!" (Luke 12:22–24).

Luke is a master of literary art—notice how he follows up the parable of the rich fool with Jesus' words to the Twelve "about God's care for the birds of the air and the lilies of the field."[8] The disciples were very aware that they abandoned possessions to follow Him, but they needed not worry. Their needs would always be met. In an illustration from the ravens, Jesus employed the forceful "how much more" argument: if something is true for the *very least*, it must certainly be true for the *very greatest*. If God feeds unclean ravens, *how much more* will He feed you?[9]

"And which of you by worrying can add a day to his life's span? Therefore if you cannot do even a very little thing, why do you worry about other things? Consider the lilies, how they grow: they neither labor nor spin; but I tell you, not even Solomon in all his glory clothed himself like one of these. Now if God so clothes the grass in the field, which is alive today and tomorrow is thrown into the furnace, how much more will He clothe you? You of little faith!" (verses 25–28).

In a second illustration from nature, Jesus talks about flowers and grasses. "Consider the lilies," He said (verse 27), thinking perhaps of the purple anemone. Its color would compare with a king's royal garb. Flowers are more beautifully clothed than Solomon. In contrast, the field grasses serve only as smoky fuel in a land where wood is scarce. If God cares enough to provide grasses for cooking fires, *how much more* will He provide for the needs of people?

"And do not seek what you are to eat and what you are to drink, and do not keep worrying. For all these things are what the nations of the world eagerly seek; and your Father knows that

you need these things. But seek His kingdom, and these things will be provided to you. Do not be afraid, little flock, for your Father has chosen to give you the kingdom" (verses 29–32).

Still addressing the disciples, Jesus reminded them again of the caring Father. They've learned to address God as their "Father" when they pray (Luke 11:1–4). But these men "of little faith" (Luke 12:8) are inclined to worry about their necessities. Jesus told them they didn't need to spend time looking for what they needed. "Do not keep worrying" (verse 29). If their first priority is advancing God's kingdom, they can trust Him to meet their needs. "Do not be afraid, little flock" (verse 31). We have the promise God gave us: "Don't worry about anything; instead, pray about everything. Tell God what you need, and thank him for all he has done. Then you will experience God's peace" (Philippians 4:6, 7, NLT).

"Sell your possessions and give to charity; make yourselves money belts that do not wear out, an inexhaustible treasure in heaven, where no thief comes near nor does a moth destroy. For where your treasure is, there your heart will be also" (Luke 12:33, 34).

Perhaps turning again to the listening crowd, Jesus summarized the topic of possessions and what greed does to one's heart. "Greed can never *get* enough, worry is afraid it may not *have* enough."[10] Remember that you can't take wealth with you. Where you place your values is a measure of what is in your heart.

Reflection

Jesus' parable of the rich fool strikes at what most of us strive for—enough savings to retire and live for decades on our surplus. Ask yourself, If I don't know what to do with this story, should I just ignore it?[11]

---

1. Leon Morris, *Luke: An Introduction and Commentary*, Tyndale New Testament Commentaries, vol. 3 (Downers Grove, IL: IVP Academic, 1988), 230.
2. *NIV Cultural Backgrounds Study Bible* (Grand Rapids, MI: Zondervan, 2016), 1773.
3. Darrell L. Bock, *Luke* (Grand Rapids, MI: Baker Academic, 1994), 1151, 1152.
4. William Barclay, *The Gospel of Luke* (Philadelphia, PA: Westminster Press, 1975), 164.
5. Joel B. Green, *The Gospel of Luke*, New International Commentary on the New Testament, vol. 3 (Grand Rapids, MI: Eerdmans, 1997), 490.
6. Bock, *Luke*, 1150.
7. Darrell L. Bock, *A Theology of Luke and Acts* (Grand Rapids, MI: Zondervan, 2012), 328, 329.
8. O. C. Edwards Jr., *Luke's Story of Jesus* (Minneapolis: Fortress, 1981), 64.
9. Green, *Gospel of Luke*, 493.
10. Morris, *Luke*, 231.
11. E. Randolph Richards and Brandon J. O'Brien, *Misreading Scripture With Western Eyes* (Downers Grove, IL: InterVarsity, 2012), 187.

Chapter 50

Be Ready and Faithful

Luke 12:35–48 (Matthew 24:42–51)

"Slavery in the Roman Empire was a fact of life. Most people could not imagine a society without slaves."[1] Paul called himself a "slave of Jesus Christ" as a sign of his devotion (Romans 1:1, NET) and described how Jesus came to the world by emptying "himself, taking the form of a slave" (Philippians 2:7, NRSV). Although slave work was often hard labor, it was sometimes skilled service like teaching or tutoring, bookkeeping, and even estate management. Masters sometimes freed slaves as a reward for obedience and loyalty. We must keep all this in mind as we continue Luke's account of Jesus' teaching in the cities and towns of Judea.

A large crowd continued to press around Jesus and the disciples. Sometimes Jesus directed His remarks to the disciples and sometimes to the crowd. The distinction is not always clear, even to the disciples, as we discover when Peter interrupted with a question (Luke 12:41). Jesus urged everyone to prepare for His future coming in glory—the "not yet" aspect of the kingdom.[2] How do we get ready for Jesus' second coming?

"Be prepared, and keep your lamps lit. You are also to be like people who are waiting for their master when he returns from the wedding feast, so that they may immediately open the door to him when he comes and knocks. Blessed are those slaves whom the master will find on the alert when he comes; truly I say to you, that he will prepare himself to serve, and have them recline at the table, and he will come up and serve them. Whether he comes in the second watch, or even in the third, and finds them so, blessed are those slaves" (verses 35–38).

The crowd probably scratched their heads when Jesus mentioned a householder serving a meal to his *slaves!* Especially if the master was dressed to the nines for a wedding banquet! Jesus used this topsy-turvy illustration to speak about readiness for His second coming, His return in glory. The cultural illustration seems strange to us, but let's put ourselves in the story. We slaves have several things we must do:

- Draw up our long outer garments and tuck them around the waist, so we can move quickly ("Let's rid ourselves of every obstacle" [Hebrews 12:1]).
- Check that we have enough oil to keep the house lamps burning, just like we would if we were expecting our master to come home from a wedding celebration that may have lasted more than a week ("Be filled with the Spirit" [Ephesians 5:18]).
- Be ready to open the door as soon as the master knocks. It might be midnight or even three in the morning ("Be on the alert then, because you do not know the day nor the hour" [Matthew 25:13]).

- Surprise! The master arrives and escorts other faithful slaves and us into heaven's banquet hall, where we will recline at a table overflowing with choice foods and wine. ("Now the Lord of armies will prepare a lavish banquet" [Isaiah 25:6]).
- Surprise again! We are individually served by the immaculately dressed master ("I am coming again and will take you to Myself" [John 14:3]).

We were born as slaves to sin, but our Master came to live with us as a fellow slave, died to give us our freedom, and lives to take us to His home.

"But be sure of this, that if the head of the house had known at what hour the thief was coming, he would not have allowed his house to be broken into. You too, be ready; because the Son of Man is coming at an hour that you do not think He will."

Peter said, "Lord, are You telling this parable to us, or to everyone else as well?" (Luke 12:39–41).

Then Jesus changed the metaphor. Now He compared His coming to a thief breaking into a house. Thieves often entered by digging through a mud-brick wall and surprising the occupants.[3] Similarly, God loves to use the element of surprise. The exact time of Jesus' coming is unknown, and the only way to be secure is to be ready for it. This vivid illustration got Peter's attention. "Are you using this illustration for the other disciples and me, or is it for the whole crowd?" Yes, Jesus wanted everyone to hear what He was saying!

And the Lord said, "Who then is the faithful and sensible steward, whom his master will put in charge of his servants, to give them their rations at the proper time? Blessed is that slave whom his master finds so doing when he comes. Truly I say to you that he will put him in charge of all his possessions" (verses 42–44).

It is not just a matter of standing around, waiting. Servants have important responsibilities. It was a familiar scene for the listening crowd because everyone knew what slaves had to do. Good stewardship means taking responsibility for the lesser members of the home or community. For those awaiting Jesus' return, it means attending to the physical needs of the poor and downtrodden in the community.

"But if that slave says in his heart, 'My master will take a long time to come,' and he begins to beat the other slaves, both men and women, and to eat and drink and get drunk; then the master of that slave will come on a day that he does not expect, and at an hour he does not know, and will cut him in two, and assign him a place with the unbelievers. And that slave who knew his master's will and did not get ready or act in accordance with his will, will receive many blows, but the one who did not know it, and committed acts deserving of a beating, will receive only a few blows. From everyone who has been given much, much will be demanded; and to whom they entrusted much, of him they will ask all the more" (verses 45–48).

There is another side to the story. Some who claim to be waiting for their master's return are unfaithful and disobedient. They will be punished. Slaves were typically subject to all sorts of interrogation, even torture, by the master. There was punishment for those who neglected their responsibilities to their households or communities, and it was scaled according to the nature of the offense.

The unwise steward made two mistakes in his thinking: "*I will do what I like while my master is away*" and "*I have plenty of time to put things right before the master comes.*"[4] "If the picture of accountability appears threatening, even gruesome, there are no grounds for fear. God has granted the kingdom to those willing to orient their hearts and lives around it."[5]

Reflection

"One of the most dangerous days in a man's life is when he discovers the word 'to-morrow.'"[6] How have you seen this maxim play out in your life?

1. Katy E. Valentine, "Slavery in the New Testament," *Bible Odyssey*, accessed September 29, 2022, https://www.bibleodyssey.org/passages/related-articles/slavery-in-the-new-testament.

2. Darrell L. Bock, *A Theology of Luke and Acts* (Grand Rapids, MI: Zondervan, 2012), 396.

3. Joel B. Green, *The Gospel of Luke*, New International Commentary on the New Testament, vol. 3 (Grand Rapids, MI: Eerdmans, 1997), 504.

4. William Barclay, *The Gospel of Luke* (Philadelphia, PA: Westminster Press, 1975), 168.

5. Green, *Gospel of Luke*, 507.

6. Barclay, *Gospel of Luke*, 168.

Chapter 51

Division

Luke 12:49–59 (Matthew 10:34–39)

Jesus was about to say something very troubling. This is not the gentle Jesus we learned about when we were young. Should we just skip these next few verses? But no, we mustn't.

"I have come to cast fire upon the earth; and how I wish it were already kindled! But I have a baptism to undergo, and how distressed I am until it is accomplished!" (Luke 12:49, 50).

When Jesus took on humanity, it came with the range of needs and emotions that you and I experience—hunger, tiredness, contentment, joy, and now, apprehension. He had been talking to His disciples and the crowds about how they should prepare for His second coming and the judgment. As He looked at the mass of people surrounding Him, He grew distressed that so many were blind to the reality of the times. They were rejecting His teaching and ignoring the warnings.

For a moment, Jesus gazed into the future. Ahead of Him are rejection and death. He would then experience the fire of His Father's anger—not for Him, no! no! but for the terrible evil that has engulfed the planet and destroyed the souls of so many people. In dying, Jesus would experience a kind of baptism by taking our sins upon Himself.[1] Paul wrote that He became sin for us: "He made Him who knew no sin to be sin on our behalf, so that we might become the righteousness of God in Him" (2 Corinthians 5:21). Only then could He fulfill the core purpose of His mission: to release humanity from the clutches of the evil one.

In truth, "those who would reduce Jesus to a sentimental savior of a doting God have not come to terms with the depth of divine passion, of the wrath and love of God which is revealed in Jesus' word, will, and obedience even unto death."[2] Only after His resurrection and departure could Jesus begin to do much of what He came to the world to do. That's when a different kind of fire would burn in the hearts of people, as the Holy Spirit energized and empowered, so that the good news of salvation would spread like wildfire across the world.

"Do you think that I came to provide peace on earth? No, I tell you, but rather division; for from now on five members in one household will be divided, three against two and two against three. They will be divided, father against son and son against father, mother against daughter and daughter against mother, mother-in-law against daughter-in-law and daughter-in-law against mother-in-law" (Luke 12:51–53).

"Peace on earth" was part of the angel's message to the shepherds at Jesus' birth (Luke 2:8–14); yet when the aged Simeon held the babe in his arms, he warned that Jesus would also bring division (verse 34). "Many Jewish people expected the Messiah to bring war against the Gentiles, but Jesus here warns that his requirements would bring division within households."[3] While peace of mind and heart may always be true for those who place their trust in God, Jesus knew that His messages would divide families. Perhaps He was borrowing from the prophet Micah:

> For son disavows father,
> Daughter rises up against her mother,
> Daughter-in-law against her mother-in-law;
> A person's enemies are the people of his own household (Micah 7:6).

"A person who yields his or her life to God may experience division on some level. It is possible a new believer's family members might experience a difficult adjustment period. The differentness of a new Christian's life may be a light that shines into the darkness of the lives of others. If you experience division because of your faith in Jesus, remember you are one with Him. That oneness with Jesus will draw others to know and love Him."[4]

Reading the time

Jesus continued by emphasizing the importance of paying attention to the time.

And He was also saying to the crowds, "Whenever you see a cloud rising in the west, you immediately say, 'A shower is coming,' and so it turns out. And whenever you feel a south wind blowing, you say, 'It will be a hot day,' and it turns out that way. You hypocrites! You know how to analyze the appearance of the earth and the sky, but how is it that you do not know how to analyze this present time?" (Luke 12:54–56).

People always wanted Jesus to give signs to prove who He was. Now, He turned it back on them—they knew very well how to read weather signs. Air masses coming in from the west, over the Mediterranean, picked up moisture and brought showers, especially in winter. At other times, winds blew in from the southern desert, bringing scorching summer temperatures. The crowd nodded affirmatively—yes, they read the weather signs. But Jesus continued, asking why they had not learned to discern the times in which they lived. Why couldn't they see "what God is doing in their midst?"[5]

"And why do you not even judge by yourselves what is right? For when you are going with your accuser to appear before the magistrate, on the way, make an effort to settle with him, so that he does not drag you before the judge, and the judge hand you over to the officer, and the officer throw you into prison. I tell you, you will not get out of there until you have paid up the very last lepton" (verses 57–59).

There is a danger for anyone who does not evaluate the times correctly. Jesus calls on people to reflect on their spiritual condition. Every individual has a losing case in the judgment—the final judgment is for real, but being repentant and trusting in Jesus now will take away that fear. You can't stake your case for the judgment on the faith of your father or anyone else. Individual repentance before a call to account at the judgment turns a lost cause into a redeemed case.

Finally, Jesus used the illustration of settling a dispute. Luke "changed its setting from a Jewish dispute, which could have been settled by a scribe . . . , to a Hellenistic one, which would have been settled by a judge," which his friend Theophilus would understand.[6] A debtor finds himself in prison until he can pay "the very last lepton." The lepton was the smallest of the coins, equal to one-eighth of a penny. Unable to pay even that small amount, the debtor would be beaten in prison as an incentive for his family or friends to come to his aid.

It is a somber picture. Better to make peace with God now while there is still time.

Reflection

What has Christ brought to your family? Division? Or peace? How can you show love under circumstances of division?

1. Darrell L. Bock, *Luke* (Grand Rapids, MI: Baker Academic, 1994), 1194.
2. David Tiede, *Luke*, Augsburg Commentary on the New Testament (Minneapolis, MN: Augsburg, 1988), 244.
3. *NIV Cultural Backgrounds Study Bible* (Grand Rapids, MI: Zondervan, 2016), 1775.
4. John Bradshaw, *The Hope of Glory* (Nampa, ID: Pacific Press®, 2021), 141.
5. Bock, *Luke*, 1197.
6. Robert H. Stein, *Luke*, The New American Commentary, vol. 24 (Nashville, TN: Broadman, 1992), 367.

Chapter 52

Call to Repentance

Luke 13:1–9

As Jesus taught, a listener brought up a recent event. I imagine it went something like this:

"Hey! Have you heard the latest? Governor Pilate killed several people as they were offering their sacrifices at the temple."
"I heard that too. They were Galileans, I believe."
"Yes. Pilate killed them and mixed their blood with their sacrifices."
"That's horrible. When did this happen?"
"Not during Passover, I'm sure, because the festival crowds would have rioted."
"No, I think it might have been during Passover because that's the only time when a lot of Galileans come down to Jerusalem."
"Those Galileans must have sinned badly to be punished like that."
"Does Jesus know about this? He's a Galilean."
"That's right. He might take up the case against the Romans."
"Someone should ask Him about it."

Whatever response the crowd was hoping for, they were likely disappointed when they heard Jesus' answer.

Now on that very occasion there were some present who reported to Him about the Galileans whose blood Pilate had mixed with their sacrifices. And Jesus responded and said to them, "Do you think that these Galileans were worse sinners than all the other Galileans just because they have suffered this fate? No, I tell you, but unless you repent, you will all likewise perish" (Luke 13:1–3).

It is on record that Pilate was known for his brutality and had massacred people on other occasions, typically at Passover when Jerusalem was crowded with pilgrims who were sometimes out of control.[1] Jesus had just finished talking about settling accounts with God before the final judgment. At the time, it was widely believed that disaster is a punishment for sin, so if some Galileans were massacred by Pilate while they were offering their sacrifices at the temple, they must have deserved it. By inference, Galileans who escaped the massacre must have been living righteous lives.

Jesus had nothing to say about the report, but He asked, "Do you think that those Galileans were worse sinners than all the other Galileans just because they died this way? No! I tell you, but unless all of you repent, you will all perish." Universal sinfulness is basic. Only heartfelt repentance will save sinners from the final, second death.[2]

The Galilean incident reminded Jesus of another reported event.

"Or do you think that those eighteen on whom the tower in Siloam fell and killed them were worse offenders than all the other people who live in Jerusalem? No, I tell you, but unless you repent, you will all likewise perish" (verses 4, 5).

The "tower in Siloam" was probably where the south and east walls of Jerusalem intersected near the Pool of Siloam. The deaths may have been caused by a scaffolding accident. Again, their deaths did not mean they were worse sinners than other Jerusalemites. We must draw the same lesson today. God's faithful are not exempt from tornadoes, floods, fires, cancer, or dementia. Faith in God is not a guarantee against sickness or suffering. These things happen because we live in a sinful world. Circumstances will test our faith. Ancient Job, not knowing that his sufferings were caused by Satan, stated his faith firmly: "Though He slay me, I will hope in Him" (Job 13:15).

Jesus used both events to remind the crowd that the first step toward faithfulness is repentance. His cousin John in the wilderness first gave that call; now, Jesus sounded the same urgent message. At Pentecost, Peter would preach the same message to the crowds in Jerusalem: "Therefore repent and return, so that your sins may be wiped away, in order that times of refreshing may come from the presence of the Lord" (Acts 3:19). Repentance is a key concept in the Gospel of Luke. "His eleven uses of the noun comprise half of the uses in the NT."[3]

The fruitless fig tree

The stories of the Galilean atrocities and the Tower of Siloam led Jesus into a parable for the listening crowd. It is a parable that has a double application—one is the urgent need for repentance; the other, God's patience.[4]

And He began telling this parable: "A man had a fig tree which had been planted in his vineyard; and he came looking for fruit on it and did not find any. And he said to the vineyard-keeper, 'Look! For three years I have come looking for fruit on this fig tree without finding any. Cut it down! Why does it even use up the ground?' But he answered and said to him, 'Sir, leave it alone for this year too, until I dig around it and put in fertilizer; and if it bears fruit next year, fine; but if not, cut it down' " (Luke 13:6–9).

Having a fig tree in a vineyard was not unusual. That scenario is cited seven times in the Old Testament. The prophet Micah looked forward to a time when "each of them will sit under his vine and under his fig tree, with no one to make them afraid" (Micah 4:4). To sit under one's vine and fig tree meant being safe at home, experiencing peace and prosperity.

The fig tree in Christ's parable represents the nation of Israel. The Jews had been given a long time to bear the fruit of righteousness, and there was an urgent need for a response. For three years, John and Jesus had been preaching repentance, and although many had listened and responded, the Jewish nation as a whole was not listening. Time was almost up. The tree was taking water and valuable nutrients from the soil, and the call to "Cut it down!" was near.

The tree was saved by the vinedresser, who represents Jesus. Let's give it one more year, he said.

I'll dig around it and fertilize it. Maybe it will bear fruit next year. If not, you can cut it down. John had given the same warning: "The axe is already being laid at the root of the trees; so every tree that does not bear fruit is cut down" (Luke 3:9). The fig tree parable shows God's displeasure with His covenant people but also His patience: "Give it one more year."

The parable was Jesus' final message to the large crowd that pressed around Him. These people represented the entire Jewish nation. He had called on them to discern the time. Would they respond to the warnings and appeals? This is *"the gospel of the second chance."*[5]

Reflection

An airplane disaster killed many people. One couple who was supposed to be on that plane had to make a last-minute flight change, and they thanked God that He rewarded their faithfulness by saving their lives. Ask yourself, How would I respond to other Christians whose relatives perished in the disaster?

1. *NIV Cultural Backgrounds Study Bible* (Grand Rapids, MI: Zondervan, 2016), 1775.

2. Joel B. Green, *The Gospel of Luke*, New International Commentary on the New Testament, vol. 3 (Grand Rapids, MI: Eerdmans, 1997), 515.

3. Darrell L. Bock, *A Theology of Luke and Acts* (Grand Rapids, MI: Zondervan, 2012), 262.

4. Leon Morris, *Luke: An Introduction and Commentary*, Tyndale New Testament Commentaries, vol. 3 (Downers Grove, IL: IVP Academic, 1988), 240.

5. William Barclay, *The Gospel of Luke* (Philadelphia, PA: Westminster Press, 1975), 176; emphasis in the original.

Chapter 53

A Sabbath Healing

Luke 13:10–21 (Matthew 13:31–33; Mark 4:30–32)

Next, we find Jesus teaching in a Judean synagogue on the Sabbath. Luke doesn't share the content of His sermon, but something made the day memorable.

Now Jesus was teaching in one of the synagogues on the Sabbath. And there was a woman who for eighteen years had had a sickness caused by a spirit; and she was bent over double, and could not straighten up at all. When Jesus saw her, He called her over and said to her, "Woman, you are freed from your sickness." And He laid His hands on her; and immediately she stood up straight again, and began glorifying God (Luke 13:10–13).

In the synagogue, Jesus saw a woman in need. She's described as "bent over double," a condition sometimes referred to "as 'spondylitis deformans; the bones of her spine were fused into a rigid mass.' "[1] It is a sad condition that rendered her socially unacceptable. She lived in a culture in which men publicly shunned even healthy women.[2] Luke says her condition was caused by a Satanic spirit.

The mission of Jesus was to release and set free (Luke 4:18), so He called her to Him and laid His hands on her, and she was freed from her body prison. She stood up straight for the first time in eighteen years and glorified God. Can you picture her joy? But not everyone was happy.

But the synagogue leader, indignant because Jesus had healed on the Sabbath, began saying to the crowd in response, "There are six days during which work should be done; so come during them and get healed, and not on the Sabbath day." But the Lord answered him and said, "You hypocrites, does each of you on the Sabbath not untie his ox or donkey from the stall and lead it away to water it? And this woman, a daughter of Abraham as she is, whom Satan has bound for eighteen long years, should she not have been released from this restraint on the Sabbath day?" (Luke 13:14–16).

The synagogue leader was angry. He felt that Jesus' action was an invasion of his prerogative as the synagogue ruler—his job was to maintain the letter of the law but not its spirit. He's angry with Jesus, but he vents it on his congregation: "You can come and get healed on any of the other six days, but don't come on Sabbath."

But Jesus was angry too. "Don't you untie your ox or donkey from the stall on Sabbath and lead it to water? Of course, you do. This poor woman has been tied up by Satan for eighteen long years. Why shouldn't I release her on the Sabbath? 'If you can take pity on . . . a stupid animal on the Sabbath, why can't you do as much for a human being, a child of God?' "[3]

Jesus' response was to the synagogue leader as well as to those who thought as he did. "You hypocrites! You put religious tradition and rules before mercy and compassion. You show mercy to your animals but not to people." The synagogue ruler was probably thinking of Deuteronomy 5:13, 14, "Six days you shall labor and do all your work, but the seventh day is a Sabbath of the LORD your God; you shall not do any work that day." Jewish teachings enumerated thirty-nine forms of human labor that were forbidden on the Sabbath.[4] Animals, however, received special treatment. Consider their crazy logic with a "how much more" scenario:[5]

If an animal, *how much more* a daughter of Abraham?

If an animal you have bound for a few hours, *how much more* a person whom Satan has bound for eighteen years?

If you can loose the bonds of an animal on the Sabbath, *how much more* is it necessary for God to loosen this woman's bond on the Sabbath?

Did Jesus perform healings on other days of the week? Of course. Most of His healing miracles were performed on days other than Sabbaths. We rarely have details of those because there was no conflict with Pharisaic rules.

And as He said this, all His opponents were being humiliated; and the entire crowd was rejoicing over all the glorious things being done by Him (Luke 13:17).

There was joy and holy excitement in the synagogue that Sabbath day. The humiliation felt by the synagogue leader and his supporters was swamped by the rejoicing of the crowd for "all the glorious things" that Jesus did. He restored the Sabbath to what God intended it to be in the beginning—a weekly day for rest, wholeness, joyful fellowship, and the practice of mercy.[6]

The healing of the bent-over woman symbolizes the nature of God's kingdom and Jesus' mission: the release of Satan's captives. The religious leaders of Judaism visualized a religiopolitical kingdom that would free Judaism from Rome and establish a Messiah-king in Jerusalem, and they expected it to happen quickly. God's kingdom is not going to be like that. Now Luke includes two simple parables that portray the nature of God's kingdom.

So He was saying, "What is the kingdom of God like, and to what shall I compare it? It is like a mustard seed, which a man took and threw into his own garden; and it grew and became a tree, and the birds of the sky nested in its branches" (verses 18, 19).

Matthew's version of this parable emphasizes the smallness of the seed (Matthew 13:32). Luke dreamed of a world for Christ, so he referenced the birds that nest in its branches.[7] The birds sheltering in the mustard tree allude to Gentiles who will be welcomed into the kingdom. True, the kingdom begins very small, like a mustard seed, followed by a gradual process of growth. The humble form of the kingdom's beginning should not deceive anyone.

And again He said, "To what shall I compare the kingdom of God? It is like leaven, which a woman took and hid in three sata of flour until it was all leavened" (verses 20, 21).

The second parable draws on a familiar image. Villagers throughout Palestine used leaven as they prepared to bake their daily bread in their ovens. As leaven invisibly permeates the bread, the growth of the kingdom will be invisible to most people. It also works that way in the life of the Christian. Feeding daily on the Bread of Life invites the presence of the Holy Spirit into one's life. He will change that life from the inside out.

Reflection

Is a weekly day of rest and fellowship relevant in today's world? What kind of Sabbath experience did Jesus portray?

1. Leon Morris, *Luke: An Introduction and Commentary*, Tyndale New Testament Commentaries, vol. 3 (Downers Grove, IL: IVP Academic, 1988), 240.

2. Darrell L. Bock, *Luke* (Grand Rapids, MI: Baker Academic, 1994), 1215, 1216.

3. O. C. Edwards Jr., *Luke's Story of Jesus* (Minneapolis: Fortress, 1981), 68, 69.

4. Bock, *Luke*, 1217.

5. Joel B. Green, *The Gospel of Luke*, New International Commentary on the New Testament, vol. 3 (Grand Rapids, MI: Eerdmans, 1997), 524.

6. Keith Clouten, *A Day for Joy* (Energion Books, 2022).

7. William Barclay, *The Gospel of Luke* (Philadelphia, PA: Westminster Press, 1975), 179.

Chapter 54

The Narrow, Open Door

Luke 13:22–35

And He was passing through one city and village after another, teaching, and proceeding on His way to Jerusalem. And someone said to Him, "Lord, are there just a few who are being saved?" (Luke 13:22, 23).

Someone had a question for Jesus: "Are only a few people going to be saved?" (verse 23, NIV). The questioner was probably assuming "that the kingdom of God was for the Jews and that gentiles would all be shut out."[1] In His response, Jesus sadly admitted that many would *not* be saved. He has talked about people's need to figure out the times in which they were living. Time was running out for the Jewish nation. People were urged to repent while the door to salvation was still open.

Christ's "journey to Jerusalem represents actual [foot] traveling, but Luke has organized this narrative primarily as a journey into God's kingdom, the 'Way.' "[2] Jesus has spoken a lot about the need for repentance, but it has now become an urgent necessity.

And He said to them, "Strive to enter through the narrow door; for many, I tell you, will seek to enter and will not be able. Once the head of the house gets up and shuts the door, and you begin standing outside knocking on the door, saying, 'Lord, open up to us!' and He then will answer and say to you, 'I do not know where you are from' " (verses 23–25).

One day, somewhere along the journey to Jerusalem, Jesus told the parable about a door that is open for anyone to enter if they wish, but it comes with two warnings—the doorway is narrow, and it won't always be open.

Imagine the main thoroughfare of a town, with buildings on each side of the street. One of these buildings has a narrow, open door to the street. Why is the doorway narrow? Is it narrow in width so that you have to breathe in and squeeze through? There is no point, then, in trying to carry your possessions in with you. Or, perhaps, the door is low in height, so you must bend down with humility and discard your self-righteousness.

Or, perhaps, part of the problem is *finding* the door. Matthew's Gospel describes a wide gate and a broad road that leads to destruction (Matthew 7:13, 14). Many people, hastening along that road, miss the narrow door that leads to salvation.[3] People are inclined to dismiss a narrow door. But besides being narrow, the door is open only for a short time. The owner of the house controls the door, and when the time is up, He will close it for good.

"Then you will begin saying, 'We ate and drank in Your presence, and You taught in our streets!' And yet He will say, 'I do not know where you are from; LEAVE ME, ALL YOU EVILDOERS.' In that place there

will be weeping and gnashing of teeth when you see Abraham, Isaac, Jacob, and all the prophets in the kingdom of God, but yourselves being thrown out. And they will come from east and west, and from north and south, and will recline at the table in the kingdom of God. And behold, some are last who will be first, and some are first who will be last" (Luke 13:26–30).

There is something very wonderful for those who choose to go through the narrow door. You will do more than kick yourself if you miss what is happening inside. There is a great banquet table, and among the guests are Abraham, Isaac, Jacob, and all the prophets. Isaiah describes the feast: "Now the LORD of armies will prepare a lavish banquet for all peoples on this mountain; a banquet of aged wine, choice pieces with marrow, and refined, aged wine" (Isaiah 25:6).

People who pride themselves in being children of Abraham will discover, as John the Baptist warned (Luke 3:8), that ancestry is not a free passage to salvation and a future life with God. It's the *faith* of Abraham that is required. Nor will it help to remind Jesus that you were in His congregation one day when He was teaching or that you once ate with Him. Table fellowship symbolizes friendship, but only a real relationship with Jesus counts.[4]

Those who find themselves outside the locked door will experience shock and anguish when they peer through the window and see the large number of Gentiles enjoying the feast. They will have come from east, west, north, and south to take their places at the table of salvation. Most Jews expected that God would exalt Israel and punish their Gentile oppressors.[5] Even the disciples were slow to catch on to what was happening; it would take Peter quite some time to discover that God has righteous followers even among Roman officers (Acts 10; 11).[6] Jesus summed up the reality with a proverb: "The last shall be first, and the first, last."

At that very time some Pharisees approached, saying to Him, "Go away and leave this place, because Herod wants to kill You." And He said to them, "Go and tell that fox, 'Behold, I am casting out demons and performing healings today and tomorrow, and on the third day I reach My goal.' Nevertheless I must go on My journey today and tomorrow and the next day; for it cannot be that a prophet would perish outside Jerusalem" (Luke 13:31–33).

Not all Pharisees are in conflict with Jesus. Even while He used the parable to warn Jewish leaders that their self-righteousness would keep them outside, some Pharisees approached Jesus to warn Him of a threat from Herod Antipas, the ruler of Galilee. Jesus instructed these Pharisees to tell Herod that He still had many things to accomplish before He reached Jerusalem. "I have nothing to fear from Herod; I am safe here, for death comes in Jerusalem."[7] Jerusalem was where the prophets met persecution and death, and it was where Jewish leaders would put Jesus to death. That was when Herod would have a part to play in His trial.

As He thought and spoke of Jerusalem, Jesus lamented the failure of that city and the Jewish nation to accept Him as their Savior.

"Jerusalem, Jerusalem, the city that kills the prophets and stones those who have been sent to her! How often I wanted to gather your children together, just as a hen gathers her young under her wings, and you were unwilling! Behold, your house is left to you desolate; and I say to you, you will not see Me until you say, "BLESSED IS THE ONE WHO COMES IN THE NAME OF THE LORD!" (verses 34–35).

Jesus' love and compassion for God's chosen people came through in this utterance, even in His repeating the name of the city: "Jerusalem! Jerusalem!" "Your house is left to you desolate." In those words, Jesus foresaw the terrible destruction of the city in AD 70.

Yet there was still time for repentance. How would Jerusalem respond to Jesus? "Will its inhabitants receive Him with pronouncements of blessing appropriate to 'one who comes in the name of the Lord'? Or will they declare Him to be a false prophet, an apostate, as they had God's earlier envoys?"[8]

"Lord, will only a few be saved?" Jesus never answered the man's question. He was not interested in numbers. The "requirement for entrance into God's kingdom is . . . [to] repent and be forgiven."[9] And the narrow door is still open.

Reflection

In a reversal of the open- or closed-door image, Jesus is pictured in Revelation as standing outside the door of your heart. "Look! I stand at the door and knock. If you hear my voice and open the door, I will come in, and we will share a meal together as friends" (Revelation 3:20, NLT). How will you respond?

---

1. William Barclay, *The Gospel of Luke* (Philadelphia, PA: Westminster Press, 1975), 183.

2. Paul Borgman, *The Way According to Luke: Hearing the Whole Story of Luke-Acts* (Grand Rapids, MI: Eerdmans, 2006), 203, 204.

3. Darrell L. Bock, *Luke* (Grand Rapids, MI: Baker Academic, 1994), 1235.

4. Joel B. Green, *The Gospel of Luke*, New International Commentary on the New Testament, vol. 3 (Grand Rapids, MI: Eerdmans, 1997), 531.

5. *NIV Cultural Backgrounds Study Bible* (Grand Rapids, MI: Zondervan, 2016), 1777.

6. Robert H. Stein, *Luke*, The New American Commentary, vol. 24 (Nashville, TN: Broadman, 1992), 378–381.

7. Bock, *Luke*, 1248.

8. Green, *Gospel of Luke*, 538.

9. Borgman, *Way According to Luke*, 211.

Chapter 55

Seats at the Table

Luke 14:1–14

It was another Sabbath in another town. As was His custom, Jesus attended the local synagogue, most likely as the guest speaker, and as was also customary, a leading Pharisee invited Him to lunch with a group of his colleagues.[1] As a special Sabbath meal, it would have been prepared the previous day in accordance with rules for Sabbath-keeping.

It happened that when He went into the house of one of the leaders of the Pharisees on the Sabbath to eat bread, they were watching Him closely. And there in front of Him was a man suffering from edema (Luke 14:1, 2).

The host is described as a "leading Pharisee"—perhaps the local synagogue ruler—which meant that his lunch guests would be of high social standing. For Pharisees, meals like this functioned to establish "in-group" boundaries. Lesser mortals were not invited, though it was a Sabbath custom to leave the door of the house open for anyone who wanted to stand inside and listen to the table conversation.[2] Because Jesus was on the move, the Pharisees here may not have met Him, but they had heard some things about Him, so they watched Him closely.

Imagine the surprise, then, when a man suffering from edema (bloating) appeared at the Pharisee's house. Was he brought there to trap Jesus? Sufferers of diseases like his were typically viewed as sinners, and the table fellowship demanded preset values and ceremonial purity.[3] To bring this sick man to the lunch is so out of character with Pharisaical values and attitudes that the idea is preposterous. More likely, the sufferer was drawn by the presence of Jesus, the Healer, and overcame his embarrassment because the door to the Pharisee's house would be open in harmony with Sabbath custom.[4] He could not join the others at the meal, of course, but he could stand behind the recliners. Recall that we encountered a similar situation in Galilee where a sinful woman came to a Pharisee's house at a Sabbath meal (Luke 7:36–39).

And Jesus responded and said to the lawyers and Pharisees, "Is it lawful to heal on the Sabbath, or not?" But they kept silent. And He took hold of him and healed him, and sent him away. And He said to them, "Which one of you will have a son or an ox fall into a well, and will not immediately pull him out on a Sabbath day?" And they could offer no reply to this (Luke 14:3–6).

The sick man was clearly not part of the group, but Jesus stood in front of him with a question for the Pharisees and lawyers: "Is it lawful to heal on the Sabbath, or not?" (verse 3). How would they answer that question? The law of Moses does not forbid it, but rabbinic Sabbath regulations permitted healing only if a person's life was in danger. Rather than appear uncompassionate, they remained silent. Whereupon Jesus placed his hands on the man, healed him, and permitted him to leave the house quietly.

Farmers often dug pits to collect groundwater or to capture predators, but sometimes their own children or animals fell into them.[5] So Jesus asked a follow-up question: "If one of your animals—or children—falls into a well on a Sabbath day, will you leave it there?" They were tempted to shake their heads, but again there was silence. Jesus asked hard questions, so it was best to keep quiet.

Now He began telling a parable to the invited guests when He noticed how they had been picking out the places of honor at the table, saying to them, "Whenever you are invited by someone to a wedding feast, do not take the place of honor, for someone more distinguished than you may have been invited by him, and the one who invited you both will come and say to you, 'Give your place to this person,' and then in disgrace you will proceed to occupy the last place. But whenever you are invited, go and take the last place, so that when the one who has invited you comes, he will say to you, 'Friend, move up higher'; then you will have honor in the sight of all who are dining at the table with you. For everyone who exalts himself will be humbled, and the one who humbles himself will be exalted" (verses 7–11).

Now the watchers were themselves being watched. Jesus observed how everyone scrambled to select the most-honored places to recline at the table. At Jewish banquets, it was typical to have several couches arranged in a U-shape around a low table. Each couch, known as a triclinium, allowed three people to recline. The bottom of the U was the head couch, with the host occupying the most-honored position at the center. The least-honored banquet seats were those furthest from the host.[6]

Addressing the group, Jesus used the example of a wedding banquet to show how pride governed table protocol in Judaism. An individual who was asked to move to a less-exalted seat would be shamed in the company of his friends. To follow Jesus means practicing humility instead of pride and being generous without any thought of payback. Those who exalt themselves will find themselves humiliated, while those who choose humility will be exalted. This is another case of the "great reversal," a very hard lesson for Pharisees.

Now He also went on to say to the one who had invited Him, "Whenever you give a luncheon or a dinner, do not invite your friends, your brothers, your relatives, nor wealthy neighbors, otherwise they may also invite you to a meal in return, and that will be your repayment. But whenever you give a banquet, invite people who are poor, who have disabilities, who are limping, and people who are blind; and you will be blessed, since they do not have the means to repay you; for you will be repaid at the resurrection of the righteous" (verses 12–14).

Luke gave special attention to the poor in his Gospel. "The 'lowly people' are especially noted as candidates for God's grace,"[7] and we may expect to find many of them at heaven's banquet table. Jesus suggested practicing that kind of table fellowship now. When you plan a luncheon or dinner, don't always invite your friends and relatives. Protocol would require them to invite you whenever they plan a dinner. Instead, invite people who are poor, disabled, or blind. For that afternoon's table audience, though, Jesus' counsel was unthinkable. "You mean I'm to have a poor or disabled person sit alongside me? I would be shamed!"[8]

"When pride comes, then comes dishonor" (Proverbs 11:2). I'm reminded of the title of a book on my library shelves: *I Know We're All Welcome at the Table, but Do I Have to Sit Next to You?*[9] Jesus was doing far more than offering sage counsel for the dinner host and table companions. "He is toppling the familiar world of the ancient Mediterranean, overturning its socially constructed reality and replacing it with what must have been regarded as a scandalous alternative."[10]

The powerful and privileged would never think to invite the poor to their meals for these reasons:

- It would endanger the social status of the host.
- It might cause embarrassment for the poor person, who could never reciprocate.
- It would thus be a wasted invitation.

Yes, it may seem like a wasted invitation, but Jesus promised blessing for practicing selfless generosity toward those who live on the margins of society. And goodness will be richly repaid "at the resurrection of the righteous." This was a meaningful promise for Pharisees, who were firm believers in the final resurrection.

Reflection

Who am I to sit with? Is she different than me? Is he dressed poorly? Does she worship at my church? Is he unclear when he speaks? Is it better for me to decline the invitation and stay home?

1. Robert H. Stein, *Luke*, The New American Commentary, vol. 24 (Nashville, TN: Broadman, 1992), 386.

2. Darrell L. Bock, *Luke* (Grand Rapids, MI: Baker Academic, 1994), 694.

3. Joel B. Green, *The Gospel of Luke*, New International Commentary on the New Testament, vol. 3 (Grand Rapids, MI: Eerdmans, 1997), 540.

4. Bock, *Luke*, 1256.

5. *NIV Cultural Backgrounds Study Bible* (Grand Rapids, MI: Zondervan, 2016), 1777.

6. Leon Morris, *Luke: An Introduction and Commentary*, Tyndale New Testament Commentaries, vol. 3 (Downers Grove, IL: IVP Academic, 1988), 249.

7. Darrell L. Bock, *A Theology of Luke and Acts* (Grand Rapids, MI: Zondervan, 2012), 248.

8. Randolph Richards and Brandon J. O'Brien, *Misreading Scripture With Western Eyes* (Downers Grove, IL: InterVarsity, 2012), 130, 131.

9. Janice Springer, *I Know We're All Welcome at the Table, but Do I Have to Sit Next to You?* (Gonzalez, FL: Energion, 2018).

10. Green, *Gospel of Luke*, 550.

Chapter 56

The Great Dinner

Luke 14:15–24 (Matthew 22:1–14)

Here we find Jesus at the home of a leading Pharisee for Sabbath lunch. There hasn't been much table conversation because Jesus asked questions that nobody wanted to answer, and He gave counsel the Pharisees didn't want to accept. It began with His Sabbath healing of a man with edema; then, He responded to the way guests looked for the seats of honor at the table; now, He wanted them to extend meal invitations to the poor and disabled—people far outside their social boundaries. Jesus acknowledged that inviting the poor would not bring reciprocal invitations on earth but reminded them that the reward for doing what is right comes at the resurrection.

Now when one of those who were reclining at the table with Him heard this, he said to Him, "Blessed is everyone who will eat bread in the kingdom of God!" (Luke 14:15).

Pharisees liked to hear about the final resurrection of the righteous. It led one dinner guest to express himself: Happy are those like himself and his table companions who would assuredly have places at the heavenly banquet table.

Seizing the topic, Jesus shared a parable with them. Once again, His humor came through wonderfully as He described a sumptuous banquet that didn't turn out the way it was planned.[1]

But He said to him, "A man was giving a big dinner, and he invited many; and at the dinner hour he sent his slave to tell those who had been invited, 'Come, because everything is ready now' " (verses 16, 17).

This dinner would be a really big affair. The householder sent invitations to a long list of his friends. "Make your reservations," he said, and they did. It would be unthinkable to ignore such an invitation. It was important for the master and his staff to know how many planned to come because it would take considerable time and effort to prepare this banquet. When everything was ready and the roast bullock piping hot, he sent his slave with the summons, "Come!" This was the kind of sumptuous meal the Pharisees loved to attend. They liked the picture Jesus described—it was their kind of event. Plus, it matched their picture of a Messianic banquet. No poor or lame people at this dinner!

"And yet they all alike began to make excuses. The first one said to him, 'I purchased a field and I need to go out to look at it; please consider me excused.' And another one said, 'I bought five yoke of oxen, and I am going to try them out; please consider me excused.' And another one said, 'I took a woman as my wife, and for that reason I cannot come.' And the slave came back and reported this to his master" (verses 18–21).

Only three examples were given, but sadly "they all alike began to make excuses." What was wrong with these people? They reserved their places at the dinner, but then they offered ridiculous excuses for not coming.

- "I purchased a field and I need to go look at it." The field would still be there tomorrow!
- "I bought five yoke of oxen and need to try them out." That's a costly purchase, so why didn't he try them out before he bought them?
- "I just got married and can't come." Weddings were planned far in advance, so this guy knew of the conflict when he agreed to come.[2] Since women didn't receive invitations to feasts, he could just leave his wife at home and come.

With this plot twist, Jesus shocked His table company. It never happened this way in real life! It's true that when Israel was in battle, Moses permitted a man to stay home if he'd just built a house or planted a vineyard or gotten married. Otherwise, he might be killed in the battle and never get to enjoy these things (Deuteronomy 20:5–7). But this was not a wartime story.

"Then the head of the household became angry and said to his slave, 'Go out at once into the streets and lanes of the city and bring in here those who are poor, those with disabilities, those who are blind, and those who are limping' " (Luke 14:21).
Of course, the host became angry. Then he sent his slave out again. Since the original invitees made excuses, the invitation now went out to the poor, the disabled, the blind, and the lame. "Bring them in!" he told his servant. This was a revolutionary idea because Jewish leadership considered people who had disabilities, including blindness, to be under God's punishment, so they were excluded from worship in the temple. But this was a banquet, so there were no such restrictions.

"And later the slave said, 'Master, what you commanded has been done, and still there is room.' And the master said to the slave, 'Go out into the roads and the hedges and press upon them to come in, so that my house will be filled' " (verses 22, 23).
A final time the slave was sent, this time outside the town precincts. There he found the homeless, the derelicts who found shelter in hedges, the beggars who had been chased out of town. After all, the master insisted that every place at the banquet table must be filled. Notice that the first ones—those of high status—were *invited*; the second group of the poor and disabled was *brought* to the feast; the third group of the "down and out" was *compelled* to come. Dirty and untidy, they felt embarrassed and ashamed, but they came. It seems likely that this last group represented Gentiles, who were diminished in the eyes of Jewish leadership.[3]

" 'For I tell you, none of those men who were invited shall taste my dinner' " (verse 24).
Finishing the story, I imagine that Jesus looked intently at the Pharisees, each one sitting in his carefully chosen place with his mouth wide open in astonishment, before He said, "I tell you, none of those who were invited shall taste my dinner."
In response, "the religious leaders squirm, perhaps: not only do they seek the wrong seats of honor at a perfectly proper party, and not only do they throw the wrong kind of parties: *they don't recognize*

the kind of feast to which they are being invited!"[4] These leaders are the very people who missed the narrow door in the earlier parable and found themselves locked outside (Luke 13:23–25).

Reflection

Jesus sometimes used what we might call shock therapy in His teaching. Why is it important to recognize that God won't always do things your way? Think about this as you read Isaiah 55:8, 9 and Romans 11:33–36.

1. O. C. Edwards Jr., *Luke's Story of Jesus* (Philadelphia, PA: Fortress Press, 1981), 69.

2. *NIV Cultural Backgrounds Study Bible* (Grand Rapids, MI: Zondervan, 2016), 1778.

3. Darrell L. Bock, *Luke* (Grand Rapids, MI: Baker Academic, 1994), 1268.

4. Paul Borgman, *The Way According to Luke: Hearing the Whole Story of Luke-Acts* (Grand Rapids, MI: Eerdmans, 2006), 198; emphasis in the original.

Chapter 57

Full-Blooded Discipleship

Luke 14:25–35 (Matthew 10:37–39)

Sabbath lunch and the conversation with a group of Pharisees ended, and Jesus continued on His way toward Jerusalem. A crowd traveled with Him, drawn to the teachings and healing miracles of this unique Rabbi. Who would not want to follow such an individual? Some amazing stories circulated about Him, like the miraculous feeding of more than five thousand people in Galilee. It was obvious that there would be many advantages to having Jesus as your Rabbi.

Now large crowds were going along with Him, and He turned and said to them, "If anyone comes to Me and does not hate his own father, mother, wife, children, brothers, sisters, yes, and even his own life, he cannot be My disciple" (Luke 14:25, 26).

Jesus told His listeners that it was not easy to be His disciple. Associating and traveling with Him was not enough. You cannot be like some of the individuals who accepted invitations to a great dinner but then made excuses that they were too busy to come. Discipleship is not like that. If I want to be a disciple, I must ask Jesus to be the center of my life—Jesus becomes my leader, and I am His follower.

In the Jewish culture of the time, family ties were close and extremely important, both historically and culturally. Breaking from the family unit was a painful thing. Those who live in Western societies today have little concept of what it means for a Muslim or a citizen of a decidedly non-Christian country to decide to follow Christ—and how it affects one's family. Most of us in the West are able to associate with Christ simply because it is culturally appropriate in our free society.[1]

This was the second occasion that Jesus spoke about families and how membership in God's kingdom would cause familial disruption. Last time, He had talked about "division" as individual family members made their choices to follow Jesus or not (Luke 12:51–53).[2] Now, He focused on priorities. What did He mean by saying a person must "hate" his parents, spouse, siblings, and children if he wanted to be Jesus' disciple? Remember that He once taught love for *enemies* as well as *neighbors*, so what can it mean to "hate" members of your *family*? Recall that Jacob "loved" Rachel but "hated" Leah, who gave birth to most of his children (Genesis 29:30, 31). "Hate" is a bad translation for us—it does *not* mean a loss of affection for one's own.

It will help us to think about "love" for a moment. There are at least four Greek words that we translate as "love." One of them is *agapē*, the predominant one in the New Testament. It does not mean affection but, rather, a conscious decision to make someone or something your priority. So, in that sense, for me to "love" my wife, mother, son, or daughter is to make each of them a priority in my life. In the same sort of way, to "hate" my wife or family, in the biblical sense, is to make *someone or something else* my highest priority. My family is still very important to me—my affection for them is strong—but my love (*agapè*) for God takes top place.

So, we don't leave feelings behind when we follow Jesus, but we must give Him first place in our hearts. "Jesus' demand is for his followers to love/obey him more than anyone else, even their own families. Being Jesus' disciple entails primary allegiance to Jesus. No one and no thing can usurp his supreme position."[3]

"Whoever does not carry his own cross and come after Me cannot be My disciple" (Luke 14:27).

Discipleship means the willingness to bear the pain of persecution. Note that "those condemned to execution would often carry the horizontal beam of their cross out to the site of their execution, through an often hostile and mocking mob."[4] Discipleship is a mind-set, a preparedness to suffer for one's identity with Jesus.

"For which one of you, when he wants to build a tower, does not first sit down and calculate the cost, to see if he has enough to complete it? Otherwise, when he has laid a foundation and is not able to finish, all who are watching it will begin to ridicule him, saying, 'This person began to build, and was not able to finish!' " (verses 28–30).

Jesus used two illustrations to show that discipleship requires careful thought and planning. At the time, it was not uncommon for a wealthy landowner to build a watchtower in his vineyard. Even today, during a visit to the rice terraces of the northern Philippines, I saw a couple of locally constructed watchtowers that were designed to keep flocks of birds from devouring the rice before its harvest. Watchtowers are built to help identify potential threats. A would-be disciple must watch out for evil influences that threaten his spiritual values. How will his discipleship affect family, income, property, and possessions? An individual should assess whether he or she is ready to take on the personal commitment and sacrifice required to follow Jesus.[5] There is no such thing as a half-disciple.

"Or what king, when he sets out to meet another king in battle, will not first sit down and consider whether he is strong enough with ten thousand men to face the one coming against him with twenty thousand? Otherwise, while the other is still far away, he sends a delegation and requests terms of peace. So then, none of you can be My disciple who does not give up all his own possessions" (verses 31–33).

The second illustration is of a king whose army of ten thousand men may not be strong enough to meet an enemy numbering twenty thousand. Clearly, he must carefully analyze the situation and consider the military equipment at his disposal and his battle strategy. Preparatory planning is required before a decision is made. Failure to think ahead leads to mockery in the first illustration and surrender in the second. So, a lack of commitment, resolve, and sober reflection results in a failed disciple. Discipleship demands prayerful preparation.

Concluding, Jesus emphasized that no one can be His disciple without making it the priority of his or her life. "If a man is daunted by the high demands of Christ let him remember that he is not left to fulfill them alone. He who called him to the steep road will walk with him every step of the way and be there at the end to meet him."[6]

"Therefore, salt is good; but if even salt has become tasteless, with what will it be seasoned? It is

useless either for the soil or the manure pile, so it is thrown out. The one who has ears to hear, let him hear" (verses 34, 35).

The true disciple is "salt" to his community. The purpose of salt is to improve the flavor. The Christian's life is supposed to do the same within their community of influence.[7]

This was a very difficult teaching from Jesus. Discipleship is demanding. "Jesus is calling for the reconstruction of one's identity, not along ancestral lines or on the basis of one's social status, but within the new community oriented toward God's purpose and characterized by faithfulness to the message of Jesus."[8] Again Jesus counseled, "He who has ears to hear, let him hear" (verse 35, ESV). He is looking for full-blooded disciples.

Reflection

Jesus is our model for discipleship. Growing as a disciple involves learning (Luke 2:46, 47), spending time alone with God (Luke 5:16), instruction and mentoring (Luke 8:1–15), and going out to serve (Luke 9:1–6, 10)

---

1. Darrell L. Bock, *Luke* (Grand Rapids, MI: Baker Academic, 1994), 1285.
2. Paul Borgman, *The Way According to Luke: Hearing the Whole Story of Luke-Acts* (Grand Rapids, MI: Eerdmans, 2006), 198, 199.
3. Robert H. Stein, *Luke*, The New American Commentary, vol. 24 (Nashville, TN: Broadman, 1992), 396.
4. *NIV Cultural Backgrounds Study Bible* (Grand Rapids, MI: Zondervan, 2016), 1778.
5. Darrell L. Bock, *A Theology of Luke and Acts* (Grand Rapids, MI: Zondervan, 2012), 321.
6. William Barclay, *The Gospel of Luke* (Philadelphia, PA: Westminster Press, 1975), 197.
7. Barclay, 198.
8. Joel B. Green, *The Gospel of Luke*, New International Commentary on the New Testament (Grand Rapids, MI: Eerdmans, 1997), 565.

Chapter 58

A Lost Sheep and a Shepherd's Joy

Luke 15:1–10

Chapter 15 contains another story that is unique to Luke's Gospel, and it is often a favorite chapter in the Bible because it is the gospel within the gospel.[1] We again find Jesus in the company of Pharisees and scribes who were observing a gathering of "sinners." This wasn't a compatible combination, so we immediately smell a conflict.

Now all the tax collectors and sinners were coming near Jesus to listen to Him. And both the Pharisees and the scribes began to complain, saying, "This man receives sinners and eats with them" (Luke 15:1, 2).

Two disparate groups were present—religious leaders and "sinners." Some Pharisees stood around to observe and criticize Jesus' behavior. He had developed a reputation for associating with tax collectors and sinners. That association was bad enough, but in the eyes of Jewish leadership, eating—that is, having "table fellowship"—with people equated to welcoming them and regarding them with value.[2] Tax collectors were dishonest and not valued because they worked for Rome. "Sinners" were the kind of people that the householder's slave had to find and compel to the "great dinner" because they knew they were unvalued and unworthy (Luke 14:23, 24). Befriending undesirables was the wrong kind of table fellowship. Now, these unclean, contemptible outsiders were responding to Jesus' final words in the preceding chapter: "If you have ears to hear, listen!" (See Luke 14:35.)[3] These "sinners" were there to listen.

And so He told them this parable, saying, "What man among you, if he has a hundred sheep and has lost one of them, does not leave the other ninety-nine in the open pasture and go after the one that is lost, until he finds it? And when he has found it, he puts it on his shoulders, rejoicing. And when he comes home, he calls together his friends and his neighbors, saying to them, 'Rejoice with me, because I have found my sheep that was lost!' I tell you that in the same way, there will be more joy in heaven over one sinner who repents than over ninety-nine righteous people who have no need of repentance" (Luke 15:3–7).

Jesus told "them"—the scribes and Pharisees who complained about Him—this parable. The story was intentionally for them, and it's about a shepherd and one lost sheep. Pharisees would never think of themselves as shepherds—who were considered outsiders too—unless the Holy Spirit impressed this prophecy of Ezekiel on their minds and hearts:

"What sorrow awaits you shepherds who feed yourselves instead of your flocks. . . . You have not taken care of the weak. You have not tended the sick or bound up the injured. You have not gone

looking for those who have wandered away and are lost. . . .

". . . I myself will search and find my sheep. I will be like a shepherd looking for his scattered flock. I will find my sheep and rescue them" (Ezekiel 34:2–12, NLT).

Ezekiel recorded God saying, "I myself will search and find my sheep," and truly, a people-seeking God was a new thought for Jewish leaders.[4] God takes the initiative in searching for His lost sheep and bringing them home. The parable pictures a modestly comfortable shepherd with one hundred sheep and no hired hand. He would likely call on other nearby herders to watch his flock while he searched for the lost one.

Luke 15 is a chapter about rejoicing. When the shepherd found the lost sheep, he carried it home on his shoulders with joy in his heart and invited friends and neighbors to what sounds like a party, saying, "Rejoice with me, because I have found my sheep that was lost!" (Luke 15:6). We may wonder why he'd throw a party for just one sheep. Jesus used this story to illustrate how heaven celebrates when one sinner repents and comes home. There is no joy over the many who consider themselves righteous but sense no need for repentance.

"Or what woman, if she has ten silver coins and loses one coin, does not light a lamp and sweep the house and search carefully until she finds it? And when she has found it, she calls together her friends and neighbors, saying, 'Rejoice with me, because I have found the coin which I had lost!' In the same way, I tell you, there is joy in the presence of the angels of God over one sinner who repents" (verses 8–10).

The second parable features a peasant woman who lost one coin, a Greek drachma, which was a working man's day wage. Her house was dark, possibly lacking a window, so she lit her lamp and used her broom of palm twigs to sweep the floor of beaten earth covered with dried reeds and rushes.[5] Talk about trying to find a needle in a haystack! But what joy she must have felt when the lost coin was discovered! She called her female friends and neighbors to rejoice with her, and they celebrated together. Again, Jesus said their joy is representative of the joy in heaven when a lost sinner is found and drawn to God.

Both stories picture God searching for the lost, but His disciples are also called to join Him in the search for lost souls. The basic motif in the two stories is search, and the basic emotion is joy. God is quick to invite others to His banquet table. In fact, "God will go to great effort and rejoice with great joy to find and restore a sinner to himself. Jesus wishes to emphasize that God is not a God of the few, a God of the wise, or a God only of those who think they pursue God. He is a God who searches, finds, and cares for the sinner."[6]

Reflection

Luke emphasized joy throughout his Gospel. What experiences bring you joy? When is it hard to experience joy? How do you celebrate a truly joyful experience?

1. William Barclay, *The Gospel of Luke* (Philadelphia, PA: Westminster Press, 1975), 199.
2. Leon Morris, *Luke: An Introduction and Commentary*, Tyndale New Testament Commentaries, vol. 3 (Downers Grove, IL: IVP Academic, 1988), 255.
3. Joel B. Green, *The Gospel of Luke*, New International Commentary on the New Testament, vol. 3 (Grand Rapids, MI: Eerdmans, 1997), 571.
4. Morris, *Luke*, 255.
5. Barclay, *Gospel of Luke*, 202.
6. Darrell L. Bock, *Luke* (Grand Rapids, MI: Baker Academic, 1994), 1295.

Chapter 59

The Forgiving Father

Luke 15:11–24

The third parable continues with the theme of lostness. Popularly known as the story of the prodigal son, it is undoubtedly one of the most beautiful stories in the Bible. The tax collectors and "sinners"—the ones with ears to hear—should see this story as a wide-open invitation from a God who welcomes home His runaway children.

And He said, "A man had two sons. The younger of them said to his father, 'Father, give me the share of the estate that is coming to me.' And so he divided his wealth between them" (Luke 15:11, 12).
Let's view this story by looking at the two characters, the son and his father, separately.

- *Son.* The boy is probably in his late teens since he is single.[1] His demand for his share of the father's estate is completely against the customs of the time. Distribution of property before a father's death was frowned upon. Essentially the son said, "Give me now what I would get anyway when you are dead, and let me out of here."[2] This is sinful behavior, and the boy's behavior casts him in a disparaging light.
- *Father.* The typical father would be authoritarian and controlling, especially for a son who has not yet reached the age of maturity. Why did he accede to the demand of his younger son? Note that the son didn't even ask respectfully. Nevertheless, the father divided his estate "between them." The younger "son would receive half of what the elder son receives, or one-third of the estate."[3] His brother would get two-thirds.

"And not many days later, the younger son gathered everything together and went on a journey to a distant country, and there he squandered his estate in wild living" (verse 13).

- *Son.* The division of an estate during the lifetime of the father is one thing; converting one's inheritance into cash is quite another. The son's shocking breach of family ties seems unforgivable. He's severing his relationship with his father. Leaving home, he trotted off to a distant country and followed a wild, undisciplined lifestyle. He squandered his resources on worthless pleasures.
- *Father.* Why did he permit the sale of his son's share of the property for cash? The Pharisees in Jesus' audience were already thinking, "What a foolish father! The boy deserves a beating."

"Now when he had spent everything, a severe famine occurred in that country, and he began doing without. So he went and hired himself out to one of the citizens of that country, and he sent him

into his fields to feed pigs. And he longed to have his fill of the carob pods that the pigs were eating, and no one was giving him anything" (verses 14–16).

- *Son.* A "severe famine" hit the distant country, and the boy was penniless—he had no money and no family. He had to do something, so he looked for employment. Nothing much was offered during a famine, but he finally found a low-paying job feeding pigs. That's the lowest possible job for a Jew—feeding unclean animals. He is shaming his family by becoming "unclean and degraded," living like a Gentile. The boy was hungry, even for some of the carob pods that he fed to the pigs, "but no one gave him anything" (verse 16, NIV).
- *Father.* The father knew nothing of what was happening. And we may rightfully wonder, *Has he given up on this totally irresponsible boy?*

"But when he came to his senses, he said, 'How many of my father's hired laborers have more than enough bread, but I am dying here from hunger! I will set out and go to my father, and will say to him, "Father, I have sinned against heaven, and in your sight; I am no longer worthy to be called your son; treat me as one of your hired laborers." ' So he set out and came to his father" (verses 17–20).

- *Son.* His tummy rumbling with hunger, the boy finally came to his senses. Squatting by the pig trough, I imagine him realizing, "I've been stupid. Back home, even my dad's hired hands have all the food they want." He knew that kind of job was temporary because it depended on the seasons, his dad only hired when he needed the help, and hired hands could be dismissed at a day's notice. "But I'll take a chance. I'm dying of starvation here." So, the boy began the long journey home. As he trudged homeward, he prepared a short speech in his mind and practiced it a few times. How would his dad receive him? It didn't matter anymore; he'd willingly take the beating, no matter how severe.
- *Father.* The caring father has not stopped watching and praying for his absent son. An open check of forgiveness is ready.

"But when he was still a long way off, his father saw him and felt compassion for him, and ran and embraced him and kissed him. And the son said to him, 'Father, I have sinned against heaven and in your sight; I am no longer worthy to be called your son.' But the father said to his slaves, 'Quickly bring out the best robe and put it on him, and put a ring on his finger and sandals on his feet; and bring the fattened calf, slaughter it, and let's eat and celebrate; for this son of mine was dead and has come to life again; he was lost and has been found.' And they began to celebrate" (verses 20–24).

- *Son.* Nearly home. Bedraggled and dirty, head down, shoeless, he didn't see his father running toward him. Suddenly, he was embraced in a great bear hug. Overwhelmed, the boy opened his mouth to begin his well-rehearsed speech, "Dad, I've sinned against God and against you. I'm sorry . . ."
- *Father.* It was undignified for an older man to run, but this father was already shouting instructions to his servants: "Bring me the best robe, and a ring. And a pair of sandals."[4] The father already knew what he would do if his son returned, and I imagine him calling over his shoulder, "Oh, and bring the fattened calf. We're going to have a grand supper! My son is alive, and he's home!"

This is yet another of Luke's "party" stories. He loved to write about Jesus dining with Pharisees or tax collectors, and he recorded several parables like this one that included festive meals.

The prodigal returned home to his father's great welcome and a party. Did the tax collectors and "sinners" in Jesus' audience connect with the story? This parable was especially for them, and the message is plain: Just come home!

Reflection

Should the father have gone looking for his son (like the shepherd did for the sheep and the woman for the coin)? Why or why not?

---

1. *NIV Cultural Backgrounds Study Bible* (Grand Rapids, MI: Zondervan, 2016), 1779.
2. William Barclay, *The Gospel of Luke* (Philadelphia, PA: Westminster Press, 1975), 204.
3. Darrell L. Bock, *Luke* (Grand Rapids, MI: Baker Academic, 1994), 1309.
4. Joel B. Green, *The Gospel of Luke*, New International Commentary on the New Testament, vol. 3 (Grand Rapids, MI: Eerdmans, 1997), 581.

Chapter 60

The Unforgiving Brother

Luke 15:25–32

However, Jesus' parable of the lost son does not finish with the father's welcome and the celebration banquet. There's more to come, and some of the listening Pharisees and scribes may start squirming before it's finished.

"Now his older son was in the field, and when he came and approached the house, he heard music and dancing. And he summoned one of the servants and began inquiring what these things could be. And he said to him, 'Your brother has come, and your father has slaughtered the fattened calf because he has received him back safe and sound' " (Luke 15:25–27).

The father was a wealthy landowner, and he had servants and slaves to care for his extensive fields. His elder son was out working in the fields and arrived home toward evening, undoubtedly wondering what celebration was happening in the house. He had every right to walk right inside—it's his home, after all—but he summoned one of the servants to find out what was happening. "Your brother has come home!" This was wonderfu/l news for his father, but was it also good news for the elder brother? Has he not missed his brother?

"But he became angry and was not willing to go in; and his father came out and began pleading with him. But he answered and said to his father, 'Look! For so many years I have been serving you and I have never neglected a command of yours; and yet you never gave me a young goat, so that I might celebrate with my friends; but when this son of yours came, who has devoured your wealth with prostitutes, you slaughtered the fattened calf for him' " (verses 28–30).

This son became angry. What thoughts might have gone through his mind at that moment?

- Huh! This is favoritism!
- I work like a slave for my father. I'm the one who deserves the party.
- Will Dad divide the estate again and give this waster a whole lot more of it?
- Is this all I get for blistered hands?

Soon the father learned that his older son had arrived home from work. He immediately left the party to find his son, only to be met with a tirade of angry words, "Now *this son of yours* has turned up. He's probably spent all your money on prostitutes, and you throw a party for him. Look! I've been slaving for you all these years. I've never disobeyed you. You've never given me even a young goat so I can celebrate with my friends. It's not fair! He's *your son*; he's not my brother!"

This is a great reversal. The son who was lost, the "outsider," is back inside. The son who was an "insider" was now outside.

"And he said to him, 'Son, you have always been with me, and all that is mine is yours. But we had to celebrate and rejoice, because this brother of yours was dead and has begun to live, and was lost and has been found' " (verses 31, 32).

The father's words were gentle and tender as he spoke to the boy he loved, "Son, you are always here with me. You remember that I divided the estate between you and your brother? So you own everything we have here. Now we can rejoice because your brother has come home. He was lost, but he's alive. We have to celebrate, don't we?"

The boy was distancing himself from his family. "Refusing to share a meal is a symbolic act of gargantuan proportions in a culture where kinship boundaries are secured through the sharing of food."[1] We wonder whether this boy has ever had a relationship with his father. In a very real sense, he might be the lost son.

And what shall we say about the scribes and Pharisees who listened to the story? "They are invited to find themselves represented in the parable as the elder son—responsible and obedient, it would seem, but failing in their solidarity with the redemptive purpose of God. Will they identify with God's will and, having done so, join repentant sinners at the table?"[2]

"The story leaves us hanging, for we are not told what the elder son does. . . . The parable is left so that Luke's readers may reflect on the proper response. Would they, if they were in the brother's shoes, go inside? Will they share in the joy? Will they join in the opportunity to help the lost find God? Will they join the Father or stay outside?"[3]

Jesus' parable presents a beautiful picture of a God who values our freedom to run away but looks and longs for us to come home. Yet the story was not supposed to end the way it did. Let's imagine a different ending. The father's older son was concerned about his lost brother. He saw the distress of his grieving dad and volunteered to go out and search for his brother. He went all the way to the distant country, found his brother feeding the pigs, assured him that his father still loved him, and brought him home. One afternoon, as the anxious father looked down the road, he saw not one but two boys coming home, and one had his arm around the other, calling, "Look, Dad, I found him, and I've brought him home."[4]

Reflection

Think about the elder son. What positive characteristics about him come to your mind? Where does he need help?

---

1. Joel B. Green, *The Gospel of Luke*, New International Commentary on the New Testament, vol. 3 (Grand Rapids, MI: Eerdmans, 1997), 584, 585.
2. Green, 586.
3. Darrell L. Bock, *Luke* (Grand Rapids, MI: Baker Academic, 1994), 1320.
4. Adapted from Keith Clouten, *Breaking Through the Wall: How God Communicates With His Lost Creation* (Calhoun, GA: TEACH Services, 2018), 257, 258.

Chapter 61

The Crafty Manager

Luke 16:1–13

Next is another of Jesus' funny stories. Our cultural blinders prevent us from seeing this story through the eyes of His Jewish audience, but Luke will help us find some important lessons.

We should note that the disciples have been absent from Luke's account for a while—perhaps they enjoyed a period of rest and recuperation at home with their families? But now Jesus was instructing them again, while some Pharisees "listened in" to the teaching.

Now He was also saying to the disciples, "There was a rich man who had a manager, and this manager was reported to him as squandering his possessions. And he summoned him and said to him, 'What is this I hear about you? Give an accounting of your management, for you can no longer be manager' " (Luke 16:1, 2).

The business situation was not particularly unusual—a wealthy landowner employing a manager. His manager might be a slave who grew up in the owner's house and has been trained for the job, or he may be a free person. In a letter to the Corinthians, Paul appeals to managers to be trustworthy stewards (1 Corinthians 4:1, 2).

There are clues from the story that the wealthy owner may have lived away from his estate—again, not unusual—and received some negative reports about his on-site manager, who was summoned for an interview to provide an account. "What is this I hear about you? I want you to give me an inventory of all the goods."[1]

"And the manager said to himself, 'What am I to do, since my master is taking the management away from me? I am not strong enough to dig; I am ashamed to beg. I know what I will do, so that when I am removed from the management people will welcome me into their homes' " (Luke 16:3, 4).

What was happening? The owner had determined that his manager was guilty of mismanagement and would be terminated as soon as he wrapped up the affairs of the estate. He would then be out on the street, but what other choices did he have? As a white-collar worker, he wouldn't relish the prospect of low-paying manual labor—digging is arduous—and begging would be shameful. He soon came up with a brilliant idea that would make him business friends and hopefully lead to some job offers. After all, ancient cultures emphasized reciprocity, or returning favors.

"And he summoned each one of his master's debtors, and he began saying to the first, 'How much do you owe my master?' And he said, 'A hundred jugs of oil.' And he said to him, 'Take your bill, and sit down quickly and write fifty.' Then he said to another, 'And how much do you owe?' And

he said, 'A hundred kors of wheat.' He said to him, 'Take your bill, and write eighty' " (verses 5–7).

The manager seized upon a clever scheme to endear himself to his master's debtors. Going through the inventory of bills, he contacted each debtor, one at a time, to determine how much they would owe at harvest time. Two of the debts are substantial. The first debtor owes 100 large jugs of oil, equivalent to roughly 871 gallons, the yield from 146 olive trees. A second owes 100 kors of wheat, which is approximately 1,000 bushels, the yield from about 100 acres.[2] It is obvious that these debtors were not mere tenant-farmers but substantial landowners. In each case, the astute manager had instructions for the debtor. What did he claim as his authority for his seemingly reckless actions? He might be establishing the new customer charges like this:[3]

- Look at your bill, and you'll see that my boss has charged interest on your loan. He is not supposed to do that because charging interest is forbidden in the Torah (Deuteronomy 23:19, 20).
- I'm also reducing some of the commission that I get for my work.
- Now I want you to write a new loan agreement with those reduced figures. You can destroy the original loan agreement. Won't that make you happy?

Yes, the affluent customer would like very much what the manager did for him, and it might land him a handsome job. Notice that he instructed each debtor to deduct the interest from his bills. It had become customary for landholders to charge interest on debts, even though it was forbidden in the Mosaic Law. Those who wished to make money from loans evaded the biblical law by reasoning that the law was only made to protect the poor from exploitation.[4] And so it went with each debtor who owed money to his master. This is "the way the world works."

"And his master complimented the unrighteous manager because he had acted shrewdly; for the sons of this age are more shrewd in relation to their own kind than the sons of light" (Luke 16:8).

Essentially, this parable is about two rascals, and the story needs to be viewed in the spirit of Jesus' humor that we saw previously in the parable of the great feast (Luke 14:15–24). The landowner had enough sense to know what was going on, what game was being played.[5] Was he happy with what his manager did? Certainly not, but perhaps the owner was now "in a difficult position. He would have the greatest difficulty in establishing his claim to the original amounts now that the first bonds were destroyed. In any case he could not repudiate the steward's action without convicting himself of [charging interest]. . . . The steward is now seen as conforming to the law of God,"[6] and his customers are happy people. Yes, his manager was patently dishonest, but instead of facing the consequences, he was complimented for his astuteness and obedience to the law.[7]

"And I say to you, make friends for yourselves by means of the wealth of unrighteousness, so that when it is all gone, they will receive you into the eternal dwellings" (Luke 16:9).

Does this mean that Jesus wants us to be like the crafty manager of the parable? No, we are not to copy his dishonesty. The phrase "wealth of unrighteousness" is an inadequate translation from Greek. Wealth itself is morally neutral; it's the "*love* of money"—selfishness, wealth used wrongly, allowing wealth to replace God as life's priority—that is the "root of all sorts of evil" (1 Timothy 6:10; emphasis added). Business methodologies, strategic planning, and technologies are respectable and praiseworthy in themselves. It is how we use them that is important. Jesus wants us to be both honest and wise in our purposes and planning.

"The one who is faithful in a very little thing is also faithful in much; and the one who is unrighteous in a very little thing is also unrighteous in much. Therefore if you have not been faithful in the use of unrighteous wealth, who will entrust the true wealth to you? And if you have not been faithful in the use of that which is another's, who will give you that which is your own? No servant can serve two masters; for either he will hate the one and love the other, or he will be devoted to one and despise the other. You cannot serve God and wealth" (Luke 16:10–13).

We may draw no less than four lessons from this parable, each dealing with an aspect of stewardship:[8]

1. Be *generous* with money. People like the wealthy landowner and his manager knew very well how to make the world work for them. It is to be different for followers of Jesus. His disciples are to be honest and wise in investing funds that can be used to further the kingdom of God. Money and wealth must not be hoarded and used selfishly. The way to "make friends with wealth" is to be generous with it, using it to meet genuine needs in the community.

2. Be *faithful* with money and in stewardship. "Upon earth you are in charge of things which are not really yours. You cannot take them with you when you die. They are only lent to you. You are only a steward over them. . . . What you get in heaven depends on how you use the things of earth."[9]

3. *Serve God*, not wealth. Your highest priority is love for God. "Hating" money or wealth means that material possessions have a lower priority than service to God.

4. No slave can serve two masters. The master possesses his slave exclusively. The slave has no spare time, "so, serving God can never be a part-time or a spare-time job."[10]

In short, "the disciple, just like the dishonest steward, should look ahead. The disciple should consider what God can do and what he has done. The follower should use money not selfishly, but generously and faithfully, so that one may possess all the future riches God has for the disciple."[11]

Reflection

Christians live *in* the world, but their behavior should not be *of* the world. Ask yourself, What business practices should I avoid?

---

1. Darrell L. Bock, *Luke* (Grand Rapids, MI: Baker Academic, 1994), 1327, 1328.
2. *NIV Cultural Backgrounds Study Bible* (Grand Rapids, MI: Zondervan, 2016), 1781.
3. Leon Morris, *Luke: An Introduction and Commentary*, Tyndale New Testament Commentaries, vol. 3 (Downers Grove, IL: IVP Academic, 1988), 263.
4. J. Duncan M. Derrett, *Law in the New Testament* (Eugene, OR: Wipf & Stock, 1970), 56–63.
5. O. C. Edwards Jr., *Luke's Story of Jesus* (Philadelphia, PA: Fortress Press, 1981), 71.
6. Morris, *Luke*, 264.
7. *NIV Cultural Backgrounds Study Bible*, 1782.
8. Bock, *Luke*, 1333–1337.
9. William Barclay, *The Gospel of Luke* (Philadelphia, PA: Westminster Press, 1975), 209.
10. Barclay, 210.
11. Bock, *Luke*, 1337.

Chapter 62

Lovers of Money and Law

Luke 16:14–18

While Jesus shared the parable of the dishonest manager with His disciples, some Pharisees were listening too. When the story finished, the Pharisees took the stage, leaving the disciples in the background.

Now the Pharisees, who were lovers of money, were listening to all these things and were ridiculing Him (Luke 16:14).

If money is morally neutral, as Jesus taught, why shouldn't Pharisees—or anyone—enjoy it in abundance? The Pharisees perceived their wealth as a blessing from God, a reward for their righteousness. They didn't buy the idea of having to choose between love for God and love for money, so they ridiculed Jesus for this teaching.[1]

As I considered this passage in Luke, I remembered my visit to a Buddhist enclave in the country of Laos, where I participated in a cultural almsgiving exercise by sharing small handfuls of cooked rice with monks who came by with bowls to collect the food. Was I meeting a genuine need? I don't think so. *Genuine* charity includes gifts of money, food, or other material goods to assist those in poverty. Like my almsgiving in Laos, Pharisees were sometimes observed giving alms as an act of virtue, but too often, they did it for the wrong reason: they wanted to impress onlookers with their righteous acts. This was not an acceptable patron-client relationship.

And He said to them, "You are the ones who justify yourselves in the sight of people, but God knows your hearts; because that which is highly esteemed among people is detestable in the sight of God" (verse 15).

Jesus read the hearts of these self-righteous almsgivers. Pride and self-exaltation have no place in service to God. Showpiece sacrifices are an offense to God; in fact, they are "detestable." The Greek word may be translated as "something that stinks."[2] The prophet Micah spoke loudly against a show-culture of sacrifices and concluded,

> He has told you, O man, what is good;
>> and what does the LORD require of you
> but to do justice, to love kindness,
>> and to walk humbly with your God? (Micah 6:8, ESV).

God gives wealth to be recycled as kindness.

Lovers of law

Continuing on, Jesus shifted the topic to the Law.

"The Law and the Prophets were proclaimed until John came; since that time the gospel of the kingdom of God has been preached, and everyone is forcing his way into it" (Luke 16:16).

When Jesus mentioned "the Law and the Prophets," He was identifying the Jewish Scriptures—what we call the Old Testament. If Jesus used the full title, as He did in Luke 24:44, He would say, "The Law, the Prophets, and the Psalms." "The Law" encompasses the five books of Moses, or the Torah. "The Prophets" incorporates the historical and prophetic books. The third division, "The Psalms" or "Writings," includes the poems and songs (Psalms, Proverbs, Job, Song of Songs). In Luke 16:16, Jesus made a division between two periods:

- The age of promise was "proclaimed until John came." The Jewish Scriptures, beginning in Genesis, promised a Messiah who would free people from the oppression of sin that had engulfed the planet. John the Baptist came "in the spirit and power of Elijah" (Luke 1:17, see also Malachi 4:5) and proclaimed the arrival of Messiah.
- The age of fulfillment came with the arrival of Jesus, bringing fulfillment of the long-awaited promise and a new age when "the gospel of the kingdom of God" would be preached throughout the world.

John the Baptist was the last of the Jewish prophets and the forerunner of Jesus Christ. As a transition figure, John had one foot in the age of promise and the other in the age of fulfillment when he announced the arrival of Jesus.[3] And when Jesus began preaching the kingdom, the most unlikely people—tax-collectors and sinners—came pushing their way through the doorway to salvation. But the scribes and Pharisees wanted to set up barriers to keep them out.[4]

All this brings up another important question. If the age of "the Law and the Prophets" had come to an end, does that mean the termination of Old Testament law? No, says Jesus.

"But it is easier for heaven and earth to pass away than for one stroke of a letter of the Law to fail" (Luke 16:17).

Pharisees were lovers of law. Historically, they emerged as a separatist party from among scribes and sages in the second century before Christ. They took a role as teachers and law-keepers, becoming arbiters of Jewish religious law and even civil law. The common people of Jesus' day believed that Pharisees and scribes had authority over the requirements and interpretation of God's law, including observance of the Sabbath, as we saw in an earlier story (Luke 6:1–5).

Jesus stated that it would be easier for "heaven and earth to pass away" than for God's law to be annulled. Referring to even the tiny "stroke of a single letter," He used hyperbole to make His point. The great moral standards of the law, spelled out in the Ten Commandments, will remain forever. At the same time, many of the ancient ceremonial laws of Moses would cease to have relevance.[5] One example is the rite of circumcision, which the early church did not require of Gentile believers (Acts 15). On occasion, Jesus ignored some of the ceremonial laws, including touching what was ceremonially unclean (Luke 5:13; 7:14).

"Everyone who divorces his wife and marries another commits adultery, and he who marries one

who is divorced from a husband commits adultery" (Luke 16:18).

To illustrate what He meant, Jesus referred to a specific moral requirement of the seventh commandment: "You shall not commit adultery" (Exodus 20:14). Jewish men sometimes interpreted the command loosely and permitted divorce if the wife burned the food or gossiped.[6] On the topic of divorce, Matthew gave a fuller treatment (Matthew 5:32 and 19:7–9). Here Luke was simply emphasizing Jesus' role and authority as the ultimate lawgiver.[7]

Reflection

Which of the following is true for you?

1. I want to help my church reach its annual offering goal.
2. Those who give more than a set amount have their names on a plaque.
3. I like the good feeling when I give to meet desperate needs.
4. God says, "It is more blessed to give than to receive" (Acts 20:35).
5. I give to receive a charitable tax receipt.
6. I want to provide basic meals for ten hungry children.

1. Leon Morris, *Luke: An Introduction and Commentary*, Tyndale New Testament Commentaries, vol. 3 (Downers Grove, IL: IVP Academic, 1988), 267.

2. Darrell L. Bock, *Luke* (Grand Rapids, MI: Baker Academic, 1994), 1350.

3. Darrell L. Bock, *A Theology of Luke and Acts* (Grand Rapids, MI: Zondervan, 2012), 360–362.

4. William Barclay, *The Gospel of Luke* (Philadelphia, PA: Westminster Press, 1975), 211.

5. Morris, *Luke*, 268; Robert H. Stein, *Luke*, The New American Commentary, vol. 24 (Nashville, TN: Broadman, 1992), 419.

6. Barclay, *Gospel of Luke*, 212.

7. Bock, *Luke*, 1356, 1357.

Chapter 63

The Rich Man and Lazarus

Luke 16:19–31

Jesus' conversation with the Pharisees was not finished. He had just confirmed that the writings of the Scriptures—the Law and the Prophets—continued to be relevant and important, specifically, the laws of Moses that stress our responsibility to care for the hungry and destitute. Jesus now told a parable to show what that responsibility looks like in real life.[1]

"Now there was a rich man, and he habitually dressed in purple and fine linen, enjoying himself in splendor every day" (Luke 16:19).

The listening Pharisees were going to like this story because it was about a man who was very wealthy, which, they thought, meant he was righteous and greatly blessed. How wealthy was he? Well, his outer garments were purple—luxurious and very expensive because purple came from a costly Tyrian dye that was obtained from sea-snails.[2] His other clothing is "fine linen," which means that even his underwear is expensive. He lives luxuriously and dines sumptuously. What a great guy! At least, the Pharisees thought so.

"And a poor man named Lazarus was laid at his gate, covered with sores, and longing to be fed from the scraps which fell from the rich man's table; not only that, the dogs also were coming and licking his sores" (verses 20, 21).

What's especially surprising is that this beggar has a name, Lazarus, while the rich man remains unnamed. The equivalent Hebrew name for Lazarus is "Lazar," which "is the Greek form of Eleazer [Abraham's servant] and means *He whom God has helped.*"[3]

While the rich man had everything, Lazarus had nothing. He was almost certainly a cripple, carried and laid outside an ornate gate by someone who figured he would be given food by the wealthy occupant—but that did not happen. Lazarus longed for the scraps that fell on the floor from the rich man's table, but nothing was given to him. He also suffered from painful ulcerated sores on his body, and he apparently lacked the ability to turn away the mongrel dogs that pestered him by licking his sores. This likely caused infections and rendered him ceremonially unclean. His situation was absolutely revolting—crippled, hungry, covered with oozing and infected sores, and considered ceremonially unclean.

"Now it happened that the poor man died and was carried away by the angels to Abraham's arms; and the rich man also died and was buried. And in Hades he raised his eyes, being in torment, and saw Abraham far away and Lazarus in his arms" (verses 22, 23).

Death came to both individuals, and it changed everything. When the rich man died, he, of course, received a dignified burial. Lazarus had no burial, which meant his body would be discarded and exposed to carrion eaters—and the same scavenger dogs that licked his sores. Beyond that, though, there is a great reversal. Lazarus was carried by angels to the arms of Abraham, while the rich man found himself in Hades, tormented by mental and physical anguish. I imagine the listening Pharisees were scowling by this point!

The imagery matched Jewish eschatology, which taught that the righteous and unrighteous could see each other in Hades, the abode of the dead.[4] Hades was the name of a Greek god, one of the three sons of the gods Cronus and Rhea. The three sons defeated a coalition of other gods and claimed rulership of the cosmos, which was divided between them: Zeus received the sky, Poseidon, the sea, and Hades got the underworld.

"And he cried out and said, 'Father Abraham, have mercy on me and send Lazarus, so that he may dip the tip of his finger in water and cool off my tongue, for I am in agony in this flame.' But Abraham said, 'Child, remember that during your life you received your good things, and likewise Lazarus bad things; but now he is being comforted here, and you are in agony. And besides all this, between us and you a great chasm has been set, so that those who want to go over from here to you will not be able, nor will any people cross over from there to us' " (verses 24–26).

Sadly, the rich man was not humbled by his new and undoubtedly startling circumstances. Instead, he decided to rely on his spiritual heritage when he saw Lazarus with Father Abraham. Though the rich man forgot the warning, we should remember the words of John the Baptist, "Do not start saying to yourselves, 'We have Abraham as our father' " (Luke 3:8). The rich man assumed that Abraham is still his "father" and that Lazarus was present with Abraham in order to carry out errands for him. So, he asked Abraham to send Lazarus to him with some drops of water. Isn't it interesting that he now knew Lazarus by name but previously didn't acknowledge his existence outside his gate?

What has happened is totally unfair to the rich man's way of thinking. "He had not ordered Lazarus to be removed from his gate. . . . He did not kick him in the passing." Nor did he object if Lazarus ate some crumbs that got swept outside by his houseboy.[5]

Nevertheless, Abraham addressed the rich man tenderly, "Child, remember how things were for yourself and Lazarus? You never gave him one scrap of food, but now you want him to be your servant and bring you a drop of water. This cannot be. There is a great chasm between us."

"And he said, 'Then I request of you, father, that you send him to my father's house—for I have five brothers—in order that he may warn them, so that they will not come to this place of torment as well.' But Abraham said, 'They have Moses and the Prophets; let them hear them' " (Luke 16:27–29).

"Well, then, Father Abraham, let's try something else. Would you send Lazarus to my five brothers so that he can tell them what I am suffering and counsel them to repent?" But Abraham reminded the rich man that the Jewish Scriptures are replete with instructions and reminders to care for the needs of the poor, the widows, and orphans. The ancient book of Deuteronomy alone has seventeen references to the poor and widows: "Cursed is one who distorts the justice due a stranger, an orphan, or a widow. And all the people shall say, 'Amen' " (Deuteronomy 27:19). But the rich man had no interest in these things.

"But he said, 'No, father Abraham, but if someone goes to them from the dead, they will repent!' But he said to him, 'If they do not listen to Moses and the Prophets, they will not be persuaded even if someone rises from the dead' " (Luke 16:30, 31).

The rich man would not take no for an answer. "Continuing to speak from his supposed position of privilege, the wealthy man insists that, for his family, more is needed, that a special envoy is required."[6] He disagreed that reading the Scriptures was sufficient. After all, he himself had failed to heed what was written there.

Finally, Abraham responds, "If they don't listen to Moses and the prophets, they will not repent even if someone rises from the dead." The rich man had not listened to God's counsel through the prophets.

Abraham's statement would also be fulfilled after the resurrection of Jesus when millions would make life choices—some to everlasting life, others to eternal death. The Scriptures point to an end-time "resurrection when all will face God."[7] Clearly, "the rich man is not condemned because he is rich, but because he slipped into the coma of callousness that wealth often produces. He became consumed with his own joy, leisure, and celebration and failed to respond to the suffering and need of others around him."[8]

Reflection

Lazarus is not lying at your gate, but there are homeless individuals in your town who sleep on the streets and search waste receptacles for food scraps. What options do you have to help them?

---

1. Darrell L. Bock, *A Theology of Luke and Acts* (Grand Rapids, MI: Zondervan, 2012), 356.
2. *NIV Cultural Backgrounds Study Bible* (Grand Rapids, MI: Zondervan, 2016), 1782.
3. Robert H. Stein, *Luke*, The New American Commentary, vol. 24 (Nashville, TN: Broadman, 1992), 423; emphasis in the original.
4. Darrell L. Bock, *Luke* (Grand Rapids, MI: Baker Academic, 1994), 1369.
5. William Barclay, *The Gospel of Luke* (Philadelphia, PA: Westminster Press, 1975), 214.
6. Joel B. Green, *The Gospel of Luke*, New International Commentary on the New Testament, vol. 3 (Grand Rapids, MI: Eerdmans, 1997), 609.
7. Bock, *Luke*, 1360.
8. Bock, 1372.

Chapter 64

More Discipleship Lessons

Luke 17:1–10 (Matthew 18:6, 7, 21, 22)

The disciples (finally) took center stage again, but as usual, we can anticipate that some Pharisees will be close by, listening. The disciples learned as they followed Jesus, watched what He did, and listened to His parables, but they still needed pep talks sometimes. So, Jesus spelled out some counsel on four different topics.[1]

1. Causing people to stumble and sin

First up, Jesus taught about His disciples' interactions with others.

Now He said to His disciples, "It is inevitable that stumbling blocks come, but woe to one through whom they come! It is better for him if a millstone is hung around his neck and he is thrown into the sea, than that he may cause one of these little ones to sin. Be on your guard!" (Luke 17:1–3).

Reflecting upon causing other people to stumble, renowned Scottish New Testament interpreter William Barclay shared the following story: "When I was a lad, . . . I often played on a wide common. Near its centre, two roads met and crossed, and, standing at the cross-roads was an old, rickety sign-post. I remember one day twisting it round in its socket, thus altering the arms and making them point in the wrong direction; and I've been wondering ever since how many travellers I sent on the wrong road."[2]

No one is perfect; we are all prone to stumble and fall into sin, so any one of us may cause someone to go in the wrong direction. Here Jesus specifically warned about causing "little ones" to sin. By "little ones," He may be referring to children; to new disciples who need role models; or to individuals like Lazarus, the beggar; the lost son in the parable; and the poor, crippled, blind, and lame—or all of the above. Were the Pharisees listening to this?[3]

Having a millstone put around one's neck and being thrown into the sea means immediate death. A millstone was the heavy upper stone in a rotary grinding mill operated by a mule or donkey. Romans sometimes executed people guilty of particularly heinous crimes by drowning them, tied down with a heavy weight, but Jewish people regarded this punishment as too inhumane.[4] "Be on your guard!" Jesus says.

2. Forgiving repentant believers

Next, Jesus addressed the issue of forgiveness.

"If your brother sins, rebuke him; and if he repents, forgive him. And if he sins against you seven times a day, and returns to you seven times, saying, 'I repent,' you shall forgive him" (verses 3, 4).

Disciples have a commitment to each other—if one sins against another, he is to be gently rebuked and forgiven.* Jesus wanted His disciples to share in one another's commitment to pursue righteousness, so we are to be accountable to one another. Faith is not solely a private affair but something the community pursues together. The disciple is to show positive, honest, and loving behavior.[5]

Does forgiveness have a limit? Jesus said "seven times a day" for one who sins against you and repents. Matthew recorded a response to Peter, who asked how many times he should forgive someone. Jesus told him "seventy-seven times" (Matthew 18:22). In Matthew's account, an unrepentant sinner might be brought before the church for counsel. Jesus' point in both stories is that forgiveness has no limit but is always offered to the one who sincerely repents.[6]

3. Exercising faith

Jesus moves on to address the growth of individual faith.

The apostles said to the Lord, "Increase our faith!" But the Lord said, "If you had faith the size of a mustard seed, you could say to this mulberry tree, 'Be uprooted and be planted in the sea'; and it would obey you" (Luke 17:5, 6).

The change of topic seems like an interruption, but when Jesus taught about forgiveness with no limits, the disciples sensed they had a way to go. So, they said, "We need more faith, Lord."

Faith, though, is better measured by its quality than its quantity. Jesus proceeds to use the illustration of the mustard seed, one of the smallest seeds known to people at the time. The seed represents just a smidgeon of faith, but "you could say to this mulberry tree, 'Be uprooted and be planted in the sea' " (verse 6). I can almost hear the disciples laughing! And Jesus may be laughing with them. The black mulberry tree was known for its deep and extensive root system that made it almost impossible to remove. To replant it in the sea would be absurd.[7] Jesus made His point, though: a little faith can do incredible things and accomplish surprising results.

4. Having a servant's attitude

Jesus closed this teaching session by describing a disciple's heart for service.

"Now which of you, having a slave plowing or tending sheep, will say to him after he comes in from the field, 'Come immediately and recline at the table to eat'? On the contrary, will he not say to him, 'Prepare something for me to eat, and properly clothe yourself and serve me while I eat and drink; and afterward you may eat and drink'? He does not thank the slave because he did the things which were commanded, does he? So you too, when you do all the things which were commanded you, say, 'We are unworthy slaves; we have done only that which we ought to have done' " (verses 7–10).

In this little parable, Jesus drew on a well-known reality of village life in Palestine to teach something more about faithfulness. The disciple was to picture himself as the sole slave of a small farmer. That meant you were expected to perform all of the outdoor and household duties that on a large estate would be accomplished by several slaves.[8] After working hard all day in the field, you would return to the house,

---

* God asks us to forgive others as we have been forgiven. When possible, repentance and forgiveness may lead to a renewed relationship. However, reconciliation may not be advisable if the offender is unrepentant or may be impossible if the offender has died.

clean yourself up, and then prepare a meal for the family before you eat. This is expected of you. Do you ask for thanks or commendation? No.

Humility is tough to practice. The attitude of the disciple is to be one of humility. Paul would introduce himself as a slave of Jesus Christ (Romans 1:1, NLT). Obedience is not a cause for merit but a fulfillment of duty. "Even as one does the right thing for another without expectation of thanks, so one does the right thing for the Master of all without doing it for special notice, special privilege, or a chance to boast or be noticed as deserving approval."[9]

God will one day show His graciousness by thanking His faithful servants. "Wait until the Lord comes, who will . . . disclose the motives of human hearts; and then praise will come to each person from God" (1 Corinthians 4:5). In short, "to do what God asks is to do one's duty. Stay true, guard against sin, be forgiving, have faith, and serve dutifully—these are the traits of a growing disciple."[10]

Reflection

Read through the above four Scripture segments again, placing yourself in each situation as a listening disciple. Think about how you would react in each case.

---

1. Darrell L. Bock, *Luke* (Grand Rapids, MI: Baker Academic, 1994), 1380.

2. William Barclay, *The Gospel of Luke* (Philadelphia, PA: Westminster Press, 1975), 216.

3. Joel B. Green, *The Gospel of Luke*, New International Commentary on the New Testament, vol. 3 (Grand Rapids, MI: Eerdmans, 1997), 611.

4. *NIV Cultural Backgrounds Study Bible* (Grand Rapids, MI: Zondervan, 2016), 1647.

5. Bock, *Luke*, 1388.

6. Robert H. Stein, *Luke*, The New American Commentary, vol. 24 (Nashville, TN: Broadman, 1992), 430.

7. Leon Morris, *Luke: An Introduction and Commentary*, Tyndale New Testament Commentaries, vol. 3 (Downers Grove, IL: IVP Academic, 1988), 273.

8. Green, *Gospel of Luke*, 614.

9. Paul Borgman, *The Way According to Luke: Hearing the Whole Story of Luke-Acts* (Grand Rapids, MI: Eerdmans, 2006), 153.

10. Bock, *Luke*, 1395.

Chapter 65

A Grateful Samaritan

Luke 17:11–19

In most of the accounts we have read, Luke gave no clues about geographical location, perhaps because he was unfamiliar with Judean geography. However, we do know that the journey began by traveling through Samaria (Luke 9:51–53), and sometime later, they visited Martha and Mary at the village of Bethany, two miles from Jerusalem. In this story, they appear to be up north again, near the borders of Galilee and Samaria.

While He was on the way to Jerusalem, He was passing between Samaria and Galilee. And as He entered a village, ten men with leprosy who stood at a distance met Him; and they raised their voices, saying, "Jesus, Master, have mercy on us!" (Luke 17:11–13).

As Jesus and His followers approached an unnamed village, a group of ten lepers attracted their attention by shouting, "Jesus! Master! Have mercy on us!" (verse 13). Their disease prevented these men from entering the village, but they had heard about Jesus and called Him by name. They also called Him "Master" because they understood that He carried authority.

When He saw them, He said to them, "Go and show yourselves to the priests." And as they were going, they were cleansed (verse 14).

Out of consideration for the people traveling with Him—who may be assuming that *ten* lepers create *ten times* the risk of being near *one* of them—Jesus did not approach or touch the lepers. Instead, He gave them this instruction: "Go and show yourselves to the priests," the "purity inspectors" of Jewish society.[1]

Jesus did not promise healing for these lepers; He only told them to go find a priest. For each leper, nothing changed until he obeyed Jesus and began a faith journey to find a priest. Perhaps one recalled the biblical story of Naaman, the leper who obeyed an instruction to go and bathe in the Jordan to be cleansed (2 Kings 5:10–15)? This encounter with the ten lepers is the second Lukan account of Jesus' healing from a distance (see Luke 7:1–10).

Now one of them, when he saw that he had been healed, turned back, glorifying God with a loud voice, and he fell on his face at His feet, giving thanks to Him. And he was a Samaritan (Luke 17:15, 16).

The ten lepers left the scene. Luke doesn't expressly say that all ten followed through on their journey to find a priest, but it's apparent they did and rejoiced when they discovered they were healed. But did any return to thank Jesus, their Healer? Only one came back to thank Jesus, his face shining with the joy he felt. Praising God loudly for his healing, the restored man fell at Jesus' feet with words of gratitude.

Now Luke dropped the bombshell, and the identity of this one thankful person would shock the Jewish audience:[2] He was a Samaritan, an outsider, a foreigner!

Let's put ourselves in the thinking of this Samaritan leper.

Jesus said to go find a priest, but I don't know where to go. I can't go to the Jerusalem temple, because I'm not a Jew. I'd be forbidden to enter.

Perhaps I could go look for a Samaritan priest in our temple on Mount Gerizim. But he wouldn't be happy when he found out that I was sent by a Jewish rabbi.

I'm discouraged. This disease makes me feel wretched and unclean.

Jesus is a kind person. Should I go back and find Him? It's my only hope. Yes, I will go back to Jesus. And suddenly I'm clean.

Where did Luke learn his story? I want to imagine that Luke met this healed Samaritan while he was interviewing people in Palestine who remembered stories about Jesus. Jews and Samaritans do not mix, but since Luke was not a Jew, it was easy or him to visit Samaria. Perhaps someone lead him to this ex-leper with a story to tell.

What a beautiful story! As this former leper knelt at Jesus' feet, his heart overflowed with gratitude.

But Jesus responded and said, "Were there not ten cleansed? But the nine—where are they? Was no one found who returned to give glory to God, except this foreigner?" And He said to him, "Stand up and go; your faith has made you well" (verses 17–19).

Yes, this man was a foreigner, a Samaritan, an outcast, and not a child of Abraham in Jewish eyes. But in faith, he received healing and salvation. When Jesus said, "Your faith has made you well," the Greek words could also be translated, "Your faith has *saved* you."[4] Nine lepers received physical healing, but they missed the spiritual cleansing and total restoration Jesus freely offered. Truly, "the manner in which one responds to God's kindness is important. Anyone is a candidate for God's acts of grace, but that does not mean one has received grace's ultimate benefit. God's grace extends to all, but only some receive the gift of salvation."[5]

Commencing with this story of the Samaritan leper, Luke showcases examples of faithfulness, and we may be surprised by the list of candidates: a persistent widow (Luke 18:1–8), a self-confessed sinner at the temple (verses 9–14), a group of little children (verses 15–17), a sightless beggar (verses 35–43), and an overseer of tax collectors (Luke 19:1–10).[6] Look for their stories in the chapters ahead.

Reflection

How does this story illustrate what faith means? Why is it important to show gratitude to God? How can you do that?

---

1. Joel B. Green, *The Gospel of Luke*, New International Commentary on the New Testament, vol. 3 (Grand Rapids, MI: Eerdmans, 1997), 624.

2. Paul Borgman, *The Way According to Luke: Hearing the Whole Story of Luke-Acts* (Grand Rapids, MI: Eerdmans, 2006), 154.

3. Green, *Gospel of Luke*, 621.

4. Robert H. Stein, *Luke*, The New American Commentary, vol. 24 (Nashville, TN: Broadman, 1992), 434.

5. Darrell L. Bock, *Luke* (Grand Rapids, MI: Baker Academic, 1994), 1406.

6. Green, *Gospel of Luke*, 617.

Chapter 66

The Already and the Not Yet

Luke 17:20–37

Some of the Pharisees were slow learners. They had a belief about God's kingdom, but they didn't associate it with Jesus. In their thinking, the kingdom would arrive when someone—namely, the promised Messiah—ushered in a kingdom and brought independence from Rome. They were looking for a new "David" who would restore the Jewish monarchy. They believed the arrival of God's kingdom would be marked with cosmic signs and wonders. Unfortunately, they had it all wrong.

The "already" kingdom of grace

Jewish people were praying for the coming of God's kingdom, and they expected cosmic signs to foreshadow its arrival.[1] Knowing what they were thinking, Jesus told the Pharisees not to look for signs and wonders to usher in His kingdom.

Now He was questioned by the Pharisees as to when the kingdom of God was coming, and He answered them and said, "The kingdom of God is not coming with signs that can be observed; nor will they say, 'Look, here it is!' or, 'There it is!' For behold, the kingdom of God is in your midst" (Luke 17:20, 21).

In fact, the kingdom of grace was already present: it came with the arrival of Jesus on the planet. In the synagogue at Nazareth in Galilee, Jesus introduced the kingdom when He clearly stated His mission of bringing good news to the poor, restoration of sight to the blind, and release from the captivity of Satan (Luke 4:17–19). Visual evidence of God's kingdom was seen in the teachings of Jesus and His miraculous healings, the most recent being the cleansing of ten lepers.

If the Pharisees had just watched what Jesus was doing and teaching, they would have discovered that "the kingdom of God is [already] in your midst" (Luke 17:21). God's kingdom of grace was happening as lost sheep were found by the Shepherd, lost sons returned home, Satan's captives were released, and sinners were drawn to repentance.

The "not yet" kingdom of glory

Beyond the present, the kingdom of glory will arrive when Jesus returns the second time. The Pharisees listened as Jesus spoke to His disciples about that future kingdom. He began by referencing its timing (Luke 17:22–25), then its nature (verses 26–30), response to the event (verses 31–36), and an image of judgment (verse 37).[2]

And He said to the disciples, "The days will come when you will long to see one of the days of the

Son of Man, and you will not see it. And they will say to you, 'Look there,' or, 'Look here!' Do not leave, and do not run after them. For just like the lightning, when it flashes out of one part of the sky, shines to the other part of the sky, so will the Son of Man be in His day. But first He must suffer many things and be rejected by this generation" (verses 22–25).

People were already longing for the glorious "day of the Lord," which Luke described as "the days of the Son of Man," but they would have to be patient. This glorious kingdom would not happen until after Jesus passed through His time of suffering, death, and resurrection. So, He told them not to listen to false claims that Jesus' return had already happened in one place or another. His coming in glory will be seen by everybody. You won't be able to miss it. When that day arrives, things will happen decisively and quickly.

"And just as it happened in the days of Noah, so will it also be in the days of the Son of Man: people were eating, they were drinking, they were marrying, and they were being given in marriage, until the day that Noah entered the ark, and the flood came and destroyed them all. It was the same as happened in the days of Lot: they were eating, they were drinking, they were buying, they were selling, they were planting, and they were building; but on the day that Lot left Sodom, it rained fire and brimstone from heaven and destroyed them all. It will be just the same on the day that the Son of Man is revealed" (verses 26–30).

Jesus chose two well-known stories from Genesis to illustrate what will happen when He returns. It will be like the time of Noah. People were conducting their lives with little attention to God when the flood came (Genesis 6–8). It was a similar situation in the time of Lot when he escaped from the city of Sodom (Genesis 19). Those were times of judgment. Failure to decide for Jesus leaves a person defenseless before God.[3] Only those who embrace Jesus will welcome His coming in power and great glory.

"On that day, the one who will be on the housetop, with his goods in the house, must not go down to take them out; and likewise the one in the field must not turn back. Remember Lot's wife. Whoever strives to save his life will lose it, and whoever loses his life will keep it. I tell you, on that night there will be two in one bed; one will be taken and the other will be left. There will be two women grinding at the same place; one will be taken and the other will be left. Two men will be in the field; one will be taken and the other will be left" (Luke 17:31–36).

How will people respond to Christ's second coming? There will be a great sense of urgency. "Jesus brings this out by speaking of the two things people might be tempted to do. A man on a housetop might think of saving something from his house; a man in the field might turn back for a similar reason."[4] Lot's wife was consumed when she thought of going back to Sodom for the things that had become her life. When Jesus returns, only those who have put their lives in God's hands will be saved. Possessions will have no value then. Wholehearted devotion to Jesus replaces the desire for material possessions. In addition, Jesus described the occurrence of ordinary activities like two people sleeping in bed—"one in that bed belongs to God's reign, the other to Satan's domain."[5] Families may be torn apart. Crucial choices must be made before the time of the end.

And responding, they said to Him, "Where, Lord?" And He said to them, "Where the body is, there also the vultures will be gathered" (verse 37).

What exactly were the disciples asking? Jesus' response intimates that they were "concerned about the location of the judgment."[6] Judgment will be visible, universal, and permanent. "To follow Jesus means not to look back to the way life was before one came to follow him."[7]

Reflection

"Whoever strives to save his life will lose it, and whoever loses his life will keep it" (verse 33, in reference to the Second Coming). Ask yourself, How will the way I live in the "already" kingdom of grace prepare me for the "not yet" kingdom of glory?

1. *NIV Cultural Backgrounds Study Bible* (Grand Rapids, MI: Zondervan, 2016), 1786.

2. Darrell L. Bock, *Luke* (Grand Rapids, MI: Baker Academic, 1994), 1425.

3. Bock, 1432.

4. Leon Morris, *Luke: An Introduction and Commentary*, Tyndale New Testament Commentaries, vol. 3 (Downers Grove, IL: IVP Academic, 1988), 278.

5. Paul Borgman, *The Way According to Luke: Hearing the Whole Story of Luke-Acts* (Grand Rapids, MI: Eerdmans, 2006), 140.

6. Bock, *Luke*, 1438.

7. Darrell L. Bock, *A Theology of Luke and Acts* (Grand Rapids, MI: Zondervan, 2012), 320.

Chapter 67

A Bold Widow

Luke 18:1–8

Jesus spoke with His disciples about His second coming, describing an apocalyptic event that would be visible throughout the whole earth. For the faithful, it will be a grand and wonderful rescue from a sin-mangled planet, but it's also a final judgment for all who neglected to make friends with Jesus as their Savior. Two questions now need clarification: Will Jesus' return happen very soon after His ascension? If there is a delay, how should the faithful respond during times of trouble and persecution? Jesus used a parable to answer these questions.

Now He was telling them a parable to show that at all times they ought to pray and not become discouraged (Luke 18:1).

For Luke, as for the disciples, the second coming of Jesus "was a vibrant hope and expectation. Although it may appear to be delayed, Luke (and believers through the centuries) expected that the blessed hope (Titus 2:13) would take place soon."[1] There was a danger that if the event did not happen "soon," Jesus' followers might "become discouraged" and develop a business-as-usual attitude, losing their faith. Luke wrote that this parable would teach the need for constant prayer during the waiting, but a second underlying purpose will teach the importance of justice.

"In a certain city there was a judge who did not fear God and did not respect any person. Now there was a widow in that city, and she kept coming to him, saying, 'Give me justice against my opponent' " (Luke 18:2, 3).

We are introduced to two very different characters who live "in a certain city." The judge is probably the local magistrate, a male of notable status with a respectable standing in the community. "The Romans allowed the Jews to manage their own legal affairs," with the exception of capital punishment.[2] The judge is a thoroughly bad man—he has no regard for God or the law requiring love for our neighbor.[3] His lack of respect for people set the stage for a problem when a widow became involved in a court case.

The widow sought justice against an opponent. We're not given the particulars of the case, which might be a financial issue, or it could be that someone was contesting her right to a property left to her by her husband. Since the ancient court system belonged to the world of men, the fact that this woman found herself before a magistrate indicates that she had no family to bring her case to the court, and she lacked the economic resources to offer an appropriate bribe that would help her get a swift settlement.[4] This being the case, we may well ask, where are the people of her community? Why are her friends and neighbors not offering support or assistance in harmony with repeated Old Testament instruction to assist widows and orphans in their struggles: "Obtain justice for the orphan, plead for the widow's case" (Isaiah 1:17)?

This helpless, powerless woman appealed over and over to someone in authority to vindicate her.

"For a while he was unwilling; but later he said to himself, 'Even though I do not fear God nor respect any person, yet because this widow is bothering me, I will give her justice; otherwise by continually coming she will wear me out' " (Luke 18:4, 5).

For how long did this woman seek a settlement from this judge? Apparently, long enough for him to feel badgered by her! This was astonishing behavior for a widow. We would have expected her to make a single attempt for a settlement and, upon refusal, to back off and become a helpless, hopeless victim. This woman is acting so out of the norm that the judge wonders whether she may be capable of assaulting him with more than words! Clearly, "the language Luke uses is startling, perhaps even humorous, borrowed as it is from the boxing ring, for it invokes images of the almighty, fearless, macho judge cornered and slugged by the least powerful in society."[5] Lest she give him a black eye, he finally gave her justice.[6]

And the Lord said, "Listen to what the unrighteous judge said; now, will God not bring about justice for His elect who cry out to Him day and night, and will He delay long for them? I tell you that He will bring about justice for them quickly" (verses 6–8).

In drawing the lesson from the parable, Jesus again used the argument from the lesser to the greater. If an unjust judge will finally grant justice, *how much more* will God do so for His faithful ones? He is willing and waiting to respond to our prayer needs. Sometimes, in our brokenness, we fail to discern what our real needs are, so God listens and waits patiently for us to accept His will for our lives.

The parable seeks to bring encouragement for those who wait for the second coming of Jesus. During the waiting time, God's people will be the object of injustice within a corrupt world. Like the widow of the parable, they must never give up. Jesus told His disciples and others who were listening that "at all times they ought to pray and not become discouraged" (verse 1). Persistence in prayerful faith is the name of the waiting game.

"However, when the Son of Man comes, will He find faith on the earth?" (verse 8).

Luke made it clear that disciples are to walk by faith, especially when they are under pressure and persecution for confessing Jesus. Truly, "these words of comfort call believers to enduring hope. As Luke has said, Jesus' hope is that when the Son of Man comes, He will find disciples still waiting for His coming."[7]

Reflection

Let's imagine the widow lives in our community. Do we have a responsibility to her? What are your options?

---

1. Robert H. Stein, *Luke*, The New American Commentary, vol. 24 (Nashville, TN: Broadman, 1992), 446.

2. Darrell L. Bock, *Luke* (Grand Rapids, MI: Baker Academic, 1994), 1447.

3. Paul Borgman, *The Way According to Luke: Hearing the Whole Story of Luke-Acts* (Grand Rapids, MI: Eerdmans, 2006), 119.

4. Joel B. Green, *The Gospel of Luke*, New International Commentary on the New Testament, vol. 3 (Grand Rapids, MI: Eerdmans, 1997), 640.

5. Green, 641.

6. William Barclay, *The Gospel of Luke* (Philadelphia, PA: Westminster Press, 1975), 222.

7. Bock, *Luke*, 1456.

Chapter 68

The Pharisee and the Tax Collector

Luke 18:9–17

Now He also told this parable to some people who trusted in themselves that they were righteous, and viewed others with contempt: "Two men went up into the temple to pray, one a Pharisee and the other a tax collector" (Luke 18:9, 10).

Like the preceding parable, this one is about prayer, but the focus has changed. Instead of prayer persistence, this story is about prayer attitude. We have Pharisees in mind because of previous incidents involving their self-righteousness and self-exaltation, but the disciples also needed to pay attention.

In the parable, we again meet two very different characters. The only thing they have in common is they're both going up to the temple to pray. "Up" is the appropriate word because the Jerusalem temple is on a hill. Upon arriving at the temple, the two men took positions of their choice.

"The Pharisee stood and began praying this in regard to himself: 'God, I thank You that I am not like other people: swindlers, crooked, adulterers, or even like this tax collector. I fast twice a week; I pay tithes of all that I get' " (verses 11, 12).

The pharisee stands, which is the usual posture in temple prayer. Notice that he managed to refer to himself five times in his prayer: "I thank," "I am," "I fast," "I pay," "I get." "His attitude was clear. God was very fortunate to have someone like him."[1] He contrasted himself with a variety of unrighteous individuals, including swindlers. Perhaps the reference to "swindlers" drew his attention to the tax collector who stood in a far corner of the temple, so he added, "I'm glad I'm not like that tax collector." This judgmental statement was based solely on the other man's occupation.

Then the Pharisee proceeded to tell God about his religious activities. First, Pharisees were fastidious about tithing. Jesus accused them of tithing even the small herbs in their gardens while ignoring love and mercy (Luke 11:42). Second, while the Jewish law required fasting only on the annual Day of Atonement, many Pharisees fasted without water on Mondays and Thursdays as evidence of their piety.[2] "No man who is proud can pray. The gate of heaven is so low that none can enter it save upon his knees."[3]

"But the tax collector, standing some distance away, was even unwilling to raise his eyes toward heaven, but was beating his chest, saying, 'God, be merciful to me, the sinner!' " (Luke 18:13).

In a far-off corner of the temple stood the tax collector, who felt unworthy to approach God. He bowed his head and beat his chest to show his penitence. Acknowledging his sinfulness as a not-always-honest collector of Roman revenue, he prayed for mercy, "God, be merciful to me, the sinner" (verse 13). He made no comparison to others; rather, "he is concerned only with improving his own spiritual health, and he knows that the only way to do so is to rely totally on God's mercy."[4]

"I tell you, this man went to his house justified rather than the other one; for everyone who exalts himself will be humbled, but the one who humbles himself will be exalted" (verse 14).

A spiritual reversal took place in that temple scene. A Pharisee who exalted himself would be humbled, while a tax collector who humbled himself and sought God's mercy would be exalted and justified before God. His prayer may remind us of David's prayer after his sin with Bathsheba:

> Have mercy on me, O God,
>   because of your unfailing love.
> Because of your great compassion,
>   blot out the stain of my sins.
> Wash me clean from my guilt (Psalm 51:1, 2, NLT).

In fact, "the security that one receives through Jesus' work is grounded in God's grace and mercy, not one's works."[5] Paul said it clearly in his letter to the Ephesians: "For by grace you have been saved through faith; and this is not of yourselves, it is the gift of God; not a result of works, so that no one may boast" (Ephesians 2:8, 9).

Babies for blessing

In what may seem at first like an abrupt transition, Luke next tells about parents who brought their children for Jesus to bless (also Matthew 19:13–15; Mark 10:13–16).

Now they were bringing even their babies to Him so that He would touch them; but when the disciples saw it, they began rebuking them. But Jesus called for the little ones, saying, "Allow the children to come to Me, and do not forbid them, for the kingdom of God belongs to such as these. Truly I say to you, whoever does not receive the kingdom of God like a child will not enter it at all" (Luke 18:15–17).

There was a high mortality rate among children in the first century. Babies were especially vulnerable to sicknesses and diseases of various kinds.[6] Besides, children possessed little, if any, intrinsic value as human beings and occupied a low status in society. Against this background, the reaction of the disciples is understandable. Why should Jesus' time be taken up by persons of little importance?

But Jesus overturned this cultural norm: "Allow the children to come to me." Why did Jesus pay special attention to the children? Because children have not lost their sense of wonder and trust. In fact, Jesus counseled His followers to cultivate a childlike spirit. For "to keep alive the sense of wonder, to live in unquestioning trust, to obey, to forgive and to forget—that is the childlike spirit."[7]

Jesus' kingdom represents a reversal of cultural values. Pride and self-serving are replaced by humility and compassion for the "little ones" of Jewish society, which include all individuals outside the boundaries of social and religious rank.

Reflection

Pride is a large part of our humanity. Why is it so dangerous to our spiritual condition?

---

1. Robert H. Stein, *Luke*, The New American Commentary, vol. 24 (Nashville, TN: Broadman, 1992), 448.

2. *NIV Cultural Backgrounds Study Bible* (Grand Rapids, MI: Zondervan, 2016), 1785.

3. William Barclay, *The Gospel of Luke* (Philadelphia, PA: Westminster Press, 1975), 224.

4. Darrell L. Bock, *Luke* (Grand Rapids, MI: Baker Academic, 1994), 1464.

5. Bock, 1466.

6. Joel B. Green, *The Gospel of Luke*, New International Commentary on the New Testament, vol. 3 (Grand Rapids, MI: Eerdmans, 1997), 650.

7. Barclay, *Gospel of Luke*, 227.

Chapter 69

The Rich Young Ruler

Luke 18:18–30 (Matthew 19:16–30; Mark 10:17–31)

While Jesus was with the group of mothers, blessing their children, a well-dressed young man stood nearby, perhaps impatiently. I'm sure he wondered, *Why is this rabbi wasting His time and energy with worthless kids?* Everyone in Jewish society knew that young children had little value to anyone. Once they were old enough to work, they grew in value as they helped with farm chores, ran errands, and obeyed commands. Finally, the young man got Jesus' attention.

A ruler questioned Him, saying, "Good Teacher, what shall I do to inherit eternal life?" But Jesus said to him, "Why do you call Me good? No one is good except God alone" (Luke 18:18, 19).

Most of the parables and stories in the recent chapters of Luke are unique to his Gospel. This story, though, is also told by Matthew and Mark, and from the three accounts, we learn that this man is young, a ruler, and wealthy.

The young man had been listening to Jesus' words about having the faith of a little child. And that exchange made him wonder, *If that is how you qualify for entry into God's kingdom, how do you gain eternal life? How can I be sure I'll be saved in the final resurrection?* What Jesus said didn't seem to make sense, so he put his question directly to Jesus, addressing Him as "Good Teacher." By labeling Him "good," the young man may be trying to say, "Teacher, you're too good to be spending time with little kids." Jesus read his thoughts and took exception to his remark.[1]

"You know the commandments, 'Do not commit adultery, Do not murder, Do not steal, Do not give false testimony, Honor your father and mother.' " And he said, "All these things I have kept since my youth" (verses 20, 21).

The ruler asked what he should *do* to get eternal life, and Jesus responded by repeating some of the Ten Commandments. You need to *do* these things. But is that all I have to *do*? It seems that the young man has forgotten that the law also says, "You shall love your neighbor as yourself" (Leviticus 19:18).

Now when Jesus heard this, He said to him, "One thing you still lack; sell all that you possess and distribute the money to the poor, and you will have treasure in heaven; and come, follow Me." But when he had heard these things, he became very sad, for he was extremely wealthy (Luke 18:22, 23).

The rich young ruler must've been scratching his head. What Jesus said did not please him. Did it not occur to him that many of his brothers, sons of Abraham like himself, were clad with rags, dying of hunger, while his house was filled with goods?[2] He's "extremely wealthy," which is what gave him status in the community and, in the eyes of many, a special status with God.

Contrary to popular opinion, Jesus taught that entry into the kingdom of God involves a great reversal of values. Selfishness and greed often go hand-in-hand with wealth, and "only a wicked person would continue to pile up 'great wealth' and so destroy others."[3] In opposition to the prevailing ideas, Jesus asked this young man to divest himself of his assets so that he could benefit the poor. Instead of trusting in his wealth, he needed to put his trust in Jesus and store his treasure in heaven.

The young ruler was perplexed by what Jesus said. *Sell all my stuff? Or even most of it? No way! Jesus is asking too much, way too much.* Jesus and His listeners watched as sadness stole across the man's face. He turned away and left, not to be seen or heard from again. His departure brings sorrow to Jesus.

And Jesus looked at him and said, "How hard it is for those who are wealthy to enter the kingdom of God! For it is easier for a camel to go through the eye of a needle, than for a rich person to enter the kingdom of God!" Those who heard Him said, "And so who can be saved?" But He said, "The things that are impossible with people are possible with God" (verses 24–27).

Now it's the disciples who are puzzled. What did Jesus Say? "It is easier for a camel to go through the eye of a needle, than for a rich person to enter the kingdom of God." That's a proverbial saying, based on a legend that somewhere in the walls of Jerusalem is a low gate where a camel's load has to be removed and the animal gets down on its knees to get through. It's a humorous expression for a purposes of exaggeration.

Selfishness is not compatible with kingdom membership. Jesus has previously talked about a "narrow door" into the kingdom (Luke 13:24), but "wealth can shrink the door of the kingdom down to an impassable peephole."[4] And "He [Jesus] also tells the disciples that although it is impossible for a rich man on his own to enter the kingdom and be saved, what is impossible for humans God can do. That is, God can change a person's heart."[5]

The disciples weren't doing very well with Jesus' teaching on this particular day. They had already rebuked mothers for bringing their children to Jesus (Luke 18:15, 16), and now they interpreted Jesus' words to mean that it is impossible to enter God's kingdom unless you dispose of everything you own.

Peter said, "Behold, we have left our own homes and followed You." And He said to them, "Truly I say to you, there is no one who has left house, or wife, or brothers, or parents, or children for the sake of the kingdom of God, who will not receive many times as much at this time, and in the age to come, eternal life" (verses 28–30).

Peter reminded Jesus that he and the other disciples had already done what He asked the young ruler to do. "We have left our own homes and followed You" (verse 28). Yes, you have, Jesus said, but discipleship is more than that. Humility, the faith of a little child, and trust in Jesus are the way to salvation.[6]

Some see this story as an echo of Jesus' parable of the good Samaritan, who used his wealth to show mercy and life to a wayside traveler beaten by robbers.[7] Those who give up all for Jesus receive "many times as much" of spiritual riches, a relationship with Jesus, and exactly what the rich young ruler was seeking—eternal life in the age to come.

Reflection

Those of us who live in North America are among the wealthiest 5 percent of the world's population. How does Jesus' advice to the rich young ruler apply to us?

1. Joel B. Green, *The Gospel of Luke*, New International Commentary on the New Testament, vol. 3 (Grand Rapids, MI: Eerdmans, 1997), 655.

2. Wilhelm Shneemelcher and R. Mel. Wilson, eds., *New Testament Apocrypha* (Louisville, KY: Westminster/John Knox Press, 1991).

3. Randolph E. Richards and Brandon J. O'Brien, *Misreading Scripture With Western Eyes* (Downers Grove, IL: InterVarsity, 2012), 42.

4. Darrell L. Bock, *Luke* (Grand Rapids, MI: Baker Academic, 1994), 1486.

5. Darrell L. Bock, *A Theology of Luke and Acts* (Grand Rapids, MI: Zondervan, 2012), 107.

6. Green, *Gospel of Luke*, 658.

7. Paul Borgman, *The Way According to Luke: Hearing the Whole Story of Luke-Acts* (Grand Rapids, MI: Eerdmans, 2006), 109, 110.

Chapter 70

The Irony of Blindness

Luke 18:31–43 (Matthew 20:17–19, 29–34; Mark 10:32–34, 46–52)

The long, winding journey to Jerusalem has reached its final segment. As Jesus approached Jerusalem via Jericho, He offered His disciples a final, detailed preview of what awaited Him there.

Now He took the twelve aside and said to them, "Behold, we are going up to Jerusalem, and all the things that have been written through the prophets about the Son of Man will be accomplished. For He will be handed over to the Gentiles, and will be ridiculed, and abused, and spit upon, and after they have flogged Him, they will kill Him; and on the third day He will rise" (Luke 18:31–33).

This is the seventh time that Jesus has talked about His passion in the presence of the disciples. On three occasions in the lead-up to their departure from Galilee, all recorded in Luke 9, Jesus broached the topic with them:[1]

1. Immediately after Peter's declaration of Jesus as "the Christ of God" (verses 20–22)
2. In Jesus' conversation with Moses and Elijah during the Transfiguration (verses 30, 31)
3. In a private conversation with the disciples shortly before their departure to Jerusalem (verses 44, 45)

Then, on three subsequent occasions, Jesus spoke about His approaching suffering and death:

1. Talking about the "baptism of fire" He was soon to undergo (Luke 12:49, 50)
2. Responding to Herod's plan to kill Him (Luke 13:32, 33)
3. Describing His future return in glory (Luke 17:25)

Now, as Jesus again spoke about His approaching death and resurrection, He said it was happening in fulfillment of Old Testament prophecies (examples include Isaiah 53 and Psalm 22). "It was God's will and plan that these events occur."[2]

The disciples understood none of these things, and the meaning of this statement was hidden from them, and they did not comprehend the things that were said (Luke 18:34).

The disciples heard the words, but their meaning did not register with them. They could not figure out how Jesus' death could fit into the divine plan. The idea of a suffering Messiah—their King—is anathema to them. It would take the cross and an empty tomb to awaken the minds of the disciples.[3] Until then, they were blind to God's unfolding plan.

Restoring Sight

Now as Jesus was approaching Jericho, a man who was blind was sitting by the road, begging. But when he heard a crowd going by, he began inquiring what this was. They told him that Jesus of Nazareth was passing by. And he called out, saying, "Jesus, Son of David, have mercy on me!" Those who led the way were sternly telling him to be quiet; but he kept crying out all the more, "Son of David, have mercy on me!" (Luke 18:35–39).

A crowd traveled with Jesus as He approached Jericho from the north. Some in the crowd might have been Galileans on their pilgrimage to Jerusalem for the annual Passover festival. As they walked along together, Jesus was probably teaching, as was typical of many a rabbi.[4] On the roadside sat a blind beggar, identified by Mark as Bartimaeus (Mark 10:46), who wondered about this crowd passing by. Someone told him, "Jesus of Nazareth is passing by"; that's how most Galileans described Jesus.

Bartimaeus had heard of Jesus and identified Him not merely as "Jesus of Nazareth" but as the promised Messiah. He called loudly, "Jesus, Son of David, have mercy on me." Jesus is indeed the promised Son of David. Isn't it remarkable that a beggar, one of the "expendables" in Jewish society, has more faith knowledge of Jesus than the religious leaders? Jesus' own "disciples are blind with regard to God's plan, just as the beggar was physically blind."[5]

Predictably, the crowd tried to make the beggar shut up, but he cried even louder, "Jesus, Son of David, have mercy on me."

And Jesus stopped and commanded that he be brought to Him; and when he came near, He asked him, "What do you want Me to do for you?" And he said, "Lord, I want to regain my sight!" And Jesus said to him, "Regain your sight; your faith has made you well." And immediately he regained his sight and began following Him, glorifying God; and when all the people saw it, they gave praise to God (Luke 18:40–43).

Jesus stopped and asked that the blind man be brought to Him. He then put a faith question to the man: "What do you want Me to do for you?" The blind man responded with faith: "I want to regain my sight" (verse 41), and Jesus responded by saying, "Regain your sight. Your faith has made you well" (verse 42). The Greek of Jesus' response can also be translated, "Your faith has *saved* you." Bartimaeus immediately became a follower of Jesus. His story is a powerful contrast to the rich young ruler. The rich man walked away with sadness, while the beggar walked forward with joy, a new disciple of Christ.

In this story, we see "the continuing resistance of some to the topsy-turvy values of the kingdom, which accord privilege to the least, the last, and the left-out of society."[6] We have again seen the great reversal: "the first," epitomized by the rich young ruler, were blinded by their riches, while "the last," represented by the tax collectors and the blind beggar, now see and enter *the kingdom*.[7]

Reflection

Jesus asked Bartimaeus, "What would you like Me to do for you?" If Jesus asked you that question today, what would you tell Him?

---

1. Joel B. Green, *The Gospel of Luke*, New International Commentary on the New Testament, vol. 3 (Grand Rapids, MI: Eerdmans, 1997), 659.

2. Darrell L. Bock, *A Theology of Luke and Acts* (Grand Rapids, MI: Zondervan, 2012), 128.

3. Leon Morris, *Luke: An Introduction and Commentary,* Tyndale New Testament Commentaries, vol. 3 (Downers Grove, IL: IVP Academic, 1988), 287.

4. William Barclay, *The Gospel of Luke* (Philadelphia, PA: Westminster Press, 1975), 232.

5. Darrell L. Bock, *Luke* (Grand Rapids, MI: Baker Academic, 1994), 1501.

6. Green, *Gospel of Luke*, 662.

7. Robert H. Stein, *Luke*, The New American Commentary, vol. 24 (Nashville, TN: Broadman, 1992), 465.

Chapter 71

Salvation in Jericho

Luke 19:1–10

Finally, Jesus and His entourage arrived at Jericho, the new city built by Herod the Great. The ruins of the old Jericho, captured by Israel under Joshua's leadership, were a short distance away. The new city is seven hundred feet below sea level, six miles from the Jordan River, and a few miles north of the Dead Sea. The city is also eighteen miles from Jerusalem, which is at a much higher altitude of 2,500 feet.[1] Jericho was a beautiful and wealthy town; known in those days as the "city of palms," it held residences for aristocratic priests and a winter palace once inhabited by Herod the Great.

Jesus entered Jericho and was passing through. And there was a man called by the name of Zaccheus; he was a chief tax collector and he was rich. Zaccheus was trying to see who Jesus was, and he was unable due to the crowd, because he was short in stature. So he ran on ahead and climbed up a sycamore tree in order to see Him, because He was about to pass through that way. And when Jesus came to the place, He looked up and said to him, "Zaccheus, hurry and come down, for today I must stay at your house." And he hurried and came down, and received Him joyfully (Luke 19:1–6).

The story of Zaccheus is another Luke original. In his creative literary style, Luke has pieced together two consecutive accounts of how Jesus responded to outcasts of society: a blind beggar on the outskirts of Jericho who cried out to Jesus and a short tax collector who worked his way up a tree to see Him. In each story, people were a problem: they tried to stop Jesus from helping the blind man, and they complained loudly when Jesus spent time with a despised tax collector. Zaccheus was an important man in Jericho, but he knew what it was like to be lonely.[2]

We have met several tax collectors in Luke's Gospel, but Zaccheus is identified as "a chief tax collector." Jericho was situated on an important Eastern trade route, and it also marked the strategic border between Judea and Perea, so customs duties there are significant.[3]

The region was also famous for the lucrative production and export of an aromatic gum known as balsam. Given the Roman tax on exports, Jericho was a regional tax center. Zaccheus was a wealthy man at the top of the tax pyramid and, therefore, especially hated by the townspeople as a "great sinner." He is a Jew, a ruler, a tax collector, and wealthy.[4]

Zaccheus hadn't met Jesus, but he was curious about Him. Being short in stature, he found it difficult to see Jesus in the large crowd, which pressed close to Him. He solved his problem by running ahead of Jesus and climbing into the branches of a street-side sycamore. This was not a dignified thing to do, but perched on a large tree branch, Zaccheus had a bird's eye view of Jesus as He came by with the crowd. It was at this moment that Jesus made a surprise move. He stopped, looked up at Zaccheus, and told him to come down from his tree:[5] "Zaccheus, I'm planning to stay at your house tonight."

When the people saw this, they all began to complain, saying, "He has gone in to be the guest of a man who is a sinner!" (verse 7).

The little man was excited and very happy, even as the pressing crowd launched into criticism. "Jesus is going to be the guest of a sinner! Can you believe it?" These people loved Jesus' miracles, but they didn't care for His personal associations. Meanwhile, Jesus followed Zaccheus to his house.

But Zaccheus stopped and said to the Lord, "Behold, Lord, half of my possessions I am giving to the poor, and if I have extorted anything from anyone, I am giving back four times as much." And Jesus said to him, "Today salvation has come to this house, because he, too, is a son of Abraham. For the Son of Man has come to seek and to save that which was lost" (verses 8–10).

It appears from the text that Zaccheus's conversation with Jesus occurred in a public setting, perhaps outside the door of his house. "Lord, I will give half of my possessions to the poor." Without a word of counsel from Jesus, this man's initiative to give half his wealth to the poor came from a heart touched by the Holy Spirit. He continued with a further unsolicited commitment to make fourfold restitution of any dishonest wealth. Considering the way Zaccheus has made his money, it is unlikely he has a short list for restitution. Fourfold restoration was the most demanding penalty of the Mosaic law. For example, someone who stole a sheep that subsequently died was to pay the owner four times the value of the animal (Exodus 22:1).[6]

Rejected by society, Zaccheus responded "with a faith that [sought] to compensate for sins previously committed."[7] Jesus' response was for everyone listening: "Salvation has come to Zaccheus and his house today." He described Zaccheus as a true "son of Abraham," or one who had "brought forth fruit in keeping with repentance," as John had characterized the true children of Abraham (Luke 3:8).[8]

Now, in the hearing of the crowd, Jesus again declared His mission: "The Son of Man has come to seek and save that which was lost" (Luke 19:10). Jesus came to Jericho to save a lost Zaccheus. Before He left the city, He had a parable to share with the people. It's a complex one that perplexes many of Luke's readers.

Reflection

Luke, more than any other Gospel writer, has recorded stories and teachings about wealth and possessions. Read 2 Corinthians 8:9 and think about God's order of values.

1. Darrell L. Bock, *Luke* (Grand Rapids, MI: Baker Academic, 1994), 1505.
2. William Barclay, *The Gospel of Luke* (Philadelphia, PA: Westminster Press, 1975), 234.
3. *NIV Cultural Backgrounds Study Bible* (Grand Rapids, MI: Zondervan, 2016), 1786.
4. Joel B. Green, *The Gospel of Luke*, New International Commentary on the New Testament, vol. 3 (Grand Rapids, MI: Eerdmans, 1997), 668.
5. Bock, *Luke*, 1517.
6. Bock, 1513.
7. Darrell L. Bock, *A Theology of Luke and Acts* (Grand Rapids, MI: Zondervan, 2012), 261.
8. Robert H. Stein, *Luke*, The New American Commentary, vol. 24 (Nashville, TN: Broadman, 1992), 469.

Chapter 72

Two Interwoven Parables

Luke 19:11–27 (Matthew 25:14–30)

Jericho was the setting for a particular teaching of Jesus—a complex story that is better interpreted as two separate parables that were interwoven by Luke.[1] The common thread is the waiting time between Jesus' departure and His future return. Each story has a unique purpose and set of characters. Common to both is a king. In this lesson, we will interpret Luke's text as two separate parables.

Parable about stewardship

Now while they were listening to these things, Jesus went on to tell a parable, because He was near Jerusalem and they thought that the kingdom of God was going to appear immediately. So He said, "A nobleman went to a distant country to receive a kingdom for himself, and then to return. And he called ten of his own slaves and gave them ten minas, and said to them, 'Do business with this money until I come back.'" But his citizens hated him and sent a delegation after him, saying, "We do not want this man to reign over us" (Luke 19:11–14).

The story has some similarities to a parable found in Matthew 25, but there are also significant differences. It is likely that Jesus talked about stewardship to different people in different settings, so we should treat Luke's account independently of Matthew's. Both Matthew's and Luke's parables are presented as told by Jesus shortly before His final arrival in Jerusalem. Luke's is told at Jericho just as Jesus begins the final leg of His journey to Jerusalem.

In the parable, Jesus is portrayed as "a nobleman" who travels to a distant country—heaven—to be crowned "KING OF KINGS AND LORD OF LORDS" when He returns in glory (Revelation 19:16). Each of His earthly subjects, represented here as slaves, are given gifts or abilities to invest in the lives of others through their works of compassion. The mina was an ancient unit of weight, equal to sixty shekels and equivalent to three months' wages for a working man. Each man is called to be a steward of the talents he has been given—the sick healed, the poor relieved, and sinners brought to repentance.

"When he returned after receiving the kingdom, he ordered that these slaves, to whom he had given the money, be summoned to him so that he would learn how much they had made by the business they had done. The first slave appeared, saying, 'Master, your mina has made ten minas more.' And he said to him, 'Well done, good slave; since you have been faithful in a very little thing, you are to have authority over ten cities.' The second one came, saying, 'Your mina, master, has made five minas.' And he said to him also, 'And you are to be over five cities'" (Luke 19:15–19).

Because few people had capital, those who did were able to lend money at significant interest, so an investor might receive five or ten times his investment. Roman law allowed slaves not only to manage estates but also to earn and hold money and receive bonuses.[2]

The parable teaches accountability. Each slave was to use wisely what he had been given, trusting in the goodness of the Master and assured of final blessing and commendation as he fulfilled his kingdom responsibilities. He must not be like the rich young ruler and hoard the wealth but be like Zacchaeus the tax collector and serve the needy. Failure to carry out God's purpose is illustrated by a slave who hoards his gift.

"And then another came, saying, 'Master, here is your mina, which I kept tucked away in a handkerchief; for I was afraid of you, because you are a demanding man; you take up what you did not lay down, and reap what you did not sow.' He said to him, 'From your own lips I will judge you, you worthless slave. Did you know that I am a demanding man, taking up what I did not lay down, and reaping what I did not sow? And so why did you not put my money in the bank, and when I came back, I would have collected it with interest?' And then he said to the other slaves who were present, 'Take the mina away from him and give it to the one who has the ten minas.' And they said to him, 'Master, he already has ten minas.' 'I tell you that to everyone who has, more shall be given, but from the one who does not have, even what he does have shall be taken away' " (verses 20–26).

When rewards were given, God's justice and beneficence were clearly manifest. In the parable, some were watching the evaluation and considered it unfair that the unfaithful servant was left with nothing—his mina was given to the one who already had ten (verse 25). The parable teaches that God's grace is abundant and knows no bounds, but "there is no such thing as standing still in the Christian life. We either get more or lose what we have."[3] We reflect on Jesus' words at an earlier time, "Take care how you listen; for whoever has, to him more will be given; and whoever does not have, even what he thinks he has will be taken away from him" (Luke 8:18). Essentially, "The parable of the pounds [minas] is a warning that Jesus will be gone for some time and that on his return he will evaluate people's faithfulness to him. Those who are faithful will be rewarded generously."[4]

Parable of the rejected king

So He said, "A nobleman went to a distant country to receive a kingdom for himself, and then to return. . . . But his citizens hated him and sent a delegation after him, saying, 'We do not want this man to reign over us' " (Luke 19:12–14).

In untangling the two parables, our understanding of this one becomes clearer when we review a historical event that the Jews knew well. When Herod the Great died in 4 BC, his three sons took a trip to Rome, where Caesar Augustus divided the Jewish nation this way:

- Herod Archelaus received the lion's share of the kingdom: Idumea, Judea, and Samaria.
- Herod Antipas received Galilee.
- Philip received the far north as a tetrarchy.

Archelaus was strongly disliked by the people, especially after he severely crushed the Pharisees. The

Jews sent a delegation of fifty men to Rome to protest Archelaus's actions, and the emperor compromised in AD 6 by diminishing his power and having the Roman governor fill his shoes.[5] Jesus' parable reflects these historical events.

So, the nobleman's departure corresponds theologically to Jesus' death, resurrection, and ascension. But even before He arrived in Jerusalem, the Jewish nation was preparing to reject Him as their future King. They would soon cry, "We have no king except Caesar" (John 19:15).

"But as for these enemies of mine who did not want me to reign over them, bring them here and slaughter them in my presence" (Luke 19:27).

The parable has short- and long-term applications. Jesus' reign commences at His departure to heaven after the Resurrection, but it will not be consummated until His return. During the waiting time before He comes back, many will reject Him as their Lord and King. When He returns, there will be judgment for the unrighteous (Revelation 20). Clearly, "There is no neutral position in relationship to Jesus: one chooses for him and sees his gracious work as unique, or one aligns against him."[6]

Those who are faithful may stand proudly as members of God's kingdom. Paul confirms this: "For He rescued us from the domain of darkness, and transferred us to the kingdom of His beloved Son, in whom we have redemption, the forgiveness of sins" (Colossians 1:13, 14).

Reflection

Ask yourself, What abilities has God given me? How will I use those abilities to share Christ's love and do His work while I await His return?

---

1. Leon Morris, *Luke: An Introduction and Commentary*, Tyndale New Testament Commentaries, vol. 3 (Downers Grove, IL: IVP Academic, 1988), 291.
2. *NIV Cultural Backgrounds Study Bible* (Grand Rapids, MI: Zondervan, 2016), 1787, 1788.
3. William Barclay, *The Gospel of Luke* (Philadelphia, PA: Westminster Press, 1975), 238.
4. Darrell L. Bock, *Luke* (Grand Rapids, MI: Baker Academic, 1994), 1543.
5. Bock, 1525, 1526.
6. Bock, 1543.

Chapter 73

Last Steps to Jerusalem

Luke 19:28

After Jesus said these things, He was going on ahead, going up to Jerusalem (Luke 19:28).

We have followed Jesus and the twelve disciples on their long, winding journey to Jerusalem. It seems so long ago that we left Galilee and worked our way through Samaria and then through many parts of Judea, watching and listening as Jesus healed and taught many on His way to Jerusalem. Throughout the narrative, we saw opposition from Jewish leaders. So many misunderstood His mission, the meaning of the Scriptures, and the nature of salvation. Would this change when Jesus arrives in Jerusalem—especially when He entered the temple, where for centuries, the Jewish leadership had claimed divine authority?[1]

For most events and activities along the Jerusalem journey, we've had no idea of their physical location. Since Luke did not grow up in Palestine, the actual relationship between Judean towns and villages likely meant little to him, and it would have had even less significance for Theophilus. Luke's narrative suddenly became geographically specific, though, when Jesus approached Jericho, and from that point, Luke gave a running commentary of His movements until He entered the Holy City.

As Jesus climbed up the long hills from Jericho, He was accompanied by people on their way to the Passover festival. It is thought that if the normal population of Jerusalem was between 70,000 and 80,000, its population during Passover swelled to half a million.[2] The throng with Jesus doubtless included Galileans who were approaching the end of their long trek. It's a long, hard climb of three thousand feet elevation gain from Jericho to Jerusalem. As their path plateaus onto the mountain summits, we can imagine the anticipation as groups break into singing, using several psalms that were known as "Songs of Ascents," celebrating the approach to the Holy City.

> I will raise my eyes to the mountains;
> From where will my help come?
> My help comes from the LORD,
> Who made heaven and earth (Psalm 121:1, 2).

> I was glad when they said to me,
> "Let's go to the house of the LORD."
> Our feet are standing
> Within your gates, Jerusalem (Psalm 122:1, 2).

> To You I have raised my eyes,
> You who are enthroned in the heavens! (Psalm 123:1).

As the mountains surround Jerusalem,
So the LORD surrounds His people (Psalm 125:2).

More than ten chapters of Luke have focused on the journey to Jerusalem, and much has happened along the way. About half of Luke's account is unique to his Gospel. Of eighteen parables taught by Jesus during the journey, sixteen are recorded nowhere else. Only four miracles were recounted—three of them on the Sabbath—and all four were unique to Luke. Let's take a few moments to summarize all that happened since we left Galilee with Jesus and His disciples.[3]

- *Teaching* occupied much of Jesus' time. It was all about a new way to follow God, not the way of the Jewish leadership. Using many parables, Jesus sought to demolish the social and religious barriers that separated men and women, Jews and Gentiles, the "sinners" from the self-righteous, the poor from the rich, and the sick and the lame from the help and dignity they needed.
- *Salvation* for all people, both Jew and Gentile, is a constant theme in Luke, as well as in its sequel, Acts. The offer of salvation for everyone is emphasized several times in Luke, but not at all in Matthew or Mark, and only once in John. Jesus was constantly seeking the lost, bringing them to salvation, as we saw in the parables of the lost sheep, the lost coin, and the lost son (Luke 15). Luke used the phrase *to save* many times.
- The *kingdom of God* is another Lukan theme. The kingdom arrived with Jesus. It involved a new way of looking at the world and understanding one's place in relation to God, prayer, forgiveness, and love. Jesus introduced the "now" kingdom of grace (Luke 12:49–59; 13:18–30), but He also taught the "not yet" kingdom of glory that will take place at His second coming (Luke 17:20–27).
- *Discipleship*. Throughout the journey, Jesus was finding and calling disciples (Luke 9:57–62; 10:1–24; 18:35–43; 19:1–10). He especially focused on training the Twelve during the journey, but they were sometimes remarkably slow to catch on. They learned about many things— mission, commitment, love for God, and love for one's neighbor (Luke 10:25–37). Jesus taught them how to pray (Luke 11:1–13; 18:1–8), the importance of faithfulness and trust (Luke 12:1–48; 17:1–10; 19:11–27), and humility (Luke 18:9–17). All this has been preparing them for active service when Jesus is no longer with them. The Holy Spirit will then be their Guide and Counselor.
- One's *relationship to wealth* is emphasized in Luke's account. Two parables—the rich fool (Luke 12:13–21) and the rich man and Lazarus (Luke 16:19–31)—were followed by two encounters with wealthy individuals—the rich young ruler (Luke 18:18–23) and Zacchaeus (Luke 19:1–10). These stories provide powerful lessons that contrast selfishness with sacrificial giving.
- *Disputes and controversy* with Pharisees and scribes have characterized the journey. These Jewish leaders questioned Jesus' authority in His healings (Luke 11:14–23; 14:1–6), demanded signs and wonders (Luke 11:29–32), and were strongly rebuked by Jesus for their hypocrisy (verses 37–54).
- The *suffering* that lies ahead for Jesus was brought to the fore several times as Jesus journeyed toward Jerusalem. This was still not understood by the disciples, whose thinking rejected the concept of a suffering Messiah (Luke 12:49–50; 14:25–35; 17:25; 18:31–34). This truth would not find lodging in their hearts and minds until after Jesus' resurrection.

- *Table fellowship* is a prominent theme in Luke. On three Sabbath days, Jesus ate with Pharisees and scribes after the morning synagogue service (Luke 7:36–50; 11:37–54; 14:1–6). He also dined with His friends, Martha and Mary, on at least one occasion (Luke 10:38–42). Several of His parables featured table fellowship in tandem with rejoicing over recovery of the lost (Luke 14:15–15:32). *Rejoice* occurs more often in Luke than in any other New Testament book.

Luke wrote especially with Gentile Christians in mind. An overall theme of his Gospel is the coming of salvation in all its fulness for all people—Jews, Gentiles, Samaritans, men, women, children, tax collectors, "sinners," lepers, the down-and-out—anyone and everyone. Just ahead of Jesus as He now approaches Jerusalem is the passion—the cross, His death, His resurrection, and final victory! There we will begin to comprehend the depth and wonder of our salvation.

Reflection

List three significant lessons or concepts you have gained through your study of Luke thus far.

---

1. Darrell L. Bock, *Luke* (Grand Rapids, MI: Baker Academic, 1994), 23–25.
2. *NIV Cultural Backgrounds Study Bible* (Grand Rapids, MI: Zondervan, 2016), 1746.
3. Joel B. Green, *The Gospel of Luke*, New International Commentary on the New Testament, vol. 3 (Grand Rapids, MI: Eerdmans, 1997), 394–399.

Part IV

Jesus at Jerusalem

Luke 19:29–Acts 1:14

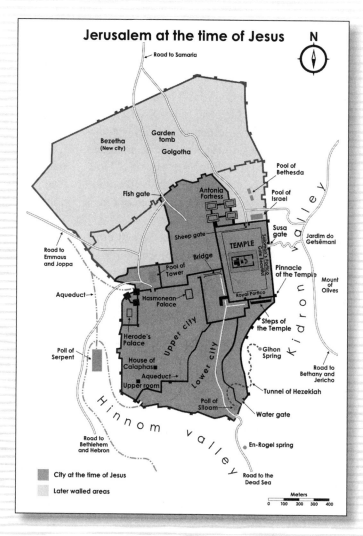

Jerusalem at the time of Jesus

N

Road to Samaria

Bezetha
(New city)

Garden
tomb

Golgotha

Pool of
Bethesda

Fish gate

Antonia
Fortress

Pool of
Israel

Sheep gate

Susa
gate

Jardim do
Getsêmani

TEMPLE

Road to
Emmaus
and Joppa

Bridge

Pool of
Tower

Pinnacle
of the Temple

Mount
of
Olives

Aqueduct

Hasmonean
Palace

Royal Portico

Steps of
the Temple

Herode's
Palace

Poll of
Serpent

House of
Calaphas

Gihon
Spring

Road to
Bethany and
Jericho

Aqueduct

Upper room

Upper city

Lower city

Tunnel of Hezekiah

Poll of
Siloam

Water gate

Hinnom valley

Kidron valley

Road to
Bethlehem
and Hebron

En-Rogel spring

Road to the
Dead Sea

City at the time of Jesus

Later walled areas

Meters
0 100 200 300 400

Chapter 74

The Greatest Story

It began with the birth of a baby in Bethlehem: "The Word became flesh, and dwelt among us" (John 1:14). Strangely, almost no one expected it or comprehended what it meant. That's because the story of sin is a story about broken relationships between God and humanity. When the first human couple yielded to a subtle invitation from Satan, who masqueraded as a serpent in a forbidden tree, humanity's free and open communication with God was lost. The separation was expressed in these words from Isaiah, "Listen! The LORD's arm is not too weak to save you, nor is his ear too deaf to hear you call. It's your sins that have cut you off from God" (Isaiah 59:1, 2, NLT).

Sin built a wall of separation between God and humankind. Across millennia, God sought to break through that wall by communicating through His prophets, but that was not enough. Prophets were struggling sinners like the rest of us, "but God had in His arsenal a startling weapon to smash through the wall of sin and distrust. The plan involved something so daring and astonishing that it left the universe spellbound with awe. God would do the unimaginable by becoming a human being, a sacrifice beyond our comprehension."[1] The Incarnation was the ultimate revelation of God's character of love to humankind. Jesus expressed it this way to a Pharisee named Nicodemus: "For God so loved the world that He gave His only begotten Son, that whoever believes in Him should not perish but have everlasting life" (John 3:16, NKJV).

So, Jesus came, but all too soon, the sent One died. Several times during His ministry, Jesus foreshadowed His suffering and death (Luke 9:22; 18:31–33). He pointed people to the Scriptures, where they could find God's communication by way of prophets, priests, kings, and poets. The Hebrew Scriptures overflow with prophecies about a promised Messiah, including His suffering and death.

So, why did Jesus have to die? The simple answer is that a human person infected by sin will inevitably die from the disease. Paul said, "The wages of sin is death" (Romans 6:23). But the Creator God, who is love (1 John 4:8), takes no joy in the death of anyone, so He conceived the plan of coming to our planet to pay the price for our sin, demonstrating beyond any doubt that He loves us and wants us to repent from our sinful ways and accept His forgiveness and His death in our place. Paul described it this way, "God made him who had no sin to be sin for us, so that in him we might become the righteousness of God" (2 Corinthians 5:21, NIV).

The greatest story ever told or written ends with a celebration when Jesus rose from the grave. It was the moment of victory in heaven's cosmic conquest against sin and evil. For eleven men, the discovery that Jesus was alive after dying on a cross was an eye-opening experience. With the promised power of the Holy Spirit, these men will be energized to tell the world that "Jesus of Nazareth" is indeed the living Son of God. Having witnessed His death and resurrection, they will be uniquely equipped to take the gospel message to the ends of the earth.

The fact of Jesus' resurrection transformed Saul the persecutor into Paul the apostle. He met the risen Christ on the Damascus road. Years later, as he wrote to believers in Philippi, Paul confessed that he was willing to discard everything as rubbish, with one proviso: "that I may know him and the power of his resurrection" (Philippians 3:8, 10, ESV). In a letter to believers in Corinth, he stated firmly, "If Christ has not been raised, your faith is worthless" (1 Corinthians 15:17). But with exuberance, he continued, "But the fact is, Christ has been raised from the dead, the first fruits of those who are asleep" (verse 20). Thank you for that affirmation, Paul! The reality of Jesus' resurrection is a guarantee that if I place my life in His hands, I can look forward to an eternity with Him.

Forty days after His resurrection, Jesus departed in a cloud. Luke, writing to his friend Theophilus and other Gentiles, made his story of Jesus complete—from the wonderful birth narrative through the years of ministry to death on the cross, followed by His resurrection and departure to heaven. No other Gospel writer accomplished that.

Joy and praise were associated with the birth of Jesus as He was presented at the temple. Joy and praise erupted again as eleven men who watched His departure went into the temple to worship Him. Luke's Gospel ends where it started, in Jerusalem.[2]

Following His physical appearance to many, Jesus ascended into a cloud and was reinstated in heaven, where the great victory is celebrated in song:

I heard every created thing which is in heaven, or on the earth, or under the earth, or on the sea, and all the things in them, saying,

"To Him who sits on the throne and to the Lamb be the blessing, the honor, the glory, and the dominion forever and ever" (Revelation 5:13).

Reflection

Luke is the only Gospel writer who chronicles the entire story of Jesus' life on earth—His birth, death, resurrection, and ascension. Is this important to you? Why or why not?

---

1. Keith Clouten, *Breaking Through the Wall: How God Communicates With His Lost Creation* (Calhoun, GA: TEACH Services, 2018), 63.

2. Darrell L. Bock, *Luke* (Grand Rapids, MI: Baker Academic, 1994), 1946.

Chapter 75

The Triumphal Entry

Luke 19:29–40 (Matthew 21:1–11; Mark 11:1–11; John 12:12–19)

With a great crowd of followers, Jesus led the way to Jerusalem. The Passover festival would begin soon, drawing large numbers of people. Jesus walked with the pilgrims in spite of a warrant for His arrest. The Jerusalem leadership had given orders that if anyone knew where Jesus was, they were to report it (John 11:57). However, His popularity with the crowds undermined this order.[1]

Among the festival pilgrims were Galileans who had taken the Jordan valley route southward to avoid Samaria. They remembered Jesus from His ministry in Galilee, and of course, they were excited to see Him again.

But something else excited the crowd of followers. If Jesus is indeed the promised Messiah, His coming to Jerusalem must surely signal His coronation as their king. So, it was a joyful crowd that accompanied Jesus to the Holy City.

When He approached Bethphage and Bethany, near the mountain that is called Olivet, He sent two of the disciples, saying, "Go into the village ahead of you; there, as you enter, you will find a colt tied, on which no one yet has ever sat; untie it and bring it here. And if anyone asks you, 'Why are you untying it?' you shall say this: 'The Lord has need of it.' " So those who were sent left and found it just as He had told them. And as they were untying the colt, its owners said to them, "Why are you untying the colt?" They said, "The Lord has need of it." And they brought it to Jesus, and they threw their cloaks on the colt and put Jesus on it (Luke 19:29–35).

Approaching the small village of Bethphage, Jesus chose two disciples for a special task. They were to go into the village and look for an "unbroken" colt. The two men followed the instructions, and it all happened exactly as Jesus described; the colt's owner made no objection.

Jesus had total foreknowledge of the event—"(1) the beast's location, (2) its tied-up state, (3) its 'unridden' history, and (4) how to procure it."[2] Throughout the events that would shortly transpire in Jerusalem, Jesus would be in control. Everything happens in accordance with the divine will.

When the two disciples brought the young donkey to Jesus, they placed their outer garments on the animal as a blanket, and Jesus sat on the colt. By doing this, they were fulfilling a royal prophecy of Zechariah:

> Rejoice greatly, daughter of Zion!
> Shout in triumph, daughter of Jerusalem!
> Behold, your king is coming to you;
> He is righteous and endowed with salvation,

Humble, and mounted on a donkey,
Even on a colt, the foal of a donkey (Zechariah 9:9).

Additionally, a more ancient reference comes from the patriarch Jacob, who spoke poetically prophetic words concerning his son, Judah, through whose line Jesus came:

"The scepter will not depart from Judah,
nor the ruler's staff from between his feet,
until he to whom it belongs shall come
and the obedience of the nations shall be his.
He will tether his donkey to a vine,
his colt to the choicest branch" (Genesis 49:10, 11, NIV).

These prophecies were fulfilled through Jesus.

Now as He was going, they were spreading their cloaks on the road. And as soon as He was approaching, near the descent of the Mount of Olives, the whole crowd of the disciples began to praise God joyfully with a loud voice for all the miracles which they had seen, shouting:

**"Blessed is the King, the One who comes in the name of the Lord;
Peace in heaven and glory in the highest!" (Luke 19:36–38).**

Reaching the summit of the Mount of Olives, the crowd gazed at Jerusalem spread out before them, and a royal procession began with a burst of praise. The excitement of the crowd was palpable. The people shouted the well-remembered words of Psalm 118:26: "Blessed is the one who comes in the name of the Lord." This psalm is part of the Hallel, which was always sung during the Passover season, but it also carried the expectation of a new Davidic king who would lead pilgrims to the temple and receive a welcome from the priests there.[3] That would not happen, but the prospect seemed glorious as people laid down their outer garments on the road for their king, the "son of David," to ride over. Matthew's account tells of people cutting palm branches and spreading them on the road (Matthew 21:8). A triumphal entry was underway!

And yet some of the Pharisees in the crowd said to Him, "Teacher, rebuke Your disciples!" Jesus replied, "I tell you, if these stop speaking, the stones will cry out!" (Luke 19:39, 40).

The joyful excitement of the crowd was not shared by some Pharisees, who caught the attention of Jesus and demanded, "Teacher, tell these disciples of Yours to stop this!"

Jesus' reply is magnificent: "If these disciples stop their praise, the creation itself will break out in song."[4]

Truly, "Jesus enters Jerusalem to a mixture of joy and tragedy as he prepares to meet his fate. He is in control of events tied to his passion. . . . Ironically, what the leadership cannot see, creation can."[5]

Reflection

How do you think the natural world shouts praise to God?

_____

1. Leon Morris, *Luke: An Introduction and Commentary* (Downers Grove, IL: IVP Academic, 1988), 293.

2. Darrell L. Bock, *Luke* (Grand Rapids, MI: Baker Academic, 1994), 1554, 1555.

3. Joel B. Green, *The Gospel of Luke*, New International Commentary on the New Testament, vol. 3 (Grand Rapids, MI: Eerdmans, 1997), 1558.

4. Bock, *Luke*, 1560.

5. Bock, 1551.

Chapter 76

The Fate of Jerusalem

Luke 19:41–48 (Matthew 21:12–17; Mark 11:15–19)

Suddenly, the crowd of happy people came to a halt—Jesus stopped the donkey, and the people quieted their shouts of praise. Spread out before them was a panorama of Jerusalem, and all eyes were drawn to the beautiful temple. Golden pillars profiled the configuration of the holy precinct where the priests would soon sacrifice the Passover lamb. But Jesus wept.

When He approached Jerusalem, He saw the city and wept over it, saying, "If you had known on this day, even you, the conditions for peace! But now they have been hidden from your eyes. For the days will come upon you when your enemies will put up a barricade against you, and surround you and hem you in on every side, and they will level you to the ground, and throw down your children within you, and they will not leave in you one stone upon another, because you did not recognize the time of your visitation" (Luke 19:41–44).

For Jesus, it had been a long road to Jerusalem. Scanning the great city, His eyes wet with tears, He pronounced judgment on a city whose very name, Jerusalem, ends with *shalom*, which means "peace." His arrival was supposed to bring the promised "peace on earth to those with whom God is pleased"—the angel's words to the shepherds (Luke 2:14, NLT)—but instead, the "coming One" will fulfill the prophetic words of Simeon: "sent as a sign from God, but many will oppose him" (verse 34, NLT). Words of warning were also spoken by the prophet Daniel: "After this period of sixty-two sets of seven, the Anointed One will be killed, appearing to have accomplished nothing, and a ruler will arise whose armies will destroy the city and the Temple. The end will come with a flood, and war and its miseries are decreed from that time to the very end" (Daniel 9:26, NLT). Truly, "Jerusalem has missed the nature of the times, which held the potential for a restoration of peace."[1]

This is the second time Luke has recorded words of judgment for Jerusalem. The first such words were spoken in the hearing of some Pharisees, "Your house is left to you desolate" (Luke 13:35). Jesus would speak words of judgment "a third time on the way to the cross (23:26–31)."[2]

Jesus spoke of a siege of Jerusalem, with barricades surrounding the city to prevent the escape of its citizens. Further, Jesus described, "They will level you to the ground, and throw down your children within you, and they will not leave in you one stone upon another" (Luke 19:44). The prediction was fulfilled in AD 70 when the Roman army led by Titus destroyed Jerusalem. The hill where Jesus now stood would be saturated with the blood of its citizens as they died painful deaths on hundreds of Roman crosses. As Luke penned his Gospel manuscript, that event was soon to take place.

During His triumphal entry, Jesus said to the Pharisees that if the people stop shouting praise, "The stones will cry out" (verse 40). In Jerusalem's destruction, the stones would cry out in a very different way as a result of the nation's rejection of Jesus.[3] The destruction of Jerusalem could have been prevented if the people "had abandoned their dreams of political power" and welcomed Jesus as the true Messiah, with changed lives and new attitudes.[4]

And Jesus entered the temple grounds and began to drive out those who were selling, saying to them, "It is written: 'AND MY HOUSE WILL BE A HOUSE OF PRAYER,' but you have made it a DEN OF ROBBERS" (verses 45, 46).

Still accompanied by the crowd, Jesus entered Jerusalem and led the way to the temple, the heart of Israel's worship. He entered the spacious area known as the Court of the Gentiles—which was a way of saying that Gentile worshipers may come here, but no further. Jesus had a job to do here—the temple leaders made this place of worship a commercial hub where sacrificial animals were purchased, along with stalls selling wine, oil, salt, and doves. There was also a money-changing table where worshipers traded their Greek and Aramaic currency for the shekels that were required to pay the temple tax. In all this buying and selling, the priestly leadership took financial advantage of the worshipers.[5]

Shock waves filled the temple as Jesus spoke with words of divine authority and drove animals, merchandise, doves, and money changers out of the building. As He sent them packing, He shouted words from Isaiah: "It is written, 'AND MY HOUSE WILL BE CALLED A HOUSE OF PRAYER,' but you have made it a DEN OF ROBBERS" (Luke 19:46, see also Isaiah 56:7 and Jeremiah 7:11). That last phrase may also be translated "a cave for bandits."

Jesus didn't quote the entire Isaiah statement, which reads, "My house will be called a house of prayer *for all the peoples*" (Isaiah 56:7; emphasis added). And we might wonder why He omitted that last phrase. Given His prediction of the coming destruction, Jesus may mean that the temple will no longer have its intended function. Gentiles would not come there to find Yahweh. God is not limited to a single territory or geographic location. Soon the call to worship will go out to all peoples through the preaching of the apostles (Acts 1:8).[6]

And He was teaching daily in the temple; but the chief priests and the scribes and the leading men among the people were trying to put Him to death, and yet they could not find anything that they might do, for all the people were hanging on to every word He said (Luke 19:47, 48).

Having cleaned up the temple of its commercial operations, Jesus was soon surrounded by a crowd "hanging on to every word" He uttered (verse 48). We are reminded of the prophetic words of the priest Zechariah: "To grant us that we, being rescued from the hand of our enemies, would serve Him without fear, in holiness and righteousness before Him all our days" (Luke 1:74, 75).

But the priests were angry. Their self-appointed temple role had been usurped by Jesus, whose popularity with the people put a temporary stop to their evil plans. But they were determined that soon this Galilean Rabbi would be exterminated.

Reflection

How and where do you worship God?

1. I go to church every week.

2. I have a regular time each day for Bible study and prayer.

3. I sing in the church choir.

4. I pray when I wake up each morning.

5. Spending time in nature draws me to God.

6. Large sanctuaries with pipe organ music give me goose bumps.

7. I say grace before meals.

8. I keep Jesus in my thoughts throughout the day.

1. Darrell L. Bock, *Luke* (Grand Rapids, MI: Baker Academic, 1994), 1561.

2. Robert H. Stein, *Luke*, The New American Commentary, vol. 24 (Nashville, TN: Broadman, 1992), 482.

3. Bock, *Luke*, 1563.

4. William Barclay, *The Gospel of Luke* (Philadelphia, PA: Westminster Press, 1975), 241.

5. Barclay, 242.

6. Joel B. Green, *The Gospel of Luke*, New International Commentary on the New Testament, vol. 3 (Grand Rapids, MI: Eerdmans, 1997), 694.

Chapter 77

The Vineyard Owner's Son

Luke 20:1–18 (Matthew 21:23–27, 33–46; Mark 11:27–33, 12:1–12)

Luke 20 describes theological warfare. Jesus faced controversy in several areas. And it all happened while He taught in the temple, where a crowd of admirers hung on to His every word. First, He was first interrupted by a group of priests, scribes, and elders. They played a dangerous game of verbal sparring.[1]

On one of the days while He was teaching the people in the temple and preaching the gospel, the chief priests and the scribes with the elders confronted Him, and they declared, saying to Him, "Tell us by what authority You are doing these things, or who is the one who gave You this authority?" (verses 1, 2).

Essentially, they asked Jesus, "Rabbi, what gives you the right to create havoc in the temple and teach here? Surely you know that *we* are the appointed purveyors of religious knowledge. Tell us, who gave you authority to usurp our place?"

But He replied to them, "I will also ask you a question, and you tell Me: Was the baptism of John from heaven or from men?" (verses 3, 4).

If the leaders wanted to play the game this way, Jesus would parley with them, so He asked them a question, "Where did John the Baptist get *his authority* to baptize people?" The truth, of course, is that both Jesus and John received their authority from God. John was sent to preach repentance and forgiveness and to point the way to Jesus.

They discussed among themselves, saying, "If we say, 'From heaven,' He will say, 'Why did you not believe him?' But if we say, 'From men,' all the people will stone us to death, since they are convinced that John was a prophet." And so they answered that they did not know where it came from. And Jesus said to them, "Neither am I telling you by what authority I do these things" (verses 5–8).

His question was too tricky for the scribes to answer. If they said that John was heaven-sent, the natural follow-up would be, why didn't they recognize his mission and heed his call to repentance? And if they said that John was just a dissident voice in the wilderness, they would face irate crowds who heard John and were led to repentance, forgiveness, and baptism. The people were convinced that John was a God-sent prophet.

So, the Jewish leaders refused to answer. They would never admit that John was God-sent because it would dislodge the foundation of *their* authority, which was bound up with their heredity, wealth, and influence.[2] Round one: Jesus wins. Then He responded to their question by telling them a story.

But He began to tell the people this parable: "A man planted a vineyard and leased it to vine-growers, and went on a journey for a long time. At the harvest time he sent a slave to the vine-growers, so that they would give him his share of the produce of the vineyard; but the vine-growers beat him and sent him away empty-handed. And he proceeded to send another slave; but they beat him also and treated him shamefully, and sent him away empty-handed. And he proceeded to send a third; but this one too they wounded and threw out. Now the owner of the vineyard said, 'What am I to do? I will send my beloved son; perhaps they will respect him.' But when the vine-growers saw him, they discussed with one another, saying, 'This is the heir; let's kill him so that the inheritance will be ours.' And so they threw him out of the vineyard and killed him. What, then, will the owner of the vineyard do to them? He will come and put these vine-growers to death, and will give the vineyard to others" (verses 9–16).

Jesus revealed the nature and source of His authority with this parable.[3] The parable draws its meaning from a passage in Isaiah: "I will sing for the one I love a song about his vineyard." "When I expected sweet grapes, why did my vineyard give me bitter grapes?" "The nation of Israel is the vineyard of the LORD" (Isaiah 5:1, 4, 7, NLT).

In Palestine, peasants worked on large estates owned by wealthy, often absentee, landlords. As tenant farmers, they lived and worked on the estates and paid their landlords a substantial portion of the harvest.[4] The parable has three clear applications, which the temple leadership saw but would not acknowledge:[5]

1. The "beloved son" of the vineyard owner represents Jesus. The father-owner has given his son full authority.
2. The tenants of the vineyard represent the Jewish leadership. The emissaries sent by the owner represent God's emissaries, His prophets.
3. Giving the vineyard to "others" represents a transfer of spiritual leadership from the Jewish nation to the Gentiles. The apostles will be given their commission, "You shall be My witnesses both in Jerusalem, and in all Judea and Samaria, and even to the remotest part of the earth" (Acts 1:8).

The parable shows how far the Jerusalem leadership had departed from their divinely appointed role. Israel was judged for its bad fruit—bloodshed, injustice, unrighteousness, absence of love, and lack of compassion for the needy.

However, when they heard this, they said, "May it never happen!" (Luke 20:16).

The leaders did not miss the obvious allusions to Isaiah's "vineyard" poem. The parable had cleverly exposed their evil plans. Of course, no one liked the way the story ended, with the Jewish vineyard being given to others. It received a noisy response, "Heaven forbid!" (verse 16, NRSV).

But Jesus looked at them and said, "Then what is this statement that has been written:

'A STONE WHICH THE BUILDERS REJECTED,
THIS HAS BECOME THE CHIEF CORNERSTONE'?

Everyone who falls on that stone will be broken to pieces; but on whomever it falls, it will crush him" (verses 17, 18).

Jesus quoted from Psalm 118:22, which is another part of the Hallel sung during the Passover season. The words would be fresh in peoples' minds at this festival time. Like a stone rejected by builders, Jesus was rejected by Israel's leadership. But the rejected stone, Jesus Christ, would become the "chief cornerstone" in the building of the Christian church.[6]

Reflection

Ask yourself, What "fruit" am I producing in my corner of Christ's vineyard?

---

1. Darrell L. Bock, *Luke* (Grand Rapids, MI: Baker Academic, 1994), 1582.

2. *NIV Cultural Backgrounds Study Bible* (Grand Rapids, MI: Zondervan, 2016), 1789.

3. Joel B. Green, *The Gospel of Luke*, New International Commentary on the New Testament, vol. 3 (Grand Rapids, MI: Eerdmans, 1997), 703.

4. *NIV Cultural Backgrounds Study Bible*, 1789.

5. Green, *Gospel of Luke*, 704.

6. Bock, *Luke*, 1603, 1604.

Chapter 78

Show Me a Denarius

Luke 20:19–26 (Matthew 22:15–22; Mark 12:13–17)

Jesus' parable about the vineyard owner and the vinedressers had hit its target, the Jewish leaders. The vinedressers' plan to kill the owner's son was exactly what the scribes, Pharisees, and chief priests planned to do with Jesus.

The scribes and the chief priests tried to lay hands on Him that very hour, and yet they feared the people; for they were aware that He had spoken this parable against them. And so they watched Him closely, and sent spies who pretended to be righteous, in order that they might catch Him in some statement, so that they could hand Him over to the jurisdiction and authority of the governor (Luke 20:19, 20).

Jesus' popularity with the people was a problem for the temple leadership. A large and joyful crowd had recently led Him to Jerusalem in a royal procession, shouting loud hosannas to their "king." Well, if He planned to be their king, He wouldn't want to be subservient to Rome, so they tested His allegiance to Caesar. They had suffered embarrassment when they directed an either-or question to Jesus (verses 2–8), so they decided to use other people to do their dirty work. They bribed some spies who would "pretend to be righteous" when they approached Jesus.

And the spies questioned Him, saying, "Teacher, we know that You speak and teach correctly, and You are not partial to anyone, but You teach the way of God on the basis of truth. Is it permissible for us to pay taxes to Caesar, or not?" (verses 21, 22).

They must surely catch Jesus with this question. After they've flattered Him by acknowledging His impartiality as a teacher of divine truth, they posed the question, "Is it right to pay taxes to Caesar, or not?"

In asking about paying taxes to Caesar, they referred to the Roman "poll tax," which required each adult male to pay one silver denarius—a day's wage—to Caesar each year to acknowledge his empirical authority.[1] Rome conducted a periodic census in each province to update the poll tax register. The amount of the tax wasn't the issue; what irked the Jews was this annual reminder that they were governed by Rome. Perhaps, for this reason, the poll tax was not collected by the Jews' own despised tax collectors but by the Jerusalem Sanhedrin. It was done that way to protect the temple from Roman interference.

Jesus was faced with what seems like a tricky question. After all, if He says, "Yes, it's OK to pay the poll tax to Rome," He would anger a lot of people, especially the growing number of Jewish nationalists who hated this requirement. Their influence on the Jewish populace was growing and had led to the formation of the Zealots, who stirred up violence against Rome. One company of nationalists intended to mint their own coinage, refusing to use the empire's currency.[2] But if He says, "No," He will immediately be branded as an insurrectionist and would likely be arrested by Pilate, the governor.

But He saw through their trickery and said to them, "Show Me a denarius. Whose image and inscription does it have?" They said, "Caesar's." And He said to them, "Then pay to Caesar the things that are Caesar's, and to God the things that are God's." And they were unable to catch Him in a statement in the presence of the people; and they were amazed at His answer, and said nothing (verses 23–26).

Instead of falling into their trap, Jesus' reply was clever. In asking them to show Him a coin, He got them to acknowledge Roman sovereignty even before He answered their question. They carried these coins for purchases and to pay laborers. Shown a denarius, Jesus asked whose inscription it displayed. Archaeologists have discovered that the inscription on the face of a silver denarius read, "Tiberius Caesar, Augustus, son of divine Augustus," and the reverse side depicted his mother, Livia.[3]

Jesus' charge to "pay to Caesar the things that are Caesar's, and to God what is God's" stunned and disappointed the espionage agents of the Jewish leadership. They were amazed at Jesus' wise answer but had nothing more to say.

Did Jesus contradict Himself? In an earlier teaching session with the Pharisees and disciples, He said, "No servant can serve two masters. . . . You cannot serve God and wealth" (Luke 16:13). If there are two masters and two kingdoms, how can we be members of both? Also, at a later time, Peter and the apostles stated clearly, "We must obey God rather than men" (Acts 5:29). "While not denying the possibility of obedience to Caesar, Jesus asserts the prior and more fundamental claim of God on all human beings, on human existence itself."[4] The apostle Paul wrote, "Every person is to be subject to the governing authorities. For there is no authority except from God, and those which exist are established by God" (Romans 13:1). The image of Caesar may be legitimately appear on the empire's coinage, but the image of God was implanted in the human soul at Creation (Genesis 1:27). When any demand conflicts with God's will for our lives, we must courageously say no.

Efforts to snare Jesus took a variety of forms. The most efficient way to get rid of Him would be for Him to challenge Rome, but Jesus clearly won this second round of theological warfare and avoided the trap. In the later trial, the Jewish leaders referred back to this confrontation and blatantly lied about what Jesus said (Luke 23:2).[5]

Reflection

Should I say no to authority when

1. the government expects me to pay tax on my charitable donations?
2. I'm forbidden to attend church?
3. voting is compulsory?
4. an academic examination is scheduled on the Sabbath?
5. I'm forbidden to share my faith outside my home?
6. government legislates morality?

7. the speed limit on the highway is ridiculously low?

---

1. Joel B. Green, *The Gospel of Luke*, New International Commentary on the New Testament, vol. 3 (Grand Rapids, MI: Eerdmans, 1997), 712.

2. Cecil Roth, "The Historical Implications of the Jewish Coinage of the First Revolt," *Israel Exploration Journal* 12, no. 1 (1962), 33–46.

3. Darrell L. Bock, *Luke* (Grand Rapids, MI: Baker Academic, 1994), 1612.

4. Green, *Gospel of Luke*, 716.

5. Bock, *Luke*, 1614.

Chapter 79

The Seven Brothers

Luke 20:27–40 (Matthew 22:23–33; Mark 12:18–27)

The scribes and Pharisees had attempted to trap Jesus but were without success. Now some Sadducees found Him in the temple and tried to confound Him. This is the only occasion in Luke's Gospel that we encounter Sadducees, and here they confront Jesus with a nonsense story. Well, it seems silly to us, but it was a serious issue for the Sadducees.

No Sadducee writings have survived, so our knowledge about them is fragmentary. They first appeared during the second century BC, finding their place within Judaism as a conservative, aristocratic priestly party. They were worldly minded, wealthy, and quite ready to cooperate with the Romans, which made them unpopular with the Jewish people as a whole.[1] Also, unlike the Pharisees, they denied the entire doctrine of the afterlife, including belief in a resurrection. Their nonbelief in the resurrection generated their question. Hoping to challenge Jesus and embarrass their Pharisee neighbors, they came up with a most unlikely scenario.

Now some of the Sadducees (who maintain that there is no resurrection) came to Him, and they questioned Him, saying, "Teacher, Moses wrote for us that if a man's brother dies, leaving a wife, and he is childless, that his brother is to marry the wife and raise up children for his brother. So then, there were seven brothers; and the first took a wife and died childless; and the second and the third married her; and in the same way all seven died, leaving no children. Finally the woman also died. Therefore, in the resurrection, which one's wife does the woman become? For all seven married her" (Luke 20:27–33).

Respectfully addressing Jesus as "Teacher," the Sadducees posed a question that was based on the Old Testament custom of levirate marriage (Deuteronomy 25:5, 6). If a man died childless, his brother was to take the widow and raise up children for the deceased. This prevented a man's name and family from dying out. By New Testament times, the custom was beginning to fall into disuse, though levirate marriage is still practiced in some African societies.*

The Sadducees were trying to show that belief in resurrection is ludicrous. Their story is about seven brothers who eventually all married the same woman, in each case without her bearing a child. Their question assumes that marriage will continue in an afterlife exactly as in the present. So, we can imagine the dilemma when this wife is faced with seven resurrected spouses![2] In response, Jesus helps the Sadducees get their theological facts straight.

Jesus said to them, "The sons of this age marry and the women are given in marriage, but those who are considered worthy to attain to that age and the resurrection from the dead, neither marry

---

* I have personally encountered this practice in tribal societies in western Kenya.

nor are given in marriage; for they cannot even die anymore, for they are like angels, and are sons of God, being sons of the resurrection" (Luke 20:34–36).

Jesus collapsed their reasoning and their clever story by revealing that the afterlife does not replicate life on earth as it has existed. He makes a clear distinction between "this age"—when people marry and "are given in marriage"—and "that age," life after the resurrection for those who prove faithful to God.[3] These "sons of the resurrection" inherit eternal life, in which there is no more death. In this world, marriage and procreation are necessary features, Jesus says, but life in the next world will be different—contemporary marriage customs will not apply in heaven's society.[4]

"But as for the fact that the dead are raised, even Moses revealed this in the passage about the burning bush, where he calls the Lord THE GOD OF ABRAHAM, THE GOD OF ISAAC, AND THE GOD OF JACOB. Now He is not the God of the dead, but of the living; for all live to Him" (verses 37, 38).

Since Sadducees placed their sole scriptural authority in the words of Moses, Jesus directed them to some words from the Torah. Remember when Moses encountered a burning bush in the desert? At that encounter, God identified Himself as "the God of your father—the God of Abraham, the God of Isaac, and the God of Jacob" (Exodus 3:6; compare verse 15). Quoting those words, Jesus explained to His Sadducee friends that God is "God of the living." The three patriarchs—Abraham, Isaac, and Jacob—are not alive now, but they will be alive together on the day of the resurrection when God's everlasting covenant sees its final fulfillment. "For both Jesus and Luke the resurrection of the dead was clearly a future event (14:14; Acts 23:6; 24:15, 21)."[5]

Some of the scribes answered and said, "Teacher, You have spoken well." For they did not have the courage to question Him any longer about anything (Luke 20:39, 40).

With their silly story, the Sadducees wanted to make Jesus and belief in resurrection look foolish, but they were the ones who now appeared foolish.[6] Some scribes, who listened to this whole episode, must have grinned as they said, "Teacher, you have spoken well."

Luke notes that Jesus had silenced his opponents. Pharisees, scribes, priestly leaders, and Sadducees have all had their turn at trapping Him, but His wisdom and knowledge were too much for them. Jesus is clearly in control.[7]

Reflection

We are so accustomed to the way life operates in the here and now that it may be perplexing and difficult to imagine eternal life beyond the grave. What does the Bible say about eternal life?

---

1. Leon Morris, *Luke: An Introduction and Commentary*, Tyndale New Testament Commentaries, vol. 3 (Downers Grove, IL: IVP Academic, 1988), 307.
2. Darrell L. Bock, *Luke* (Grand Rapids, MI: Baker Academic, 1994), 1616.
3. Joel B. Green, *The Gospel of Luke*, New International Commentary on the New Testament, vol. 3 (Grand Rapids, MI: Eerdmans, 1997), 720.
4. Morris, *Luke*, 309.
5. Robert H. Stein, *Luke*, The New American Commentary, vol. 24 (Nashville, TN: Broadman, 1992), 500.
6. Paul Borgman, *The Way According to Luke: Hearing the Whole Story of Luke-Acts* (Grand Rapids, MI: Eerdmans, 2006), 221.
7. Bock, *Luke*, 1626.

Chapter 80

A Riddle and a Widow's Giving

Luke 20:41–21:4 (Mark 12:35–44)

While Jesus was still in the temple, surrounded by people who hung on to His every word, some scribes who were listening were impressed and said to Jesus, "Teacher, You have spoken well" (Luke 20:39). Jesus did not reply, but He challenged the scribes with a theological puzzle. They took pride in being the ultimate authority in interpreting Scripture.

But He said to them, "How is it that they say the Christ is David's son? For David himself says in the book of Psalms,

> 'THE LORD SAID TO MY LORD,
> "SIT AT MY RIGHT HAND,
> UNTIL I MAKE YOUR ENEMIES A FOOTSTOOL FOR YOUR FEET." '

Therefore David calls Him 'Lord,' and so how is He his son?" (verses 41–44).

I think Jesus may have been grinning as He asked the question, "Why do people say that the Messiah is David's son?"[1] He's quoting from Psalm 110, one of King David's royal psalms. What David wrote appears at first reading to lack logic. But the scribes needed to revise their idea of what "Son of David" means. If Jesus was the expected Messiah, they thought He'd come as a political Messiah, a fighter, like David. They anticipated an earthly king who would be called the "Son of David" and who would take the throne of David. In the style of King David, he would throw off the jurisdiction of Rome and restore the Jewish nation to its former glory.

Let's unpack the riddle:

- David referred to the Messiah as "Lord," which meant someone greater than him.
- But the Messiah was expected to come as the "*Son* of David."
- In Jewish thinking, no son can ever be greater than his father, so how could the Messianic "Son of David" be greater than David himself?[2]

No one ventured to explain the riddle. The answer is that the Messiah is here, but He's much more than a "son of David"—He is God in the flesh.[3] As Messiah, He is the Anointed One. Jesus is infinitely greater than David or any other earthly individual. He will sit at His Father's right hand and witness the final destruction of *all* enemies of God's kingdom.

Having confounded the scribes, Jesus had something to say about them to His disciples:

And while all the people were listening, He said to the disciples, "Beware of the scribes, who like to walk around in long robes, and love personal greetings in the marketplaces, and chief seats in the synagogues and places of honor at banquets, who devour widows' houses, and for appearance's sake offer long prayers. These will receive all the more condemnation" (verses 45–47).

Essentially, He's saying, "Don't be like the scribes. Their long, flowing robes mark them as gentlemen of leisure. They revel in public respect, choosing the highest seats in the synagogues and places of honor at banquets. They are self-centered and not worthy examples to follow."

Their "devouring" of "widows' houses" referred to practices that resulted in loss to widows, society's most vulnerable individuals. Widows often had debts and lacked influential people to advocate for them. People in leadership, if unscrupulous, could seize a widow's property more readily, often through legal means.[4] Temple authorities sometimes managed the property of widows in ways that took advantage of them.[5]

A widow's offering

As He spoke about scribes and widows, Jesus observed something that was happening close to where He was standing.

Now He looked up and saw the wealthy putting their gifts into the temple treasury. And He saw a poor widow putting in two lepta coins. And He said, "Truly I say to you, this poor widow put in more than all of them; for they all contributed to the offering from their surplus; but she, from her poverty, put in all that she had to live on" (Luke 21:1–4).

In the temple forecourt, people watched as wealthy individuals dropped money into special receptacles. Their offerings were used to underwrite the costs of temple worship.[6] Just then, a poor widow stepped up to toss in two copper coins. A lepton was the smallest currency, worth one-eighth of a penny, or one-hundredth of the denarius, a day's wage.

To everyone's surprise, Jesus commended the widow. What others gave to God cost them little. In contrast, the widow gave everything—all she had to live on. "God does not look at the number of contributions we make or the amount contained within them, but at the way we make them. He does not count, he weighs."[7]

Reflection

We often hear the expression, "Give until it hurts." What does that mean, and why?

---

1. Joel B. Green, *The Gospel of Luke*, New International Commentary on the New Testament, vol. 3 (Grand Rapids, MI: Eerdmans, 1997), 723.

2. Green, 724.

3. Paul Borgman, *The Way According to Luke: Hearing the Whole Story of Luke-Acts* (Grand Rapids, MI: Eerdmans, 2006), 221.

4. *NIV Cultural Backgrounds Study Bible* (Grand Rapids, MI: Zondervan, 2016), 1791.

5. Leon Morris, *Luke: An Introduction and Commentary*, Tyndale New Testament Commentaries, vol. 3 (Downers Grove, IL: IVP Academic, 1988), 311.

6. Darrell L. Bock, *Luke* (Grand Rapids, MI: Baker Academic, 1994), 1645.

7. Bock, 1648.

Chapter 81

The Way Ahead

Luke 21:5–19 (Matthew 24:1–51; Mark 13:1–37)

The week leading up to Passover began with a literal "cleansing" of the temple of its misuse as a place of business, followed by the inevitable backlash from Jewish leaders—priests, Pharisees, scribes, Sadducees—and their unsuccessful attempts to undermine Jesus' authority before a crowd of His followers. As Jesus left the temple, He was accompanied by the disciples and others.

And while some were talking about the temple, that it was decorated with beautiful stones and vowed gifts, He said, "As for these things which you are observing, the days will come when there will not be left one stone upon another, which will not be torn down" (Luke 21:5, 6).

Yes, indeed, the temple was beautiful. "After Solomon's temple was destroyed by the Babylonians in 587 B.C., [the Jews who returned] from exile . . . replaced it with a smaller [edifice] . . . which was clearly inferior to Solomon's." However, soon after Herod the Great took the throne in 37 BC, he commenced a massive reconstruction of the temple, making it much larger.[1] Josephus described foundation stones that measured thirty-five feet by twelve feet. Pilgrims who poured into Jerusalem from places near and far were overwhelmed by the temple's size and magnificence, revealed by a façade of gold plates and white marble.[2]

As people spoke with admiration about the temple's beauty, Jesus made the dire prediction that it would be destroyed, leaving not "one stone upon another" (verse 6), echoing what He had said earlier (Luke 19:44). His prediction would be fulfilled in AD 70 when the Roman army would level the temple, and it would never be rebuilt.

They asked Him questions, saying, "Teacher, when therefore will these things happen? And what will be the sign when these things are about to take place?" (Luke 21:7).

The disciples asked the obvious questions: When? And how will we know?

And He said, "See to it that you are not misled; for many will come in My name, saying, 'I am He,' and, 'The time is near.' Do not go after them. And when you hear of wars and revolts, do not be alarmed; for these things must take place first, but the end will not follow immediately."

Then He continued by saying to them, "Nation will rise against nation, and kingdom against kingdom, and there will be massive earthquakes, and in various places plagues and famines; and there will be terrible sights and great signs from heaven" (verses 8–11).

In the early Christian church, there was an expectation that the return of Jesus would be soon. Luke wrote just prior to Jerusalem's destruction in AD 70, and he understood from Jesus' words that there might be a long gap between that destruction and the return of Jesus. In fact, Luke records Jesus' clear statement,

"These things must take place first, but the end will not follow immediately" (verse 9). Soon, in a more private talk with the disciples, He spoke more about the time of the end.[3]

Jesus warned that after His death and departure, some would appear and claim to be Christ. Josephus confirmed there were such false prophets before the fall of Jerusalem.[4] Jesus also told His disciples not to be terrified when they heard of wars and revolts, such as the Zealot revolt and the violence that would happen in AD 68. Social chaos would then occur. Natural phenomena, including earthquakes and famines, happened before AD 70 as well as afterward.[5]

"But before all these things, they will lay their hands on you and persecute you, turning you over to the synagogues and prisons, bringing you before kings and governors on account of My name. It will lead to an opportunity for your testimony. So make up your minds not to prepare beforehand to defend yourselves; for I will provide you eloquence and wisdom which none of your adversaries will be able to oppose or refute. But you will be betrayed even by parents, brothers and sisters, other relatives, and friends, and they will put some of you to death, and you will be hated by all people because of My name. And yet not a hair of your head will perish. By your endurance you will gain your lives" (verses 12–19).

Jesus warned of tough times ahead for the disciples who have followed Him faithfully. They needed to be prepared for persecution, betrayal, and even death. Luke's sequel, Acts of the Apostles, confirms how His words were fulfilled in the years following His departure:

- "They will lay their hands on you" (Acts 4:3; 5:18; 12:1; 21:27)
- "And persecute you" (Acts 11:19)
- "Turning you over to synagogues and prisons" (Acts 5:19, 22, 25; 8:3; 9:2; 12:4–6; 16:16–40; 22:19; 26:10, 11)
- "Bringing you before kings and governors" (Acts 12:1–11; 23:24–24:27; 25:1–26)
- "Make up your minds" (Acts 19:21)
- "I will provide you eloquence and wisdom" (Acts 4:8–12; 5:29–32; 6:10)
- "They will put some of you to death" (Acts 7:54–60; 12:1, 2; 26:10)[6]

All this was fulfilled in the early church. Throughout this part of Luke's Gospel, we find Jesus directing the minds of His disciples to God's strong control and purpose. "It is this that determines whether they live or die, not the machinations of their enemies."[7] Perseverance to the end is what is required.

Reflection

We tend to think "time of the end" whenever the world and our existence are threatened by wars, violence, or natural disasters. How does it impact our faith? Why?

---

1. Robert H. Stein, *Luke*, The New American Commentary, vol. 24 (Nashville, TN: Broadman, 1992), 510.
2. Joel B. Green, *The Gospel of Luke*, New International Commentary on the New Testament, vol. 3 (Grand Rapids, MI: Eerdmans, 1997), 733.
3. Darrell L. Bock, *Luke* (Grand Rapids, MI: Baker Academic, 1994), 1658, 1659. Luke makes a clearer distinction between the two events than does either Matthew or Mark.
4. Stein, *Luke*, 513.

5. Morten H. Jensen, "Climate, Droughts, Wars, and Famines in Galilee as a Background for Understanding the Historical Jesus," *Journal of Biblical Literature* 131, no. 2 (2012): 307–324. See also *NIV Cultural Backgrounds Study Bible* (Grand Rapids, MI: Zondervan, 2016), 1792.

6. Stein, *Luke*, 516, 517.

7. Leon Morris, *Luke: An Introduction and Commentary*, Tyndale New Testament Commentaries, vol. 3 (Downers Grove, IL: IVP Academic, 1988), 315.

Chapter 82

Jerusalem's Destruction

Luke 21:20–24 (Matthew 24:15–28; Mark 13:14–23)

Twice before, Jesus had described Jerusalem's future doom. At one time, while in conversation with some Pharisees, Jesus uttered, "Jerusalem, Jerusalem, the city that kills the prophets and stones those who have been sent to her! . . . Behold, your house is left to you desolate" (Luke 13:34, 35). More recently, during His triumphal entry, Jesus wept for the city and made similar predictions: "The days will come upon you when your enemies will put up a barricade against you, and surround you and hem you in on every side, and they will level you to the ground, and throw down your children within you, and they will not leave in you one stone upon another, because you did not recognize the time of your visitation" (Luke 19:41–44).

Now, as Jesus and the Twelve walked away from the temple at the end of the day, Jesus responded to their remarks of admiration about its magnificence with another prediction of its coming destruction (Luke 21:5, 6). This third statement created a sad, somber picture.

"But when you see Jerusalem surrounded by armies, then recognize that her desolation is near" (verse 20).

Luke's reference to Jerusalem's "desolation" echoes the prophetic words of Daniel about the abomination that makes desolate in a time prophecy that came to fulfillment in the Incarnation (Daniel 9:24–27). Both Matthew and Mark cite the exact words from Daniel (Matthew 24:15; Mark 13:14), but Luke didn't, perhaps "because his Gentile readers would not have understood this expression."[1]

Luke, more than the other Gospel writers, understood that there would be a significant time gap between the time of his writing and the second coming of Jesus.[2] Clearly, "for Luke, Jerusalem is not the city of the end-time. His symbolic world does not picture the nations swarming to Jerusalem to receive the gospel."[3] He carefully separated the account of Jerusalem's destruction from the signs of the end time.[4] He omitted portions of Matthew's and Mark's accounts that failed to make this distinction.[5] Luke intentionally separates the two events because his non-Jewish readers will want to focus on signs of the end more than on what happened to Jerusalem.

"Then those who are in Judea must flee to the mountains, and those who are inside the city must leave, and those who are in the country must not enter the city; because these are days of punishment, so that all things which have been written will be fulfilled. Woe to those women who are pregnant, and to those who are nursing babies in those days; for there will be great distress upon the land, and wrath to this people" (Luke 21:21–23).

As the city came under siege by the Roman armies, people in the city were to leave while they could, and those living in the surrounding villages and towns were warned not to go into Jerusalem. Judeans were counseled to "flee to the mountains" (verse 21). Eusebius, an early Christian historian, told how Christians fled to the remote town of Pella east of the Jordan River during the Jewish wars that led up to AD 70.[6]

Jesus expressed special compassion for pregnant women and those nursing babies at that terrible time. Matthew's account counseled people to pray that their flight from the city will not happen in the winter or on a Sabbath day (Matthew 24:20). In each account, a time of great distress is envisaged.

"And they will fall by the edge of the sword, and will be led captive into all the nations; and Jerusalem will be trampled underfoot by the Gentiles until the times of the Gentiles are fulfilled" (Luke 21:24).

Josephus recorded that more than one million Jews were killed by the Romans and 97,000 taken as slaves. Even children were cooked for food in the midst of the siege and famine. Sadly, "when they went in numbers into the lanes of the city, with their swords drawn, they slew those whom they overtook, without mercy, and set fire to the houses whither the Jews were fled, and burnt every soul in them, and laid waste a great many of the rest; and when they were come to the houses to plunder them, they found in them entire families of dead men, and the upper rooms full of dead corpses, that is of such as died by the famine."[7]

Thus, Jerusalem was "trampled underfoot by the Gentiles." Did its destruction mean the end of Israel's role within the divine purpose? Paul asked the same question in his letter to the Romans, "I say, then, God has not rejected his people, has He? Far from it! . . . God has not rejected His people whom He foreknew" (Romans 11:1, 2). Drawing lessons from the prophets and king David, Paul sees God drawing a remnant of Israel into His faithful church: "You will say then, 'Branches were broken off so that I might be grafted in' " (verse 23).

Reflection

As a follower of Jesus, what is my attitude toward people of other faiths, such as Buddhists, Hindus, Jews, or Muslims? How might that change?

1. Robert H. Stein, *Luke*, The New American Commentary, vol. 24 (Nashville, TN: Broadman, 1992), 519.
2. Mikeal C. Parsons, *Luke: Storyteller, Interpreter, Evangelist* (Peabody, MA: Hendrickson, 2007), 94.
3. Parsons, 40.
4. Darrell L. Bock, *A Theology of Luke and Acts* (Grand Rapids, MI: Zondervan, 2012), 401, 402.
5. Darrell L. Bock, *Luke* (Grand Rapids, MI: Baker Academic, 1994), 1675.
6. Bock, 1678.
7. Flavius Josephus, *The Works of Flavius Josephus: In Four Volumes*, trans. William Whiston (London: Lackington, Allen, and Co., 1811), 265.

Chapter 83

The Return of Christ

Luke 21:25–38 (Matthew 24:24–44; Mark 13:24–37)

Luke now looked far ahead to the return of Jesus and the world conditions that would precede it. In this Lucan account, Jesus was again with the Twelve as He heralded the apocalypse—an outburst of climactic events at the end of time. Hear these words from Isaiah:

> Behold, the day of the LORD is coming,
> Cruel, with fury and burning anger,
> To make the land a desolation;
> And He will exterminate its sinners from it.
> For the stars of heaven and their constellations
> Will not flash their light;
> The sun will be dark when it rises
> And the moon will not shed its light (Isaiah 13:9, 10).

Also,

> The earth is broken apart,
> The earth is split through,
> The earth is shaken violently.
> The earth trembles like a heavy drinker (Isaiah 24:19, 20).

And "the sky will be rolled up like a scroll" (Isaiah 34:4).

"There will be signs in the sun and moon and stars, and on the earth distress among nations, in perplexity at the roaring of the sea and the waves, people fainting from fear and the expectation of the things that are coming upon the world; for the powers of the heavens will be shaken" (Luke 21:25, 26).

The signs preceding the coming of Jesus are cosmic in nature. The entire creation reacts to the event of Jesus' return. The upheaval of the earth and sky produces fear and dismay in the hearts of people. "When one considers how helpless people feel in the face of the full fury of a natural disaster, one can see the mood Jesus conveys here."[1] Jesus had already given His disciples a limited preview of the event (Luke 17:23, 24, 37).

"And then they will see the Son of Man coming in a cloud with power and great glory. But when these things begin to take place, straighten up and lift up your heads, because your redemption is drawing near" (Luke 21:27, 28).

Jesus will come "in a cloud with power and great glory" (verse 27). God's presence with Israel in their wilderness journey was seen as a cloud by day and a pillar of fire by night (Exodus 13:21). Similarly, He came in a cloud when He met Moses on the mount (Exodus 34:5), and there was a cloud of glory at Jesus' transfiguration (Luke 9:34, 35). David wrote, "He makes the clouds His chariot" (Psalm 104:3). Riding on a cloud presents a regal picture of Jesus returning in power and splendor.

When Jesus again referred to Himself as "the Son of Man," we are reminded of the Daniel 7:

> "I kept looking in the night visions,
> And behold, with the clouds of heaven
> One like a son of man was coming,
> And He came up to the Ancient of Days
> And was presented before Him.
> And to Him was given dominion,
> Honor, and a kingdom. . . .
> His dominion is an everlasting dominion
> Which will not pass away" (verses 13, 14).

The vision continued: "Then the sovereignty, the dominion, and the greatness of all the kingdoms under the whole heaven will be given to the people of the saints of the Highest One; His kingdom will be an everlasting kingdom" (verse 27).

At this great moment, the faithful are to "lift up their heads" (Luke 21:28), in total contrast to the nations who cower with foreboding. The reason is, "your redemption is drawing near" (verse 28). In response to these words, Peter will later preach a message of repentance to the crowds: "Therefore repent and return, so that your sins may be wiped away" (Acts 3:19).

And He told them a parable: "Look at the fig tree and all the trees: as soon as they put forth leaves, you see for yourselves and know that summer is now near. So you too, when you see these things happening, recognize that the kingdom of God is near" (Luke 21:29–31).

Next, Jesus told a short parable about a fig tree that grows widely in Palestine. The tree is bare during the winter, so the appearance of buds and leaves is a sure sign of the coming summer. Luke's audience may not be familiar with the fig tree, so he added "and all the trees" as they produce new leaves each spring. As the coming of new leaves is an early sign of summer, Jesus' followers are to look for the signs that His return is imminent.

Throughout His teaching, Jesus introduced His kingdom in two ways: the "now" or "already" kingdom (Luke 10:9, 11; 11:20; 17:21; 19:11) and the "not yet" (Luke 11:2; 14:15; 17:20). Speaking about His return in glory, Jesus describes the "not yet" kingdom that will finally become a reality. The unfolding of the event is told in Revelation 19:11–22:15.

"Truly I say to you, this generation will not pass away until all things take place. Heaven and earth

will pass away, but My words will not pass away" (Luke 21:32, 33).

What did Jesus mean by "this generation"? His disciples? The Jews living at that time? Or humanity in general, along with all the problems that sin has caused?[2] In Luke's Gospel, "this generation" has previously signified a *category of people* who are resistant to God's purposes (Luke 7:31; 9:41; 11:29–32, 50, 51; 16:8; 17:25). So, "this generation" refers not to a particular time in history but to people who stubbornly turn their backs on the divine purpose.[3] Finally, Jesus emphasized the certainty of His words—creation is less permanent than the truth He teaches.

"But be on your guard, so that your hearts will not be weighed down with dissipation and drunkenness and the worries of life, and that this day will not come on you suddenly, like a trap; for it will come upon all those who live on the face of all the earth. But stay alert at all times, praying that you will have strength to escape all these things that are going to take place, and to stand before the Son of Man" (Luke 21:34–36).

"Be on your guard," counseled Jesus. Since we don't know when Jesus will return, there is danger in waiting because we are impatient by nature and prone to get careless, believing that He will never come or that it makes no difference how we live.[4] The day will come suddenly, unexpectedly, Jesus warned, and it will catch those who are not ready, like a trap. This is a call to faithfulness and to a wonderful reward for those who stand firm. The faithful will have the joy of standing before Jesus and hearing His approving words, "Well done!"

Now during the day He was teaching in the temple, but at evening He would go out and spend the night on the mountain that is called Olivet. And all the people would get up very early in the morning to come to Him in the temple to listen to Him (verses 37, 38).

We can see a pattern during Passion Week. During each day, Jesus taught an approving crowd in the temple. Each evening, He left the city to spend the night at the Mount of Olives, bivouacking there with His disciples and crowds of people who had come to Jerusalem for Passover. On some evenings, Jesus walked to the welcoming home of Mary, Martha, and Lazarus at Bethany (Matthew 21:17).

Reflection

How do I live while I wait for Jesus to return?

1. When I see the signs Jesus talked about, then I will get ready.
2. I try to live faithfully every day.
3. I want to complete my education and get married before He comes.
4. I've memorized the promises of His soon return.
5. I'm waiting to see the events of Revelation happening before I get excited.
6. I just go about my life, sick of waiting.
7. I will spend some of my time helping people in need.

---

1. Darrell L. Bock, *Luke* (Grand Rapids, MI: Baker Academic, 1994), 1683.
2. Robert H. Stein, *Luke*, The New American Commentary, vol. 24 (Nashville, TN: Broadman, 1992), 526.
3. Joel B. Green, *The Gospel of Luke*, New International Commentary on the New Testament, vol. 3 (Grand Rapids, MI: Eerdmans, 1997), 742.
4. Bock, *Luke*, 1693.

Chapter 84

Preparation and Betrayal

Luke 22:1–13 (Matthew 26:1–5, 14–19; Mark 14:1, 2, 10–16)

As we open Luke 22, we enter the final phase of the Incarnation, the event to which the entire story of Jesus has been leading.

All through the week leading up to Passover, the Jewish leaders were very angry with this Man who rid the temple of its commercial income and attracted the poorer classes, who congregated around Him in the temple courts every day. Behind the scenes, they sought an opportunity to arrest Jesus. They tried all week to trap Him with their questions, but it didn't work. In fact, everything has worked to His advantage! However, an opportunity is about to open up.

Now the Feast of Unleavened Bread, which is called the Passover, was approaching. And the chief priests and the scribes were trying to find a way to put Him to death, since they were afraid of the people (verses 1, 2).

Originally, the seven-day Feast of Unleavened Bread commenced one day after the Passover (Numbers 28:16, 17), but by the time of Jesus, the two festivals were merged together as a single event. Passover is the most celebrated of the annual Jewish festivals, harkening back to the Exodus from Egypt, led by Moses. On the night before the Israelites left Egypt, each household slaughtered a lamb and ate it along with unleavened bread. Before midnight, some of the lamb's blood was spread on the doorposts, a sign that the occupants trusted God for their deliverance from slavery. That night, the firstborn of Egypt died while the firstborn of Israel were "passed over." God promised, "When I see the blood I will pass over you" (Exodus 12:13).

Truly, "the Passover was Almighty God's preview of His mercy and grace to send His Son, the Messiah, Yahshua (Jesus), as the Ultimate Lamb of God."[1] And remember the way John the Baptist introduced Jesus to the crowds gathered at the Jordan: "Behold, the Lamb of God who takes away the sin of the world!" (John 1:29).

Passover, then, is the time when the Jewish nation commemorated its past deliverance from bondage. The emphasis placed on the Passover is exemplified in that "it was the ambition of every Jew in every part of the world . . . to come to the Passover in Jerusalem at least once in his lifetime."[2] During the festival, families ate together, sang, and offered thanks and sacrifices to God. But while a huge influx of pilgrims experienced joy in celebrating life, the nation's leadership was scheming to bring death to the One who is the source of life.[3]

And Satan entered Judas, the one called Iscariot, who belonged to the number of the twelve. And he left and discussed with the chief priests and officers how he was to betray Him to them. And they

were delighted, and agreed to give him money. And so he consented, and began looking for a good opportunity to betray Him to them away from the crowd (Luke 22:3–6).

We've seen the motif of conflict throughout Luke's narrative, previewed in Simeon's prophetic words to Joseph and Mary (Luke 2:34). We saw it happen in the imprisonment and subsequent death of John the Baptist (Luke 3:18–20; 9:7–9), and again when Jesus was warned that Herod sought to kill Him (Luke 13:31–35).

The atmosphere of Jerusalem was highly charged. Perhaps half a million pilgrims[4] swarmed the city for the festival that celebrated their identity as a nation, and because of the crowds, Rome was also well represented. Judea's governor, Pilate, whose palace was in Caesarea on the coast, came to Jerusalem with a supportive band of soldiers for the duration.[5]

Jesus' disciples were present, and we may watch them with uncertainty. One of them, Judas Iscariot, betrayed his Master. Peter came perilously close to failure when he denied Jesus at the trial, and during their last meal together, all of them tried to figure out which one of them was the greatest. We must wait for Luke's account in Acts to see these men in decisive action for God.

The opportunity the leaders wanted came unexpectedly when Satan entered the heart of Judas when he surrendered his soul to the devil. Time and again, we see that "there is no handle on the outside of the door of the human heart. It must be opened from within."[6] What happened next was being orchestrated in the cosmic sphere. "The account shows that the events surrounding Jesus' ministry are part of a larger, cosmic drama between great spiritual powers. Heaven and hell are interested in the fate of Jesus. In the great chess match, this is Satan's major move to remove Jesus from the game."[7]

Why did Judas betray His Master? Was he disappointed that Jesus hadn't set up a political kingdom? Perhaps, but there is also evidence that Judas was covetous, a lover of money. At Bethany, a few days before Passover, Judas condemned the waste of perfume that Mary used to anoint Jesus: "He did not say this because he cared about the poor but because he was a thief; as keeper of the money bag, he used to help himself to what was put into it" (John 12:6, NIV). So, what the Jewish leadership could not engineer was achieved with the help of one of Jesus' own disciples. Judas ostensibly sold his Master for a sum of money when in fact, he sold himself to Satan.

Now the first day of Unleavened Bread came, on which the Passover lamb had to be sacrificed. And so Jesus sent Peter and John, saying, "Go and prepare the Passover for us, so that we may eat it." They said to Him, "Where do You want us to prepare it?" (Luke 22:7–9).

It's Thursday of Passion Week, the day before Passover, according to the official calendar.* All four Gospels agree that Jesus died on Friday afternoon (Matthew 26:45–50, Mark 15:33–37, Luke 23:44–46, and John 19:28–31), at the time of the evening sacrifice at the temple.[8] But before His arrest, Jesus asked Peter and John to prepare Passover for the group, and they responded with a logical question: "Where?"

And He said to them, "When you have entered the city, a man carrying a pitcher of water will meet you; follow him into the house that he enters. And you shall say to the owner of the house, 'The

---

* See Exodus 12 for the story of the first Passover. Leviticus 23:4–8 describes the feast of the Passover and Unleavened Bread, which began at sundown on the fourteenth day of the first month (verse 5). An additional resource to read about the Last Supper on Thursday and the Friday sacrifice is found in "A Servant of Servants" and "Calvary," two chapters in *The Desire of Ages*, by Ellen G. White.

Teacher says to you, "Where is the guest room in which I may eat the Passover with My disciples?" ' And he will show you a large, furnished upstairs room; prepare it there." And they left and found everything just as He had told them; and they prepared the Passover (verses 10–13).

Throughout the passion story, Jesus remains in control of the situation. Since Peter and John were Galileans, the layout of Jerusalem wasn't familiar to them, so Jesus gave very specific instructions. Every pilgrim knew that the Passover meal must be eaten within the city walls, and Jesus participated like any other pious pilgrim.

Entering the city, Peter and John would meet a man carrying a large jar of water—this is especially unusual because women normally had that role. They were to follow this man to a house, which they would enter and ask the owner for a properly furnished upper room. Everything took place just as Jesus outlined. Then the two disciples prepared the Passover meal. They went to the temple late afternoon to procure a lamb and then had it slain at the temple before they purchased bitter herbs, unleavened bread, and wine for the meal. Thus, Peter and John prepared the fellowship meal for the group in the upper room.[9]

Reflection

Luke showed us that Jesus followed a divine plan in everything. Does God have a plan and purpose for you? How do you discover what it is?

1. *NIV Cultural Backgrounds Study Bible* (Grand Rapids, MI: Zondervan, 2016), 1793.
2. William Barclay, *The Gospel of Luke* (Philadelphia, PA: Westminster Press, 1975), 263.
3. Darrell L. Bock, *Luke* (Grand Rapids, MI: Baker Academic, 1994), 1703.
4. *NIV Cultural Backgrounds Study Bible*, 1746.
5. Joel B. Green, *The Gospel of Luke*, New International Commentary on the New Testament, vol. 3 (Grand Rapids, MI: Eerdmans, 1997), 744, 745.
6. Barclay, *Gospel of Luke*, 263.
7. Bock, *Luke*, 1706.
8. Ellen G. White, *The Desire of Ages* (Nampa, ID: Pacific Press®, 2005), 756, 757.
9. Bock, *Luke*, 1711.

Chapter 85

The Last Supper

Luke 22:14–20 (Matthew 26:26–29; Mark 14:22–25)

This is the seventh meal scene with Jesus recorded in Luke. We should also note that Jesus included table scenes in some of the parables (Luke 14:7–14, 16–24; 15:11–24). As we review the previous dining events with Jesus, we observe that His sharing a meal with others served one or both of these purposes:

- Community-building—with Levi and sinners (Luke 5:29), with a crowd of five thousand (Luke 9:12), and with Mary and Martha (Luke 10:38).
- Boundary-marking—with Pharisees and a sinful woman (Luke 7:36), with Pharisees and scribes (Luke 11:37), and with Pharisees after a Sabbath healing (Luke 14:1).

Some form of conflict is observable in all six of those table settings, and it will be evident again in this farewell meal with the disciples.[1]

When the hour came, He reclined at the table, and the apostles with Him. And He said to them, "I have eagerly desired to eat this Passover with you before I suffer; for I say to you, I shall not eat it again until it is fulfilled in the kingdom of God" (Luke 22:14–16).

It was early Thursday evening when Jesus and the Twelve sat together in the upper room in Jerusalem. Peter and John had faithfully prepared the Passover for the group, but as everyone arrived, they expected that a slave would be on hand to remove their sandals and wash their dirty feet. But no slave appeared, so Jesus took the initiative. Taking a basin and a towel, He knelt behind these men, one by one, and did the work of a slave by washing each pair of soiled feet (John 13:5–11). What humility!

Reclining on cushions around a low table was characteristic of a festive meal. Jews had adopted the Greco-Roman "symposium" style for their Passover meal.[2] There, in the upper room, the disciples partook of the lamb, not yet conscious that their Master was preparing to offer Himself as the ultimate Passover Lamb.

And when He had taken a cup and given thanks, He said, "Take this and share it among yourselves; for I say to you, I will not drink of the fruit of the vine from now on until the kingdom of God comes" (Luke 22:17, 18).

According to ancient sources, the order of celebration at a Passover meal went as follows:[3]

- The head of the family—Jesus on this occasion—pronounced a blessing over the first cup, which is shared, followed by herbs dipped in a sauce. Luke 22:17 reflects this beginning.
- Before the second cup was taken, the youngest son asked why this meal was special; in reply, the head of the family told the story of the Exodus. This was followed by the singing of part of the Hallel (Psalms 113; 114).
- The head of the family then took the unleavened bread, blessed it, broke it, and handed it to the others (Luke 22:19). This was followed by the meal itself.
- At the end, there was the third cup of wine (verse 20), along with the singing of the second part of the Hallel (Psalms 115–118).

And when He had taken some bread and given thanks, He broke it and gave it to them, saying, "This is My body, which is being given for you; do this in remembrance of Me." And in the same way He took the cup after they had eaten, saying, "This cup, which is poured out for you, is the new covenant in My blood" (Luke 22:19, 20).

As they followed steps three and four of the traditional order, Jesus introduced something entirely new in the breaking of the bread and in the third and final cup. Traditionally, as the family head broke the bread, he would explain its significance by saying something like, "This is the bread of affliction which our ancestors ate when they came out of Egypt."[4] Jesus, however, surprised His hearers with new meanings.[5] As He broke the bread, He handed pieces to each disciple, and as they ate and drank, they learned three things:

1. The bread now represents His body, which will be broken in His death verse 19).
2. The cup represents Jesus' spilled blood (verse 20).
3. They are to do this often as a way of remembering that His death was for them.

In taking the cup (verse 20), Jesus announced that the wine represented His shed blood. More than this, though, it inaugurated a "new covenant." God's salvation plan has reached a new phase. Those who ally themselves with Jesus receive the benefits of salvation through His sacrifice.

Luke is the only Gospel writer who followed the traditional order of the meal, as outlined above, and included Christ's instruction that His followers are to partake often of these emblems of His death for the sinner.[6] Interestingly, Paul almost duplicated the words of Luke when he wrote to the Corinthian believers, "The Lord Jesus, on the night when He was betrayed, took bread; and when He had given thanks, He broke it and said, 'This is My body, which is for you; do this in remembrance of Me.' In the same way He also took the cup after supper, saying, 'This cup is the new covenant in My blood; do this, as often as you drink it, in remembrance of Me.' For as often as you eat this bread and drink the cup, you proclaim the Lord's death until He comes" (1 Corinthians 11:23–26). "It [Jesus' death] has repercussions for the fate of the Twelve and others like them who have tied their fate to Jesus. He dies for them. He gives himself up for them. Here is not only deep theological truth, but great love."[7] And Paul encourages readers, "But God showed his great love for us by sending Christ to die for us while we were still sinners" (Romans 5:8, NLT).

Reflection

Does your church practice Communion? How might it help you spiritually to look backward? And then how might it help you look forward?

1. Joel B. Green, *The Gospel of Luke* (Grand Rapids, MI: Eerdmans, 1997), 756.

2. *NIV Cultural Backgrounds Study Bible* (Grand Rapids, MI: Zondervan, 2016), 1793.

3. Green, *Gospel of Luke*, 758; Darrell L. Bock, *Luke* (Grand Rapids, MI: Baker Academic, 1994), 1722.

4. See Deuteronomy 16:3 and "Passover Foods: What's Kosher?" Haggadot.com, accessed November 2, 2022, https://www.haggadot.com/passover101/food.

5. *NIV Cultural Backgrounds Study Bible*, 1794.

6. Bock, *Luke*, 1725–1727.

7. Bock, 1725.

Chapter 86

The Farewell Discourse

Luke 22:21–38 (Matthew 26:21–25, 30–35; Mark 14:18–21, 26–31; John 13:21–30, 36–38)

When the Passover was finished, Jesus continued to share with His disciples some of what was on His mind. Five chapters of John's Gospel are filled with Jesus' conversation and prayers with His disciples that evening (John 13–17).

In contrast, Luke's account is concise and unique. He introduces a type of "table talk" with which he, as a Gentile, was familiar. Luke's model was the Greco-Roman Symposium which began with a shared meal—like the Last Supper—followed by words from a guest who would select one or more topics to engage the group in conversation.[1] Here, Jesus is the guest. The disciples listened, made comments, asked questions, and discussed. But Jesus began with a statement that shocked His listeners.

"But behold, the hand of the one betraying Me is with Mine on the table. For indeed, the Son of Man is going as it has been determined; but woe to that man by whom He is betrayed!" And they began to debate among themselves which one of them it was who was going to do this (Luke 22:21–23).

The one who would betray their Master sat among them—he had eaten food and shared the cup with them. He heard Jesus interpret the bread and wine as His own body and blood to be broken and spilled for them. Though present, Judas had not yet been identified as the betrayer. I'm sure the startled disciples looked at each other with astonishment and began to ask among themselves, *Is it me? Which one of us would do this thing?* Jesus made it clear that this betrayal was inevitable because it was part of God's plan.

When Jesus said, "the Son of Man is going as it has been determined" (verse 22), He was referencing words from a vision of the prophet Daniel (Daniel 7:13, 14, 21, 22). Judas, though responsible for his actions, is also a player in a cosmic controversy.[2] What thoughts crowded his mind as he participated in the shared meal and heard Jesus' deeply meaningful words? We cannot know, but when he quietly rose from the table, left the upper room, and descended the outside steps to the dark streets of Jerusalem, his mind was made up. He would sell Jesus for thirty silver coins—the price of a slave.

And a dispute also developed among them as to which one of them was regarded as being the greatest. And He said to them, "The kings of the Gentiles domineer over them; and those who have authority over them are called 'Benefactors.' But it is not this way for you; rather, the one who is the greatest among you must become like the youngest, and the leader like the servant. For who is greater, the one who reclines at the table or the one who serves? Is it not the one who reclines at the table? But I am among you as the one who serves" (Luke 22:24–27).

Disputes about status had bothered the disciples for a long time. That night, though, they were shocked to discover that Judas had betrayed their Master. And he was the treasurer! That gave him status. Who would take over his role? I imagine this may have influenced the argument over which disciple was the greatest. It is noteworthy that "although one of the twelve will 'betray' Jesus, Luke suggests in this ironic way that all twelve of them 'betray' his basic kingdom message with its immediate implications for issues of status and position."[3] Their thinking mimicked the scribes and Pharisees who selected their table places according to their self-determined status within a group (Luke 14:7–14), but it was almost inconceivable that Jesus' own followers were so out of step with His teaching and example. In this very room, they had sheepishly watched as Jesus bathed and dried their soiled feet.

So, Jesus drew an important lesson for them. The ways of God's kingdom are totally at odds with the ways of the world, where "Gentiles" practice status in the way they manage affairs and people. Jesus emphasized, "But it is not this way for you" (Luke 22:26). Greatness is conferred not by age or position but by humble service. Jesus had just given them a prime example of what it means to be a servant-leader. The disciples must learn, "if Jesus is great and he does not live like the world, how should his followers live? The call is clear: live by serving."[4]

"You are the ones who have stood by Me in My trials; and just as My Father has granted Me a kingdom, I grant you that you may eat and drink at My table in My kingdom, and you will sit on thrones judging the twelve tribes of Israel" (verses 28–30).

Jesus foresaw that these men, right now struggling with daunting issues, would become faithful leaders for gospel advance and have fellowship with Him in His future kingdom. As He observed their troubled thoughts, He mercifully expressed appreciation for their loyalty to Him, with the promise of a glorious future.

Sadly, they still weren't ready to hear everything that Jesus wanted to tell them (John 16:12). Mark records Jesus saying that "all of you will desert me" this night (Mark 14:27, NLT), including Peter.

"Simon, Simon, behold, Satan has demanded to sift you men like wheat; but I have prayed for you, that your faith will not fail; and you, when you have turned back, strengthen your brothers." But he said to Him, "Lord, I am ready to go with You both to prison and to death!" But He said, "I tell you, Peter, the rooster will not crow today until you have denied three times that you know Me" (Luke 22:31–34).

However, Peter was not the only one in danger. Satan was "demanding" to take all eleven remaining disciples just as he took Judas. But Jesus was praying for His flock, including Peter, who remained adamant about his loyalty to his Master. He would never play false with his Lord as Judas had, asserting, "Even though everyone else deserts You, I will never do that! I don't care if I have to go to prison with You—or even die with You—I will never deny You! Never!"

How encouraging to note that Jesus prayed for Peter: "I have pleaded in prayer for you, Simon, that your faith should not fail. So when you have repented and turned to me again, strengthen your brothers" (verse 32, NLT). Although Peter would deny his Lord three times before the next day dawned, he would "turn back" and lead multitudes to Jesus through the power of the Holy Spirit.

And He said to them, "When I sent you out without money belt and bag and sandals, you did not lack anything, did you?" They said, "No, nothing" (verse 35).

Life in Galilee was comparatively peaceful and secure. When Jesus sent the disciples on their first missionary journey, they were cared for and protected. But that was then. Their future ministry would be different.

And He said to them, "But now, whoever has a money belt is to take it along, likewise also a bag, and whoever has no sword is to sell his cloak and buy one. For I tell you that this which is written must be fulfilled in Me: 'AND HE WAS COUNTED WITH WRONGDOERS'; for that which refers to Me has its fulfillment." They said, "Lord, look, here are two swords." And He said to them, "It is enough" (verses 36–38).

Whoa! What did Jesus just say? As their time together drew to a close, Jesus sought to prepare His disciples for the challenging days ahead. He was about to pass through an ordeal of suffering and death, and He told them that He would be treated like a criminal and hung on a cross between two condemned men (Isaiah 53:12). In the future, the disciples also faced times of suffering and death, and I'm sure they wondered if they must equip themselves with swords for their defense.[5]

But William Barclay believed the talk about swords was simply "a vivid eastern way of telling the disciples that their very lives were at stake."[6] Praise God for the promise of the Holy Spirit to guide and empower them as they taught and preached the gospel (John 14:15–17). They would be armed with prayer and faith in God. Jesus had once said, "I did not come to bring peace, but a sword" (Matthew 10:34). He used the *sword* as a figure of speech, a symbol of preparation for opposition. But the disciples were edgy that night, and they took the remark literally: "Look, Lord! Here are two swords." He responded, "Enough of this!" Thankfully, "by the time of the Book of Acts, they will understand what Jesus meant. They will learn to look constantly to God."[7]

Reflection

Under pressure, will I be faithful to my convictions? How will I achieve that?

1. Joel B. Green, *The Gospel of Luke*, New International Commentary on the New Testament, vol. 3 (Grand Rapids, MI: Eerdmans, 1997), 766.
2. *NIV Cultural Backgrounds Study Bible* (Grand Rapids, MI: Zondervan, 2016), 1794.
3. Green, *Gospel of Luke*, 766.
4. Darrell L. Bock, *Luke* (Grand Rapids, MI: Baker Academic, 1994), 1739.
5. *NIV Cultural Backgrounds Study Bible*, 1794.
6. William Barclay, *The Gospel of Luke* (Philadelphia, PA: Westminster Press, 1975), 270.
7. Bock, *Luke*, 1751.

Chapter 87

In the Garden

Luke 22:39–53 (Matthew 26:36–56; Mark 14:32–52; John 18:1–12)

And He came out and went, as was His habit, to the Mount of Olives; and the disciples also followed Him (Luke 22:39).

Late Thursday night, Jesus left the upper room with the eleven disciples. They went out of the city and followed a path to the Mount of Olives (Luke 21:37). Like many other festival pilgrims, they left the city each night and found quiet sleeping places in the garden area among the olive groves. But the mood was noticeably different that night—somber and troubled.

All twelve disciples had shared a meal together in the upper room, after which Jesus shared a farewell message with them. Soon He would be leaving them to go to His Father, He said. But don't be afraid, He told them, because one day He would come back and take His followers home with Him (John 14:1–3). Naturally, they had many questions: "Where are you going? Why can't we go with you? Is the Father anything like you?" (see John 14:5–13).

Now when He arrived at the place, He said to them, "Pray that you do not come into temptation." And He withdrew from them about a stone's throw, and He knelt down and began to pray, saying, "Father, if You are willing, remove this cup from Me; yet not My will, but Yours be done." [Now an angel from heaven appeared to Him, strengthening Him. And being in agony, He was praying very fervently; and His sweat became like drops of blood, falling down upon the ground] (Luke 22:40–44).

Arriving at the customary site, Jesus asked the eleven remaining disciples to pray. When testing came, they must depend on God to give them strength (Luke 11:1–4). Jesus walked a short distance away and knelt in prayer to His Father. Jews normally stood to pray—recall the Pharisee and tax collector in the temple—but kneeling emphasized submission to the will of God. That night, Jesus uttered a prayer of wholehearted obedience: "Father, if You are willing, remove this cup from Me; yet not My will, but Yours be done" (Luke 22:42). The cup symbolizes suffering, and that night reality pressed in. "He was only thirty-three; and no one wants to die at thirty-three. He knew what crucifixion was like; he had seen it. . . . There is no scene like this in all history."[1]

There are several ways to say, "Your will be done"; you can say it with a feeling of hopelessness, or of frustration, or as one who's been "battered into submission"—or "with the accent of perfect trust." Jesus spoke to the One in whom He has full confidence, His Father.[2]

The struggle in the Garden that night was cosmic; it was Satan's last focused opportunity to accomplish what he failed to do at the outset of Jesus' ministry (Luke 4:1–13). Authority is again in the balance. Now, as then, Jesus maintained His oneness with the Father. That oneness between God and Jesus is something

259

that humans will forever contemplate but never fully understand. Eventually, an angel came to strengthen Jesus in His hour of spiritual agony,* measured as tears (Hebrews 5:7) and sweat that has the appearance of blood. In submitting to the will of His Father, Jesus chose to die, to endure the cross of shame. Satan also wants Jesus to die, but on *his* terms.[3]

When He rose from prayer, He came to the disciples and found them sleeping from sorrow, and He said to them, "Why are you sleeping? Get up and pray that you do not come into temptation" (Luke 22:45, 46).

It was customary on Passover to stay awake and talk of God's acts of redemption, but after His prayer, Jesus found the disciples asleep.[4] It had been an exhausting time, their shock and mental stress were great, and they were beat. They awakened as He again urged them to pray. But His words were interrupted by voices of approaching men in the darkness.

While He was still speaking, behold, a crowd came, and the one called Judas, one of the twelve, was leading the way for them; and he approached Jesus to kiss Him. But Jesus said to him, "Judas, are you betraying the Son of Man with a kiss?" (verses 47, 48).

Judas led "a crowd" through the olive grove to the familiar spot where he confidently expected to find Jesus. Coming upon Him and the disciples, Judas believed he was in charge. He had told the soldiers to arrest the one he kissed. But his plans were intercepted because Jesus took control of the situation with a pointed question, "Judas, are you betraying Me with a kiss?"

When those who were around Him saw what was going to happen, they said, "Lord, shall we strike with the sword?" And one of them struck the slave of the high priest and cut off his right ear. But Jesus responded and said, "Stop! No more of this." And He touched his ear and healed him (Luke 22:49–51).

Jesus entered this situation composed and confident after wrestling in prayer, but the disciples had slept, and they responded with agitation and miscomprehension.[5] Dimly remembering the evening discussion about swords, they were ready to defend their Master and asked Him, "Shall we strike with the sword?" (verse 49). The words were hardly uttered before one of them, Peter (John 18:10), unpracticed, struck out with the sword and missed the head of the high priest's servant but sliced off his right ear. "Stop!" exclaimed Jesus, "No more of this!" (Luke 22:51). And in that highly stressful moment, He performed His last recorded healing by restoring the servant's ear. Jesus acted with compassion and demonstrated His love for His enemies (Luke 6:27, 28).[6]

And Jesus said to the chief priests and officers of the temple and elders who had come against Him, "Have you come out with swords and clubs as you would against a man inciting a revolt? While I was with you daily in the temple, you did not lay hands on Me; but this hour and the power of darkness are yours" (Luke 22:52, 53).

Among the crowd with Judas were chief priests, temple officers, elders, servants, and soldiers. "You

---

* Similarly, the Old Testament shares stories of an angel sent to help Elijah (1 Kings 19:5–8) and Daniel (Daniel 3:24–26; 10:17–19).

are treating Me like a revolutionary," Jesus said. "Why didn't you lay hands on Me while I taught in the temple each day?" Then, knowing the cosmic nature of all this, He added, "This hour and the power of darkness belong to you." "He [Jesus] notes that the tone of the arrest is all wrong, for he is not a criminal (as his healing proves). He describes the nature of the times as darkness, rejection, and evil. A mood of somber description falls upon the account like a dark cloud. Jesus is headed to trial. But the reader is to note who is in control. The hour of darkness, too, will pass."[7]

Reflection

How does the story of Jesus wrestling in prayer affect you? Consider the following:

1. Circumstances sometimes cause me to doubt God's goodness.
2. The humanity of Jesus gives me hope.
3. I need a Savior who knows what it's like to have big questions.
4. His mental anxiety exceeded anything that I will ever experience.
5. The future of the world hung in the balance as He wrestled.
6. His disciples had abandoned Him.
7. I can also wrestle in prayer when I feel angry or overwhelmed.

---

1. William Barclay, *The Gospel of Luke* (Philadelphia, PA: Westminster Press, 1975), 271.
2. Barclay, 272.
3. Joel B. Green, *The Gospel of Luke*, New International Commentary on the New Testament, vol. 3 (Grand Rapids, MI: Eerdmans, 1997), 779.
4. *NIV Cultural Backgrounds Study Bible* (Grand Rapids, MI: Zondervan, 2016), 1795.
5. Green, *Gospel of Luke*, 782.
6. Darrell L. Bock, *Luke* (Grand Rapids, MI: Baker Academic, 1994), 1771.
7. Bock, 1774.

Chapter 88

"The Power of Darkness"

Luke 22:54–71 (Matthew 26:57–27:1; Mark 14:53–72; John 18:12–27)

In the darkness of the garden, Jesus was arrested and taken to the high priest's house. Stunned by what happened, the disciples scattered—all except Peter, who followed the arresting party to the palace.

Now they arrested Him and led Him away, and brought Him to the house of the high priest; but Peter was following at a distance. After they kindled a fire in the middle of the courtyard and sat down together, Peter was sitting among them (Luke 22:54, 55).

The high priest's mansion was likely built around a central courtyard. Perhaps, while Jesus was questioned in the apartment of Annas (the associate high priest), a motley group of soldiers and slaves remained in the courtyard, where they kindled a fire to keep warm during the pre-dawn hours. And there, Peter found a place to sit by the fire.

And a slave woman, seeing him as he sat in the firelight, and staring at him, said, "This man was with Him as well." But he denied it, saying, "I do not know Him, woman!" And a little later, another person saw him and said, "You are one of them too!" But Peter said, "Man, I am not!" And after about an hour had passed, some other man began to insist, saying, "Certainly this man also was with Him, for he, too, is a Galilean." But Peter said, "Man, I do not know what you are talking about!" And immediately, while he was still speaking, a rooster crowed (Luke 22:56–60).

Less than twelve hours before, Peter had voiced a loud commitment to be faithful to Jesus—even to death if necessary. But now, under pressure and with Satan's promptings, he denied his Master three times:[1]

1. In the first occurrence, Peter denied his *relationship with Jesus*. There was recognition when a slave girl looked at him, "This man was with Him." Peter responded, "I do not know Him!" (verses 56, 57).
2. A little later, Peter denied his *relationship with his colleagues*. "You are one of them too," came from a man in the group. Peter responded, "Man, I am not!" (verse 58).
3. An hour goes by—enough time for Peter to reconsider his responses in light of his earlier commitment. Another man at the fireside insisted, "Certainly, this man was with Him. I can tell because he's a Galilean." This time Peter denied his *relationship to his past*, to the day on the shores of Galilee when Jesus called him to follow Him. Responding to the man's accusations,

Peter said, "I don't know what you are talking about!" (verses 59, 60). Immediately, Peter heard the crowing of a rooster.

And then the Lord turned and looked at Peter. And Peter remembered the word of the Lord, how He had told him, "Before a rooster crows today, you will deny Me three times." And he went out and wept bitterly (verses 61, 62).

This third denial may have happened just when Jesus was transferred from Annas's apartment to that of Caiaphas, the high priest (John 18:12–27). As Peter remembered his Master's prophetic words, Jesus looked at His failed disciple. Peter immediately left the scene and cried his heart out. I think he waited, alone and miserable, through Friday and Sabbath, but he also recalled Jesus' promise that he "would turn again" and be a strength to the people (Luke 22:32). Sure enough, Luke would later record Peter's powerful sermon to the Jews at Pentecost (Acts 2).

The men who were holding Jesus in custody began mocking Him and beating Him, and they blindfolded Him and repeatedly asked Him, saying, "Prophesy, who is the one who hit You?" And they were saying many other things against Him, blaspheming (Luke 22:63–65).

Some soldiers, who were probably tired and bored by all that was going on, mocked and abused Jesus. Their behavior violated all official legal ethics, though the abuse of prisoners was common.[2] Matthew describes spitting, striking, and slapping (Matthew 26:67). Isaiah predicted of Jesus,

> I offered my back to those who beat me,
>   my cheeks to those who pulled out my beard;
> I did not hide my face
>   from mocking and spitting (Isaiah 50:6, NIV).

That night, the guards beat Jesus and mocked His prophetic gift with a cruel game of "play the prophet,"[3] repeatedly demanding, "Tell us who hit you."

Meanwhile, dawn transitioned into day as Jesus was led to the council of judges known as the Sanhedrin. Called at this early hour on Passover Friday, the Jewish leaders were hard-pressed to get Jesus condemned before Jerusalem awakened to a festival day. What they were about to do was a travesty of justice.

The Sanhedrin was the supreme court of Judaism; it comprised seventy-one judges made up of chief priests, scribes, and elders. It met in a room within the temple complex, but not normally on a feast day. Technically, their meeting during Passover was illegal, but the alternative of holding Jesus through Friday and Sabbath was too risky for them to contemplate. They were afraid of what the crowds might do. So, they called together the chief priests and scribes for an urgent meeting and then brought Jesus before this group.

When it was day, the Council of elders of the people assembled, both chief priests and scribes, and they led Him away to their council chamber, saying, "If You are the Christ, tell us." But He said to them, "If I tell you, you will not believe; and if I ask a question, you will not answer. But from now on the Son of Man will be seated at the right hand of the power of God." And they

all said, "So You are the Son of God?" And He said to them, "You say correctly that I am." And then they said, "What further need do we have of testimony? For we have heard it ourselves from His own mouth!" (Luke 22:66–71).

The trial was a sham. Jesus said very little, claiming only that He would exercise authority over those who were judging Him. Matthew describes false witnesses that testified, but Jesus still remained silent (Matthew 26:59–63). Finally, the high priest demanded an answer from Jesus: "Are you the Son of God?" They wanted Jesus to incriminate Himself by claiming to be the Messiah.[4] "The trial proceeds . . . with only one witness (Jesus), only one answer (his claim that he will sit at God's right hand), and only one result (conviction). The leadership convicts Jesus on the basis of his own testimony. . . . Jesus drives the events that lead to his death. The issue is simply who he is."[5] With His clear statement, they charged Him with blasphemy.

Everything that happened was the outworking of the divine purpose. Note the double irony here. In calling for Jesus' execution, the Jewish leaders thought they were doing away with someone who opposed God's purpose for the temple and the nation. Yet, in sending Jesus to the cross, they unwittingly served God's plan to have the Son of God die for the sins of the whole world.[6] Earlier, Jesus Himself tried to prepare His disciples for this: "The Son of Man must suffer many things and be rejected by the elders and chief priests and scribes, and be killed and be raised on the third day" (Luke 9:22). But only afterwards would the disciples remember His words. Clearly, "the power of darkness would be allowed to do what it wanted with Jesus. Yet what took place was not their will but God's. . . . The opponents of Jesus had been granted this hour in order to fulfill God's plan as foretold in Scripture."[7] Satan tried to control the event, but in the end, he was only an instrument in God's hand.

Reflection

Put yourself in Peter's shoes after his three denials of his relationship with Jesus. Then read Mark 16:5–7. What does this tell you?

---

1. Joel B. Green, *The Gospel of Luke*, New International Commentary on the New Testament, vol. 3 (Grand Rapids, MI: Eerdmans, 1997), 787.

2. *NIV Cultural Backgrounds Study Bible* (Grand Rapids, MI: Zondervan, 2016), 1795.

3. Green, *Gospel of Luke*, 786.

4. Leon Morris, *Luke: An Introduction and Commentary* (Downers Grove, IL: IVP Academic, 1988), 335.

5. Darrell L. Bock, *Luke* (Grand Rapids, MI: Baker Academic, 1994), 1775.

6. James M. Dawsey, *The Lukan Voice: Confusion and Irony in the Gospel of Luke* (Macon, GA: Mercer University Press, 1986), 8, 9.

7. Robert H. Stein, *Luke*, The New American Commentary, vol. 24 (Nashville, TN: Broadman, 1992), 563.

Chapter 89

Before Pilate and Herod

Luke 23:1–12 (Matthew 27:2, 11–14; Mark 15:1–5; John 18:28–38)

The Jewish leaders engineered a conviction. Jesus had stated the truth that He is the Son of God, which to their Jewish ears was blasphemy and deserved death. But Roman law prevailed in Judea, so they could not put Jesus to death without a guilty verdict by the Roman governor, Pontius Pilate, who was conveniently in Jerusalem. So, the leaders made an early morning visit to Pilate.

Then the entire assembly of them set out and brought Him before Pilate. And they began to bring charges against Him, saying, "We found this man misleading our nation and forbidding us to pay taxes to Caesar, and saying that He Himself is Christ, a King" (Luke 23:1, 2).

It required only one or two men in authority to bring a case before Pilate, but believing that there's authority in numbers, the entire assembly set out with Jesus to the Fortress of Antonia in the northeastern sector of Jerusalem. The Jewish leadership planned to bring three charges against Jesus:

1. He "misleads our nation," which was another way of saying that many of Jesus' teachings, like loving one's enemies, lacked divine sanction in the thinking of scribes and Pharisees. Therefore, Jesus was a "false prophet" who deserved a death sentence, according to Deuteronomy 13.[1] Pilate, however, had no interest in this peculiar mix of Jewish customs and teachings.
2. He "forbids us to pay taxes to Caesar," which was a blatant lie, as they well knew (see Luke 20:25). This accusation might interest Pilate, except the Jews had no choice in the matter of paying taxes to Rome.
3. He "says that He is Messiah, a king." The terms *Christ* and *Messiah* were Jewish titles with little meaning to the Romans. But if Jesus claimed "kingship," that was a different story. If Jesus was a threat to Rome, He could be convicted as a revolutionary.[2]

This final charge was the only one to which Pilate responded.

Now Pilate asked Him, saying, "So You are the King of the Jews?" And He answered him and said, "It is as you say." But Pilate said to the chief priests and the crowds, "I find no grounds for charges in the case of this Man" (Luke 23:3, 4).

In his account, John records a lengthy exchange between Pilate and Jesus on this issue, concluding with Jesus' declaration that His kingship is not of this world (John 18:33–38). Luke simply records Jesus' response to Pilate's question by saying, "You have said so" (Luke 23:3, NIV). Pilate wasn't impressed with the charges brought against Jesus and perhaps regarded him as a harmless eccentric. He told the priests and leaders, "I find no grounds for charges against Him."

But they kept on insisting, saying, "He is stirring up the people, teaching all over Judea, starting from Galilee, as far as this place!"

Now when Pilate heard this, he asked whether the man was a Galilean. And when he learned that He belonged to Herod's jurisdiction, he sent Him to Herod, since he also was in Jerusalem at this time (Luke 23:5–7).

But the Jewish leaders were insistent, "Jesus stirs up the people everywhere—even in Galilee, with His teachings." That comment prompted Pilate to ask Jesus, "Are you a Galilean?" Receiving an affirmative, Pilate knew what to do. Although the Province of Galilee was ultimately under the authority of Rome, Herod Antipas had jurisdiction over that area. Herod also happened to be in Jerusalem at that time, ostensibly to show his support for the Passover festival. So, perhaps breathing a sigh of relief, Pilate decided to pass the buck by sending Jesus to Herod at his Jerusalem locale.

Now Herod was overjoyed when he saw Jesus; for he had wanted to see Him for a long time, because he had been hearing about Him and was hoping to see some sign performed by Him. And he questioned Him at some length; but He offered him no answer at all (verses 8, 9).

What made Herod so happy when the Jewish leaders brought Jesus to him? It turns out that for a long time, he had wanted to meet this wonder-worker. While the disciples were on their Galilean mission assignment, Herod tried unsuccessfully to meet Jesus (Luke 9:7–9). Then he was later reported as wanting to kill Jesus (Luke 13:31). Herod now seized the opportunity to interview Jesus, hoping for some entertainment by having Jesus perform miraculous wonders for him. He plied Jesus with questions but was met with total silence. Jesus would not answer Herod because His power was to be used in accordance with God's will, not for selfish whims and entertainment.[3]

Now the chief priests and the scribes stood there, vehemently charging Him. And Herod, together with his soldiers, treated Him with contempt and mocked Him, dressing Him in a brightly shining robe, and sent Him back to Pilate. And so Herod and Pilate became friends with one another that very day; for previously, they had been enemies toward each other (Luke 23:10–12).

In this encounter, Jesus again exhibited self-control, but Herod reacted with contempt. Herod and his guards mocked Jesus and finally dressed Him in some regal-looking clothing and sent Him back to Pilate. Justice was nonexistent. "Indifference to Jesus is as dangerous as opposition to him, for it allows injustice to continue and ignores God's activity and presence. Rationality is lacking in assessing Jesus. Frivolity is everywhere. People do not reckon seriously with his claims and wave them aside. Jesus' death makes no sense, if the scales of justice are applied. Such is the blindness of human sin."[4]

Reflection

How important is it to you that you serve a God of justice?

---

1. Joel B. Green, *The Gospel of Luke*, New International Commentary on the New Testament, vol. 3 (Grand Rapids, MI: Eerdmans, 1997), 800.

2. Darrell L. Bock, *Luke* (Grand Rapids, MI: Baker Academic, 1994), 1810, 1811.

3. Leon Morris, *Luke: An Introduction and Commentary* (Downers Grove, IL: IVP Academic, 1988), 339.

4. Bock, *Luke*, 1822.

Chapter 90

Sentencing by Pilate

Luke 23:13–25 (Matthew 27:15–26; Mark 15:6–15; John 18:38–40)

Pilate, the Roman governor, has already made two attempts to release Jesus, having declared Him innocent of any crime. In his first meeting with the Jewish leaders, very early in the morning, Pilate listened to their charges. He then sent Jesus to Herod, who also quizzed Jesus and probably believed Him to be innocent. Pilate tried three more times to get Jesus released.

Now Pilate summoned to himself the chief priests, the rulers, and the people, and he said to them, "You brought this man to me on the ground that He is inciting the people to revolt; and behold, after examining Him before you, I have found no basis at all in the case of this man for the charges which you are bringing against Him. No, nor has Herod, for he sent Him back to us; and behold, nothing deserving death has been done by Him. Therefore I will punish Him and release Him" (Luke 23:13–16).

Pilate called for something like a town meeting to present his report. Unfortunately, those people will not be the ones who listened to Jesus and hung on to His every word. Remember that during Passover, Jerusalem was a very crowded city, and the common people were forced to camp outside the city every night.[1] So it is safe for us to assume that the people who found places to stay in the city were the well-to-do, elite class, who mostly honored and respected the priests and Jewish leadership. In all likelihood, these are the people who responded to the summons and made their way to the Praetorium that Friday morning. Pilate reiterated his previous conclusion, essentially, "You brought this man to me with the accusation that He's a revolutionary leader. I have examined Him and found no basis for this charge against Him. Now Herod has also examined Him and sent Him back to us. He has done nothing deserving of death. I will scourge Him and then release Him."

[Now he was obligated to release to them at the feast one prisoner.]

But they cried out all together, saying, "Away with this Man, and release to us Barabbas!" (He was one who had been thrown into prison for a revolt that took place in the city, and for murder) (verses 17–19).

Responding to a request from the Jews, Pilate introduced the practice of releasing a Jewish prisoner at Passover time each year. The most notorious prisoner awaiting execution at this time was Barabbas, who had recently led an insurrection in Jerusalem and committed murder. He was awaiting crucifixion.

Given a choice, Pilate felt confident the people would not want the violent Barabbas back on the streets. Instead, the crowd called for his release! The man's name comes from two Greek words: *bar*, which means "son," and *abbas*, which means "papa." This son-of-a-father is being thrown into the ring with the real "Son of the Father," Jesus. Even more interesting are some New Testament manuscripts that give his name as "Jesus Barabbas" (Matthew 27:17, NIV). It's interesting to note that "some manuscripts include the name Jesus before the surname Barabbas, others do not. Given a clear disposition by Christian scribes copying the New Testament to hold Jesus' name in reverence, it is easy to understand how they might omit that name when used to refer to a criminal."[2]

But Pilate, wanting to release Jesus, addressed them again, but they kept on crying out, saying, "Crucify, crucify Him!" And he said to them a third time, "Why, what has this man done wrong? I have found in His case no grounds for a sentence of death; therefore I will punish Him and release Him" (Luke 23:20–22).

Pilate made two more attempts to release Jesus, but in vain. The crowd, egged on by the high priests and leaders, became noisy and insistent. With emotions stirred, it was a classic case of crowd psychology.

But they were insistent, with loud voices, demanding that He be crucified. And their voices began to prevail. And so Pilate decided to have their demand carried out. And he released the man for whom they were asking, who had been thrown into prison for a revolt and murder; but he handed Jesus over to their will (verses 23–25).

Finally, despite his certainty that Jesus was innocent, Pilate gave in to the will of the people. Barabbas, the revolutionary and murderer, would be set free, while the One who "went about doing good and healing" (Acts 10:38) would go to His death. Jesus was handed over to the Jewish leaders to do with Him as they would.[3]

I imagine that when Barabbas heard the jangling of keys and chains, he took a deep breath. His crucifixion was about to take place, and he knew he deserved his fate. But then the guard unlocked his door and told him, "Another fellow is to be crucified in your place. Another revolutionary, I think. His name is Jesus."

Yes, both men are revolutionaries. One used weapons, bloody violence, and murder in an effort to overthrow the might of Rome. The other uses even more powerful weapons—love and forgiveness. He will shed His own blood to lead a kingdom that is "not of this world" and will last forever.[4]

Reflection

Paul wrote, "For the wages of sin is death, but the gracious gift of God is eternal life in Christ Jesus our Lord" (Romans 6:23). Barabbas received this free gift. Have you?

---

1. Robert H. Stein, *Luke*, The New American Commentary, vol. 24 (Nashville, TN: Broadman, 1992), 531.
2. Jeannine K. Brown, *Matthew*, Teach the Text Commentary Series (Grand Rapids, MI: Baker Books, 2015), 306.
3. Stein, *Luke*, 583.
4. Randy Roberts, "Barabbas: Liberated Witness | Randy Roberts 03-13-21 (part 2 of 6)," Loma Linda University Church, posted March 13, 2021, YouTube video, 32:19, https://www.youtube.com/watch?v=3dRX-bXSOX4.

Chapter 91

Calvary

Luke 23:26–43 (Matthew 27:32–44; Mark 15:21–32; John 19:17–27)

All four Gospel writers tell the story of Jesus' crucifixion, death, and resurrection, but as we would expect, the accounts highlight different details. The variations show that there was no attempt to fabricate the story; if there were, we would assume there'd be total agreement between the four accounts. The fact that each writer recounted the stunning events as he observed them or was informed by an eyewitness is an important factor in confounding skeptics.

Luke's account includes some unique aspects of Jesus' crucifixion and death. First, he describes Jesus stopping to address some women who were weeping for Him. Second, Luke records His prayer of forgiveness for those who condemned Him and the soldiers who crucified Him. Third, a crucified criminal who declared Jesus innocent and righteous received assurance of salvation from Jesus.

And when they led Him away, they seized a man, Simon of Cyrene, as he was coming in from the country, and placed on him the cross to carry behind Jesus (Luke 23:26).

From Pilate's judgment hall, Jesus was led away by Roman soldiers to the place of execution. It was customary for an accused individual to carry his own cross, but when, in His weakened condition, Jesus was unable to support it across His lacerated back, the soldiers looked for a substitute and quickly grabbed a bystander, a Passover pilgrim, to carry the shameful instrument. Simon is from a Jewish community in Cyrene (near modern Tripoli, Libya) and very likely was visiting Jerusalem for his once-in-a-lifetime attendance at Passover. Forced to carry a cross, Simon was publicly shamed. However, "his bitterness turned to wonder and to faith; . . . in the thing that seemed to be his shame he found a Saviour."[1] The fact that Mark identified two of his sons, Alexander and Rufus, is evidence that Simon and his family became Christians (Mark 15:21).

Now following Him was a large crowd of the people, and of women who were mourning and grieving for Him. But Jesus turned to them and said, "Daughters of Jerusalem, stop weeping for Me, but weep for yourselves and for your children. For behold, days are coming when they will say, 'Blessed are those who cannot bear, and the wombs that have not given birth, and the breasts that have not nursed.' Then they will begin TO SAY TO THE MOUNTAINS, 'FALL ON US,' AND TO THE HILLS, 'COVER US.' For if they do these things when the tree is green, what will happen when it is dry?" (Luke 23:27–31).

Among a large crowd accompanying Jesus to Golgotha were several women who wept for Him. These were not from the crowd who, moments ago, were shouting for crucifixion. More than likely, these women were among those who spent time with Jesus in His daily teaching at the temple.

Certainly, they were compassionate women who were deeply moved as they saw Jesus' suffering.

Amazingly, Jesus paused to speak to these "daughters of Jerusalem." "Don't weep for Me," He told them. And then, with prophetic insight into the horrors that this city would experience in its coming destruction, He said, "Weep for yourselves and your children" (verse 28). British historian Simon Segab Montefiore has unearthed archives that describe the invasion of Jerusalem by Titus in AD 70. The records note that approximately five hundred Jews were crucified each day. The details are gruesome.[2] If they are crucifying the One who preached about love and peace, what will they do to an entire city filled with revolutionary violence? Jesus was unjustly executed, but intense bloodshed was coming for the people of Jerusalem.

Now two others, who were criminals, were also being led away to be put to death with Him. And when they came to the place called The Skull, there they crucified Him and the criminals, one on the right and the other on the left (verses 32, 33).

Crucifixion was one of the most inhumane methods of execution ever devised. Besides the intense physical pain, the public humiliation of being strung up naked brought shame. Victims were often tied to the cross, but other times their hands and feet were nailed to the cross as was done with Jesus (John 20:25; Colossians 2:14). A tablet specifying the crime was hung around the neck of the accused.[3] Pilate wrote the sign above Jesus, "THIS IS THE KING OF THE JEWS"—words intended to embarrass the Jewish leadership (Luke 23:38). Both the Jews and the Romans share the blame for Jesus' death (Acts 4:24–28). We can be thankful that the Gospel writers shielded us from the physical horrors of the crucifixion.

[But Jesus was saying, "Father, forgive them; for they do not know what they are doing."] And they cast lots, dividing His garments among themselves. And the people stood by, watching. And even the rulers were sneering at Him, saying, "He saved others; let Him save Himself if this is the Christ of God, His Chosen One." The soldiers also ridiculed Him, coming up to Him, offering Him sour wine, and saying, "If You are the King of the Jews, save Yourself!" Now there was also an inscription above Him, "THIS IS THE KING OF THE JEWS" (Luke 23:34–38).

Jesus was mocked and ridiculed as He hung on the cross. Soldiers gambled for His clothing nearby, fulfilling Psalm 22:18, "They divide my garments among them, and they cast lots for my clothing," while people shouted, "Save yourself if you are the Christ of God." Jesus expressed love and forgiveness for those very people: "Father, forgive them, for they do not know what they are doing." While people taunted Him to "save" Himself, it is the fact that He stayed on the cross that laid the groundwork for saving *them*. He did what they mocked Him for *not* doing![4] Bystanders watched, mocked, sneered, confessed, mourned, and blasphemed—"a cameo of the world's reactions to Jesus."[5]

One of the criminals who were hanged there was hurling abuse at Him, saying, "Are You not the Christ? Save Yourself and us!" But the other responded, and rebuking him, said, "Do you not even fear God, since you are under the same sentence of condemnation? And we indeed are suffering justly, for we are receiving what we deserve for our crimes; but this man has

done nothing wrong." And he was saying, "Jesus, remember me when You come into Your kingdom!" And He said to him, "Truly I say to you, today you will be with Me in Paradise" (Luke 23:39–43).

Besides recounting the mocking and hate-filled words of a variety of people at the cross, Luke also tells us of those who affirmed Jesus. Even while He was dying, Jesus continued His ministry of intercession, love, and forgiveness for His enemies.

One of the criminals crucified with Jesus added his voice to the mocking, "So you're the Messiah, are you? Prove it by saving yourself—and us, too, while you're at it!" (verse 39, NLT).

But the criminal hanging on the other side of Jesus rebuked his compatriot. "Don't you fear God? We deserve our suffering, but this Man is innocent." The man's brief observation of Jesus on the cross led him to repent and ask for salvation. Specifically, he asked to be remembered when Jesus returned in glory. Jesus responded, "I am saying to you today that you will be with Me in Paradise."[6] Additionally, Jesus' references to "today" and "paradise" are uncertain; " 'today' could have meant within 24 hours or it could have been intended as an eschatological reference to the new age that Jesus inaugurated."[7]

Glory in the cross

Let's pause and ask what Paul meant when he wrote, "God forbid that I should glory, save in the cross of our Lord Jesus Christ" (Galatians 6:14, KJV). Did he glory in the crucifixion of Jesus? One of my favorite preachers, Randy Roberts, draws sharp contrasts between "Cross" and "crucifixion." He references the one Person, Jesus Christ, but there are two realities and two experiences. Consider the following:[8]

- The Cross reflects the love of God; crucifixion, the hatred of humanity.
- The Cross reveals God's glory; crucifixion, human shame.
- The Cross shows God at His highest; crucifixion, humanity at its lowest.
- The Cross reveals the magnanimity of God; crucifixion, the offensive repugnance of sin.
- The Cross says, "I will save you"; crucifixion says, "I will kill you."
- The Cross shows God at His best; crucifixion, man at his worst.
- The Cross is the supreme manifestation of the love of God; crucifixion, the deepest hatred of Satan.

In this way, we can all glory in the Cross of Jesus along with Paul.

Reflection

My God hanging naked on a Roman cross? How does that make me feel? Paul wrote to believers in Rome: "I am *not ashamed* of the gospel, because it is the power of God that brings salvation to everyone who believes" (Romans 1:16, NIV; emphasis added; see also 1 Corinthians 1:18).

Why did Jesus die? What do you believe?

1. His death demonstrated God's love for humanity.
2. His time on earth was up.
3. He died to satisfy the demands of an angry God.

4. He died to save me.

5. He died to pay the penalty that Satan demanded.

6. He died to buy back what Adam lost through disobedience.

7. I can't comprehend such love for me, a sinner.

---

1. William Barclay, *The Gospel of Luke* (Philadelphia, PA: Westminster Press, 1975), 283.

2. Simon Segab Montefiore, *Jerusalem, the Biography* (London: Weidenfeld & Nicolson, 2011).

3. Darrell L. Bock, *Luke* (Grand Rapids, MI: Baker Academic, 1994), 1830, 1831.

4. Darrell L. Bock, *A Theology of Luke and Acts* (Grand Rapids, MI: Zondervan, 2012), 258.

5. Bock, *Luke*, 1836.

6. Bock, *Theology of Luke and Acts*, 404. Where is the placement of "today" in Jesus' response to the criminal? There are no commas in the original Greek text. Luke uses the word *today* twenty times in his Gospel. Half of those have the meaning of immediacy, where *today* means "at this moment," so the text of verse 43 may also be read, "I say to you today [*at this moment*], you will be with Me in Paradise."

7. O. C. Edwards Jr., *Luke's Story of Jesus* (Philadelphia, PA: Fortress Press, 1981), 93.

8. Randy Roberts, "Daughters of Jerusalem: Weeping Witness," Loma Linda University Church, March 27, 2021, YouTube video, 26:39, https://www.youtube.com/watch?v=n-cKFIgLd7w.

Chapter 92

Death and Burial

Luke 23:44–56 (Matthew 27:45–66; Mark 15:33–47; John 19:28–42)

It was now about the sixth hour, and darkness came over the entire land until the ninth hour, because the sun stopped shining; and the veil of the temple was torn in two (Luke 23:44, 45).

Without clocks and watches, people in Bible times figured out the time of day by looking at the sky. The day in Palestine was divided into twelve hours, so the third hour was mid-morning, the sixth hour was about noon, and the ninth was mid-afternoon. Jesus was nailed to the cross sometime late morning. Luke records two things that happened at noon:

1. Creation reacted to the sight of its Creator on a cross with three hours of darkness across all of Judea[1] and an earthquake (see also Matthew 27:51).
2. God demonstrated His displeasure by ripping the temple curtain from top to bottom (see also Mark 15:38).

Darkness in the Old Testament is often associated with judgment, as happened in Egypt before the Exodus (Exodus 10:21–23). Speaking through Amos, God declared, "It will come about on that day . . . that I will make the sun go down at noon, and make the earth dark in broad daylight" (Amos 8:9). A prophecy of Joel (Joel 2:10, 30, 31) points to the great "day of the LORD" at the end of time, but there is partial fulfillment of both prophecies at Jesus' death. His sacrificial ordeal is also the fulfillment of Isaiah 52:13–53:12.[2]

The high, heavy temple veil hung across the entrance to the Holy of Holies, which was entered only once each year, by the high priest, on the Day of Atonement, when a sacrifice was offered for the sins of all the people. The rending of the veil from top to bottom prefigured the temple's destruction, and it symbolized a new reality—that Jesus was offering His life as the ultimate sacrifice for not only the Jewish nation but also the entire world. Access to God is found no longer through a temple but through open hearts and the Holy Spirit.

And Jesus, crying out with a loud voice, said, "Father, INTO YOUR HANDS I ENTRUST MY SPIRIT." And having said this, He died. Now when the centurion saw what had happened, he began praising God, saying, "This man was in fact innocent" (Luke 23:46, 47).

The last words of Jesus are a cry of faith and confidence, uttered with the assurance of resurrection. One person who watched Jesus throughout the day was a Roman centurion, a Gentile, charged with overseeing the crucifixion and ultimately confirming that death had occurred. As Jesus' life passed away, he praised God, declaring, "This man was innocent!" The centurion confirmed that a terrible injustice had occurred.

And all the crowds who came together for this spectacle, after watching what had happened, began to return home, beating their breasts. And all His acquaintances and the women who accompanied Him from Galilee were standing at a distance, seeing these things (verses 48, 49).

As daylight returned in the late afternoon, the crowds that watched the event turned toward their homes, but their attitude had changed. Some who had shouted for the crucifixion or hurled insults now became strangely silent, and many beat their breasts in shame or fear. Among those who watched from a distance were Jesus' disciples. They had scattered when Jesus was arrested, and their minds were still in turmoil. They didn't understand.

Also "at a distance" were several women from Galilee—Mary Magdalene, Mary the mother of Clopas, and Joanna, the wife of King Herod's steward (Luke 8:3). The disciple John was also there, but he stood near the cross with Jesus' mother, Mary. He recorded a conversation that occurred between Jesus and himself: "When Jesus saw his mother there, and the disciple whom he loved standing nearby, he said to her, 'Woman, here is your son,' and to the disciple, 'Here is your mother.' From that time on, this disciple took her into his home" (John 19:26, 27, NIV).

And a man named Joseph, who was a member of the Council, a good and righteous man (he had not consented to their plan and action), a man from Arimathea, a city of the Jews, who was waiting for the kingdom of God—this man went to Pilate and asked for the body of Jesus. And he took it down and wrapped it in a linen cloth, and laid Him in a tomb cut into the rock, where no one had ever lain. It was a preparation day, and a Sabbath was about to begin. Now the women who had come with Him from Galilee followed, and they saw the tomb and how His body was laid. And then they returned and prepared spices and perfumes.

And on the Sabbath they rested according to the commandment (Luke 23:50–56).

Among the "secret" disciples of Jesus was Joseph, a wealthy man from Arimathea—a place virtually unknown outside Judea. Luke surprises us by sharing that Joseph is a member of the Sanhedrin, and we can guess that he'd been intentionally excluded from that day's ugly session.

Once the Roman centurion confirmed that Jesus was dead, and with Sabbath approaching, Joseph had no time to waste. As a respected Jew, he approached Pilate and received permission to take Jesus' body for burial. Removing Jesus' body from the cross, he cleaned, washed, anointed with oil, and clothed Him with expensive linen.[3] Joseph connected with some of the Galilean women, who then accompanied him to a new tomb excavated from the rock. The women watched as the body was carefully placed within, then they returned to their lodgings as the Sabbath began. The women rested on Sabbath, but then they prepared perfumes and spices that they would take to the tomb early on Sunday morning. Jesus died a criminal's death, but He was honored in His burial. He would rest in Joseph's tomb until the call of God sounded on Resurrection morning.

Meanwhile, the chief priests and Pharisees remembered what Jesus had said about rising again after three days, so they asked Pilate to make the grave site secure. Pilate told them to "go, make it as secure as you know how" (Matthew 27: 65). A guard of soldiers was placed there, and a seal was placed on the entrance stone (verses 62–66).

Luke didn't dwell on the salvific purpose of Jesus' death because "Luke does not understand the crucifixion in terms of vicarious atonement, or of sacrificial death on behalf of others."[4] To get that, we go to the writings of the apostles:

- Peter: " 'He himself bore our sins' in his body on the cross, so that we might die to sins and live for righteousness; 'by his wounds you have been healed' " (1 Peter 2:24, NIV).
- Peter: "There is salvation in no one else, for there is no other name under heaven given among mortals by which we must be saved" (Acts 4:12, NRSV).
- Paul: "He made Him who knew no sin to be sin in our behalf, so that we might become the righteousness of God in Him" (2 Corinthians 5:21).
- Paul: "For I am not ashamed of the gospel, for it is the power of God for salvation to everyone who believes" (Romans 1:16).
- Author of Hebrews: "Therefore he is able also to save completely those who come to God through him, because he always lives to intercede for them" (Hebrews 7:25, NIV).

Reflection

Many bystanders left the crucifixion scene "beating their breasts." What thoughts might have been going through their minds? Read Acts 2:36, 37.

---

1. Darrell L. Bock, *Luke* (Grand Rapids, MI: Baker Academic, 1994), 1858.
2. Joel B. Green, *The Gospel of Luke*, New International Commentary on the New Testament, vol. 3 (Grand Rapids, MI: Eerdmans, 1997), 827.
3. Green, *Gospel of Luke*, 830.
4. O. C. Edwards Jr., *Luke's Story of Jesus* (Philadelphia, PA: Fortress Press, 1981), 79.

Chapter 93

"He Is Not Here!"

Luke 24:1–12 (Matthew 28:1–7; Mark 16:1–8; John 20:1, 2)

Sunday morning, the women set out to Jesus' tomb, and I'm sure they wondered whether they would find help to move the stone that covered the entrance. The disc-shaped stone used to seal a tomb's entrance was large and heavy, normally requiring several men to move it in the groove.[1]

But on the first day of the week, at early dawn, they came to the tomb bringing the spices which they had prepared. And they found the stone rolled away from the tomb, but when they entered, they did not find the body of the Lord Jesus (Luke 24:1–3).

Arriving at the tomb, the women were surprised to find the stone already removed! But surprise became bewilderment when they discovered that the tomb was empty. They expected to find a corpse to anoint and wondered what had happened!

While they were perplexed about this, behold, two men suddenly stood near them in gleaming clothing; and as the women were terrified and bowed their faces to the ground, the men said to them, "Why are you seeking the living One among the dead? He is not here, but He has risen. Remember how He spoke to you while He was still in Galilee, saying that the Son of Man must be handed over to sinful men, and be crucified, and on the third day rise from the dead" (verses 4–7).

Didn't they remember Jesus' words, "The Son of Man must suffer many things and be rejected by the elders and chief priests and scribes, and be killed and be raised on the third day" (Luke 9:22)?

And they remembered His words, and returned from the tomb and reported all these things to the eleven, and to all the rest. Now these women were Mary Magdalene, Joanna, and Mary the mother of James; also the other women with them were telling these things to the apostles (Luke 24:8–10).

Finally, the women remembered the words of Jesus and believed. Their fear transformed into excitement. The angels had instructions for the women, with special recognition for Peter, the one who denied his Master: "But go, tell His disciples and Peter" (Mark 16:7).

The eleven disciples, likely with other followers, were in hiding. Luke doesn't share where the women would find the men, but they were probably huddled together in the same upper room where the Twelve ate the Passover meal with Jesus less than three days before. This was possibly a secure place for the sad and disillusioned men.

The women had incredible news to share with them. "Let's hurry! These men may not even know where our Master was buried. 'Go and tell the disciples' is what the angels told us to do. Just imagine when we tell them that the Lord has risen from the dead! He is alive!"

In a male-dominated society, women were not highly esteemed.[2] In first-century Palestine, two groups of people were not allowed to testify in a court of law due to their low social status—shepherds and women.[3] Luke told us that shepherds were the first witnesses of Jesus' birth (Luke 2:8–20). And now, women are the first witnesses of His resurrection.

But these words appeared to them as nonsense, and they would not believe the women. Nevertheless, Peter got up and ran to the tomb; and when he stooped and looked in, he saw the linen wrappings only; and he went away to his home, marveling at what had happened (Luke 24:11, 12).

We should not be surprised when the women's story of the empty tomb is met with unbelief by the male disciples. They regarded the women's testimony as nothing more than idle chatter. The women likely felt affronted, but they knew what men were like. Sadly, the disciples failed to remember and grasp Jesus' teaching regarding His suffering, death, and resurrection:

- Before they left Galilee: " 'The Son of Man is going to be handed over to men.' But they did not understand this statement, . . . and they were afraid to ask Him" (Luke 9:44, 45)
- As they were on their way to Jericho, Jesus, speaking of Himself, said, " 'For He will be handed over to the Gentiles, . . . and after they have flogged Him, they will kill Him; and on the third day He will rise.' The disciples understood none of these things" (Luke 18:32–34).

So, the men could not make sense of the news the women shared with them. Their dreams about God's kingdom had been shattered—Thomas was not the only doubting disciple.[4]

If the other male disciples continued to be obtuse, Peter wanted certainty. He very recently learned "that what Jesus says is not only surprising, but right."[5] Ignoring the others, he ran to the tomb and found it empty except for the grave clothes. Wonder must have coursed through his mind as his faith began to germinate.

Reflection

Ask yourself, Why is the resurrection of Jesus critical to my salvation?

---

1. *NIV Cultural Backgrounds Study Bible* (Grand Rapids, MI: Zondervan, 2016), 1798.
2. Leon Morris, *Luke: An Introduction and Commentary*, Tyndale New Testament Commentaries, vol. 3 (Downers Grove, IL: IVP Academic, 1988), 50.
3. *NIV Cultural Backgrounds Study Bible*, 1779.
4. Joel B. Green, *The Gospel of Luke*, New International Commentary on the New Testament, vol. 3 (Grand Rapids, MI: Eerdmans, 1997), 839.
5. Darrell L. Bock, *Luke* (Grand Rapids, MI: Baker Academic, 1994), 1900.

Chapter 94

On the Road to Emmaus

Luke 24:13–32

The story of two travelers on the road to Emmaus is a beautiful example of Luke's craftsmanship as a writer—he told the story with drama and detail.

And behold, on that very day two of them were going to a village named Emmaus, which was sixty stadia from Jerusalem. And they were talking with each other about all these things which had taken place (Luke 24:13, 14).

Sunday afternoon, two men trudged the seven miles* from Jerusalem to the village of Emmaus. Although evidently not numbered among the eleven, they were part of the group of disillusioned men who spent hours together in bewilderment. These two were sad as they walked and talked together, rehashing the events of the weekend.

While they were talking and discussing, Jesus Himself approached and began traveling with them. But their eyes were kept from recognizing Him. And He said to them, "What are these words that you are exchanging with one another as you are walking?" And they came to a stop, looking sad (verses 15–17).

A stranger caught up with the two as they walked—it was Jesus, but they were kept from recognizing Him. He asked them, "What is the topic of your conversation as you walk along together?" They stopped, their faces no doubt reflecting their despondency. Less than forty-eight hours ago, they had stood on a hillside outside Jerusalem, paralyzed with fear as they saw their beloved Master stripped, tortured, and crucified.

One of them, named Cleopas, answered and said to Him, "Are You possibly the only one living near Jerusalem who does not know about the things that happened here in these days?" And He said to them, "What sort of things?" And they said to Him, "Those about Jesus the Nazarene, who proved to be a prophet mighty in deed and word in the sight of God and all the people, and how the chief priests and our rulers handed Him over to be sentenced to death, and crucified Him. But we were hoping that it was He who was going to redeem Israel. Indeed, besides all this, it is now the third day since these things happened. But also some women among us left us bewildered. When they were at the tomb early in the morning, and did not find His body, they came, saying that they had also seen a vision of angels who said that He was alive. And so some of those who were with us went

---

* One Roman "stadion" is equal to approximately 607 feet.

to the tomb, and found it just exactly as the women also had said; but Him they did not see (Luke 24:18–24).

Let's re-create the story.

The Stranger: What is this you speak of as you walk along?

Cleopas: You've come from Jerusalem, haven't you? How is it you don't know what has happened there in the last couple of days? Have you had your head in the sand or something?

The Stranger: No. Tell me what happened.

Cleopas: About Jesus of Nazareth. He was a prophet. He did many wonderful things. We listened to His teachings.

Other Disciple: Yes, but the chief priests and rulers took Him and handed Him over to be sentenced to death.

Cleopas: In fact, they crucified Him.

Other disciple: That happened on Friday, during Passover.

Cleopas: (*Deep sigh*) We were hoping He was one sent from God to redeem Israel, to deliver us from the Romans, but—now we're not sure. Anyway, on top of all this, just this morning, some of our women shocked us. They went to the tomb early this morning and told us Jesus' body was not there. Then they claimed they saw a vision of angels who told them that He was alive.

Other disciple: But how can we believe their story?

Cleopas: Well, I don't know. Some of our men went to the tomb to see for themselves. They found the tomb empty, just like the women said. But there was no sign of Jesus (verses 17–21, author's paraphrase).

The Stranger: "Come on, men! Why are you being so foolish? Why are your hearts so sluggish when it comes to believing what the prophets have been saying all along? Didn't it have to be this way? Didn't the Anointed One have to experience these sufferings in order to come into His glory?" (verses 25, 26, *The Voice*).

Luke concludes the story,

And then He said to them, "You foolish men and slow of heart to believe in all that the prophets have spoken! Was it not necessary for the Christ to suffer these things and to come into His glory?" Then beginning with Moses and with all the Prophets, He explained to them the things written about Himself in all the Scriptures (verses 25–27).

First-century Judaism did not anticipate a suffering Messiah. People read and liked Messianic prophecies that pictured Israel's future restoration and glory (Ezekiel 37:24–27; Isaiah 9:1–4; Psalms 2; 118), but they overlooked scriptures that portrayed the suffering One (Psalm 22; Isaiah 53). So, that afternoon on the Emmaus road, Jesus reminded these men of scriptures that balanced the picture they had.

And they approached the village where they were going, and He gave the impression that He was going farther. And so they strongly urged Him, saying, "Stay with us, for it is getting toward evening, and the day is now nearly over." So He went in to stay with them (Luke 24:28, 29).

As the three approached the village of Emmaus, home to the two travelers, the men marveled as they considered the great prophetic revelations that tell the whole story of Messianic expectations. Obviously, "God reversed in dramatic style the thinking of Cleopas and his companion. They would never be the same as they learned that death could be overcome and that God's plan had moved ahead. Jesus was alive, and as a result their hope was renewed."[1] Arriving at their village at evening time, they persuaded the stranger to stay with them.

And it came about, when He had reclined at the table with them, that He took the bread and blessed it, and He broke it and began giving it to them. And then their eyes were opened and they recognized Him; and He vanished from their sight. They said to one another, "Were our hearts not burning within us when He was speaking to us on the road, while He was explaining the Scriptures to us?" (verses 30–32).

Throughout Luke's Gospel, we've seen that table fellowship with Jesus generated revelatory discourse. Once He sat at the table with the two men, Jesus' role shifted.[2] He was no longer the honored guest but the Host of the meal. He took the bread, blessed it, broke it, and gave it to them, just like He did in Galilee at the miraculous feeding of the five thousand (Luke 9:16). As Jesus blessed and broke the bread, the eyes of the two disciples suddenly opened, and they discovered that the stranger is Jesus Himself! Then He disappeared.[*]

Reflection

Ask yourself, How often am I blind to the truths of Scripture? How may the Holy Spirit be my teacher and guide?

---

1. Darrell L. Bock, *Luke* (Grand Rapids, MI: Baker Academic, 1994), 1903.
2. Joel B. Green, *The Gospel of Luke*, New International Commentary on the New Testament, vol. 3 (Grand Rapids, MI: Eerdmans, 1997), 849.

---

[*] I like to think that Luke found Cleopas and interviewed him during his investigation in Judea.

Chapter 95

Jesus Is Alive!

Luke 24:33–49

I imagine Cleopas and his friend were wild with excitement as they hiked, or maybe ran, along the road back to Jerusalem. Their weariness was gone, and they covered the seven miles in record time. They had incredible news to share with the rest of the disciples, who remained hunkered down in the upper room behind locked doors (John 20:19), scared they'd be recognized if they were seen outside.

And they got up that very hour and returned to Jerusalem, and found the eleven gathered together and those who were with them, saying, "The Lord has really risen and has appeared to Simon!" They began to relate their experiences on the road, and how He was recognized by them at the breaking of the bread (Luke 24:33–35).

It was late when they arrived at the upper room in Jerusalem; even so, the two were admitted. Hang on, though—it seems the upper-room group has equally exciting news to share with *them*!

> *Jerusalem group*: Come in, you two. Hey! Jesus is alive!
>
> *Two from Emmaus*: Yes, we know. We *saw* Him!
>
> *Jerusalem group*: You *saw* Him? Where?
>
> *Two from Emmaus*: He walked with us most of the way to Emmaus this afternoon. Have *you* seen Him too?
>
> *Jerusalem group*: No. But we know He's alive because Simon saw Him. He told us that Jesus appeared to Him, alive. Can you believe it?
>
> *Two from Emmaus*: Yes, it's true. We didn't know it was Jesus when He walked with us to Emmaus. We didn't recognize Him. It was getting dark when we got to our house, so we invited Him to stay and eat with us. When He blessed and broke the bread, we saw it was Jesus. Then He suddenly disappeared.

Peter was the first of the eleven disciples to see their Master alive, which was recorded by Paul (1 Corinthians 15:5). It's a beautiful thing that Jesus appeared so soon to the one who denied Him and then spent two lonely days full of remorse.[1]

Now while they were telling these things, Jesus Himself suddenly stood in their midst and said to them, "Peace be to you." But they were startled and frightened, and thought that they were looking at a spirit (Luke 24:36, 37).

Jesus' appearance in the upper room was as sudden as His disappearance at Emmaus. Their immediate reaction was fear—the doors were locked! Obviously, "the disciples are not operating with expectations of the miraculous."[2] They are portrayed as slow to accept the Resurrection. Jesus' first words are a blessing of peace. It's the peace that angels promised to shepherds at His birth (Luke 2:14).

And He said to them, "Why are you frightened, and why are doubts arising in your hearts? See My hands and My feet, that it is I Myself; touch Me and see, because a spirit does not have flesh and bones as you plainly see that I have." And when He had said this, He showed them His hands and His feet. While they still could not believe it because of their joy and astonishment, He said to them, "Have you anything here to eat?" They served Him a piece of broiled fish; and He took it and ate it in front of them (Luke 24:38–42).

"Why are you frightened?" Jesus knew that everyone was uncertain about Him. They had never before encountered their Master appearing and disappearing like this. The disciples wondered, *How could He get inside when the doors were locked? Is He real, or some sort of spirit? Is this the same Jesus I have known? How can I understand His resurrection?* So, Jesus proceeded to demonstrate His humanness in two ways:

1. "Touch me and see." He showed them His hands and feet where the nail prints were clearly visible and urged them to touch and feel.
2. "I'm hungry. Do you have something to eat?" Yes, they had broiled fish. So, Jesus suggested, "Let's eat together." He really was in their midst, their resurrected Friend and risen Savior!

The joy continued as Jesus shared with them. They'd listened to Him so many times, but mostly without understanding. Now their minds were opened. It's like when the two Emmaus pilgrims found "their hearts burning within them" while Jesus opened the Word to them on the road.

Now He said to them, "These are My words which I spoke to you while I was still with you, that all the things that are written about Me in the Law of Moses and the Prophets and the Psalms must be fulfilled" (verse 44).

Happy disciples listened with an eagerness they'd not felt before. Jesus led them on a tour of discovery through the entire Hebrew Scriptures—the "Law of Moses" (the first five books of our Bible), "the Prophets" (the historical books from Joshua to Chronicles as well as the major and minor prophets), "and the Psalms" (the poetic books from Job through Song of Solomon). Now, for the first time, they understood how the suffering One had become their Savior through His death and resurrection.

Then He opened their minds to understand the Scriptures, and He said to them, "So it is written, that the Christ would suffer and rise from the dead on the third day, and that repentance for forgiveness of sins would be proclaimed in His name to all the nations, beginning from Jerusalem. You are witnesses of these things. And behold, I am sending the promise of My Father upon you; but you are to stay in the city until you are clothed with power from on high" (verses 45–49).

As Jesus opened to them the promises of the Scriptures, He used three significant words that summarized the fulfillment of God's plan for Him and the disciples: *suffer, rise,* and *witness.*[3] His words about repentance and forgiveness take us way back to the proclamation of John the Baptist when his baptismal candidates experienced repentance and forgiveness of their sins. John's commission now becomes the commission of Jesus' followers. The story of His appearance to the group emphasized four things:[4]

1. The necessity of the cross
2. The reality of the Resurrection
3. The urgency of the task
4. The secret of power

Undoubtedly, "Luke desires his readers to see that the resurrection is real. He wants them to understand that God's plan goes on. That plan and promise are now realized in the new community God has formed in disciples that come from every nation. This community is going to be equipped to carry out a task until the consummation of promise comes in Jesus' return."[5]

As Luke approaches the end of his story, we can see that it has an open ending because the wait for the Holy Spirit leads us right into Luke's second volume—the Acts of the Apostles. There we will learn the details of Jesus' departure into heaven and the empowerment of the Holy Spirit as a new community of faith begins its activity under God's direction.

Reflection

Thomas was not present the first time Jesus appeared to the disciples. He insisted he would not believe unless he touched the nail holes and the wounded side of Jesus. Read Thomas' story in John's Gospel (John 20:24–29).

1. William Barclay, *The Gospel of Luke* (Philadelphia, PA: Westminster Press, 1975), 296.
2. Darrell L. Bock, *Luke* (Grand Rapids, MI: Baker Academic, 1994), 1932.
3. Darrell L. Bock, *A Theology of Luke and Acts* (Grand Rapids, MI: Zondervan, 2012), 131.
4. Barclay, *Gospel of Luke*, 298.
5. Bock, *Luke*, 1947.

Chapter 96

The Departure

Luke 24:50–53; Acts 1:1–14

Luke tells the story of Christ's ascension to heaven twice—briefly in the last four verses of his Gospel but more fully in the first chapter of his sequel, Acts. We will look at both accounts and observe some small differences.

It is interesting that neither Matthew nor John wrote anything about the departure of Jesus, and Mark has only this sentence: "So then, when the Lord Jesus had spoken to them, He was received up into heaven and sat down at the right hand of God" (Mark 16:19). So, we are dependent on our beloved historian, Luke, for both the beginning and the ending of Jesus' story—His birth in Bethlehem, and His return to glory. In writing the gospel story, Luke demonstrates clearly that God has vindicated Jesus and has now taken Him home to share in the promised rule of His great kingdom. Truly, "Theophilus can be assured that Jesus is who he claimed to be and is what the church proclaims about him."[1]

And He led them out as far as Bethany, and He lifted up His hands and blessed them. While He was blessing them, He parted from them and was carried up into heaven. And they, after worshiping Him, returned to Jerusalem with great joy, and were continually in the temple praising God (Luke 24:50–53).

These are the last four verses of Luke's Gospel. The final scene of Jesus' departure to heaven is so brief. Luke had already written more than the length of most papyrus rolls, so he was "hastening to the end of this volume."[2] This ascension account seems like it is taking place right after Jesus' appearance to the disciples in the upper room.* In fact, though, Jesus was alive on earth for forty days after resurrection Sunday, as Luke confirms in the first chapter of Acts.

We must go to John's Gospel to learn about some of the things Jesus did during those forty days after His resurrection (John 20; 21). Also, the apostle Paul tells us that as many as five hundred people saw Jesus alive during that time (1 Corinthians 15:3–8). The Lord's final instruction to the disciples was to wait in Jerusalem for the indwelling of the Holy Spirit, which would activate their ministry.

Luke's Gospel story for Theophilus concluded with joy and praise. After Jesus blessed the disciples, they worshiped Him as He rose into the sky. It is noteworthy that this is "the first time Luke speaks of anyone worshipping Jesus."[3] Then, returning to Jerusalem "with great joy," the eleven are found "continually in the temple praising God." Giving glory and praise to God for His work through Jesus are Luke's final words of his Gospel.

---

* Luke's Gospel account gives Bethany as the place where the ascension took place. His account in Acts 1 gives the location as Olivet. Bethany was located on the south slopes of the Mount of Olives.

For the story in more detail, we move on to Luke's second account:

The first account I composed, Theophilus, about all that Jesus began to do and teach, until the day when He was taken up to heaven, after He had given orders by the Holy Spirit to the apostles whom He had chosen. To these He also presented Himself alive after His suffering, by many convincing proofs, appearing to them over a period of forty days and speaking of things regarding the kingdom of God. Gathering them together, He commanded them not to leave Jerusalem, but to wait for what the Father had promised, "Which," He said, "you heard of from Me; for John baptized with water, but you will be baptized with the Holy Spirit not many days from now."

So, when they had come together, they began asking Him, saying, "Lord, is it at this time that You are restoring the kingdom to Israel?" But He said to them, "It is not for you to know periods of time or appointed times which the Father has set by His own authority; but you will receive power when the Holy Spirit has come upon you; and you shall be My witnesses both in Jerusalem and in all Judea, and Samaria, and as far as the remotest part of the earth" (Acts 1:1–8).

With Jesus standing alive in front of them, the eleven disciples were anxious to know what would happen next. Would Jesus now establish His kingdom in Jerusalem, as they have thought and talked about so much? No. Jesus told them He was following His Father's plan, and He had clear and important instructions for them: "You are to wait for the Holy Spirit to come upon you. Then you will have power that you've never had before. You are living witnesses to My life, death, and resurrection, so you will be able to assure people that these things really took place. You will be My witnesses, starting here in Jerusalem and Judea, but later to the most remote parts of the earth." The promise of the Holy Spirit ties together the last words of Luke and the first words of Acts.[4] Now, "the disciples were linked to Someone who was forever independent of space and time."[5]

And after He had said these things, He was lifted up while they were watching, and a cloud took Him up, out of their sight. And as they were gazing intently into the sky while He was going, then behold, two men in white clothing stood beside them, and they said, "Men of Galilee, why do you stand looking into the sky? This Jesus, who has been taken up from you into heaven, will come in the same way as you have watched Him go into heaven."

Then they returned to Jerusalem from the mountain called Olivet, which is near Jerusalem, a Sabbath day's journey away. When they had entered the city, they went up to the upstairs room where they were staying (Acts 1:9–13).

As the men watched, spellbound, a cloud took Jesus away from them. It is a wonderful, divine moment—the glorious finality of three years spent with the Son of God. As they stood there on Olivet, mouths wide open in wonder, two angels suddenly stood with them. The eleven disciples were still the "men of Galilee," but they were not the same as they were when Jesus first called them. Now, given the assurance that Jesus would come back as He has already told them so many times, the eleven made their way through the olive groves, into Jerusalem, and to the upper room that now carried a kaleidoscope of memories.

The ascension is not just a departure. It is also an arrival, marking the beginning of Jesus' heavenly reign. "God has acted in history through Jesus. The Gospel's ending is open-ended because it portrays Jesus reigning at God's side while the disciples rejoice in the knowledge that this authoritative Jesus cares for them. Such is the opportunity for blessing that Jesus brings. Such is the disciples' call as they bear the message of hope to all races. He is alive and in their midst, offering hope and blessing to those who will come to Him. Now is the time for all to decide where they stand."[6]

The Christian community that exploded after the resurrection of Jesus was confronted, as are people in every age, "with the paradox of Jesus' identity. Jesus is the Christ—but not the expected Christ. He is the Son of David, born in Bethlehem, the king of Israel; He is the new Joshua, a prophet like Moses; and He is like Elijah. But Jesus is also the one who refuses to be a new David, Moses, and Elijah." Jesus is the fulfillment of the Scriptures, but in a way that Judaism did not recognize. He announced a kingdom that turned the world downside up. "At once, Jesus is the rejected man, hung on the cross, and the Son of God; simultaneously humiliated and exalted."[7]

Reflection

Consider the words of the two angels to the disciples: "This Jesus, who has been taken up from you into heaven, will come in the same way as you have watched Him go into heaven" (Acts 1:11). What does this promise mean to you?

---

1. Darrell L. Bock, *A Theology of Luke and Acts* (Grand Rapids, MI: Zondervan, 2012), 79.

2. Leon Morris, *Luke: An Introduction and Commentary*, Tyndale New Testament Commentaries, vol. 3 (Downers Grove, IL: IVP Academic, 1988), 364.

3. Morris, 364.

4. Bock, *Theology of Luke and Acts*, 129.

5. William Barclay, *The Gospel of Luke* (Philadelphia, PA: Westminster Press, 1975), 299.

6. Darrell L. Bock, *Luke* (Grand Rapids, MI: Baker Academic, 1994), 1947.

7. James M. Dawsey, *The Lukan Voice: Confusion and Irony in the Gospel of Luke* (Macon, GA: Mercer University Press, 1986), 156.

The Reality of the Resurrection

The claim that Jesus resurrected from the dead and lives again is attacked by atheists and even some Christians, more so than any other story from the Bible. However, without this belief in a risen Christ, Christianity is a sham and a worthless ideology. Paul made this clear when he wrote to the Greek Christians in Corinth: "If Christ has not been raised, our preaching is useless and so is your faith" (1 Corinthians 15:14, NIV).

Belief in the Bible's Creation story is consistent with belief in the Resurrection. God made the human person as a holistic being, a oneness of body, mind, and spirit (Genesis 2:7). The Hebrew word *nephesh*, translated as "soul" in the King James Bible, has the meaning of "a living being," as in the newer translations. Ancient Job understood that all life comes from the Creator God:

> "But ask the animals, and they will teach you,
>   or the birds in the sky, and they will tell you;
> or speak to the earth, and it will teach you,
>   or let the fish in the sea inform you.
> Which of all these does not know
>   that the hand of the Lord has done this?
> In his hand is the life of every creature
>   and the breath of all mankind" (Job 12:7–10, NIV).

Lee Strobel's research

In researching the resurrection story, Lee Strobel, an atheist-turned-Christian and a *New York Times* best-selling author, conducted tough interviews with four well-recognized authorities on the subject.[1] Here is a summary of his significant conclusions about the resurrection of Jesus:

- The medical evidence, based on historical records of Roman floggings and crucifixions, proves beyond a doubt that Jesus died on the cross. One of the tasks of the Roman centurion who supervised the crucifixion of Jesus was to confirm that death had occurred. It was a cold, dead body that Joseph of Arimathea placed in his tomb late on Friday afternoon.
- Early sources provide strong evidence that the tomb was empty on Sunday morning. The site of the tomb was known to both Jews and Christians, so it could have been checked by anyone who was skeptical. "In fact, nobody, not even the Roman authorities or Jewish leaders, ever claimed that the tomb still contained Jesus' body. Instead they were forced to invent the absurd story that the disciples, despite having no motive or opportunity, had stolen the body—a theory

that not even the most skeptical critic believes today."[2]

- Jesus was seen alive after His death on the cross. Paul made a firm declaration when he wrote to the Corinthian believers: "I handed down to you as of first importance what I also received, that Christ died for our sins according to the Scriptures, and that He was buried, and that He was raised on the third day according to the Scriptures, and that He appeared to Cephas [Peter], then to the twelve. After that He appeared to more than five hundred brothers and sisters at one time, most of whom remain until now, but some have fallen asleep; then He appeared to James, then to all the apostles; and last of all, as to one untimely born, He appeared to me also" (1 Corinthians 15:3–8).

- From Luke's account in the book of Acts, we have remarkable evidence that Christianity developed and spread like wildfire immediately after the resurrection of Christ. "This Jesus whom God raised up, a fact to which we are all witnesses" (Acts 2:32). What kind of movement would spread throughout the world celebrating a dead man killed on a Roman cross?

- The disciples went to their deaths proclaiming the resurrected Jesus. Skeptics like James, Jesus' half-brother who initially didn't believe in Him, and Paul, who persecuted Christians, were converted and proclaimed the gospel until their deaths. Who would knowingly and willingly die for a lie?

Jesus' closest followers did not anticipate His death, let alone His resurrection. Several times during His ministry, Jesus tried to prepare His disciples for these events, but they did not comprehend His words. Obviously, their situation changed dramatically when they encountered the risen Jesus. Truly, "the Incarnation is the most glorious event this planet has ever experienced. The incredible journey undertaken by God two thousand years ago makes possible the greatest journey that any human being can ever take—a single, faltering step toward Jesus Christ and salvation."[3]

Reflection

What does Jesus' resurrection mean to you?

1. It gives me hope of eternal life.
2. I look forward to being reunited with family members who have died.
3. It gives me assurance that Jesus will return.
4. I wish I could be sure that it really happened.
5. Jesus has conquered death.
6. I can't think of any better news.
7. "Victory in Jesus, my Savior forever."[4]

---

1. Lee Strobel, *The Case for Christ* (Grand Rapids, MI: Zondervan, 1998).
2. Strobel, 263.
3. Keith Clouten, *Breaking Through the Wall* (Calhoun, GA: TEACH Services, 2018), 71.
4. Eugene M. Bartlett, "Victory in Jesus" (Albert E. Bromley & Sons, 1967).